CY-BELIEVERS

VOL.4

Shioko Mizuk

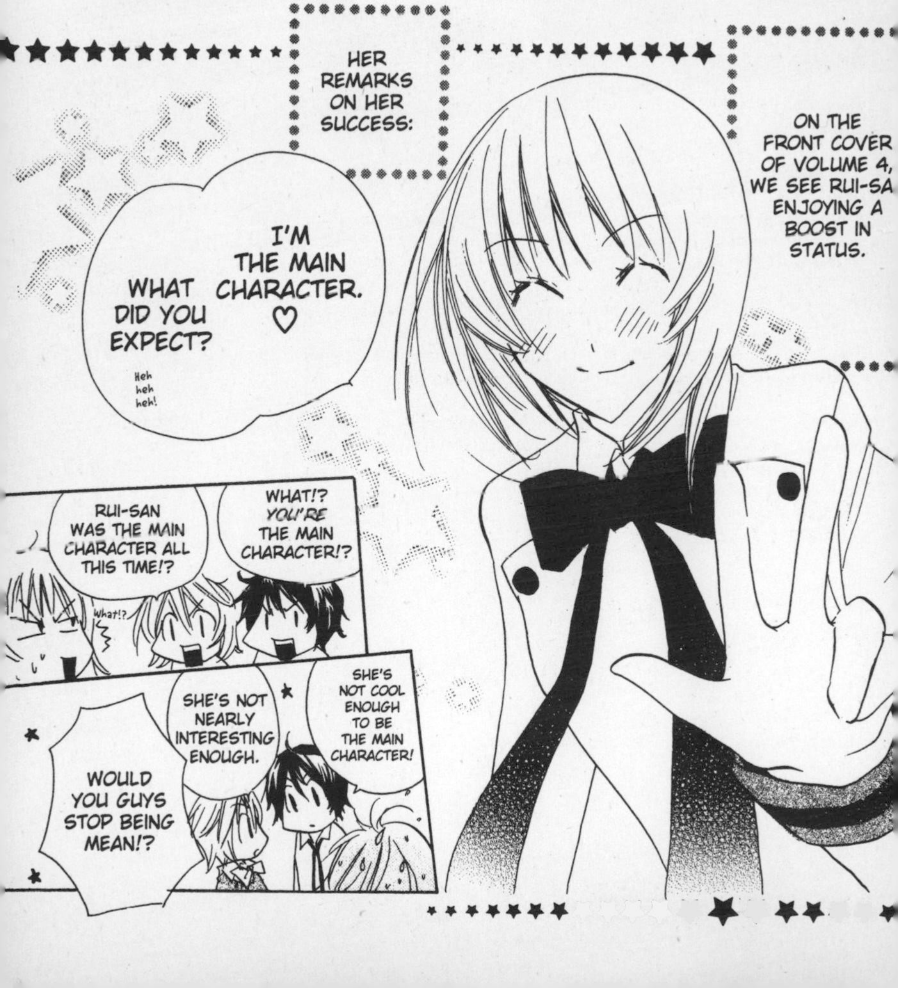
ON THE FRONT COVER OF VOLUME 4, WE SEE RUI-SA ENJOYING A BOOST IN STATUS.
HER REMARKS ON HER SUCCESS:
I'M THE MAIN CHARACTER. ♡
WHAT DID YOU EXPECT?
Heh heh heh!
WHAT!? YOU'RE THE MAIN CHARACTER!?
RUI-SAN WAS THE MAIN CHARACTER ALL THIS TIME!?
What!?
SHE'S NOT COOL ENOUGH TO BE THE MAIN CHARACTER!
SHE'S NOT NEARLY INTERESTING ENOUGH.
WOULD YOU GUYS STOP BEING MEAN!?

Translation – Christine Schilling
Adaptation – Kai Connick
Lettering and Retouch – Jennifer Skarupa
Production Assistant – Suzy Wells
Editorial Assistant – Mallory Reaves
Production Manager – James Dashiell
Editor – Brynne Chandler

A Go! Comi manga

Published by Go! Media Entertainment, LLC

Denno Believers Volume 4
© SHIOKO MIZUKI 2008
Originally published in Japan in 2008 by Akita Publishing Co., Ltd., Tokyo.
English translation rights arranged with Akita Publishing Co., Ltd. through
TOHAN CORPORATION, Tokyo

English Text © 2008 Go! Media Entertainment, LLC. All rights reserved.

Visit us online at www.gocomi.com
e-mail: info@gocomi.com

ISBN 978-1-60510-025-8

First printed in December 2008

1   2   3   4   5   6   7   8   9

Manufactured in the United States of America

CY-BELIEVERS

By
Shioko Mizuki

VOLUME 4

go!comi

Vol.4

CONTENTS

Story so far - Rui Kobayakawa, daughter of the king of a multi-million dollar hotel chain, has always dreamt of living on her own, so she enters a boarding school for high school. Now the super-sadist Natori Nijo and computer geeks Azumi Takano and Rio Kisaragi are looking for an opportunity to take advantage of her. With help from the student council, "Cy-Believers" is recognized as a legitimate club and Rui works hard to keep the members' list growing, becoming a real threat to the public safety commission. Meanwhile, Rui's father comes for a visit. He tells Natori that if he wants Rui, he has to let her win. That sends Natori into a desperate frenzy, and he tries to take Rui by force, only to fail miserably. However, in the end, they gain an understanding, and see each other with a little more compassion. ♥ But then, Rui and Azumi get into a big fight...

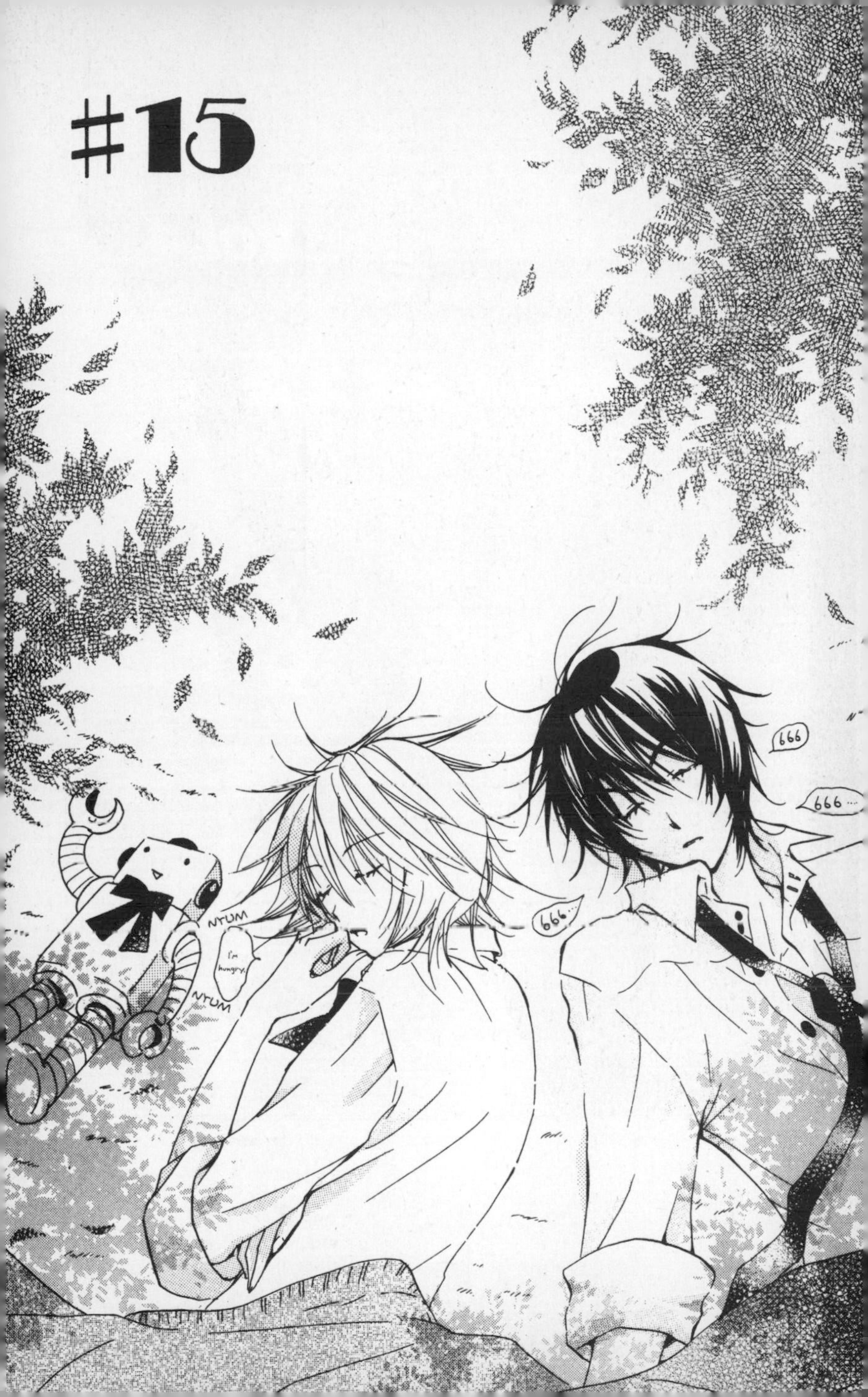
#15
666
666...
666...
NTUM
I'm hungry.
NTUM

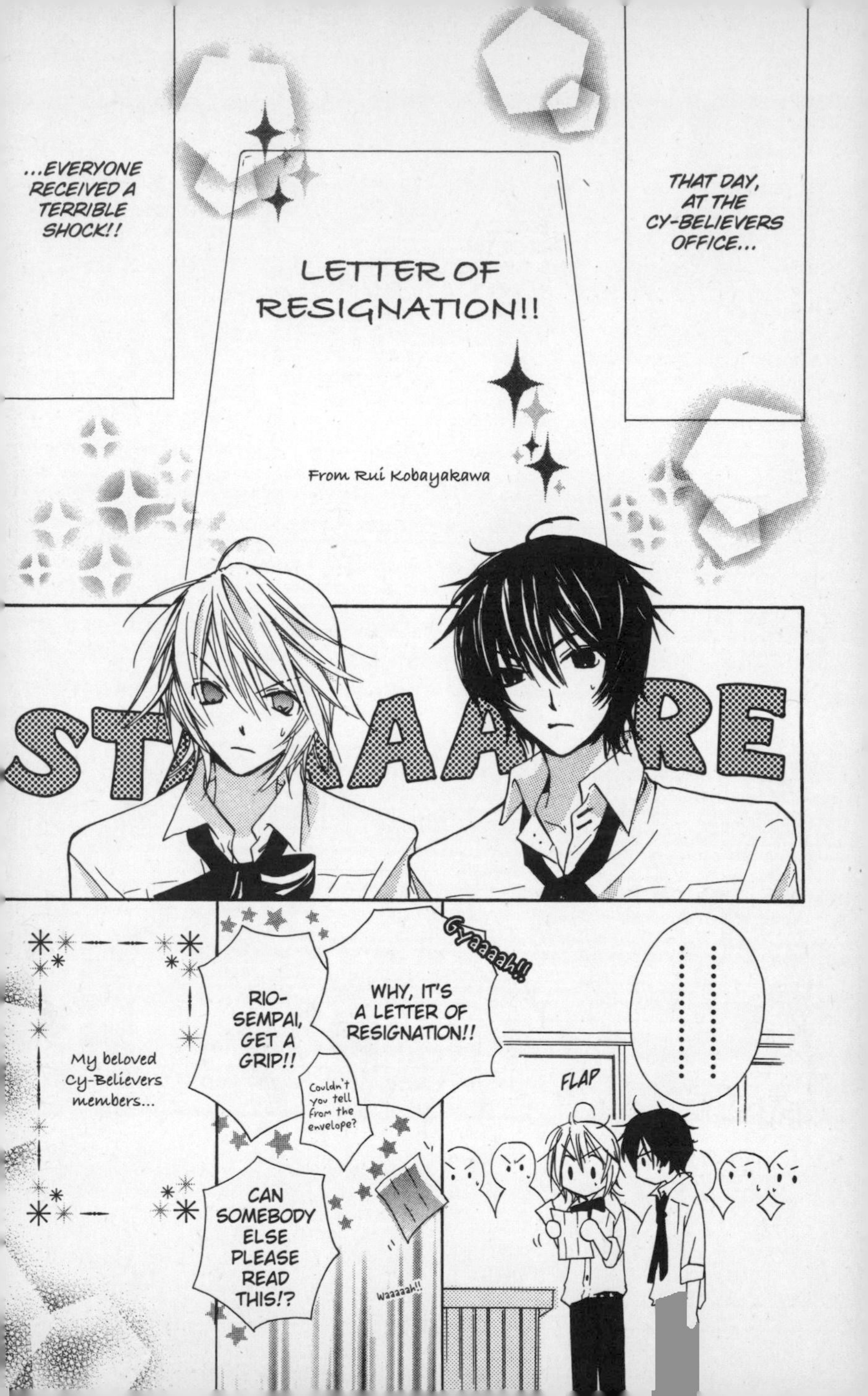
THAT DAY, AT THE CY-BELIEVERS OFFICE...
LETTER OF RESIGNATION!!
From Rui Kobayakawa
...EVERYONE RECEIVED A TERRIBLE SHOCK!!
FLAP
Gyaaaah!!
WHY, IT'S A LETTER OF RESIGNATION!!
RIO-SEMPAI, GET A GRIP!!
Couldn't you tell from the envelope?
CAN SOMEBODY ELSE PLEASE READ THIS!?
Waaaaah!!
My beloved Cy-Believers members...

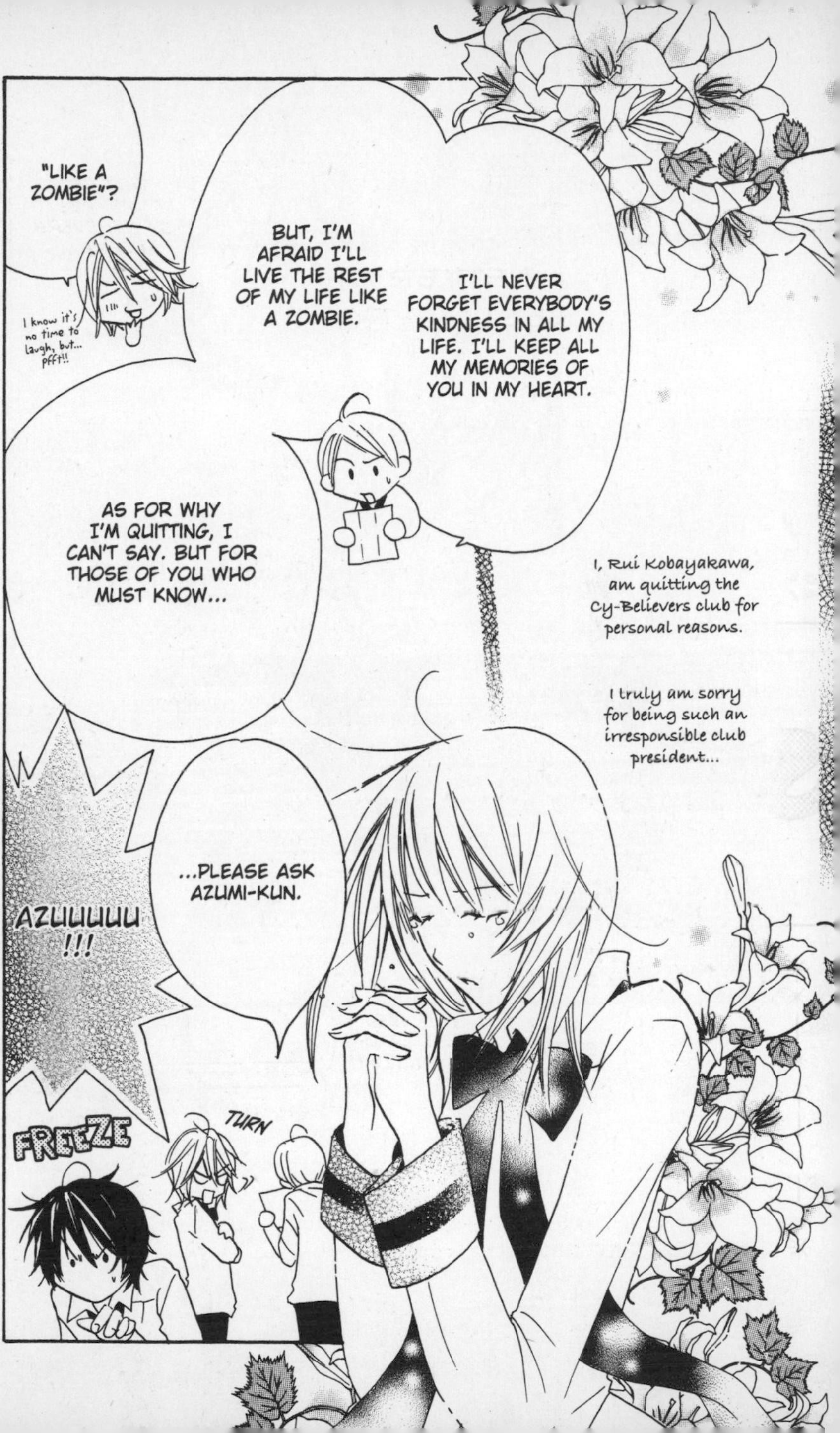

I, Rui Kobayakawa, am quitting the Cy-Believers club for personal reasons.
I truly am sorry for being such an irresponsible club president...
I'LL NEVER FORGET EVERYBODY'S KINDNESS IN ALL MY LIFE. I'LL KEEP ALL MY MEMORIES OF YOU IN MY HEART.
BUT, I'M AFRAID I'LL LIVE THE REST OF MY LIFE LIKE A ZOMBIE.
"LIKE A ZOMBIE"?
I know it's no time to laugh, but... pfft!!
AS FOR WHY I'M QUITTING, I CAN'T SAY. BUT FOR THOSE OF YOU WHO MUST KNOW...
...PLEASE ASK AZUMI-KUN.
AZULUUUU !!!
TURN
FREEZE

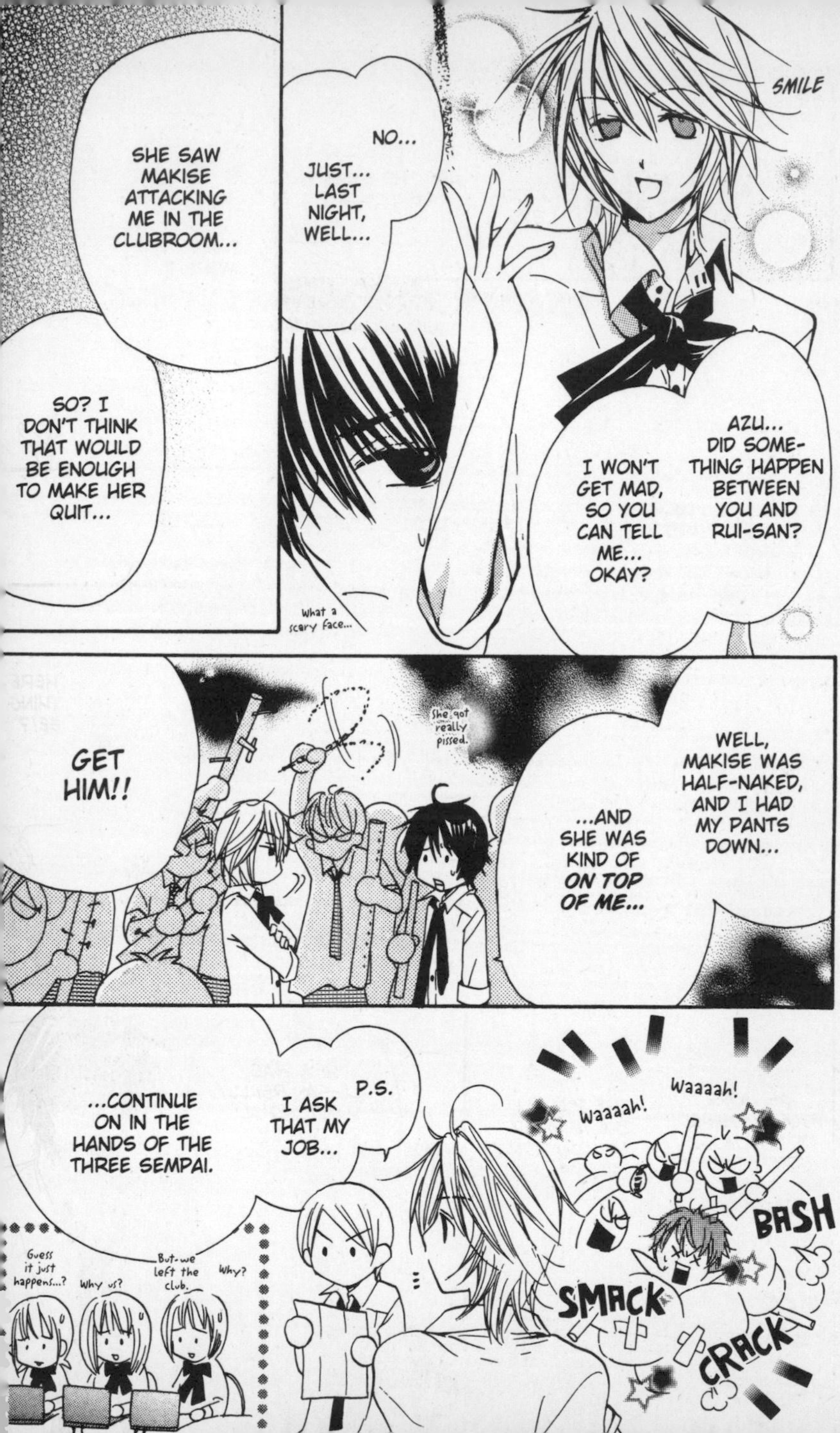
SMILE
NO... JUST... LAST NIGHT, WELL...
AZU... DID SOMETHING HAPPEN BETWEEN YOU AND RUI-SAN?
I WON'T GET MAD, SO YOU CAN TELL ME... OKAY?
What a scary face...
SHE SAW MAKISE ATTACKING ME IN THE CLUBROOM...
SO? I DON'T THINK THAT WOULD BE ENOUGH TO MAKE HER QUIT...
WELL, MAKISE WAS HALF-NAKED, AND I HAD MY PANTS DOWN...
...AND SHE WAS KIND OF ON TOP OF ME...
She got really pissed.
GET HIM!!
Waaaah!
Waaaah!
BASH
SMACK
CRACK
P.S.
I ASK THAT MY JOB...
...CONTINUE ON IN THE HANDS OF THE THREE SEMPAI.
Why?
But-we left the club.
Why us?
Guess it just happens...?

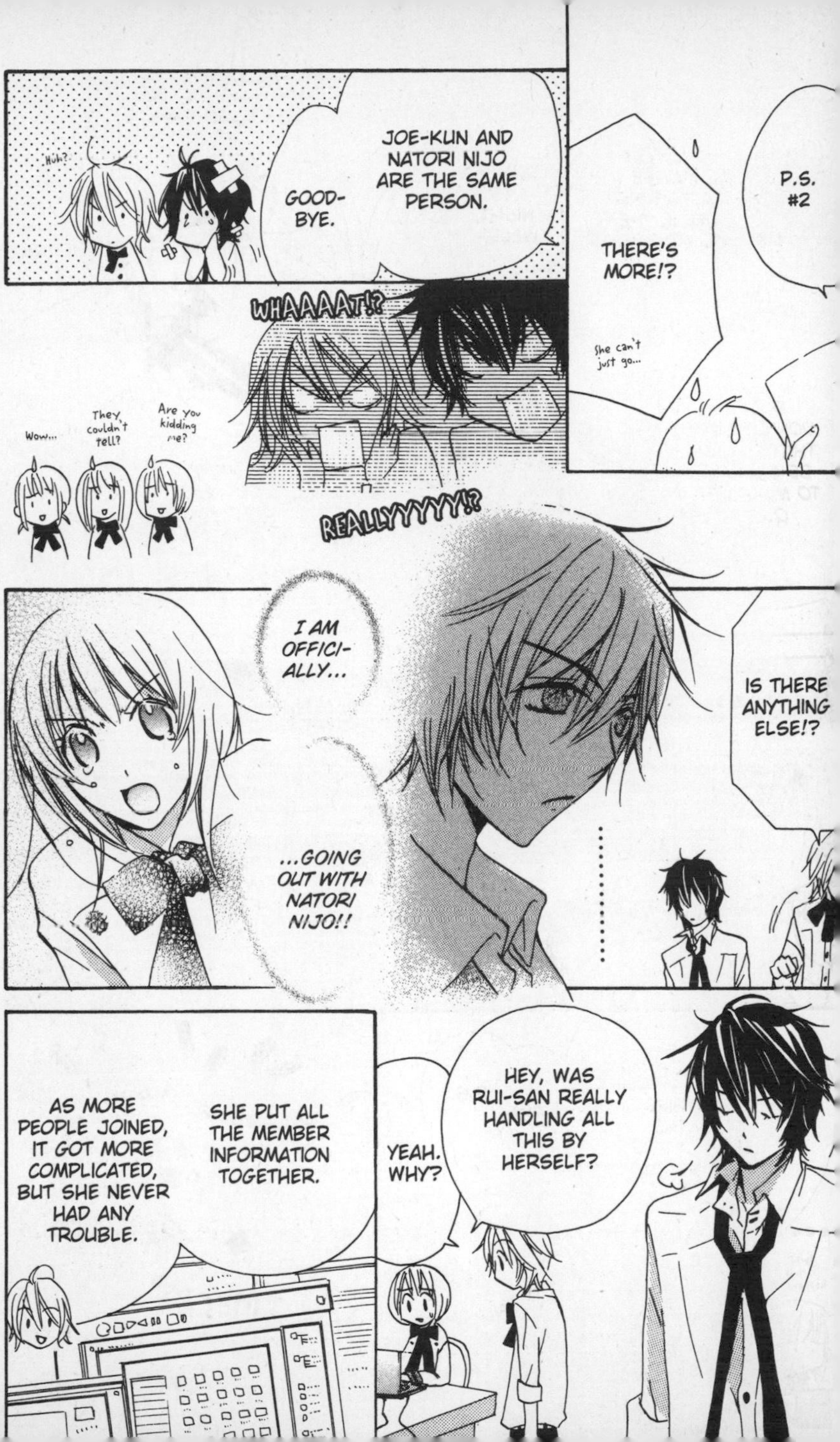
P.S. #2
THERE'S MORE!?
She can't just go...
JOE-KUN AND NATORI NIJO ARE THE SAME PERSON.
GOOD-BYE.
Huh?
WHAAAAT!?
REALLYYYYY!?
Are you kidding me?
They couldn't tell?
Wow...
IS THERE ANYTHING ELSE!?
......
I AM OFFICI-ALLY...
...GOING OUT WITH NATORI NIJO!!
HEY, WAS RUI-SAN REALLY HANDLING ALL THIS BY HERSELF?
YEAH. WHY?
SHE PUT ALL THE MEMBER INFORMATION TOGETHER.
AS MORE PEOPLE JOINED, IT GOT MORE COMPLICATED, BUT SHE NEVER HAD ANY TROUBLE.

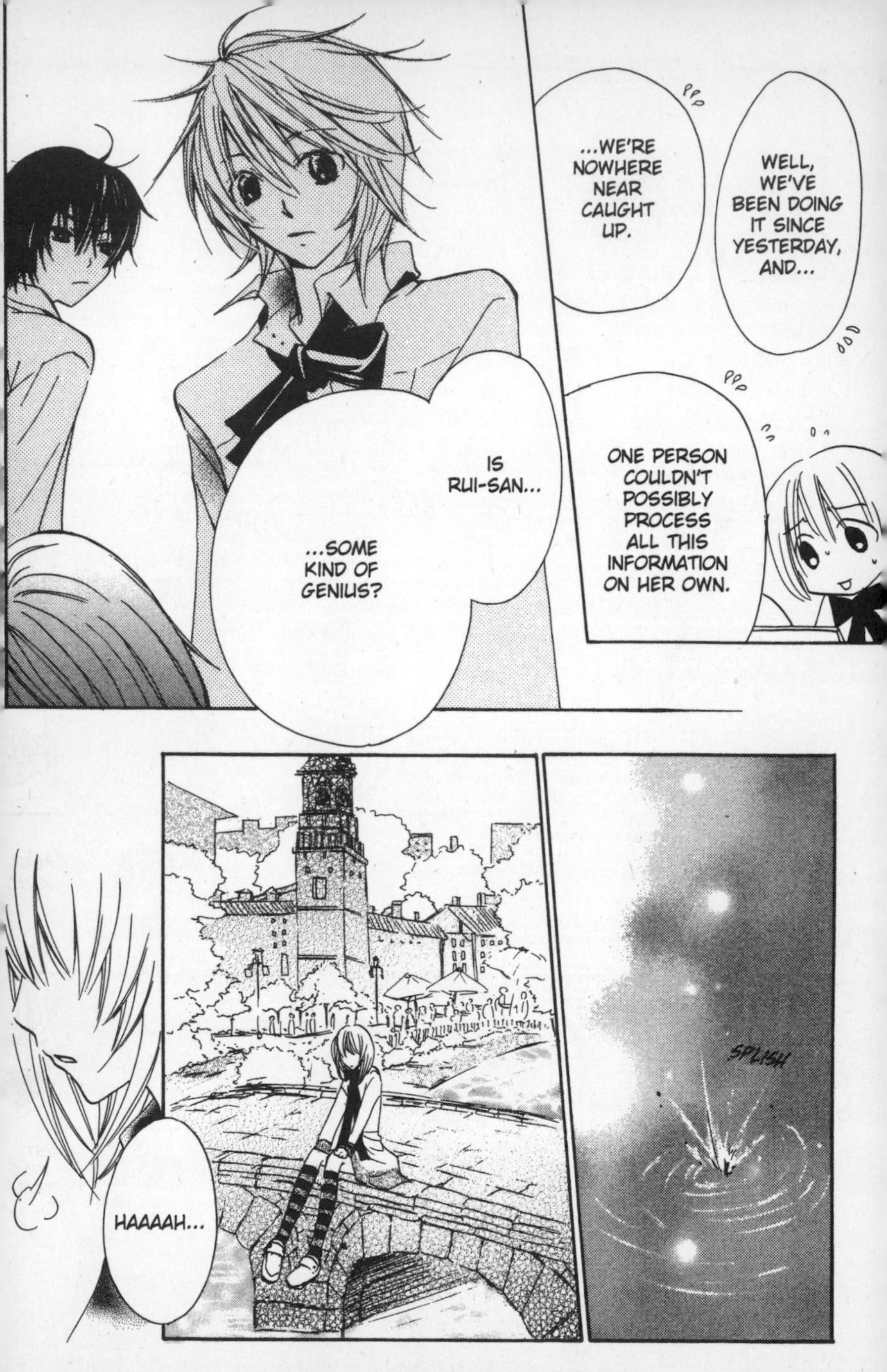
WELL, WE'VE BEEN DOING IT SINCE YESTERDAY, AND...
...WE'RE NOWHERE NEAR CAUGHT UP.
ONE PERSON COULDN'T POSSIBLY PROCESS ALL THIS INFORMATION ON HER OWN.
IS RUI-SAN...
...SOME KIND OF GENIUS?
SPLISH
HAAAAH...

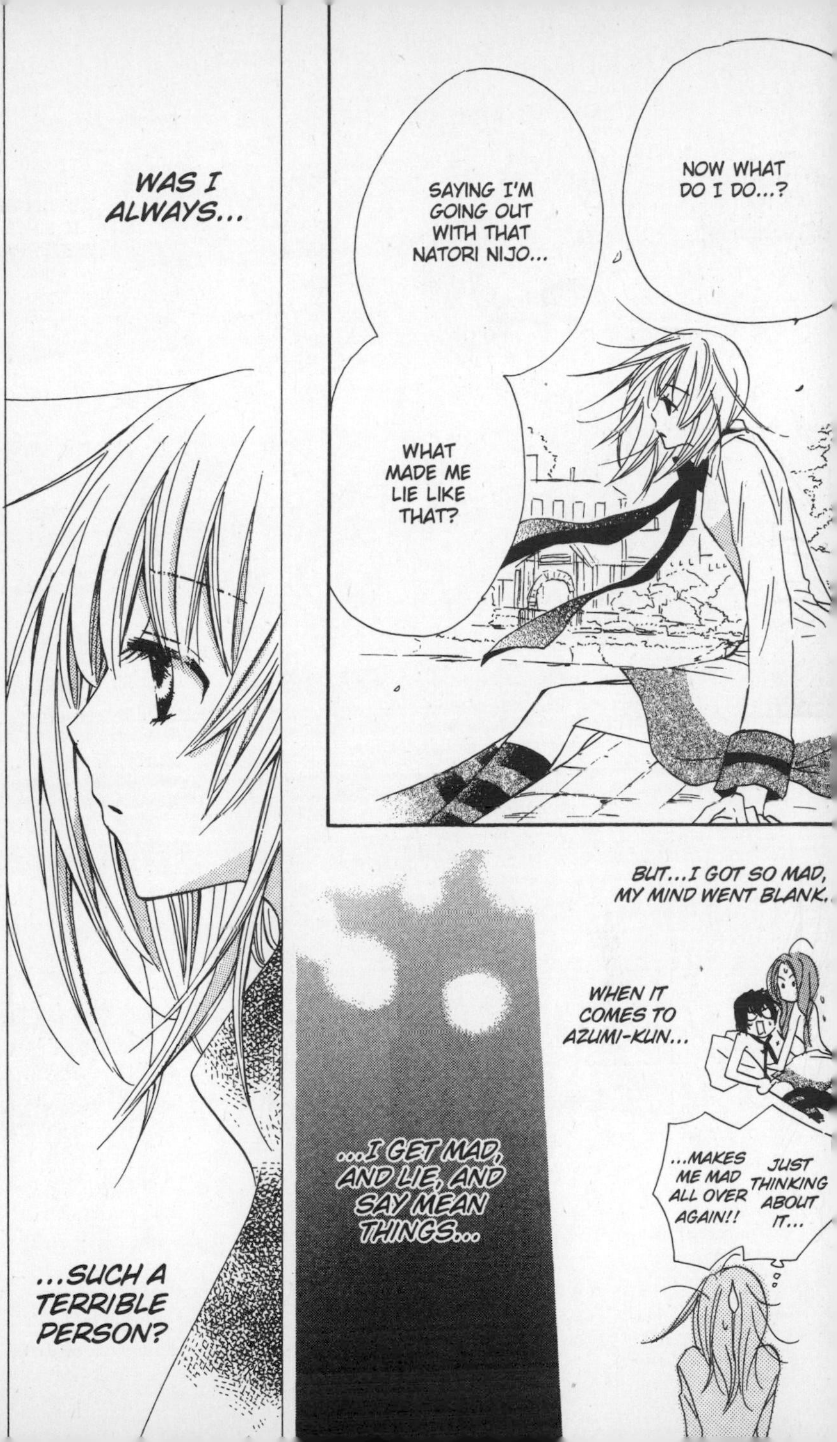
NOW WHAT DO I DO...?
SAYING I'M GOING OUT WITH THAT NATORI NIJO...
WHAT MADE ME LIE LIKE THAT?
BUT...I GOT SO MAD, MY MIND WENT BLANK.
WHEN IT COMES TO AZUMI-KUN...
JUST THINKING ABOUT IT...
...MAKES ME MAD ALL OVER AGAIN!!
...I GET MAD, AND LIE, AND SAY MEAN THINGS...
WAS I ALWAYS...
...SUCH A TERRIBLE PERSON?

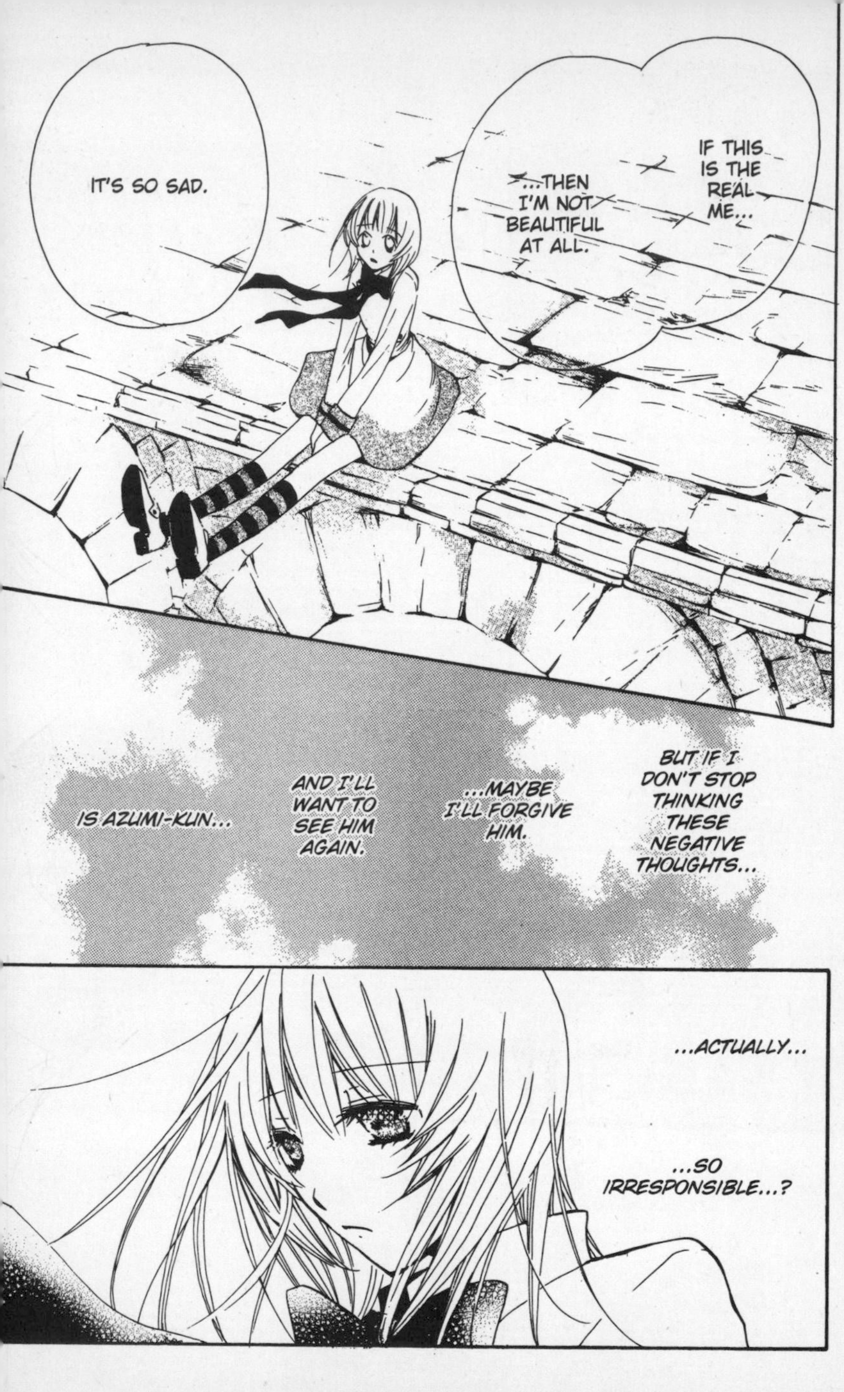
IF THIS IS THE REAL ME...
...THEN I'M NOT BEAUTIFUL AT ALL.
IT'S SO SAD.
BUT IF I DON'T STOP THINKING THESE NEGATIVE THOUGHTS...
...MAYBE I'LL FORGIVE HIM.
AND I'LL WANT TO SEE HIM AGAIN.
IS AZUMI-KUN...
...ACTUALLY...
...SO IRRESPONSIBLE...?

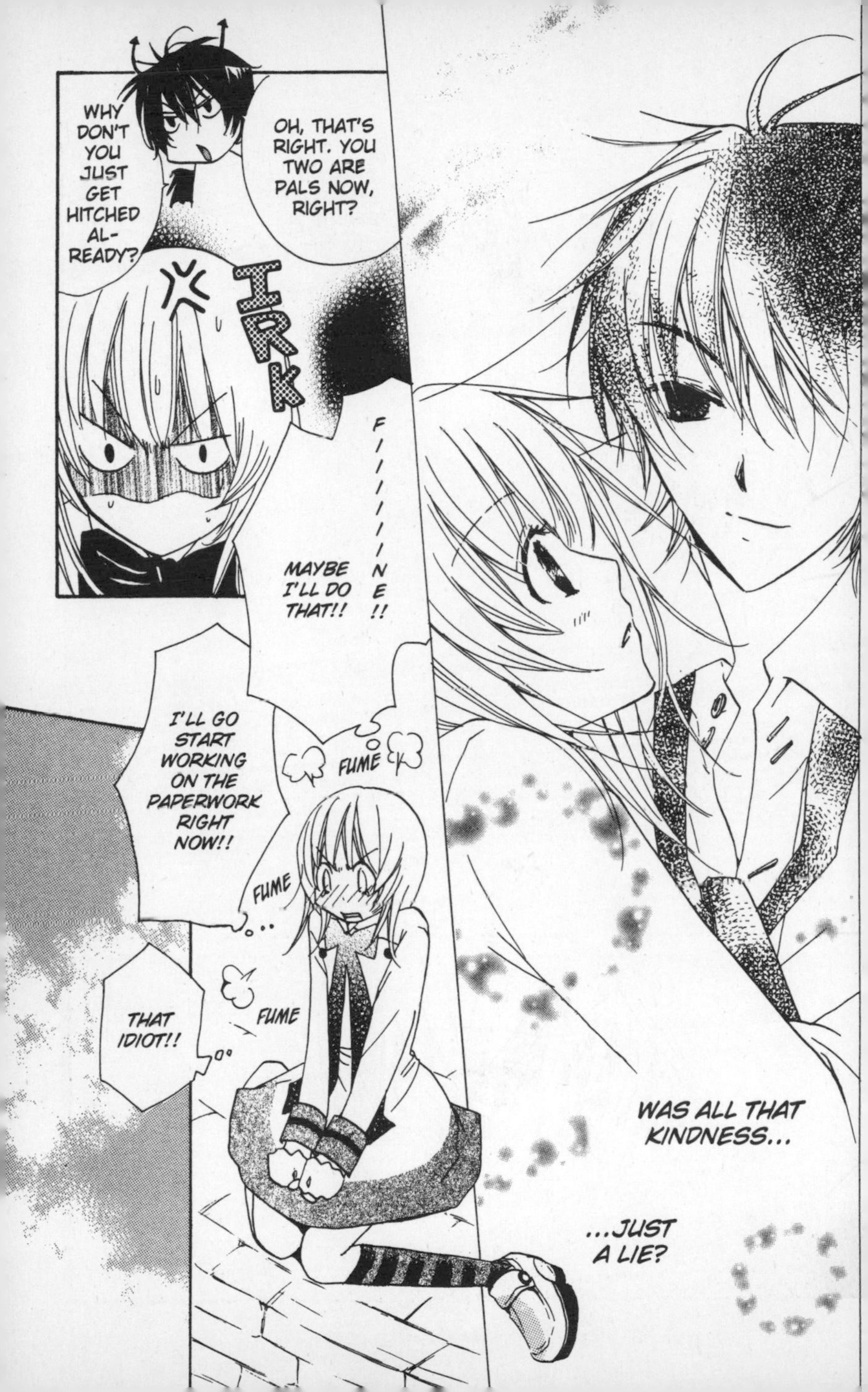
WAS ALL THAT KINDNESS...
...JUST A LIE?
OH, THAT'S RIGHT. YOU TWO ARE PALS NOW, RIGHT?
WHY DON'T YOU JUST GET HITCHED AL-READY?
IRK
F-I-I-I-I-I-I-N-E!!
MAYBE I'LL DO THAT!!
FUME
I'LL GO START WORKING ON THE PAPERWORK RIGHT NOW!!
FUME
FUME
THAT IDIOT!!

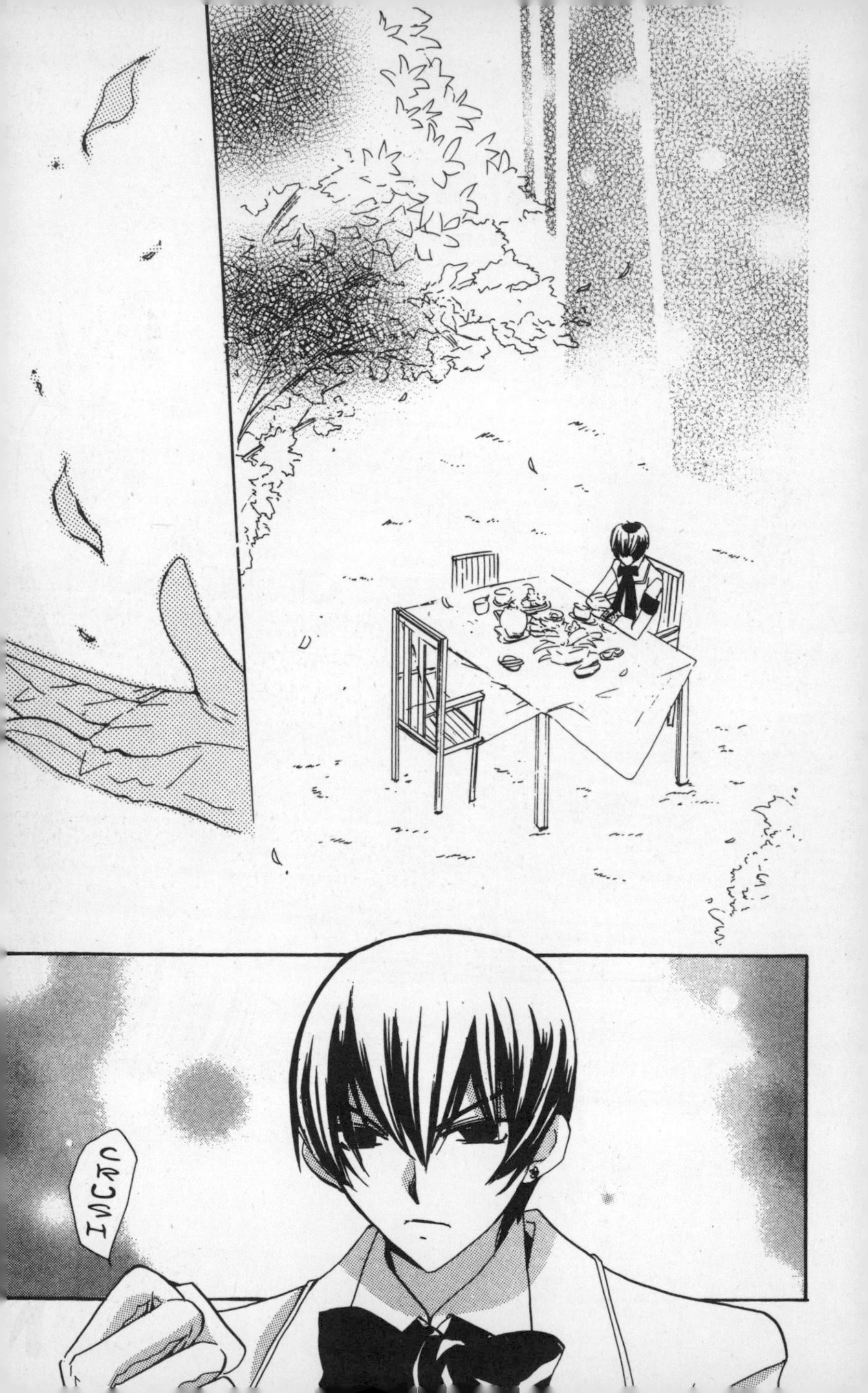

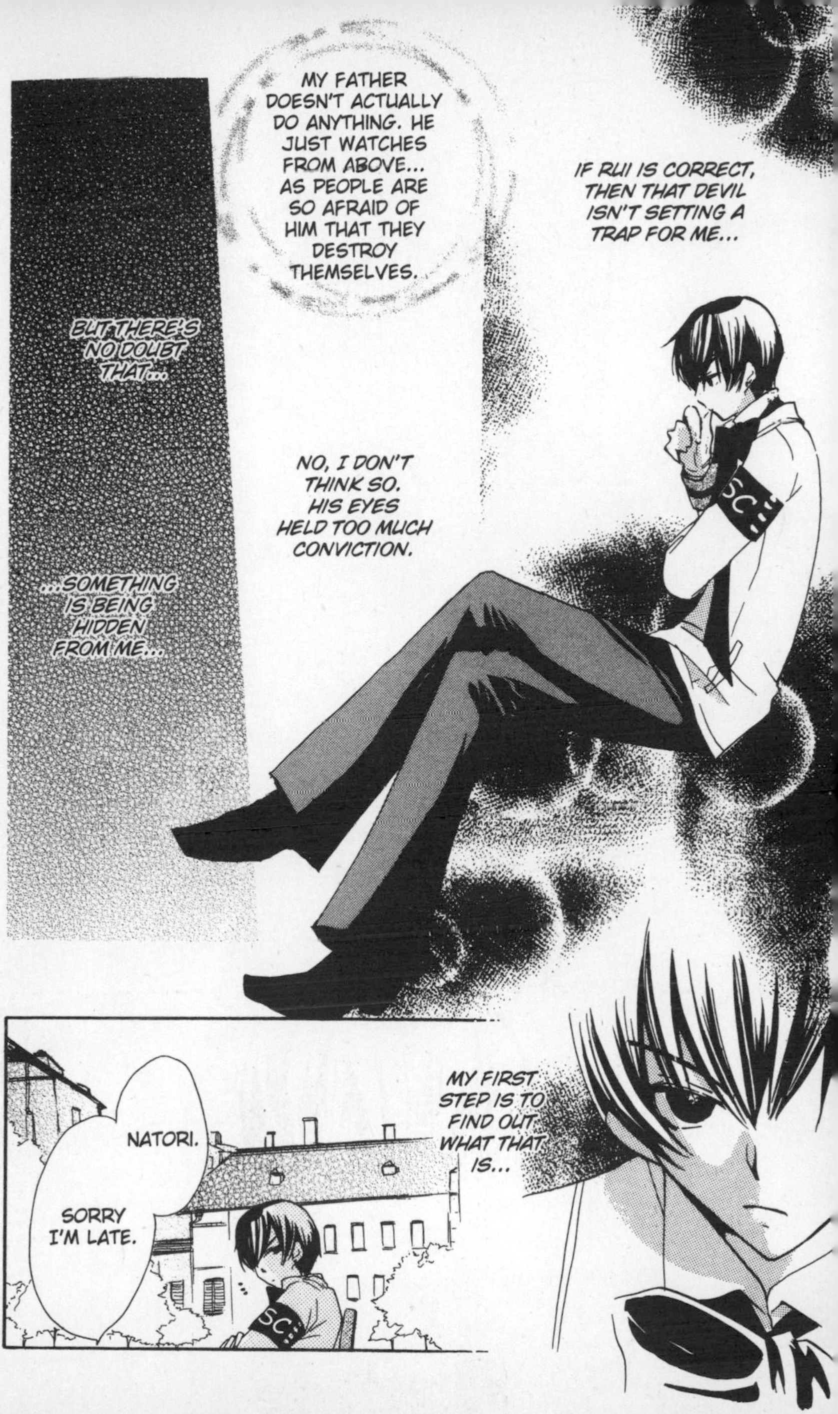
MY FATHER DOESN'T ACTUALLY DO ANYTHING. HE JUST WATCHES FROM ABOVE... AS PEOPLE ARE SO AFRAID OF HIM THAT THEY DESTROY THEMSELVES.
IF RUI IS CORRECT, THEN THAT DEVIL ISN'T SETTING A TRAP FOR ME...
NO, I DON'T THINK SO. HIS EYES HELD TOO MUCH CONVICTION.
BUT THERE'S NO DOUBT THAT...
...SOMETHING IS BEING HIDDEN FROM ME...
MY FIRST STEP IS TO FIND OUT WHAT THAT IS...
NATORI.
SORRY I'M LATE.

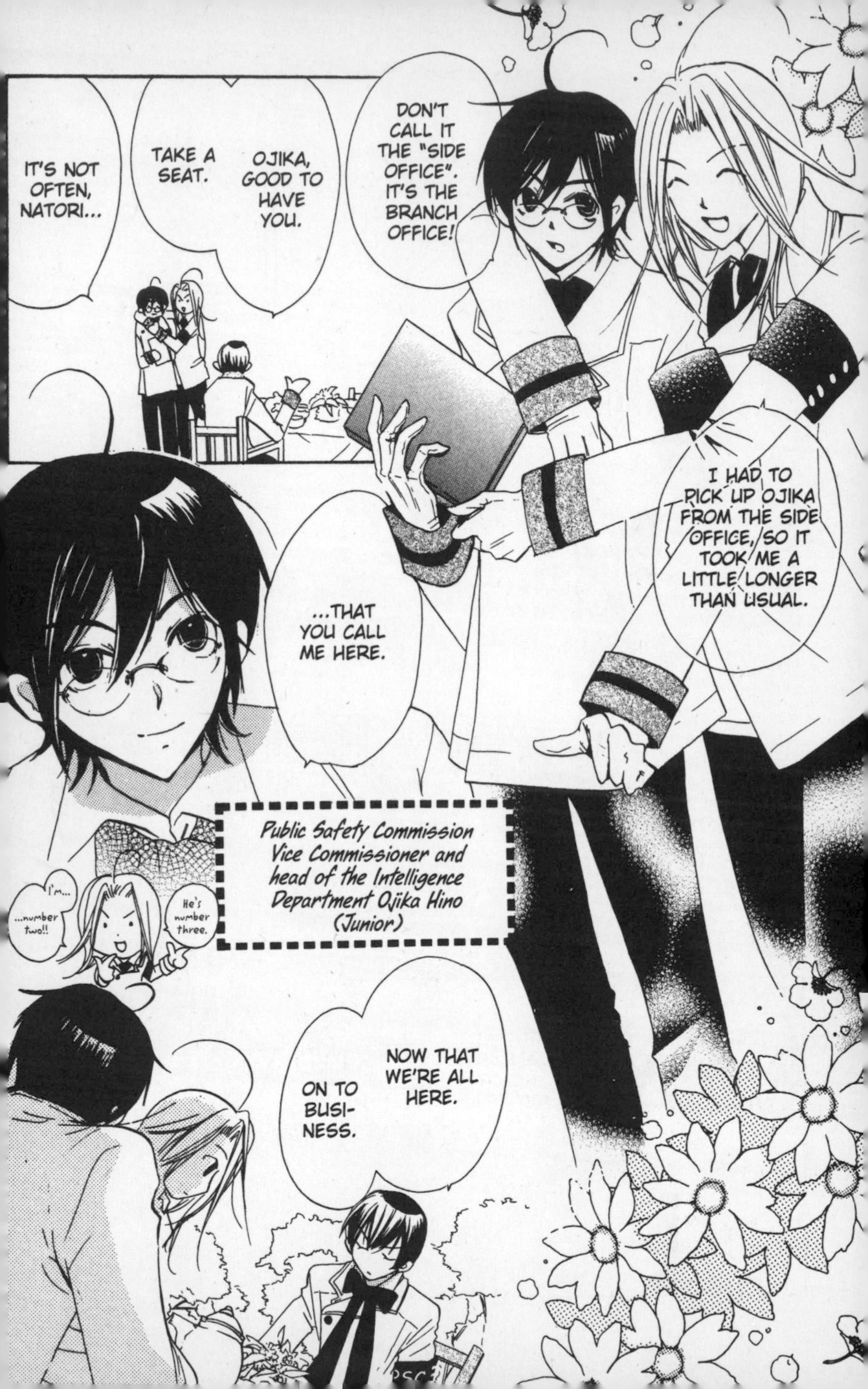
DON'T CALL IT THE "SIDE OFFICE". IT'S THE BRANCH OFFICE!
OJIKA, GOOD TO HAVE YOU.
TAKE A SEAT.
IT'S NOT OFTEN, NATORI...
I HAD TO PICK UP OJIKA FROM THE SIDE OFFICE, SO IT TOOK ME A LITTLE LONGER THAN USUAL.
...THAT YOU CALL ME HERE.
Public Safety Commission Vice Commissioner and head of the Intelligence Department Ojika Hino (Junior)
He's number three.
I'm... ...number two!!
NOW THAT WE'RE ALL HERE.
ON TO BUSINESS.

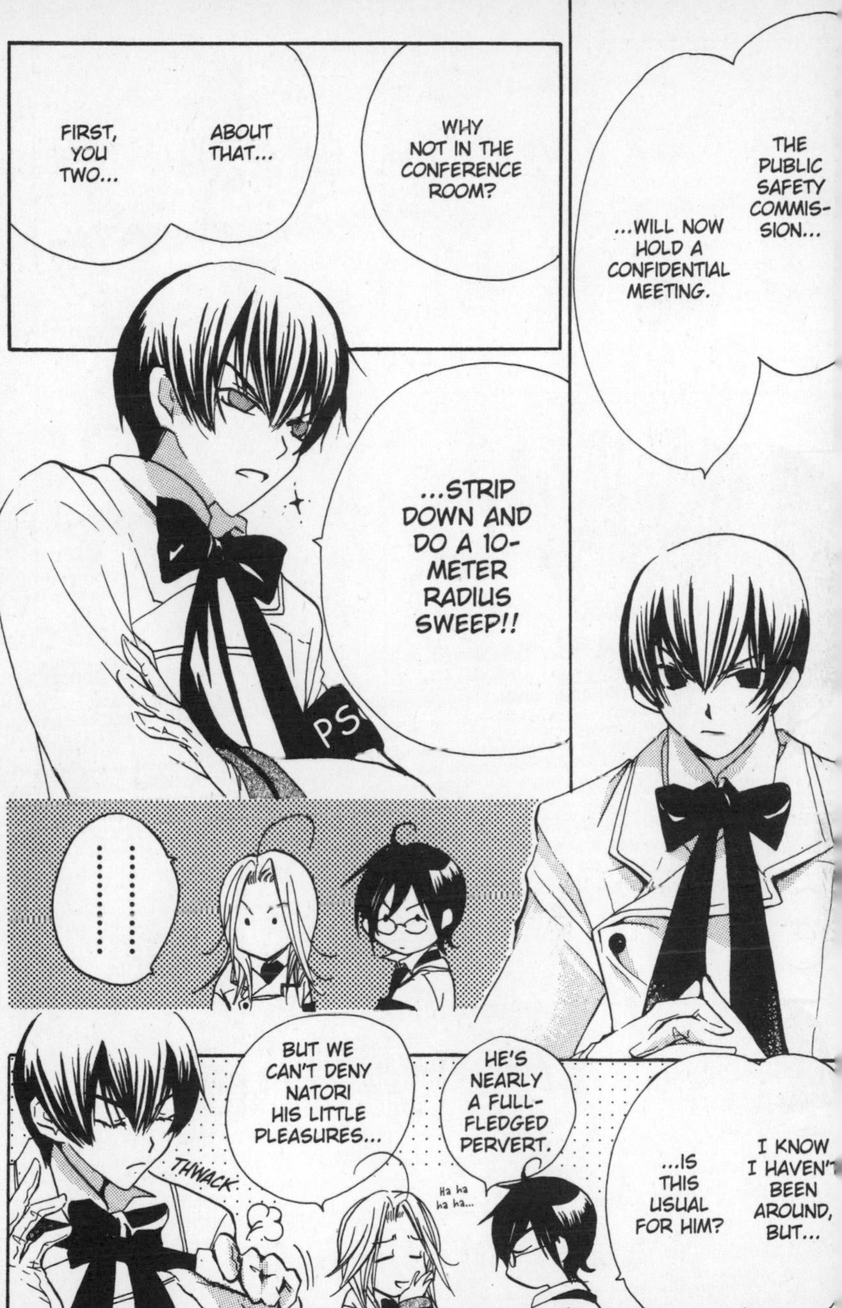
THE PUBLIC SAFETY COMMISSION...
...WILL NOW HOLD A CONFIDENTIAL MEETING.
WHY NOT IN THE CONFERENCE ROOM?
ABOUT THAT...
FIRST, YOU TWO...
...STRIP DOWN AND DO A 10-METER RADIUS SWEEP!!
PS
......
I KNOW I HAVEN'T BEEN AROUND, BUT...
...IS THIS USUAL FOR HIM?
HE'S NEARLY A FULL-FLEDGED PERVERT.
Ha ha ha ha...
BUT WE CAN'T DENY NATORI HIS LITTLE PLEASURES...
THWACK

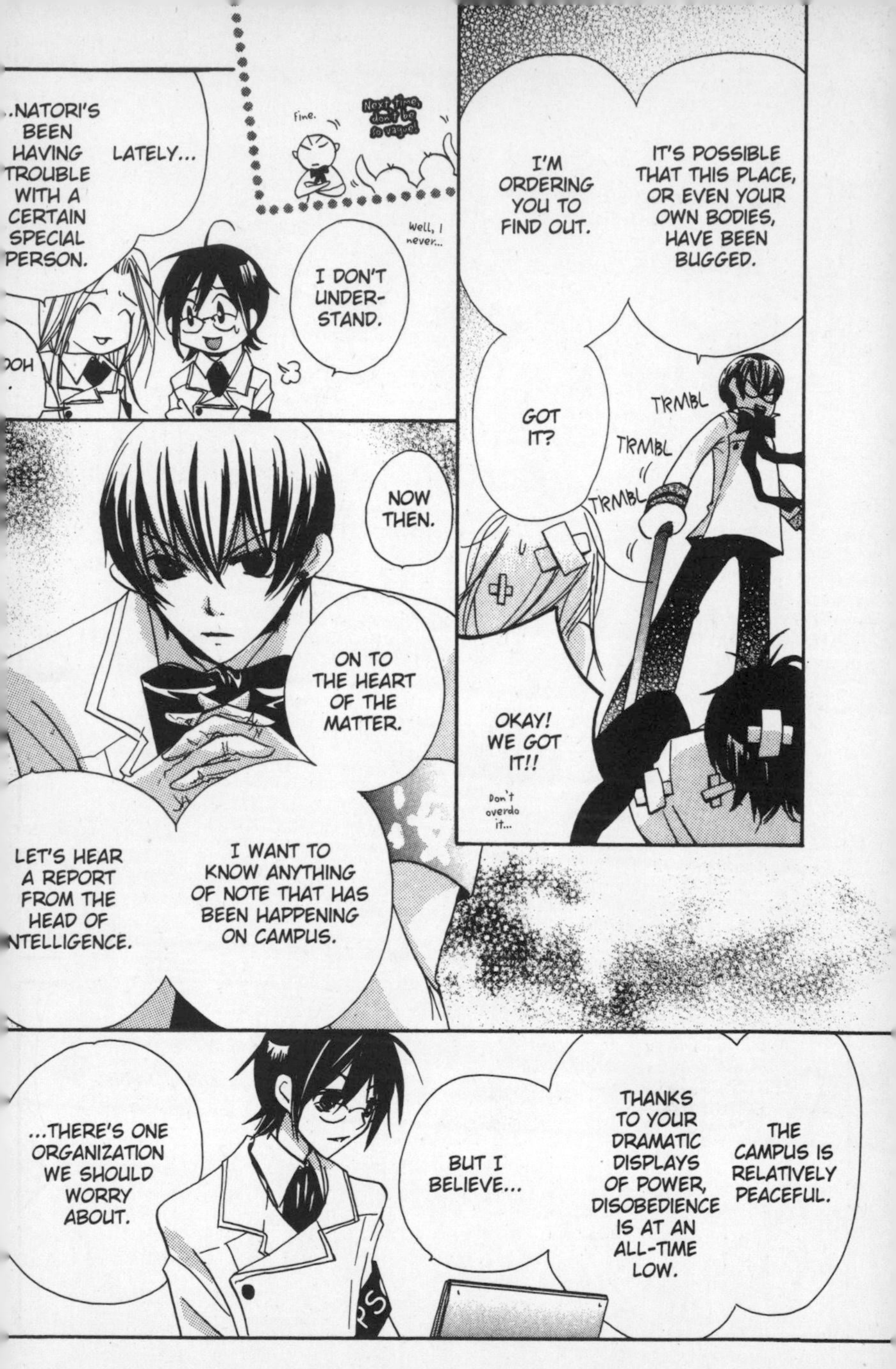
IT'S POSSIBLE THAT THIS PLACE, OR EVEN YOUR OWN BODIES, HAVE BEEN BUGGED.
I'M ORDERING YOU TO FIND OUT.
GOT IT?
TRMBL
TRMBL
TRMBL
OKAY! WE GOT IT!!
Don't overdo it...
Next time, don't be so vague!
Fine.
LATELY...
..NATORI'S BEEN HAVING TROUBLE WITH A CERTAIN SPECIAL PERSON.
Well, I never...
I DON'T UNDERSTAND.
NOW THEN.
ON TO THE HEART OF THE MATTER.
I WANT TO KNOW ANYTHING OF NOTE THAT HAS BEEN HAPPENING ON CAMPUS.
LET'S HEAR A REPORT FROM THE HEAD OF NTELLIGENCE.
THE CAMPUS IS RELATIVELY PEACEFUL.
THANKS TO YOUR DRAMATIC DISPLAYS OF POWER, DISOBEDIENCE IS AT AN ALL-TIME LOW.
BUT I BELIEVE...
...THERE'S ONE ORGANIZATION WE SHOULD WORRY ABOUT.

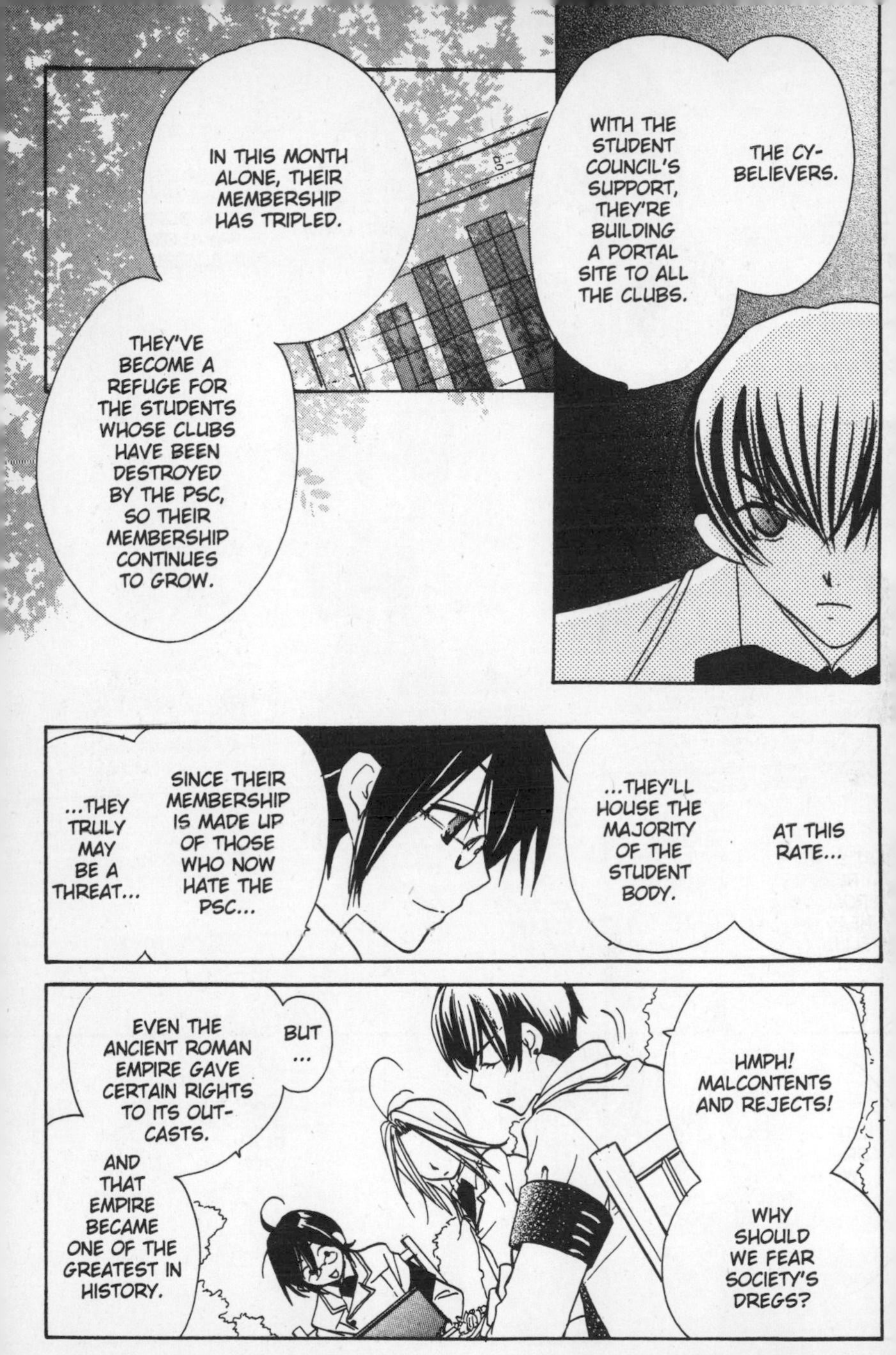
THE CY-BELIEVERS.
WITH THE STUDENT COUNCIL'S SUPPORT, THEY'RE BUILDING A PORTAL SITE TO ALL THE CLUBS.
IN THIS MONTH ALONE, THEIR MEMBERSHIP HAS TRIPLED.
THEY'VE BECOME A REFUGE FOR THE STUDENTS WHOSE CLUBS HAVE BEEN DESTROYED BY THE PSC, SO THEIR MEMBERSHIP CONTINUES TO GROW.
AT THIS RATE...
...THEY'LL HOUSE THE MAJORITY OF THE STUDENT BODY.
SINCE THEIR MEMBERSHIP IS MADE UP OF THOSE WHO NOW HATE THE PSC...
...THEY TRULY MAY BE A THREAT...
HMPH! MALCONTENTS AND REJECTS!
WHY SHOULD WE FEAR SOCIETY'S DREGS?
BUT...
EVEN THE ANCIENT ROMAN EMPIRE GAVE CERTAIN RIGHTS TO ITS OUT-CASTS.
AND THAT EMPIRE BECAME ONE OF THE GREATEST IN HISTORY.

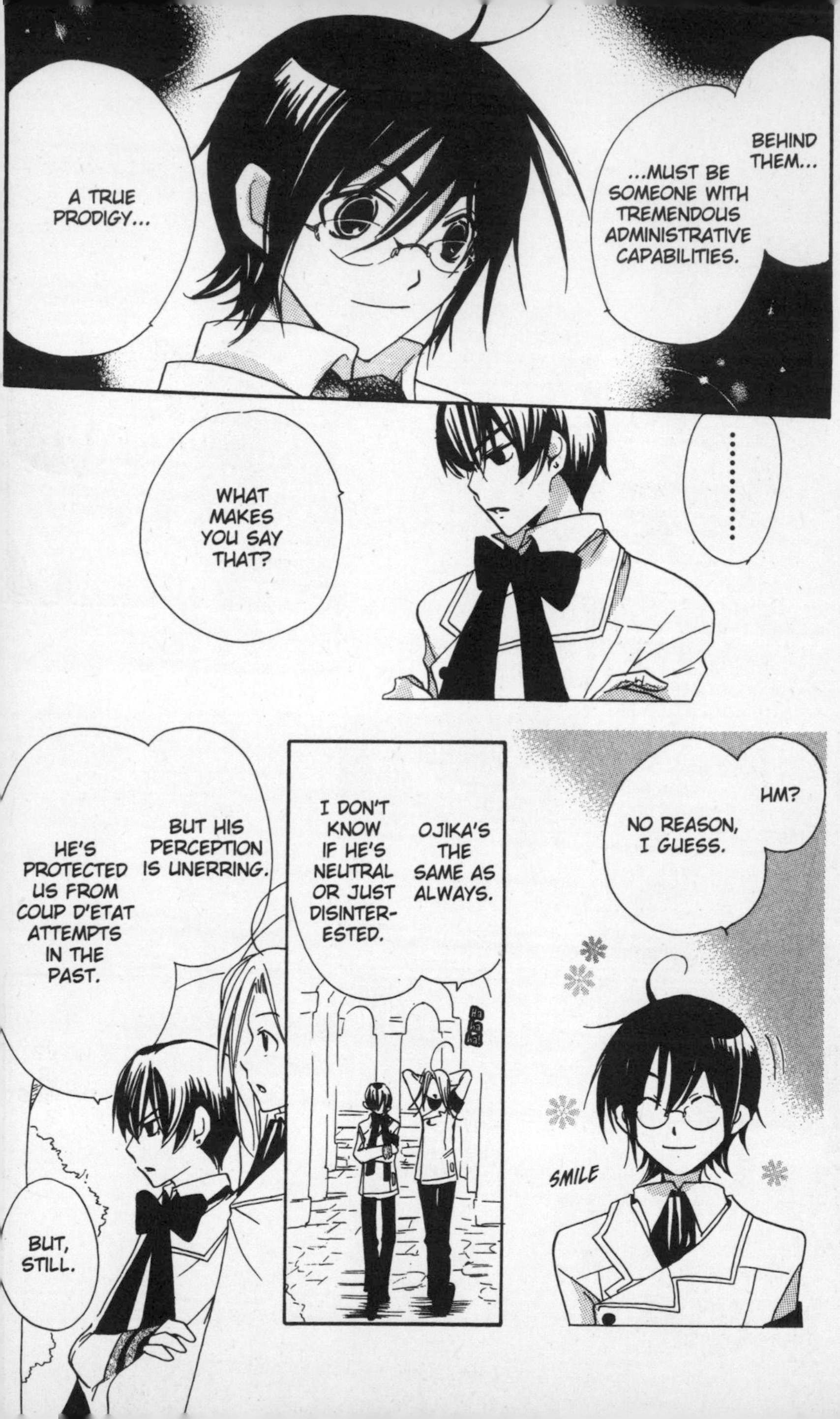
BEHIND THEM...
...MUST BE SOMEONE WITH TREMENDOUS ADMINISTRATIVE CAPABILITIES.
A TRUE PRODIGY...
......
WHAT MAKES YOU SAY THAT?
HM?
NO REASON, I GUESS.
SMILE
OJIKA'S THE SAME AS ALWAYS.
I DON'T KNOW IF HE'S NEUTRAL OR JUST DISINTER-ESTED.
Ha ha ha!
BUT HIS PERCEPTION IS UNERRING.
HE'S PROTECTED US FROM COUP D'ETAT ATTEMPTS IN THE PAST.
BUT, STILL.

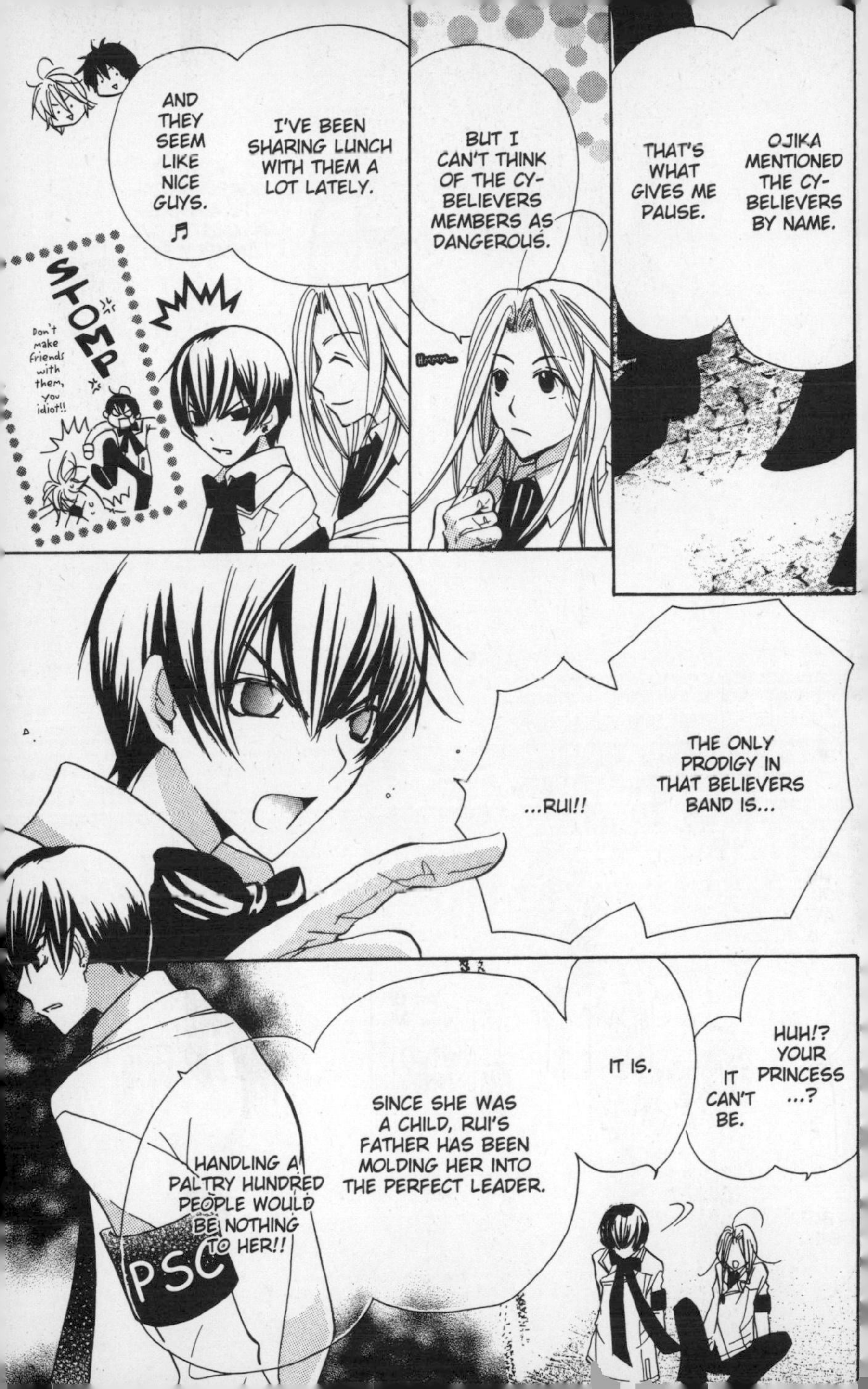
OJIKA MENTIONED THE CY-BELIEVERS BY NAME.
THAT'S WHAT GIVES ME PAUSE.
BUT I CAN'T THINK OF THE CY-BELIEVERS MEMBERS AS DANGEROUS.
HMMM...
I'VE BEEN SHARING LUNCH WITH THEM A LOT LATELY.
AND THEY SEEM LIKE NICE GUYS. ♫
STOMP
Don't make friends with them, you idiot!!
THE ONLY PRODIGY IN THAT BELIEVERS BAND IS...
...RUI!!
HUH!? YOUR PRINCESS ...?
IT CAN'T BE.
IT IS.
SINCE SHE WAS A CHILD, RUI'S FATHER HAS BEEN MOLDING HER INTO THE PERFECT LEADER.
HANDLING A PALTRY HUNDRED PEOPLE WOULD BE NOTHING TO HER!!
PSC

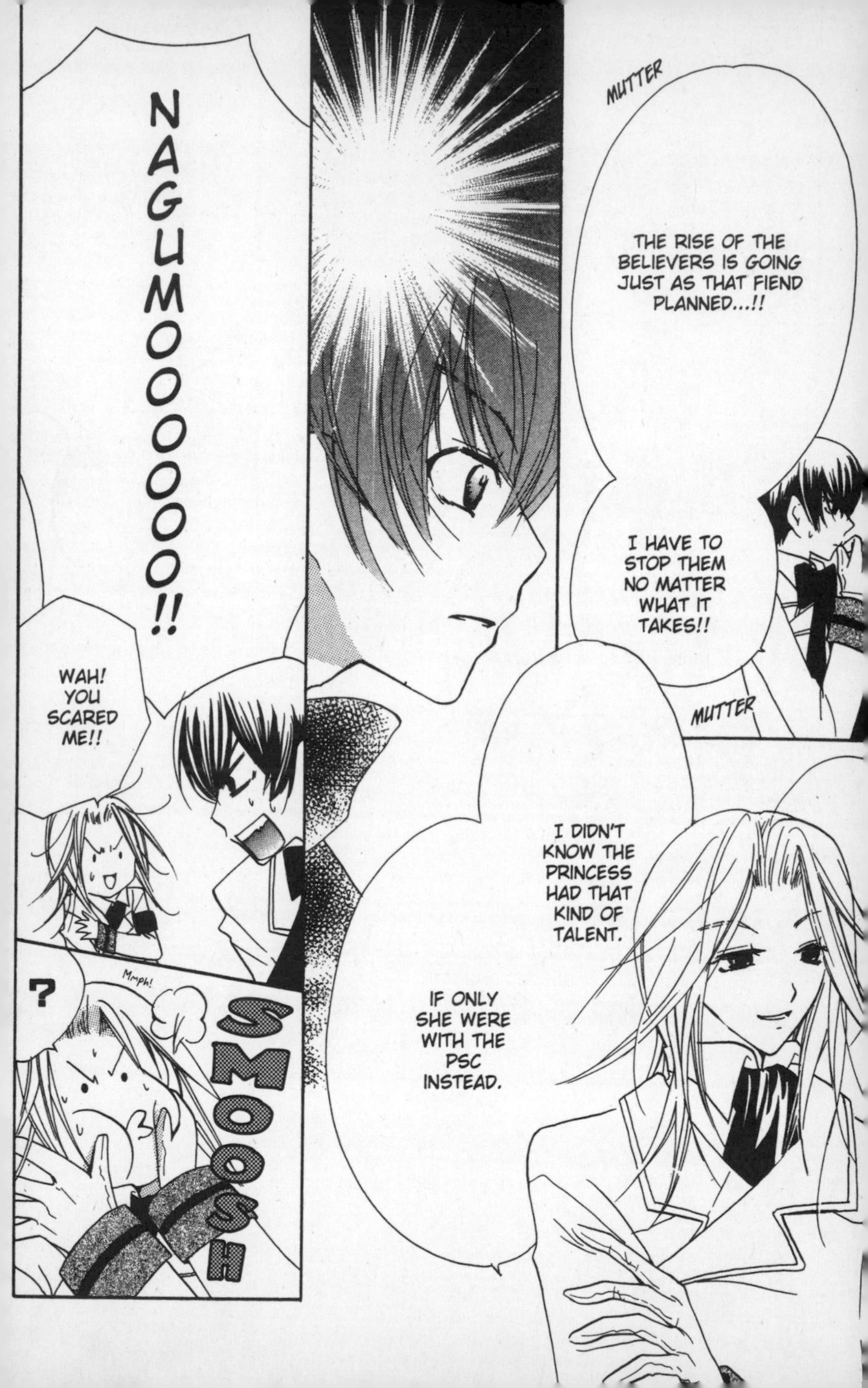
MUTTER
THE RISE OF THE BELIEVERS IS GOING JUST AS THAT FIEND PLANNED...!!
I HAVE TO STOP THEM NO MATTER WHAT IT TAKES!!
MUTTER
I DIDN'T KNOW THE PRINCESS HAD THAT KIND OF TALENT.
IF ONLY SHE WERE WITH THE PSC INSTEAD.
NAGUMOOOOOOO!!
WAH! YOU SCARED ME!!
?
Mmph!
SMOOOSH

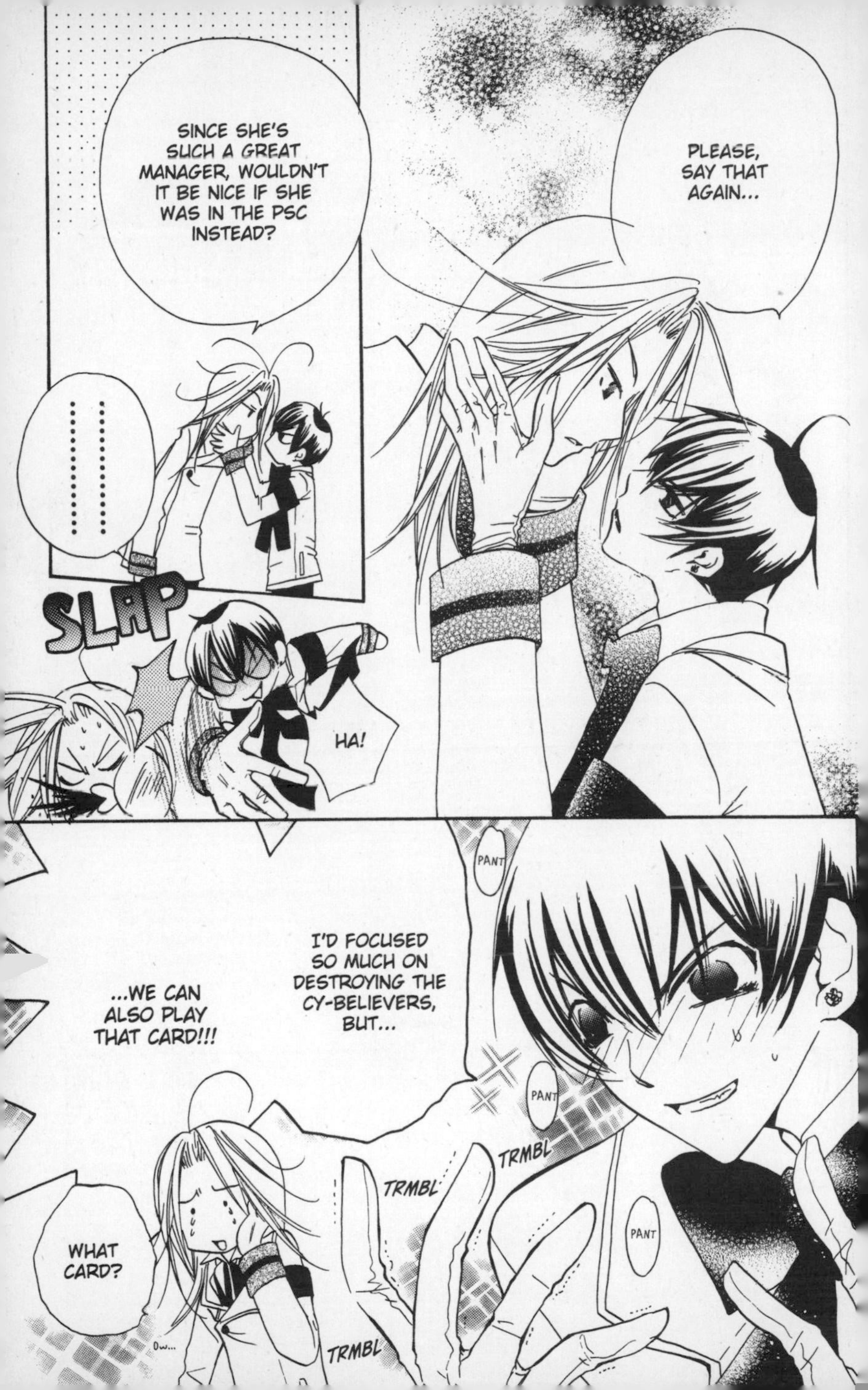
PLEASE, SAY THAT AGAIN...
SINCE SHE'S SUCH A GREAT MANAGER, WOULDN'T IT BE NICE IF SHE WAS IN THE PSC INSTEAD?
......
SLAP
HA!
PANT
I'D FOCUSED SO MUCH ON DESTROYING THE CY-BELIEVERS, BUT...
...WE CAN ALSO PLAY THAT CARD!!!
PANT
TRMBL
TRMBL
PANT
WHAT CARD?
OW...
TRMBL

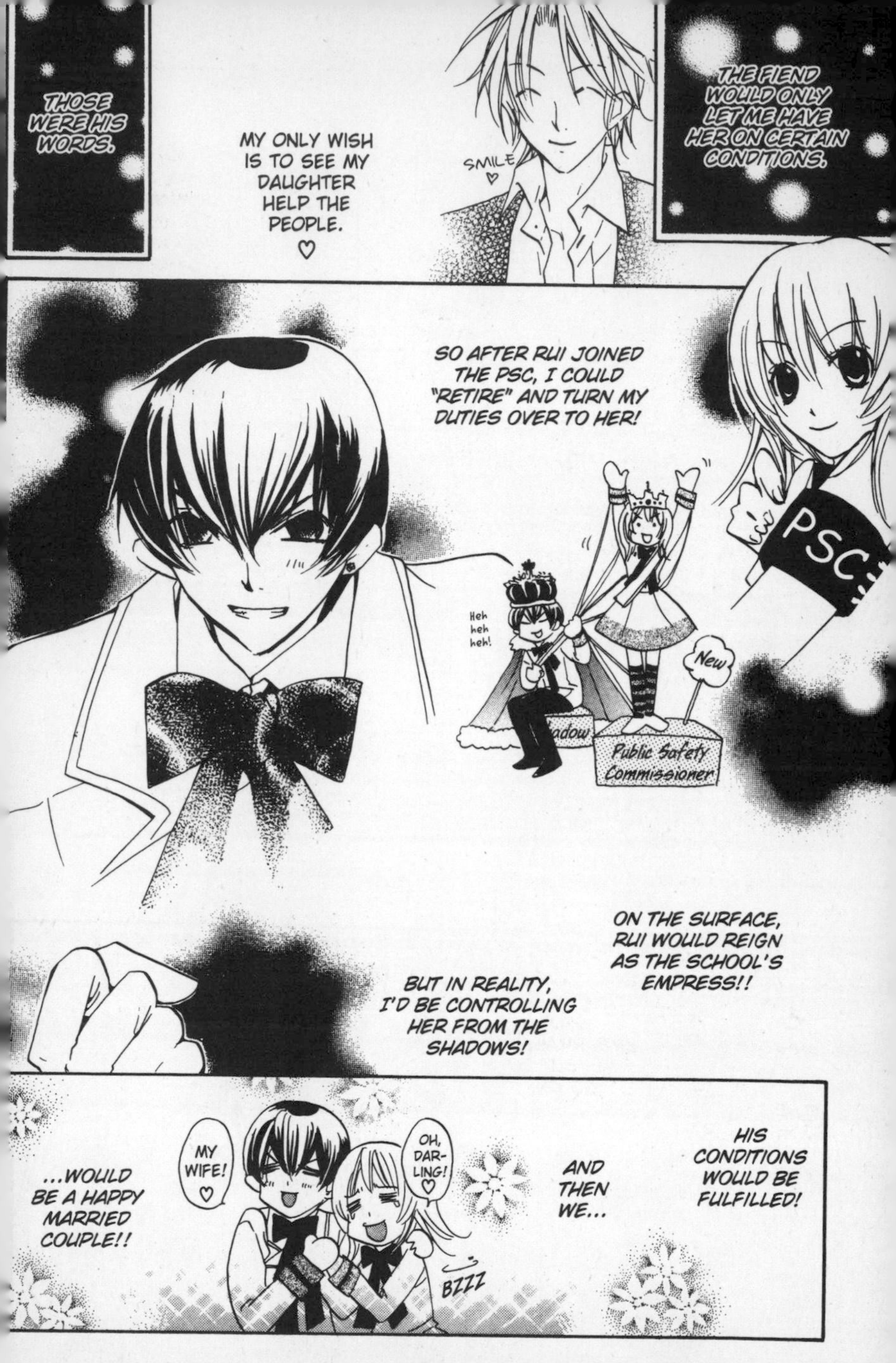

THE FIEND WOULD ONLY LET ME HAVE HER ON CERTAIN CONDITIONS.
SMILE ♡
MY ONLY WISH IS TO SEE MY DAUGHTER HELP THE PEOPLE. ♡
THOSE WERE HIS WORDS.
PSC
SO AFTER RUI JOINED THE PSC, I COULD "RETIRE" AND TURN MY DUTIES OVER TO HER!
New
Public Safety Commissioner
Heh heh heh!
ON THE SURFACE, RUI WOULD REIGN AS THE SCHOOL'S EMPRESS!!
BUT IN REALITY, I'D BE CONTROLLING HER FROM THE SHADOWS!
HIS CONDITIONS WOULD BE FULFILLED!
AND THEN WE...
OH, DARLING! ♡
BZZZ
MY WIFE! ♡
...WOULD BE A HAPPY MARRIED COUPLE!!

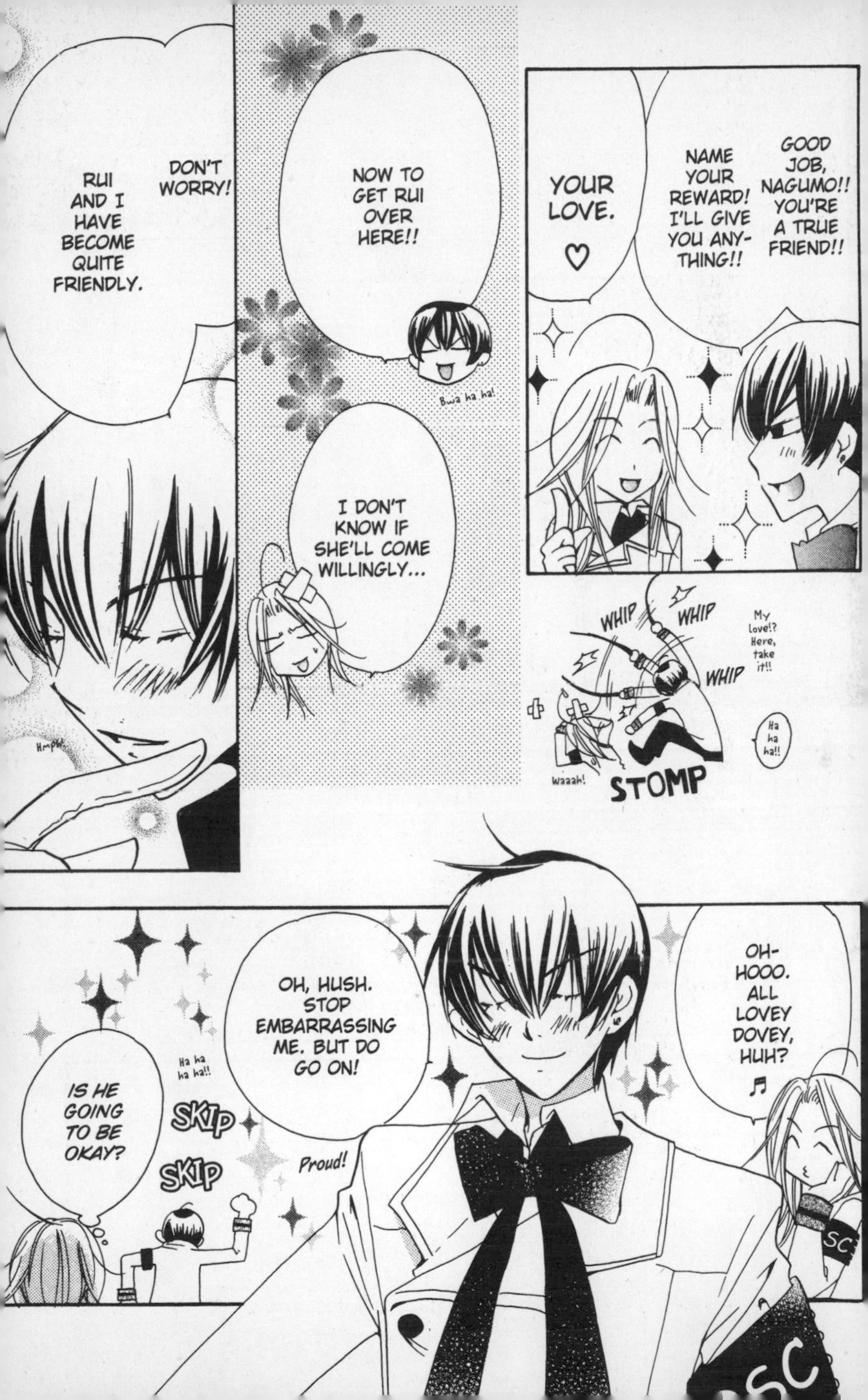
GOOD JOB, NAGUMO!! YOU'RE A TRUE FRIEND!!
NAME YOUR REWARD! I'LL GIVE YOU ANY-THING!!
YOUR LOVE. ♡
My love!? Here, take it!!
WHIP
WHIP
WHIP
Ha ha ha!!
Waaah!
STOMP
NOW TO GET RUI OVER HERE!!
Bwa ha ha!
I DON'T KNOW IF SHE'LL COME WILLINGLY...
DON'T WORRY!
RUI AND I HAVE BECOME QUITE FRIENDLY.
Hmph!
OH-HOOO. ALL LOVEY DOVEY, HUH? ♫
OH, HUSH. STOP EMBARRASSING ME. BUT DO GO ON!
Proud!
Ha ha ha ha!!
SKIP
SKIP
IS HE GOING TO BE OKAY?

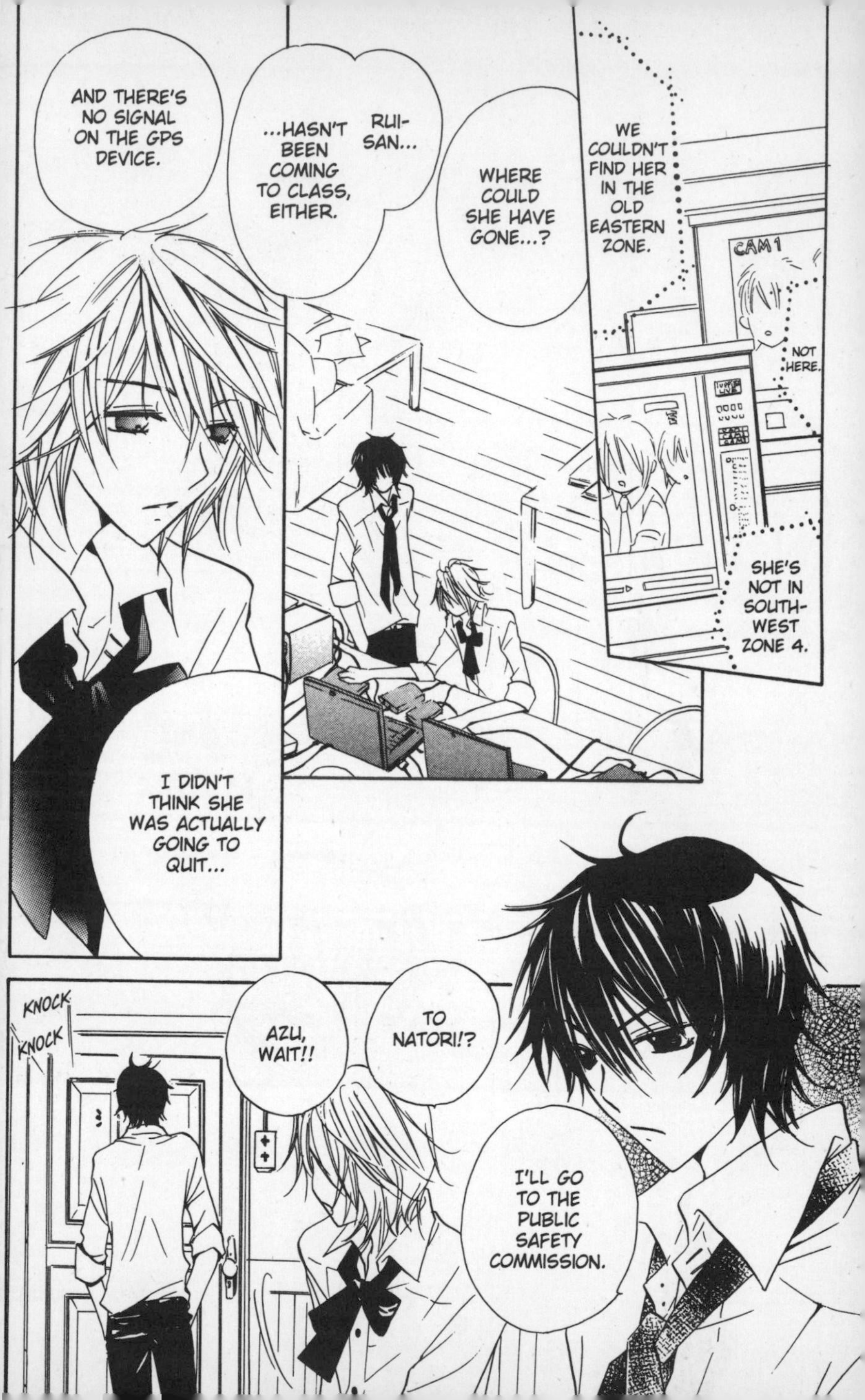
WE COULDN'T FIND HER IN THE OLD EASTERN ZONE.
CAM 1
NOT HERE.
SHE'S NOT IN SOUTH-WEST ZONE 4.
WHERE COULD SHE HAVE GONE...?
RUI-SAN...
...HASN'T BEEN COMING TO CLASS, EITHER.
AND THERE'S NO SIGNAL ON THE GPS DEVICE.
I DIDN'T THINK SHE WAS ACTUALLY GOING TO QUIT...
I'LL GO TO THE PUBLIC SAFETY COMMISSION.
TO NATORI!?
AZU, WAIT!!
KNOCK
KNOCK

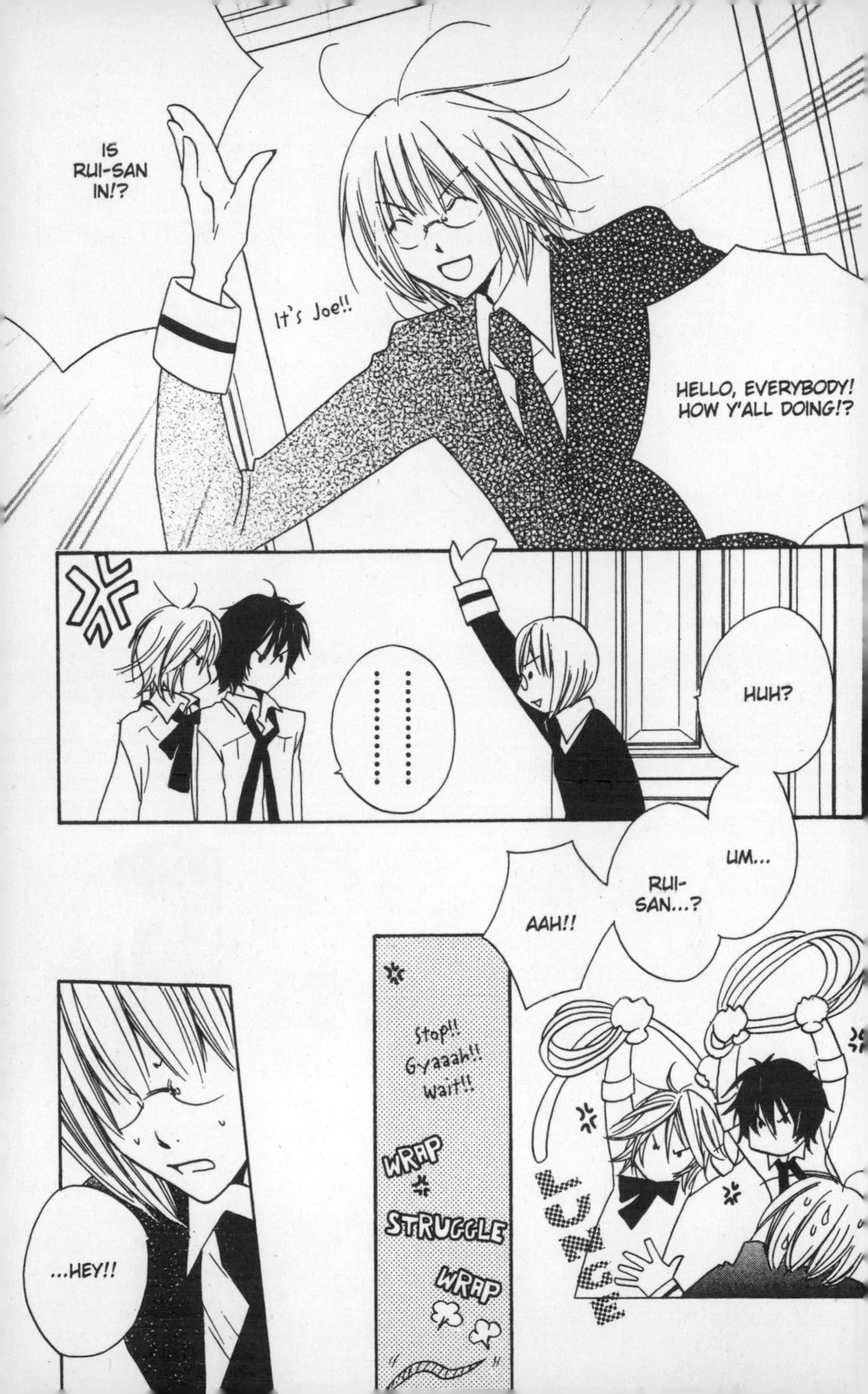
HELLO, EVERYBODY! HOW Y'ALL DOING!?
It's Joe!!
IS RUI-SAN IN!?
HUH?
......
UM... RUI-SAN...?
AAH!!
LUNGE
Stop!! Gyaaah!! Wait!!
WRAP
STRUGGLE
WRAP
...HEY!!

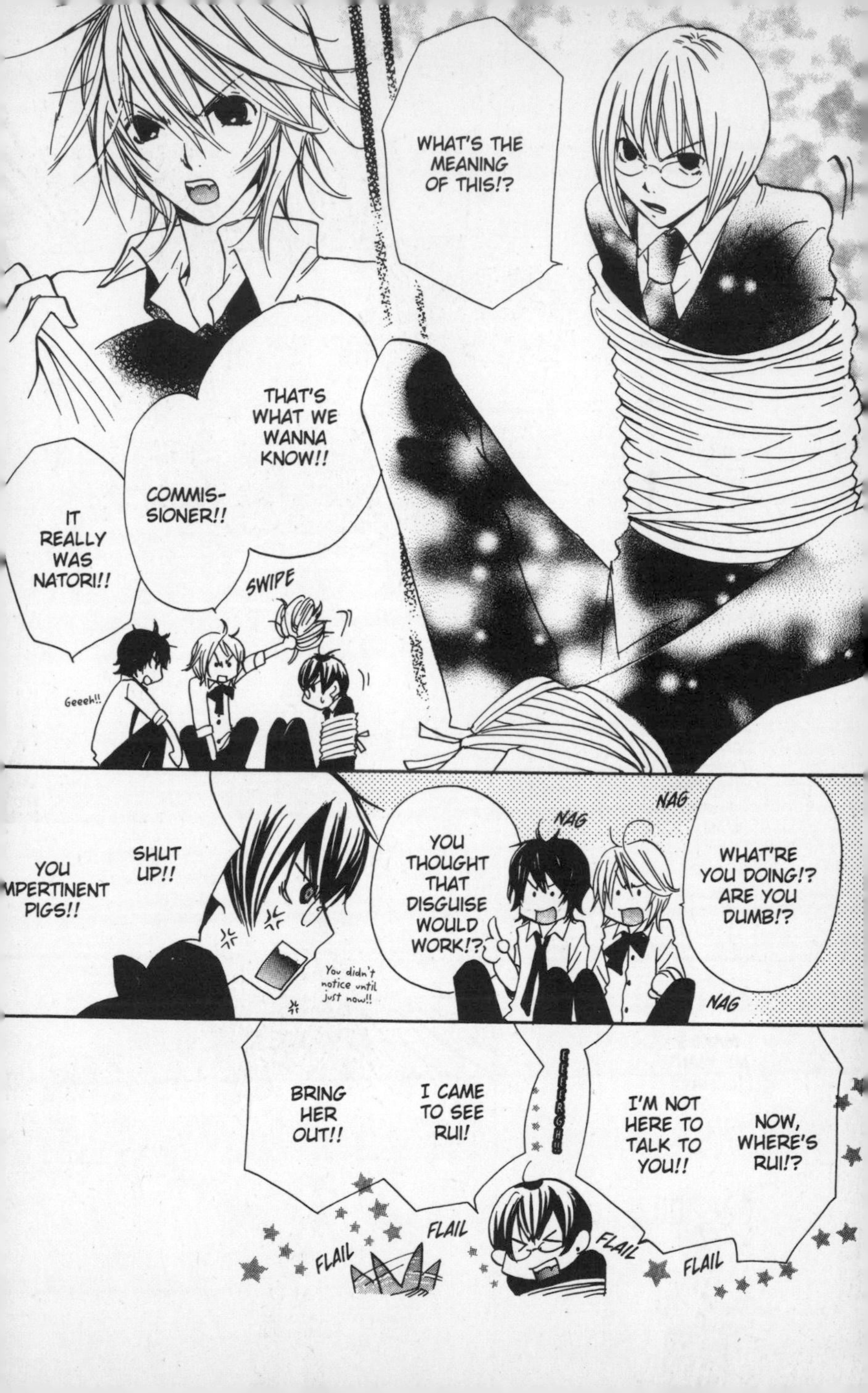
WHAT'S THE MEANING OF THIS!?
THAT'S WHAT WE WANNA KNOW!!
COMMIS-SIONER!!
IT REALLY WAS NATORI!!
SWIPE
Geeeh!!
NAG
WHAT'RE YOU DOING!? ARE YOU DUMB!?
NAG
YOU THOUGHT THAT DISGUISE WOULD WORK!?
NAG
SHUT UP!!
YOU IMPERTINENT PIGS!!
You didn't notice until just now!!
NOW, WHERE'S RUI!?
I'M NOT HERE TO TALK TO YOU!!
EEEERGH!!
I CAME TO SEE RUI!
BRING HER OUT!!
FLAIL
FLAIL
FLAIL
FLAIL

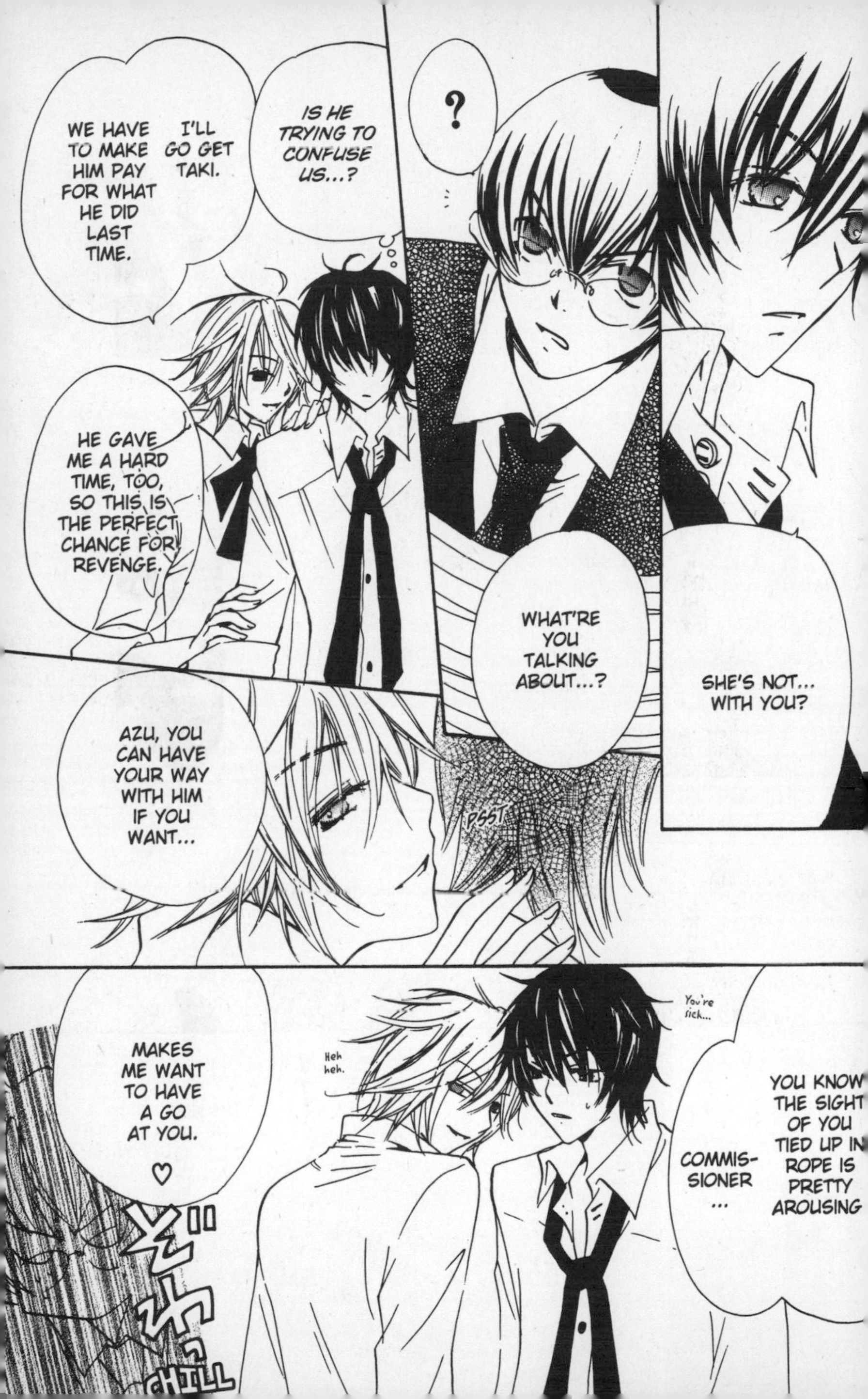
SHE'S NOT... WITH YOU?
?
WHAT'RE YOU TALKING ABOUT...?
IS HE TRYING TO CONFUSE US...?
I'LL GO GET TAKI.
WE HAVE TO MAKE HIM PAY FOR WHAT HE DID LAST TIME.
HE GAVE ME A HARD TIME, TOO, SO THIS IS THE PERFECT CHANCE FOR REVENGE.
PSST
AZU, YOU CAN HAVE YOUR WAY WITH HIM IF YOU WANT...
COMMISSIONER...
YOU KNOW THE SIGHT OF YOU TIED UP IN ROPE IS PRETTY AROUSING
You're sick...
Heh heh.
MAKES ME WANT TO HAVE A GO AT YOU. ♡
CHILL

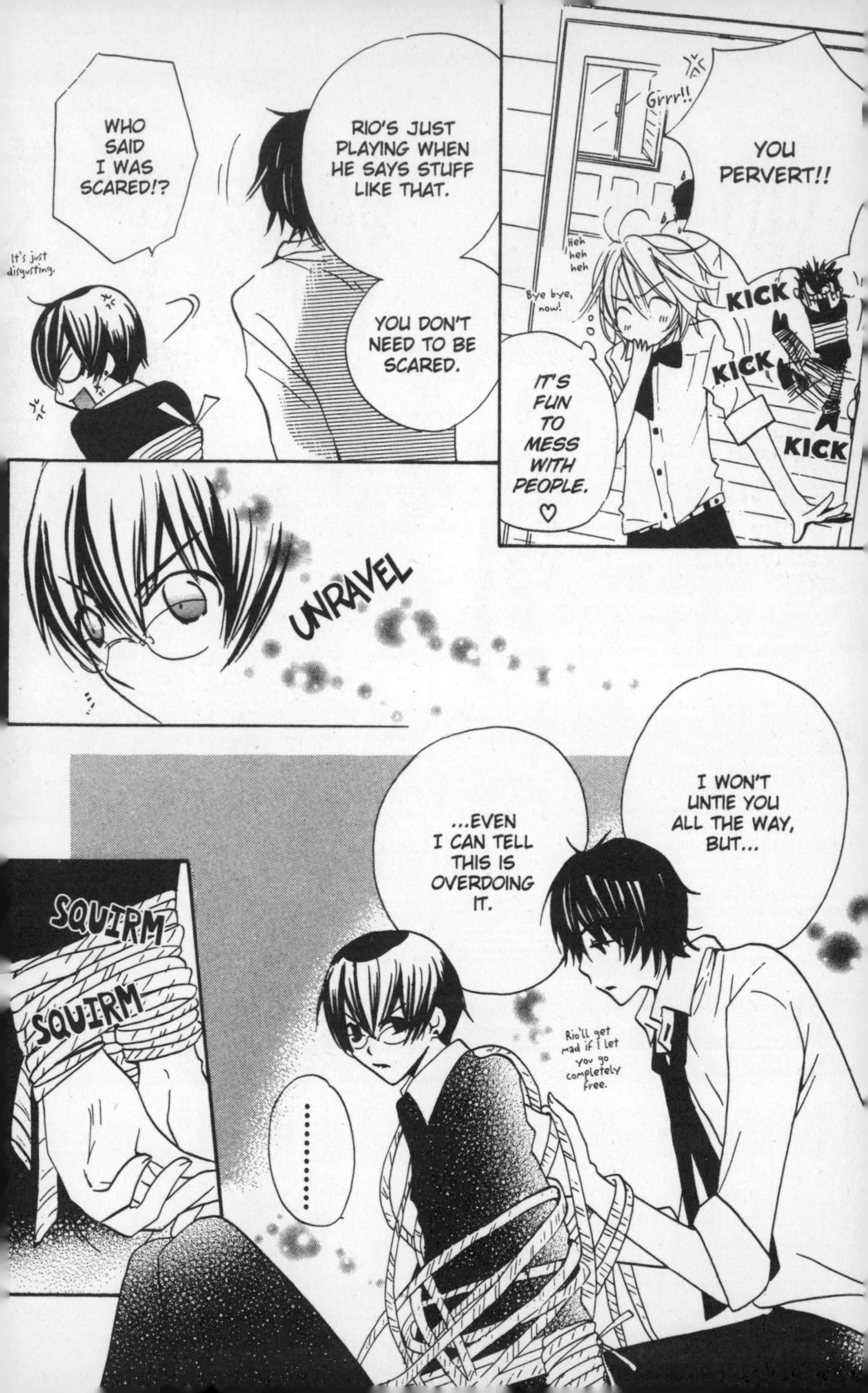
Grrr!!
YOU PERVERT!!
Heh heh heh
Bye bye, now!
KICK
KICK
KICK
IT'S FUN TO MESS WITH PEOPLE. ♡
RIO'S JUST PLAYING WHEN HE SAYS STUFF LIKE THAT.
YOU DON'T NEED TO BE SCARED.
WHO SAID I WAS SCARED!?
It's just disgusting.
UNRAVEL
I WON'T UNTIE YOU ALL THE WAY, BUT...
...EVEN I CAN TELL THIS IS OVERDOING IT.
Rio'll get mad if I let you go completely free.
....
SQUIRM
SQUIRM

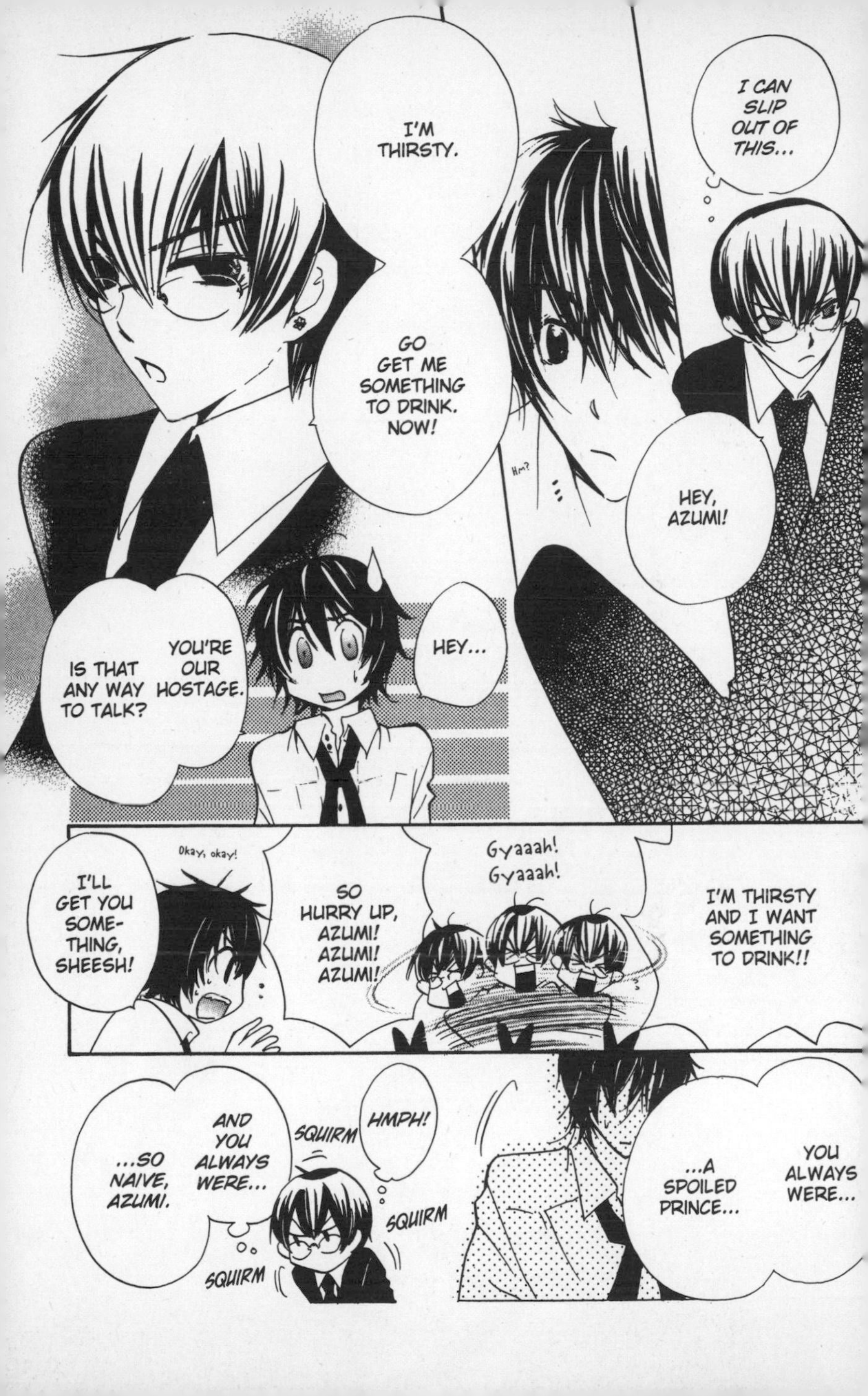
I CAN SLIP OUT OF THIS...
HEY, AZUMI!
Hm?
I'M THIRSTY.
GO GET ME SOMETHING TO DRINK. NOW!
HEY...
YOU'RE OUR HOSTAGE.
IS THAT ANY WAY TO TALK?
I'M THIRSTY AND I WANT SOMETHING TO DRINK!!
Gyaaah! Gyaaah!
SO HURRY UP, AZUMI! AZUMI! AZUMI!
Okay, okay!
I'LL GET YOU SOME-THING, SHEESH!
YOU ALWAYS WERE...
...A SPOILED PRINCE...
HMPH!
SQUIRM
SQUIRM
SQUIRM
AND YOU ALWAYS WERE...
...SO NAIVE, AZUMI.

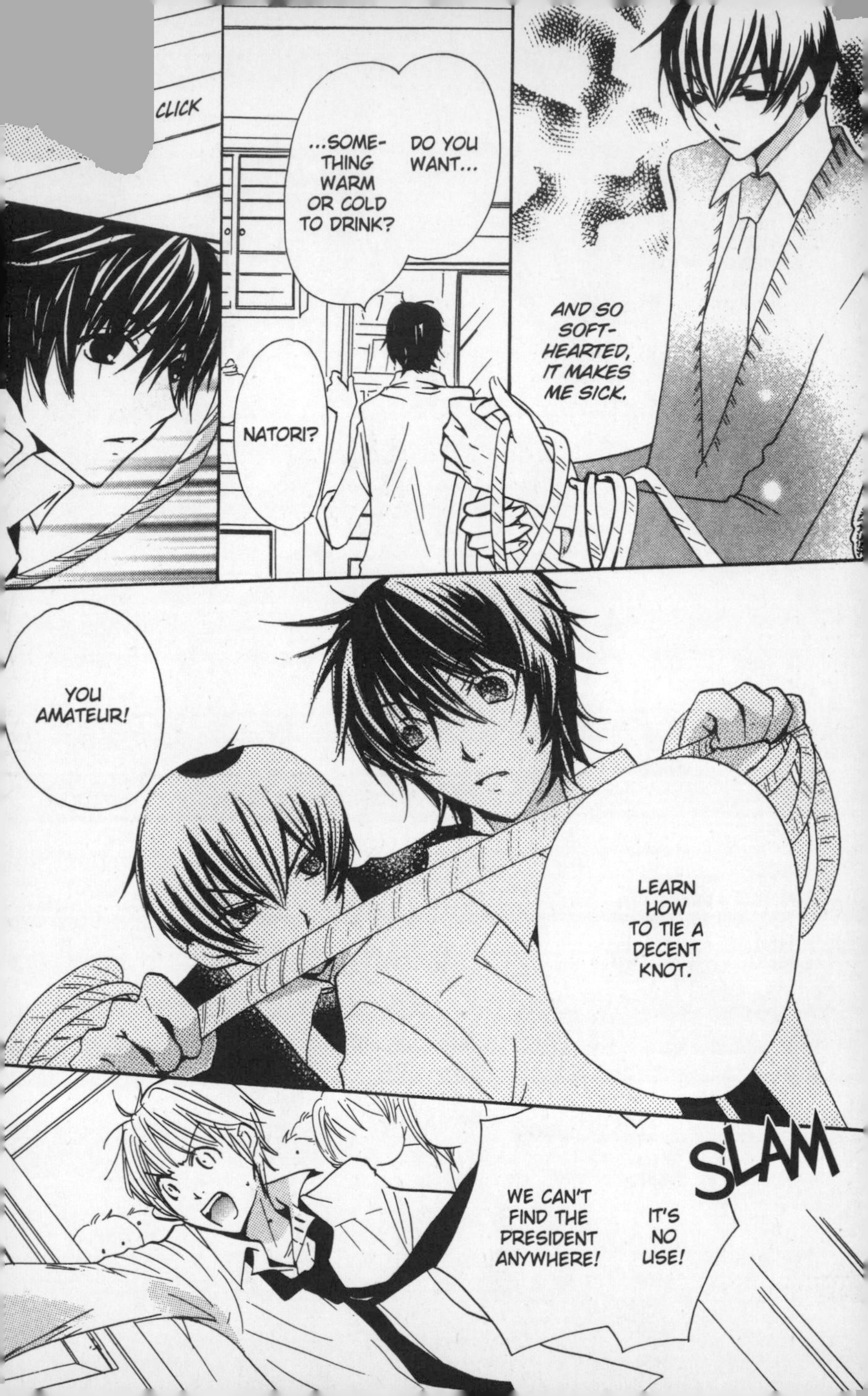
AND SO SOFT-HEARTED, IT MAKES ME SICK.
DO YOU WANT... ...SOMETHING WARM OR COLD TO DRINK?
NATORI?
CLICK
LEARN HOW TO TIE A DECENT KNOT.
YOU AMATEUR!
SLAM
IT'S NO USE!
WE CAN'T FIND THE PRESIDENT ANYWHERE!

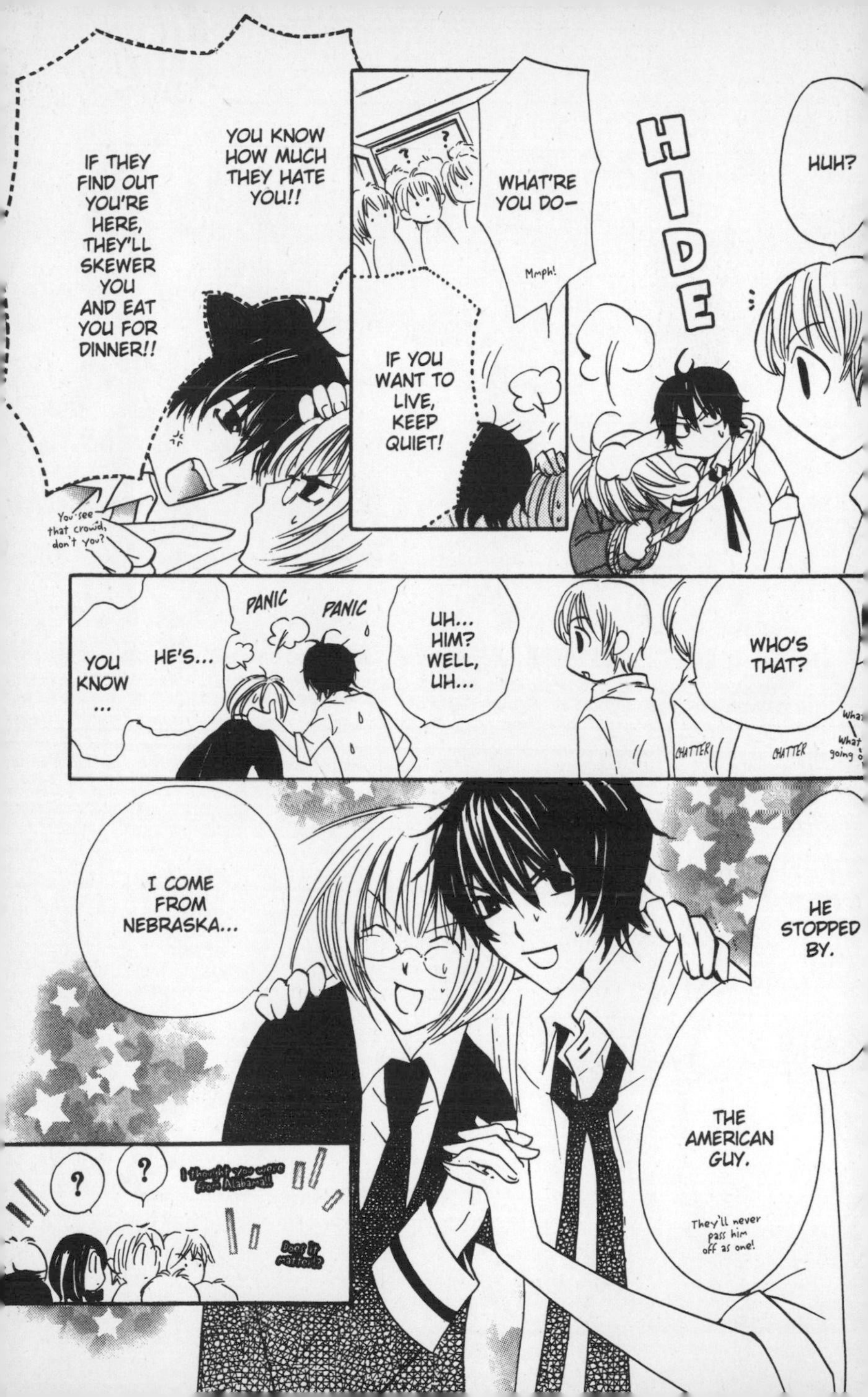
HUH?
HIDE
WHAT'RE YOU DO-
Mmph!
IF YOU WANT TO LIVE, KEEP QUIET!
YOU KNOW HOW MUCH THEY HATE YOU!!
IF THEY FIND OUT YOU'RE HERE, THEY'LL SKEWER YOU AND EAT YOU FOR DINNER!!
You see that crowd, don't you?
WHO'S THAT?
What
What going
CHATTER
CHATTER
UH... HIM? WELL, UH...
PANIC
PANIC
HE'S...
YOU KNOW ...
HE STOPPED BY.
THE AMERICAN GUY.
They'll never pass him off as one!
I COME FROM NEBRASKA...
I thought you were from Alabama!!
Does it matter!?
?
?

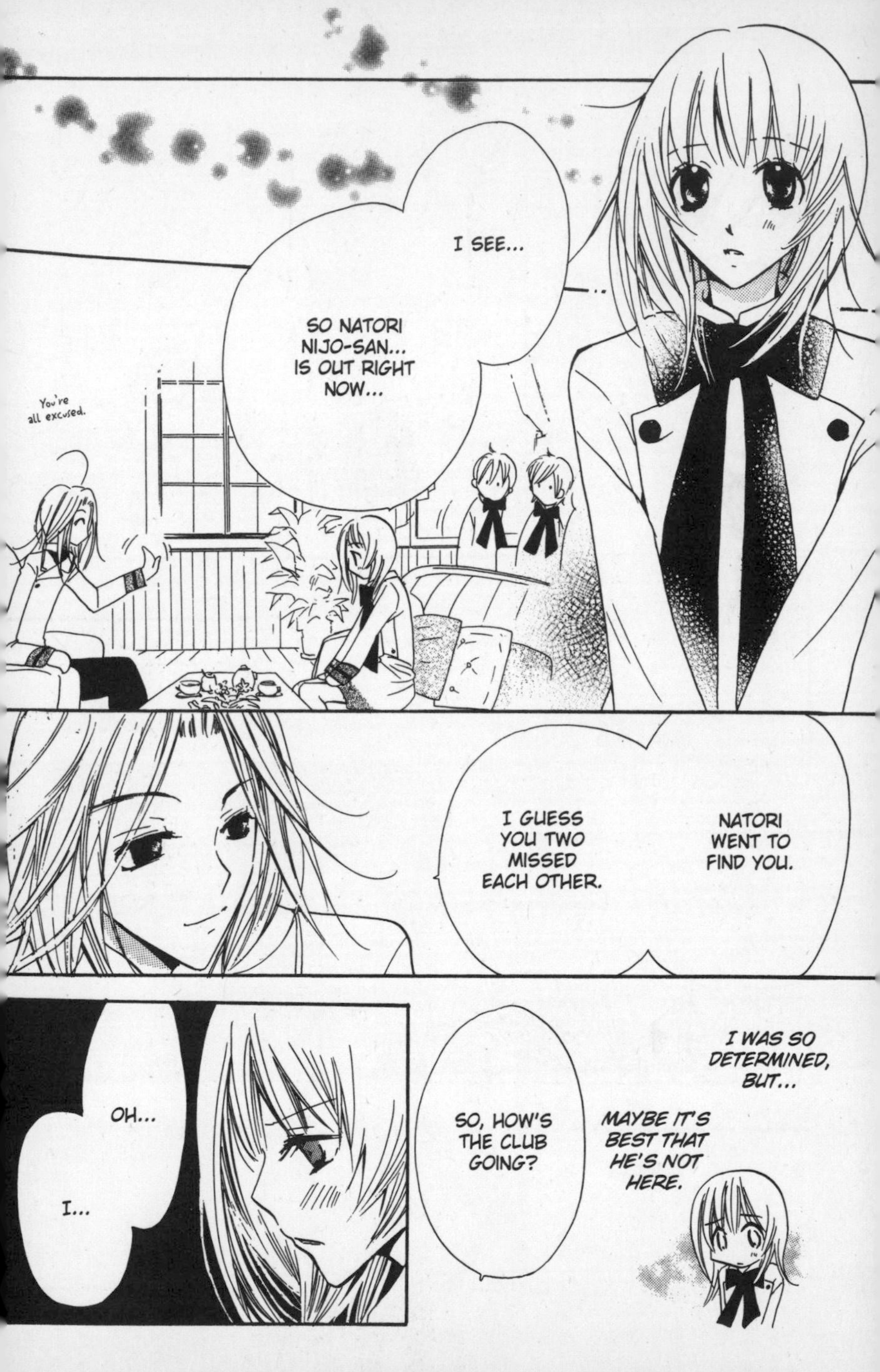
I SEE...
SO NATORI NIJO-SAN... IS OUT RIGHT NOW...
You're all excused.
NATORI WENT TO FIND YOU.
I GUESS YOU TWO MISSED EACH OTHER.
I WAS SO DETERMINED, BUT...
MAYBE IT'S BEST THAT HE'S NOT HERE.
SO, HOW'S THE CLUB GOING?
OH...
I...

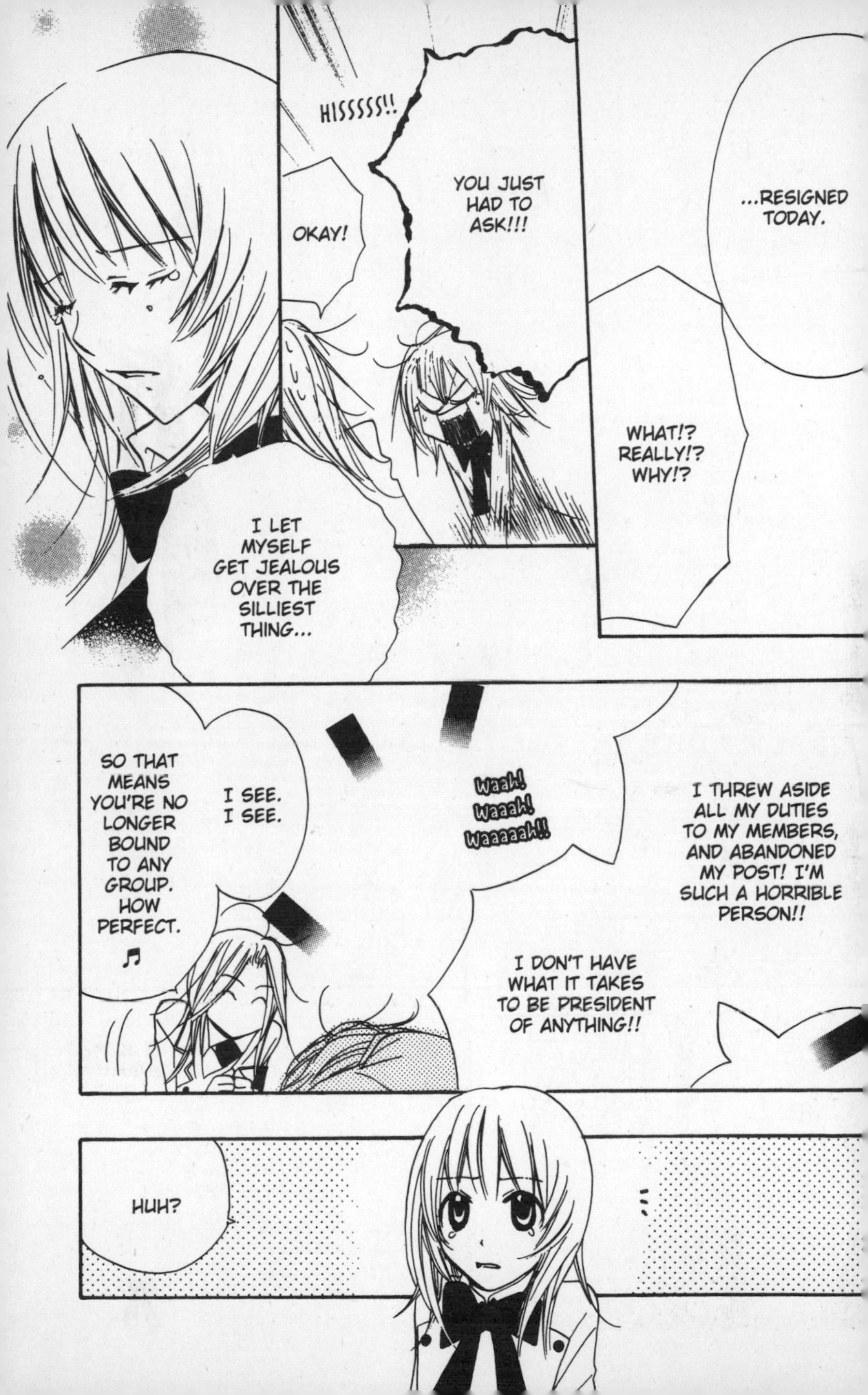
...RESIGNED TODAY.
WHAT!? REALLY!? WHY!?
HISSSSSS!!
YOU JUST HAD TO ASK!!!
OKAY!
I LET MYSELF GET JEALOUS OVER THE SILLIEST THING...
I THREW ASIDE ALL MY DUTIES TO MY MEMBERS, AND ABANDONED MY POST! I'M SUCH A HORRIBLE PERSON!!
Waah! Waaah! Waaaaah!!
I DON'T HAVE WHAT IT TAKES TO BE PRESIDENT OF ANYTHING!!
I SEE. I SEE.
SO THAT MEANS YOU'RE NO LONGER BOUND TO ANY GROUP. HOW PERFECT. ♫
...
HUH?

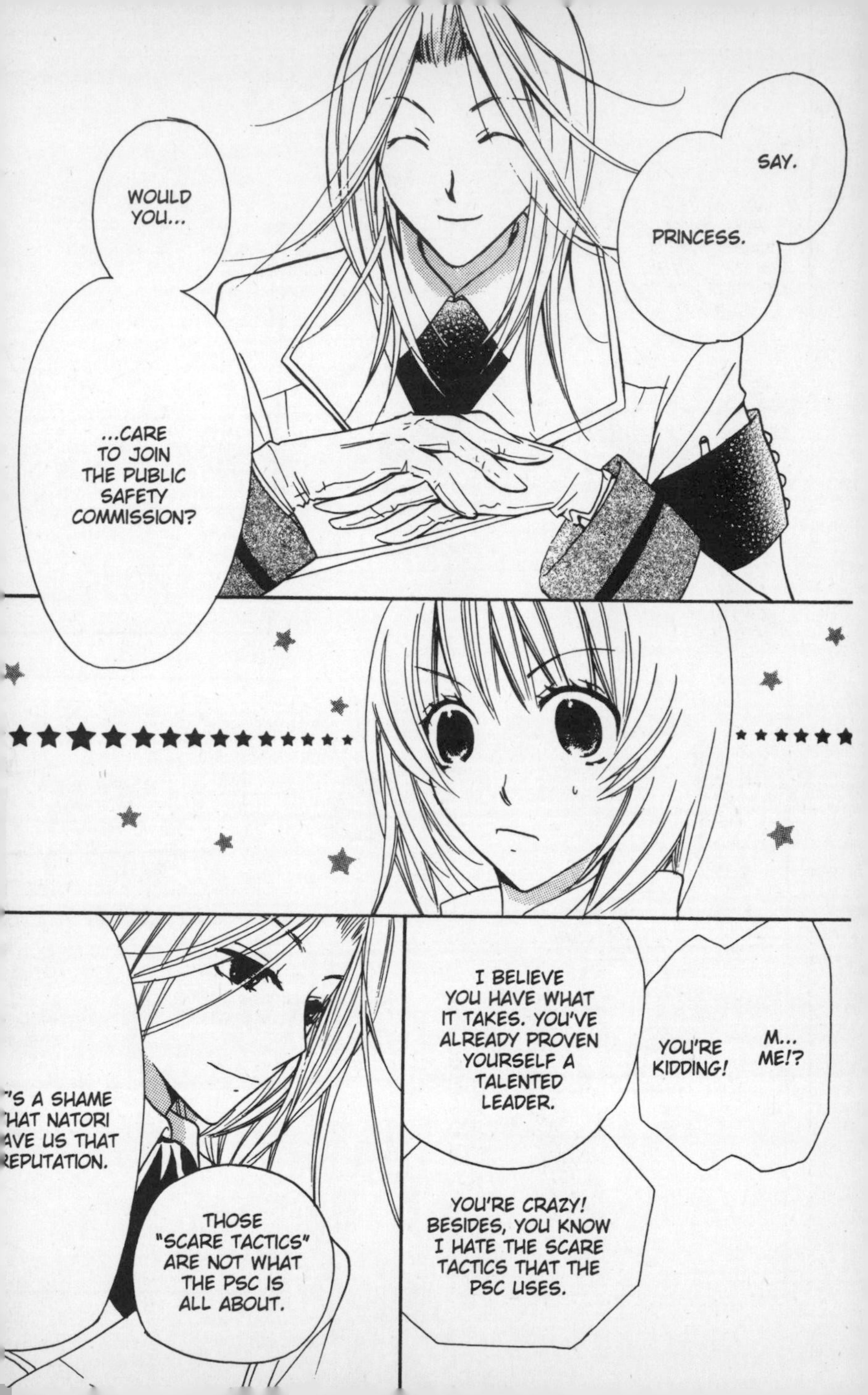
SAY. PRINCESS.
WOULD YOU...
...CARE TO JOIN THE PUBLIC SAFETY COMMISSION?
M... ME!?
YOU'RE KIDDING!
I BELIEVE YOU HAVE WHAT IT TAKES. YOU'VE ALREADY PROVEN YOURSELF A TALENTED LEADER.
YOU'RE CRAZY! BESIDES, YOU KNOW I HATE THE SCARE TACTICS THAT THE PSC USES.
THOSE "SCARE TACTICS" ARE NOT WHAT THE PSC IS ALL ABOUT.
'S A SHAME HAT NATORI AVE US THAT REPUTATION.

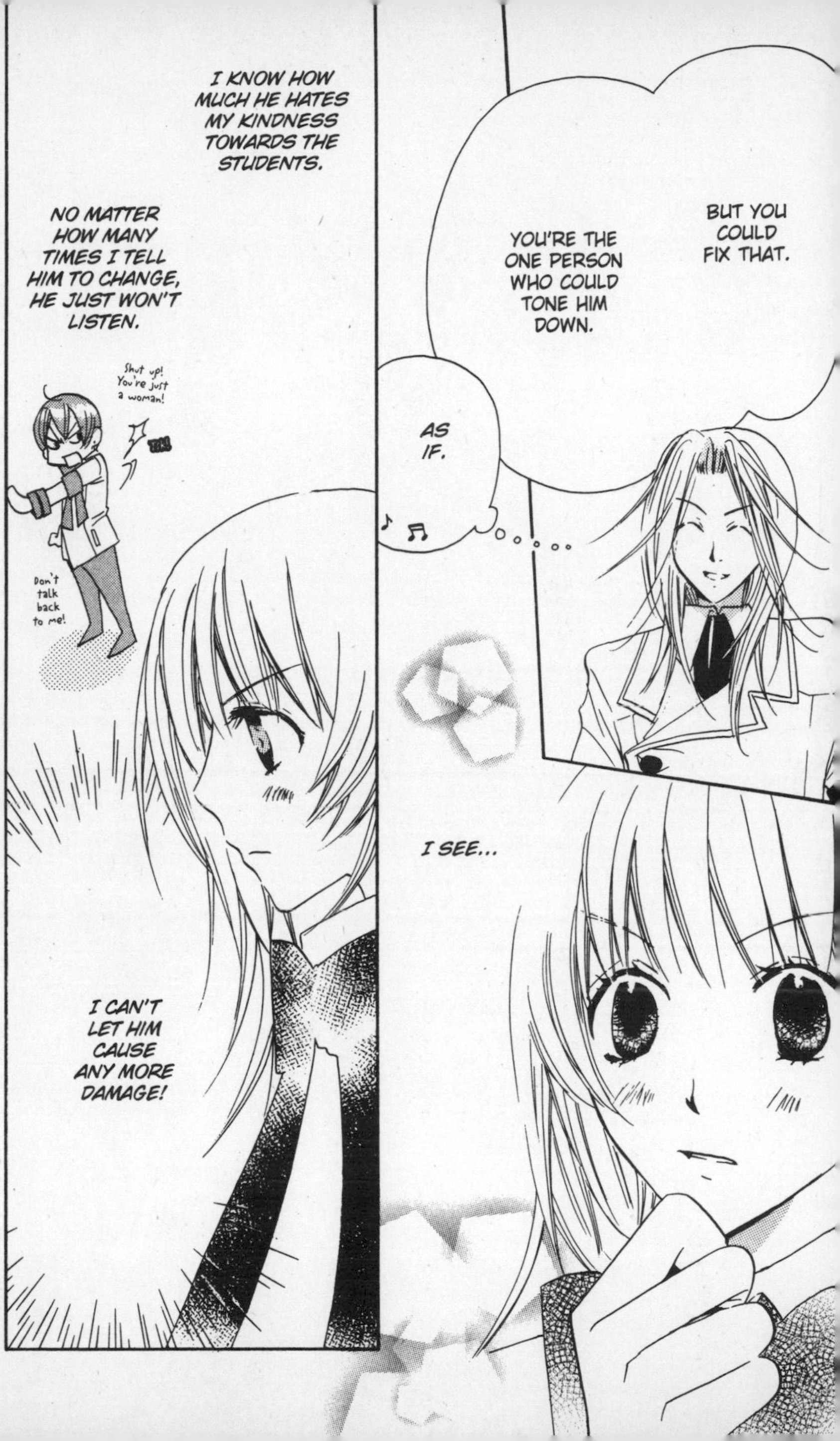
YOU'RE THE ONE PERSON WHO COULD TONE HIM DOWN.
BUT YOU COULD FIX THAT.
AS IF.
I SEE...
I KNOW HOW MUCH HE HATES MY KINDNESS TOWARDS THE STUDENTS.
NO MATTER HOW MANY TIMES I TELL HIM TO CHANGE, HE JUST WON'T LISTEN.
Shut up! You're just a woman!
Don't talk back to me!
I CAN'T LET HIM CAUSE ANY MORE DAMAGE!

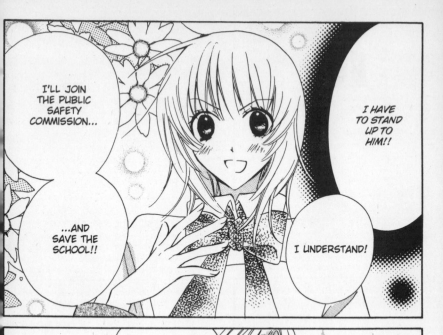

I HAVE TO STAND UP TO HIM!!
I UNDERSTAND!
I'LL JOIN THE PUBLIC SAFETY COMMISSION...
...AND SAVE THE SCHOOL!!
BREEEW
Huh?
UM, THIS SHOULD BE FINE...
...JUST LIKE WE PLANNED. RIGHT?
THAT WAS HOW I JOINED THE PUBLIC SAFETY COMMISSION...
...WHILE NATORI NIJO WORKED WITH THE CY-BELIEVERS IN MY PLACE.
WHY AM I DOING THIS!?
JUST WORKED OUT THAT WAY, I GUESS.
CLIK
CLIK
CLIK
CLIK
You're so good at that.
You're a real life saver.

#15 / END

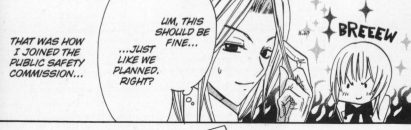

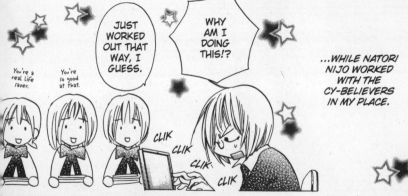

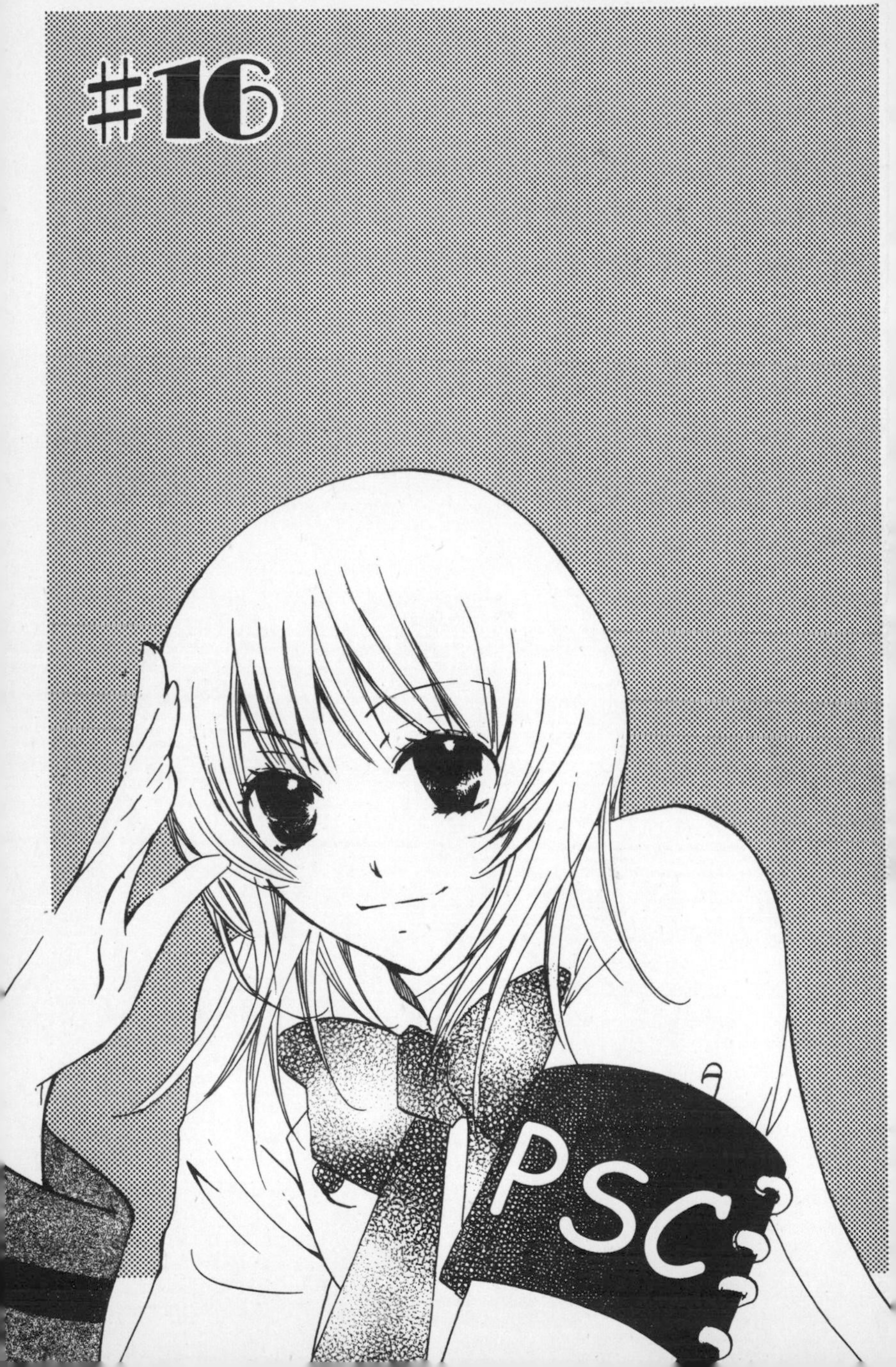
#16
PSC

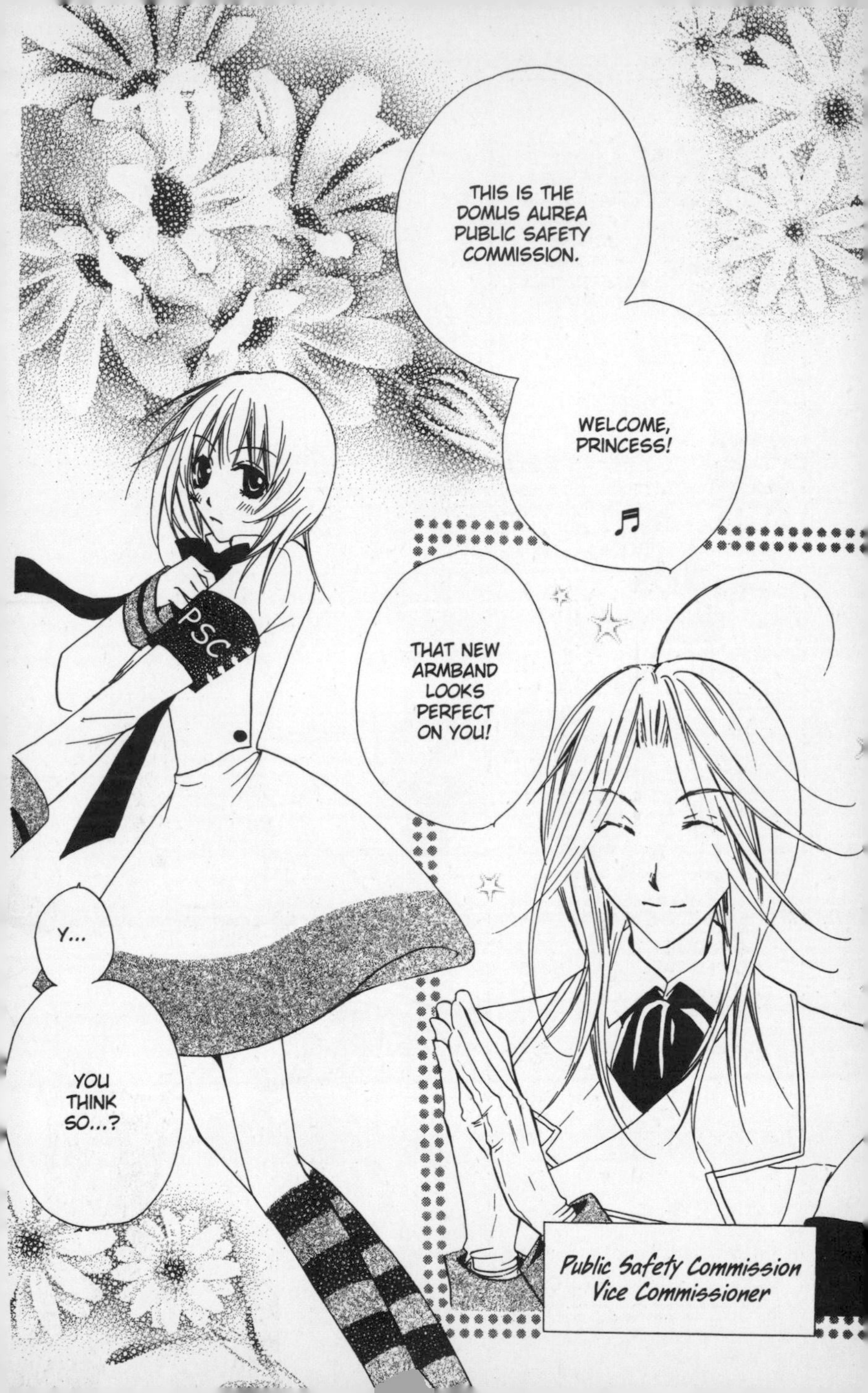
THIS IS THE DOMUS AUREA PUBLIC SAFETY COMMISSION.
WELCOME, PRINCESS! ♬
THAT NEW ARMBAND LOOKS PERFECT ON YOU!
Public Safety Commission Vice Commissioner
PSC
Y...
YOU THINK SO...?

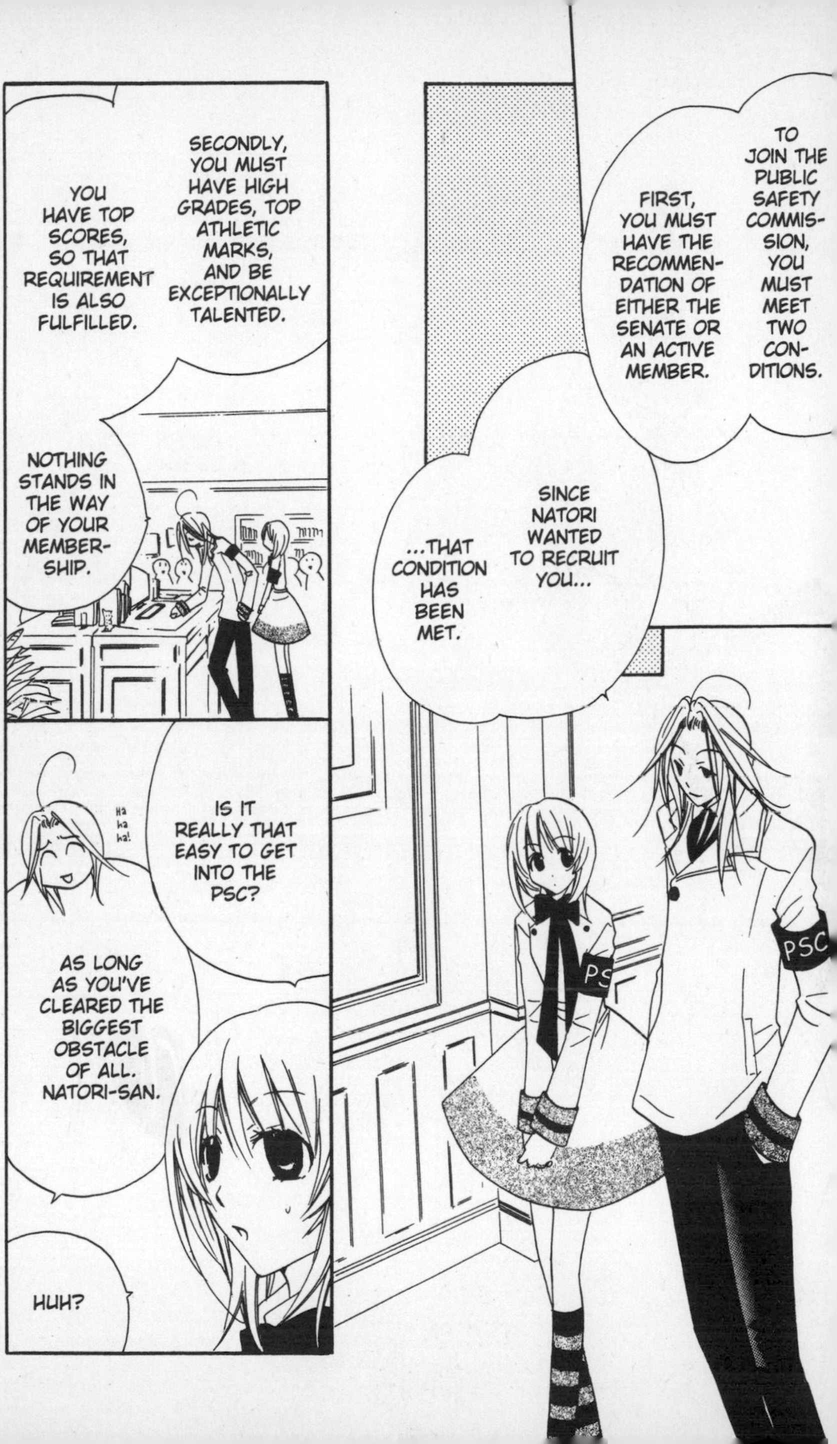
TO JOIN THE PUBLIC SAFETY COMMISSION, YOU MUST MEET TWO CONDITIONS.
FIRST, YOU MUST HAVE THE RECOMMENDATION OF EITHER THE SENATE OR AN ACTIVE MEMBER.
SINCE NATORI WANTED TO RECRUIT YOU...
...THAT CONDITION HAS BEEN MET.
PSC
PS
SECONDLY, YOU MUST HAVE HIGH GRADES, TOP ATHLETIC MARKS, AND BE EXCEPTIONALLY TALENTED.
YOU HAVE TOP SCORES, SO THAT REQUIREMENT IS ALSO FULFILLED.
NOTHING STANDS IN THE WAY OF YOUR MEMBERSHIP.
IS IT REALLY THAT EASY TO GET INTO THE PSC?
Ha ha ha!
AS LONG AS YOU'VE CLEARED THE BIGGEST OBSTACLE OF ALL. NATORI-SAN.
HUH?

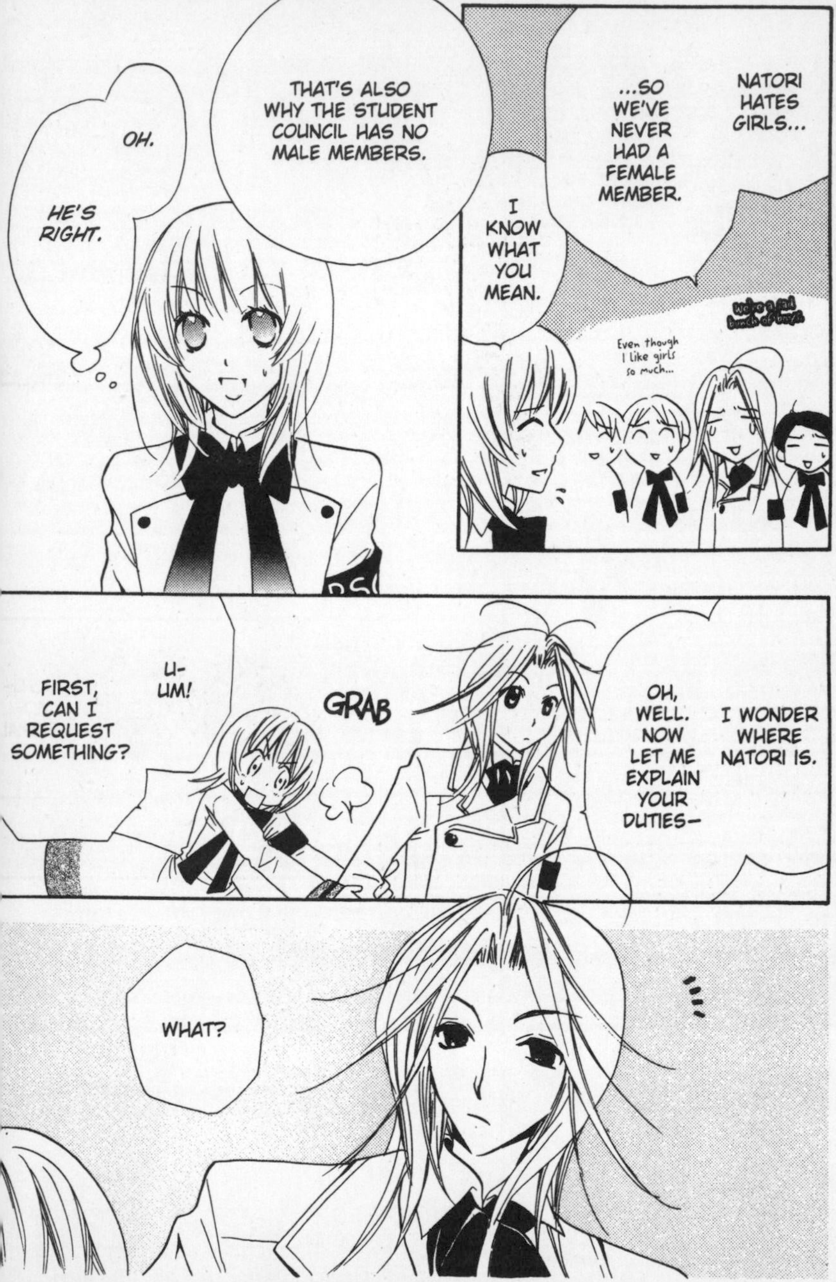
NATORI HATES GIRLS...
...SO WE'VE NEVER HAD A FEMALE MEMBER.
I KNOW WHAT YOU MEAN.
We're a sad bunch of boys.
Even though I like girls so much...
THAT'S ALSO WHY THE STUDENT COUNCIL HAS NO MALE MEMBERS.
OH.
HE'S RIGHT.
I WONDER WHERE NATORI IS.
OH, WELL. NOW LET ME EXPLAIN YOUR DUTIES–
GRAB
U-UM!
FIRST, CAN I REQUEST SOMETHING?
WHAT?

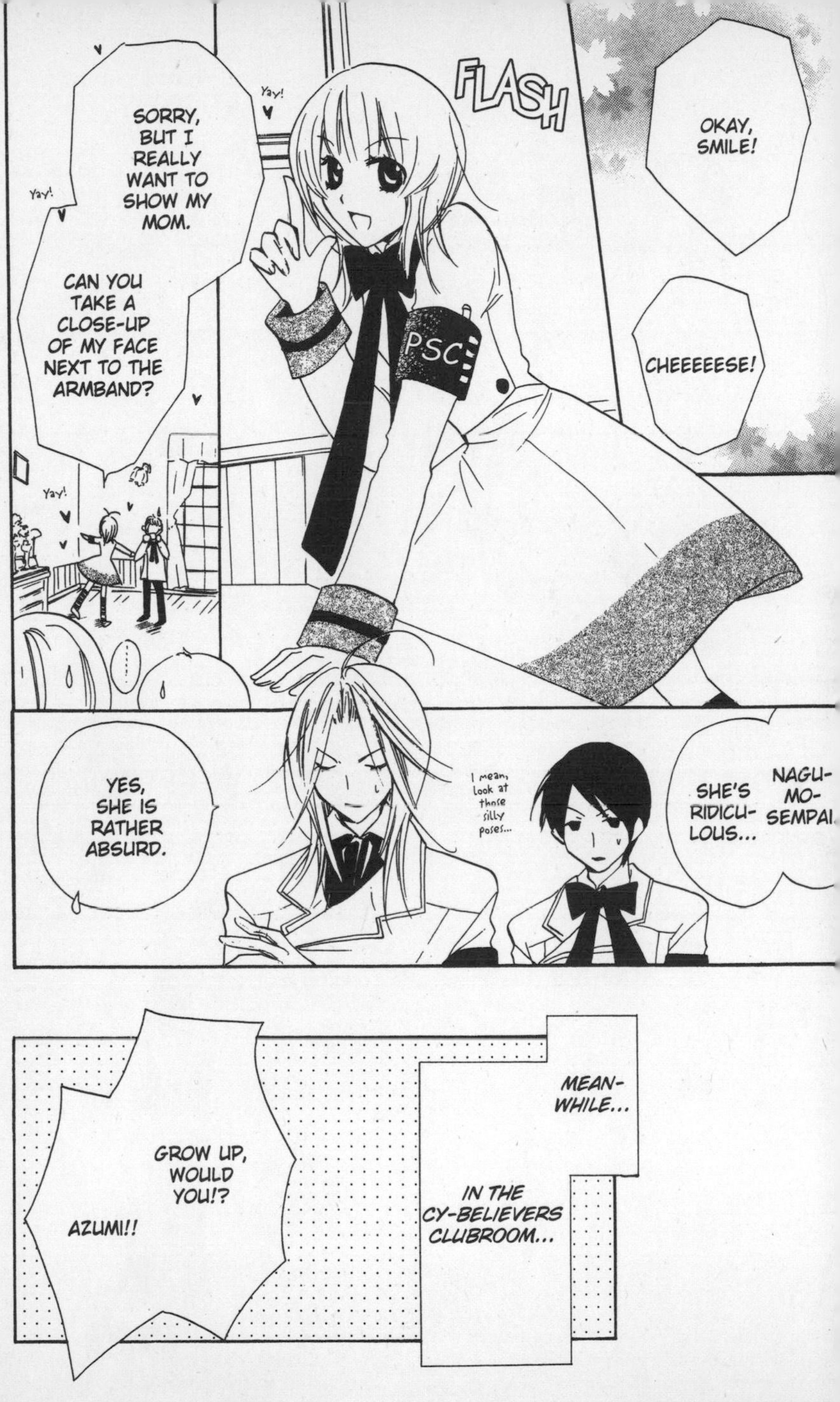

OKAY, SMILE!
FLASH
CHEEEEESE!
Yay!
SORRY, BUT I REALLY WANT TO SHOW MY MOM.
CAN YOU TAKE A CLOSE-UP OF MY FACE NEXT TO THE ARMBAND?
Yay!
Yay!
PSC
...
NAGUMO-SEMPAI.
SHE'S RIDICULOUS...
I mean, look at those silly poses...
YES, SHE IS RATHER ABSURD.
MEANWHILE...
IN THE CY-BELIEVERS CLUBROOM...
GROW UP, WOULD YOU!?
AZUMI!!

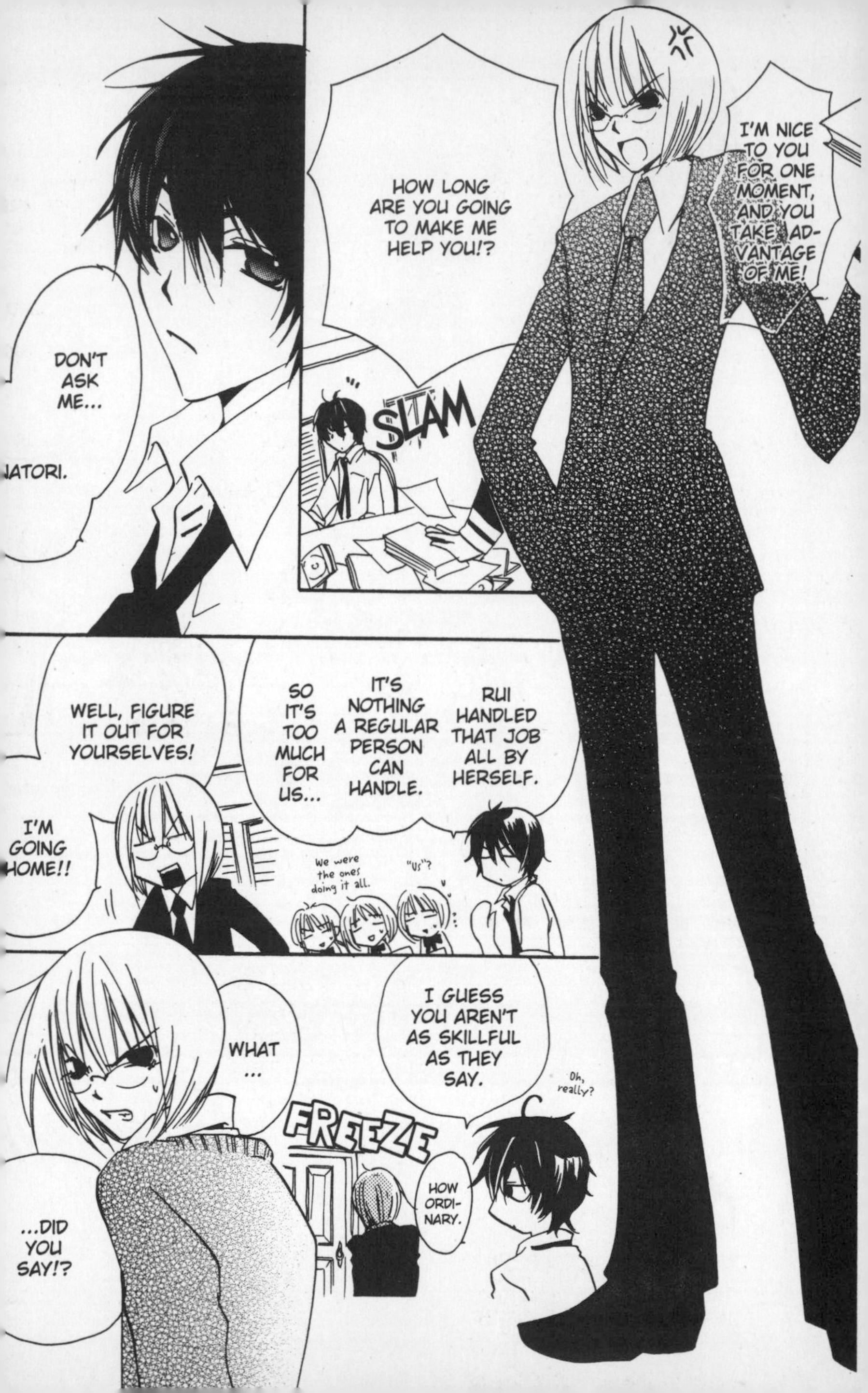
I'M NICE TO YOU FOR ONE MOMENT, AND YOU TAKE ADVANTAGE OF ME!
HOW LONG ARE YOU GOING TO MAKE ME HELP YOU!?
SLAM
DON'T ASK ME...
NATORI.
RUI HANDLED THAT JOB ALL BY HERSELF.
IT'S NOTHING A REGULAR PERSON CAN HANDLE.
SO IT'S TOO MUCH FOR US...
"Us"?
We were the ones doing it all.
WELL, FIGURE IT OUT FOR YOURSELVES!
I'M GOING HOME!!
I GUESS YOU AREN'T AS SKILLFUL AS THEY SAY.
Oh, really?
HOW ORDINARY.
FREEZE
WHAT...
...DID YOU SAY!?

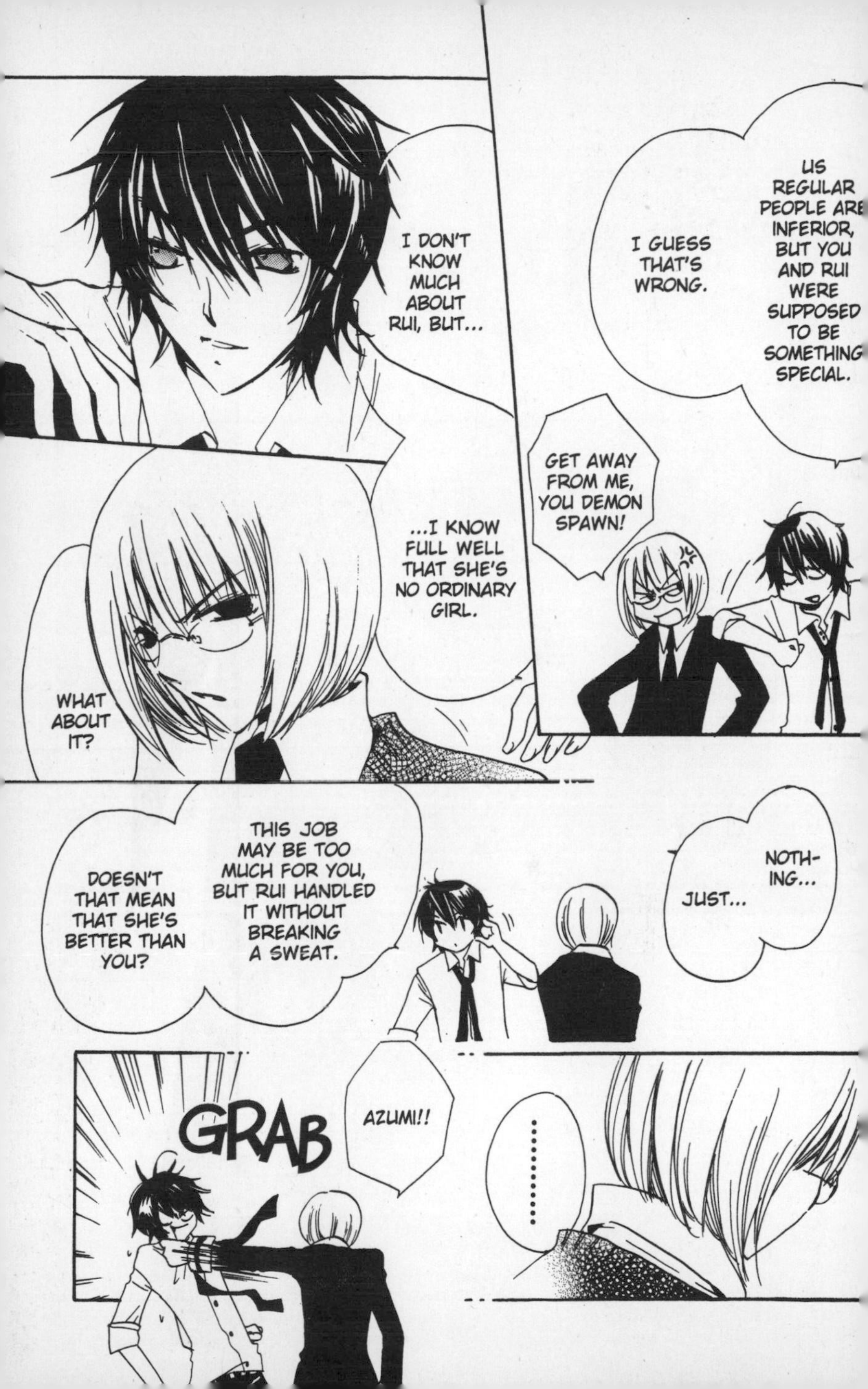
US REGULAR PEOPLE ARE INFERIOR, BUT YOU AND RUI WERE SUPPOSED TO BE SOMETHING SPECIAL.
I GUESS THAT'S WRONG.
GET AWAY FROM ME, YOU DEMON SPAWN!
I DON'T KNOW MUCH ABOUT RUI, BUT...
...I KNOW FULL WELL THAT SHE'S NO ORDINARY GIRL.
WHAT ABOUT IT?
NOTH-ING...
JUST...
THIS JOB MAY BE TOO MUCH FOR YOU, BUT RUI HANDLED IT WITHOUT BREAKING A SWEAT.
DOESN'T THAT MEAN THAT SHE'S BETTER THAN YOU?
....
AZUMI!!
GRAB

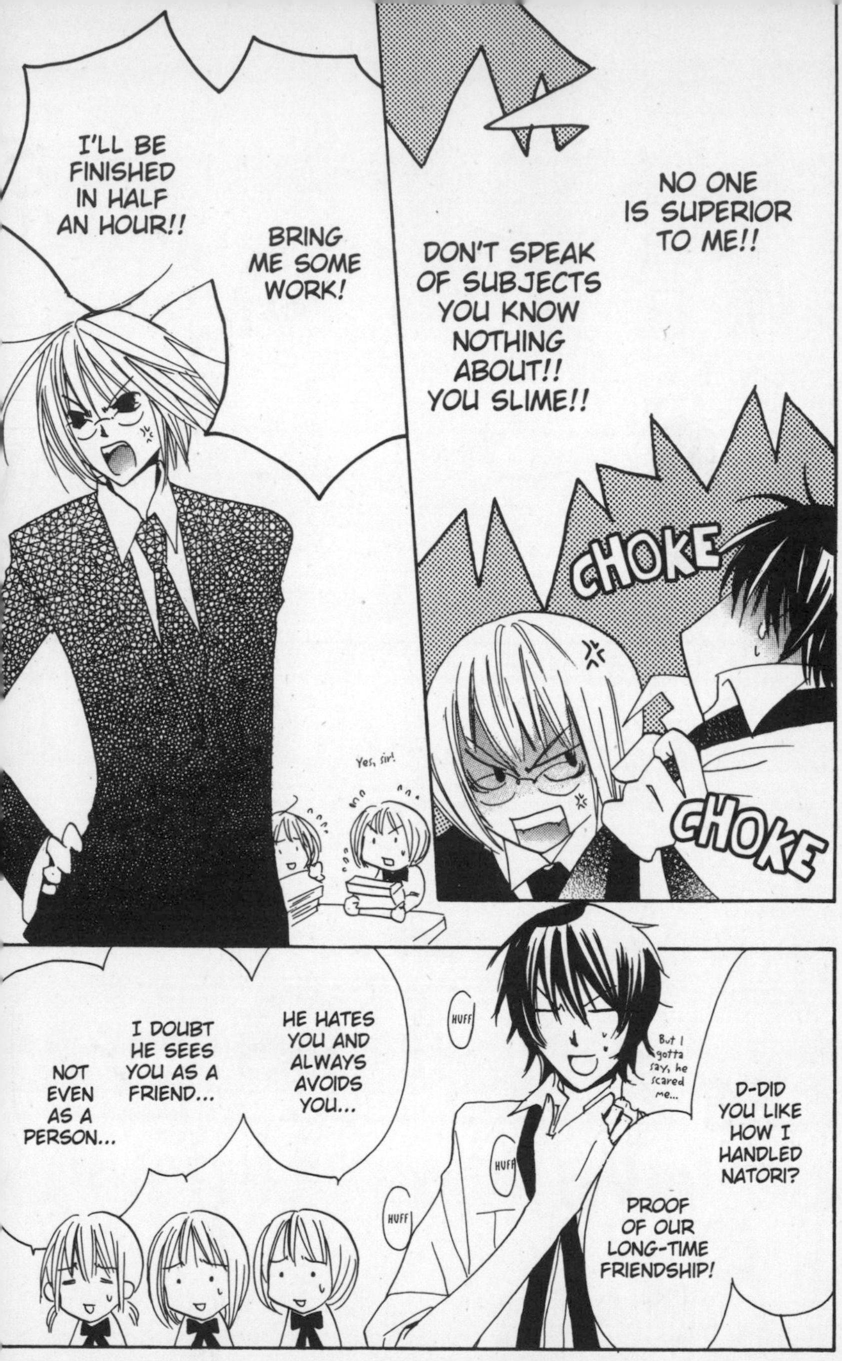

NO ONE IS SUPERIOR TO ME!!
DON'T SPEAK OF SUBJECTS YOU KNOW NOTHING ABOUT!! YOU SLIME!!
CHOKE
CHOKE
I'LL BE FINISHED IN HALF AN HOUR!!
BRING ME SOME WORK!
Yes, sir!
D-DID YOU LIKE HOW I HANDLED NATORI?
PROOF OF OUR LONG-TIME FRIENDSHIP!
But I gotta say, he scared me...
HUFF
HUFF
HUFF
HE HATES YOU AND ALWAYS AVOIDS YOU...
I DOUBT HE SEES YOU AS A FRIEND...
NOT EVEN AS A PERSON...

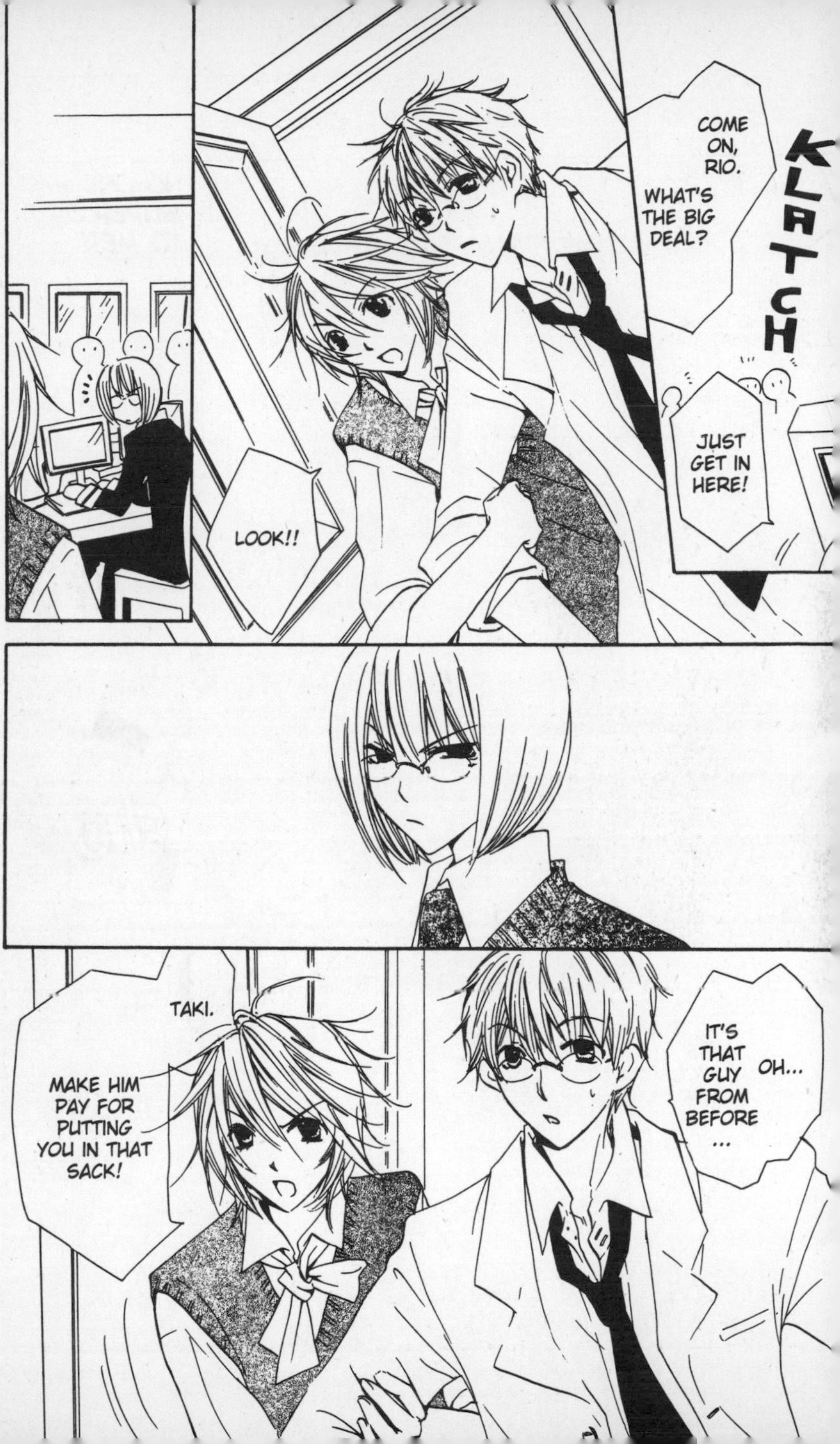
COME ON, RIO. WHAT'S THE BIG DEAL?
KLATCH
JUST GET IN HERE!
LOOK!!
OH...
IT'S THAT GUY FROM BEFORE...
TAKI.
MAKE HIM PAY FOR PUTTING YOU IN THAT SACK!

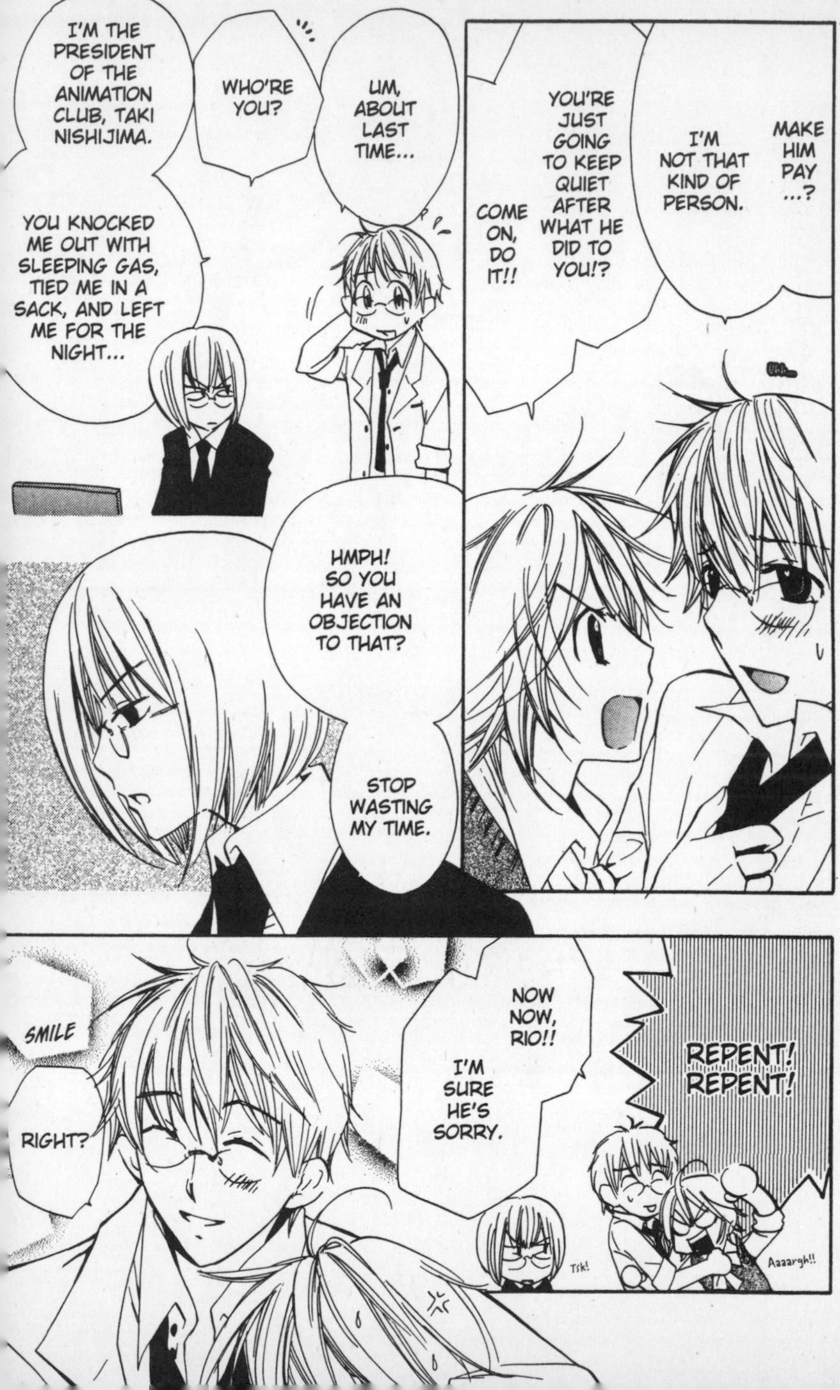
MAKE HIM PAY ...?
I'M NOT THAT KIND OF PERSON.
YOU'RE JUST GOING TO KEEP QUIET AFTER WHAT HE DID TO YOU!?
COME ON, DO IT!!
Uhh...
UM, ABOUT LAST TIME...
WHO'RE YOU?
I'M THE PRESIDENT OF THE ANIMATION CLUB, TAKI NISHIJIMA.
YOU KNOCKED ME OUT WITH SLEEPING GAS, TIED ME IN A SACK, AND LEFT ME FOR THE NIGHT...
HMPH! SO YOU HAVE AN OBJECTION TO THAT?
STOP WASTING MY TIME.
REPENT! REPENT!
Aaaargh!!
Tsk!
NOW NOW, RIO!!
I'M SURE HE'S SORRY.
SMILE
RIGHT?

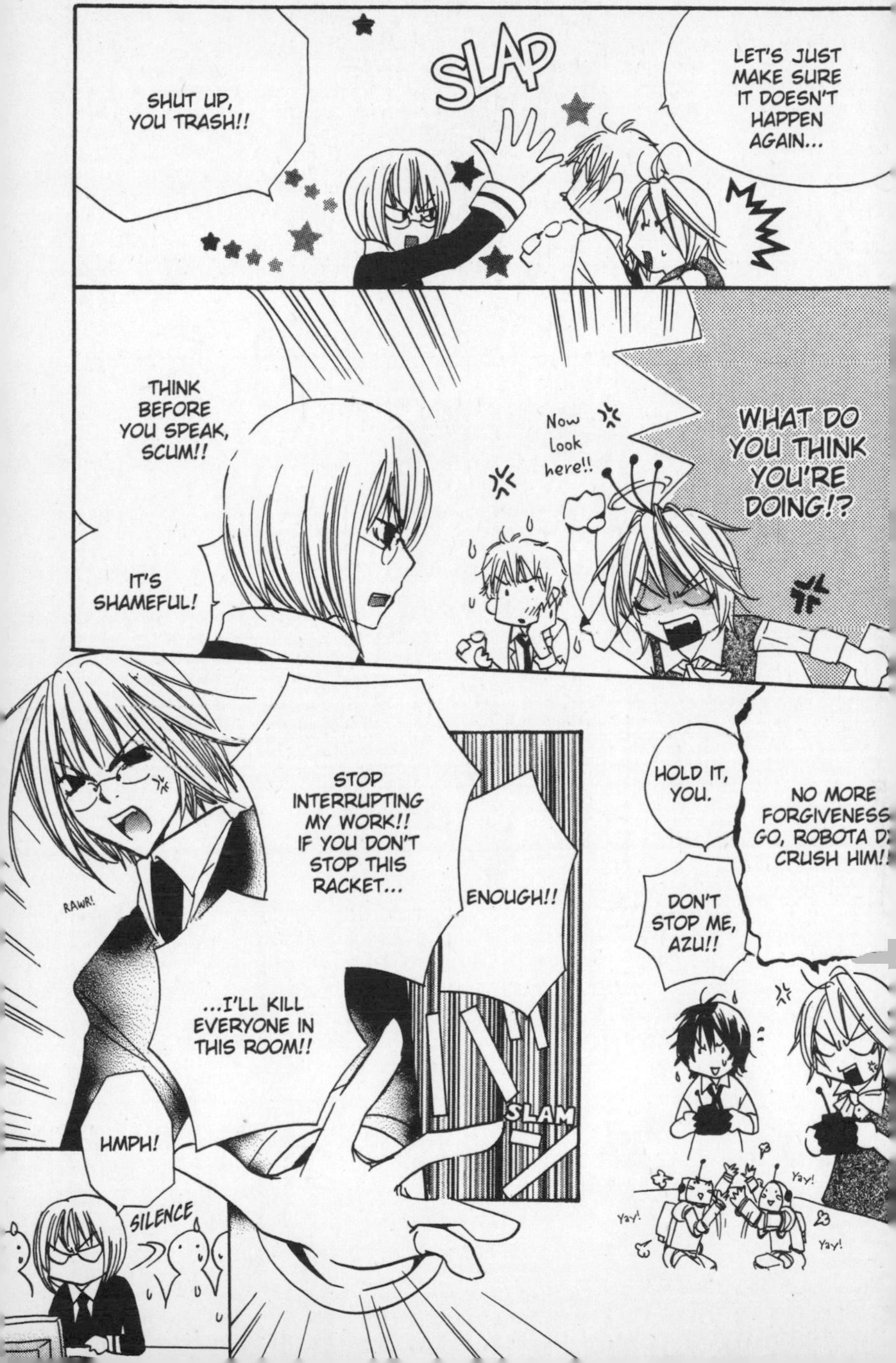
LET'S JUST MAKE SURE IT DOESN'T HAPPEN AGAIN...
SLAP
SHUT UP, YOU TRASH!!
WHAT DO YOU THINK YOU'RE DOING!?
Now look here!!
THINK BEFORE YOU SPEAK, SCUM!!
IT'S SHAMEFUL!
NO MORE FORGIVENESS
GO, ROBOTA D
CRUSH HIM!!
HOLD IT, YOU.
DON'T STOP ME, AZU!!
Yay!
Yay!
Yay!
ENOUGH!!
STOP INTERRUPTING MY WORK!! IF YOU DON'T STOP THIS RACKET...
RAWR!
...I'LL KILL EVERYONE IN THIS ROOM!!
SLAM
HMPH!
SILENCE

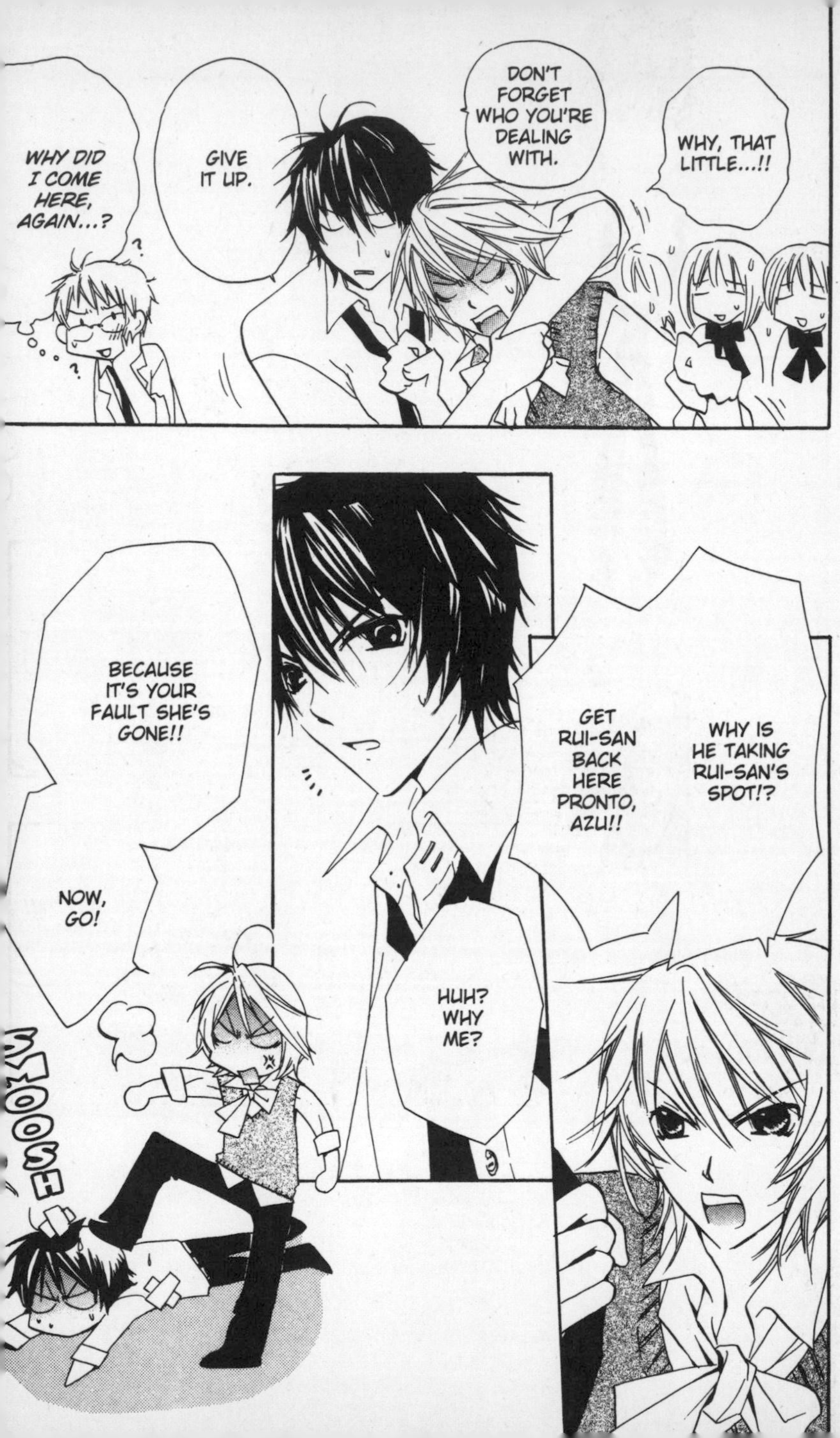
WHY, THAT LITTLE...!!
DON'T FORGET WHO YOU'RE DEALING WITH.
GIVE IT UP.
WHY DID I COME HERE, AGAIN...?
WHY IS HE TAKING RUI-SAN'S SPOT!?
GET RUI-SAN BACK HERE PRONTO, AZU!!
HUH? WHY ME?
BECAUSE IT'S YOUR FAULT SHE'S GONE!!
NOW, GO!
WHOOSH

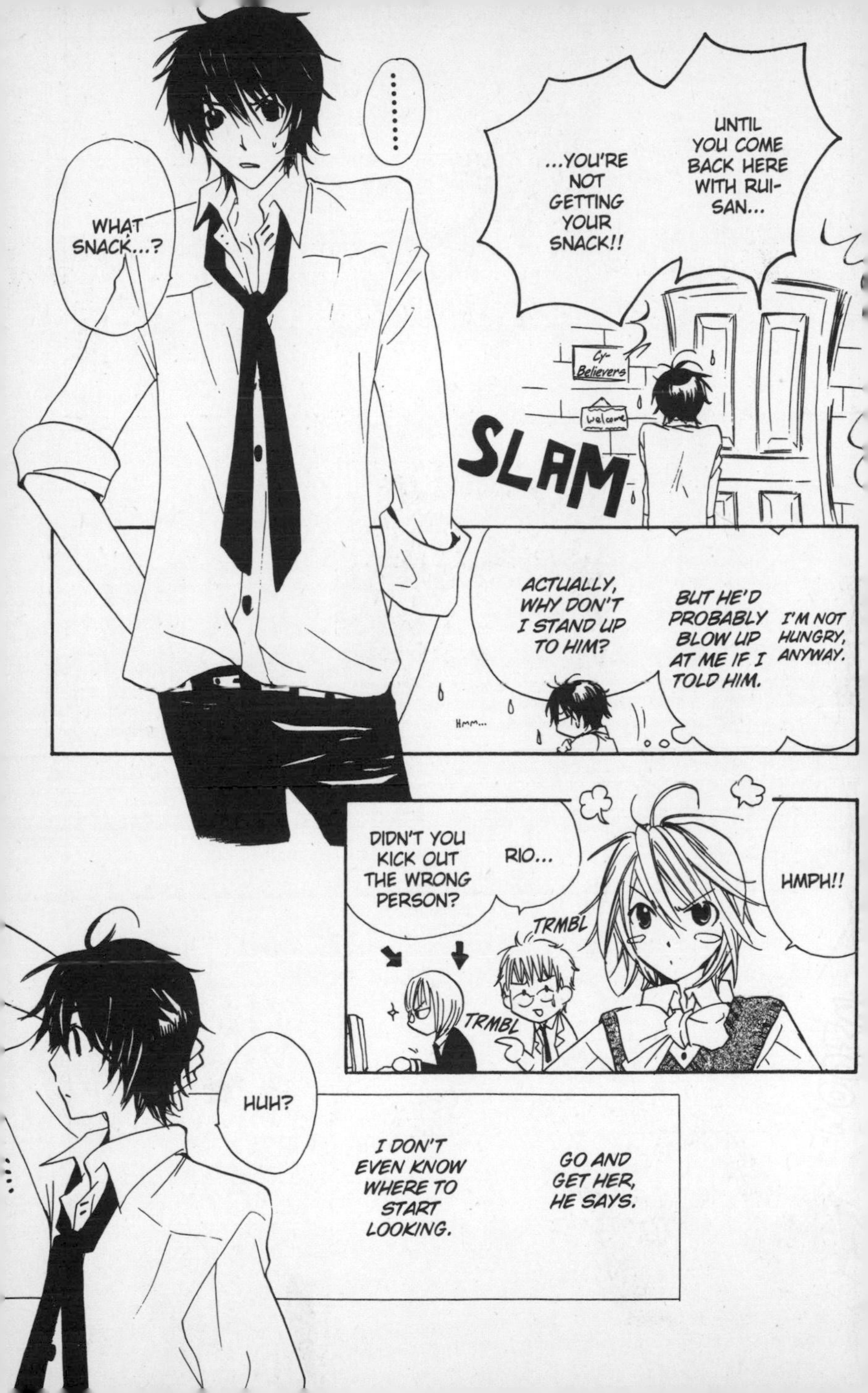
UNTIL YOU COME BACK HERE WITH RUI-SAN...
...YOU'RE NOT GETTING YOUR SNACK!!
Cy-Believers
Welcome
SLAM
......
WHAT SNACK...?
I'M NOT HUNGRY, ANYWAY.
BUT HE'D PROBABLY BLOW UP AT ME IF I TOLD HIM.
ACTUALLY, WHY DON'T I STAND UP TO HIM?
Hmm...
HMPH!!
RIO...
DIDN'T YOU KICK OUT THE WRONG PERSON?
TRMBL
TRMBL
GO AND GET HER, HE SAYS.
I DON'T EVEN KNOW WHERE TO START LOOKING.
HUH?
....

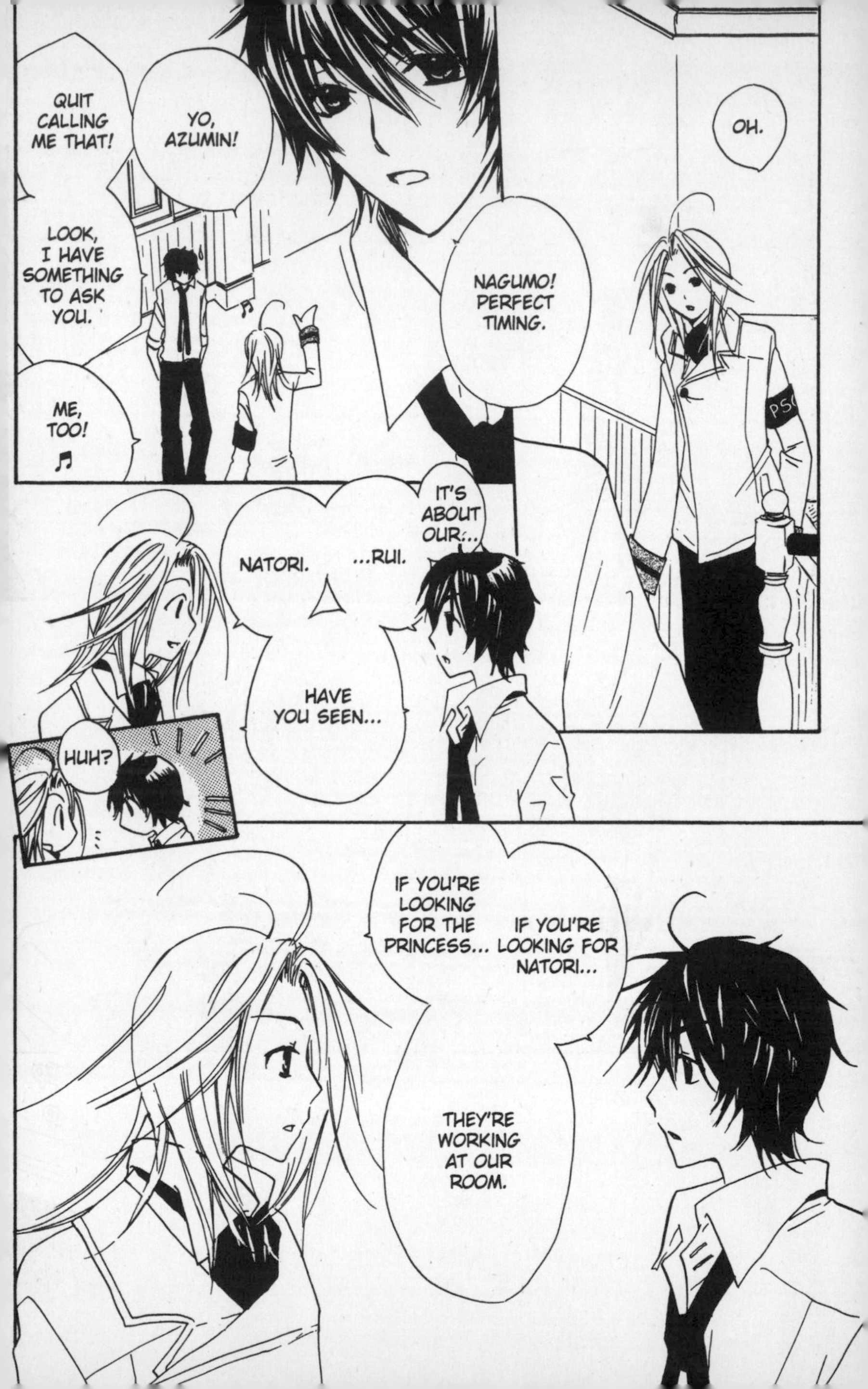

OH.
NAGUMO! PERFECT TIMING.
YO, AZUMIN!
QUIT CALLING ME THAT!
LOOK, I HAVE SOMETHING TO ASK YOU.
ME, TOO! ♪
IT'S ABOUT OUR...
NATORI.
...RUI.
HAVE YOU SEEN...
HUH?
IF YOU'RE LOOKING FOR NATORI...
IF YOU'RE LOOKING FOR THE PRINCESS...
THEY'RE WORKING AT OUR ROOM.

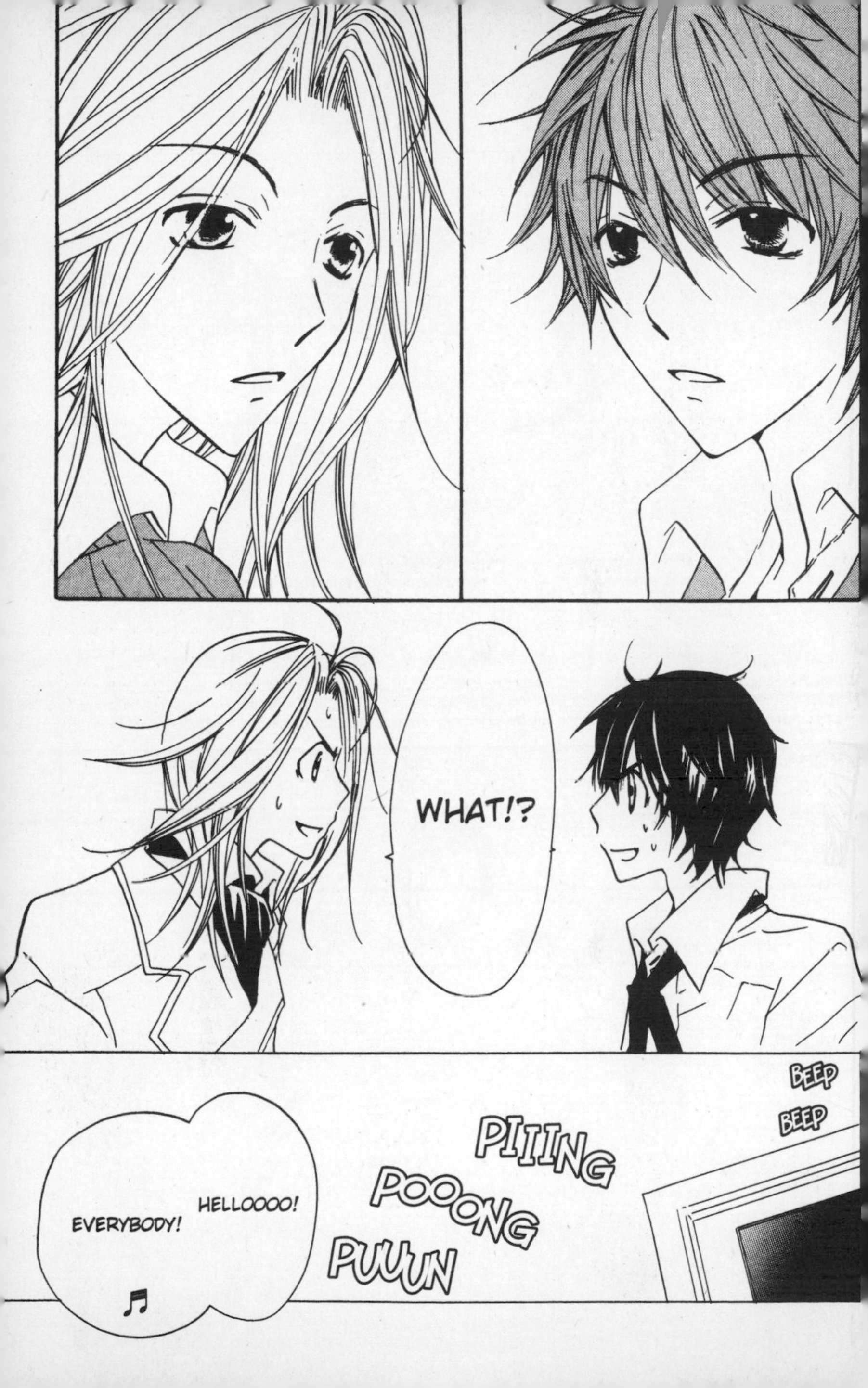
WHAT!?
BEEP
BEEP
PIIING
POOONG
PUUUN
HELLOOOO!
EVERYBODY! ♬

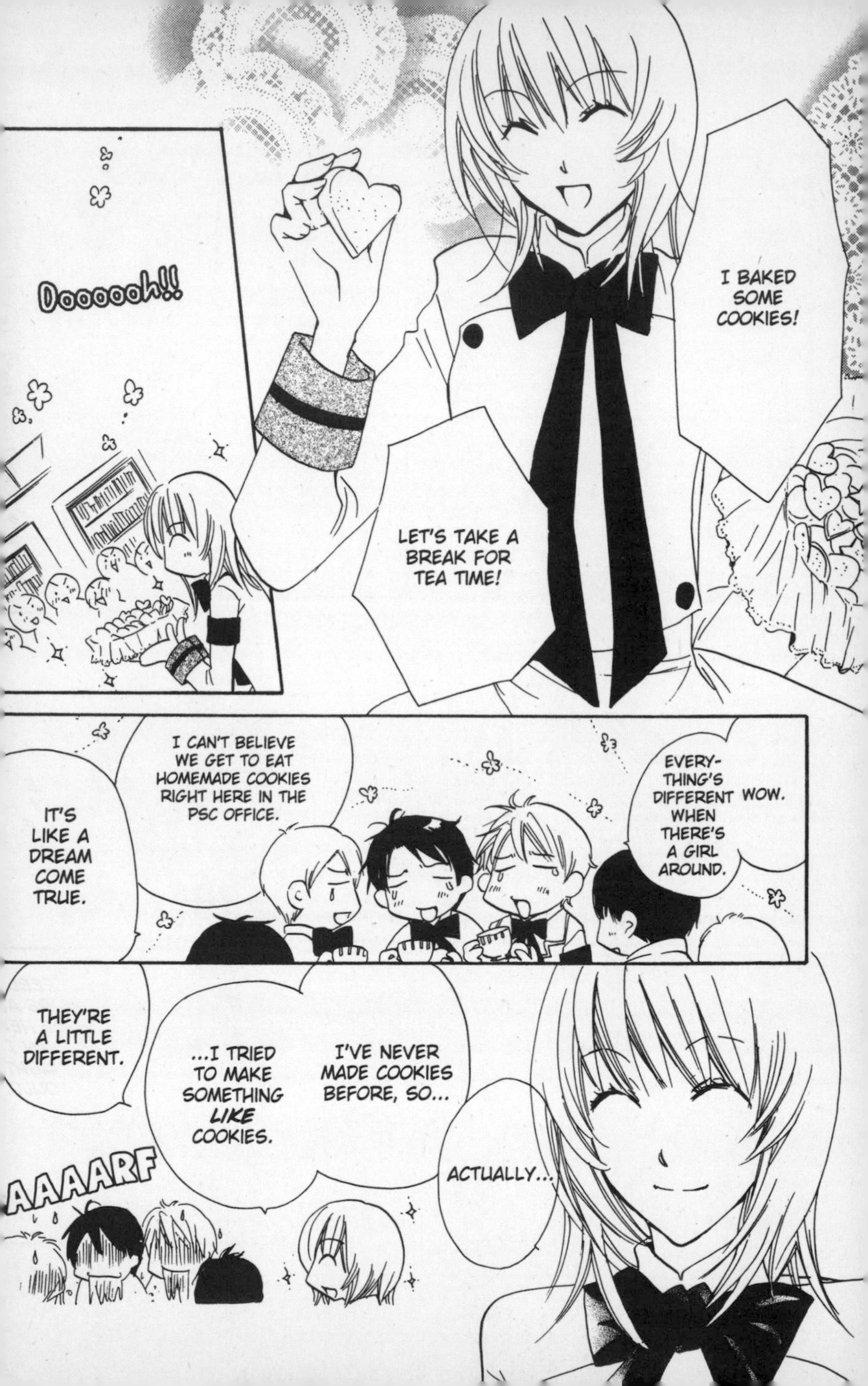
I BAKED SOME COOKIES!
LET'S TAKE A BREAK FOR TEA TIME!
Doooooh!!
WOW.
EVERY-THING'S DIFFERENT WHEN THERE'S A GIRL AROUND.
I CAN'T BELIEVE WE GET TO EAT HOMEMADE COOKIES RIGHT HERE IN THE PSC OFFICE.
IT'S LIKE A DREAM COME TRUE.
ACTUALLY...
I'VE NEVER MADE COOKIES BEFORE, SO...
...I TRIED TO MAKE SOMETHING *LIKE* COOKIES.
THEY'RE A LITTLE DIFFERENT.
AAAARF

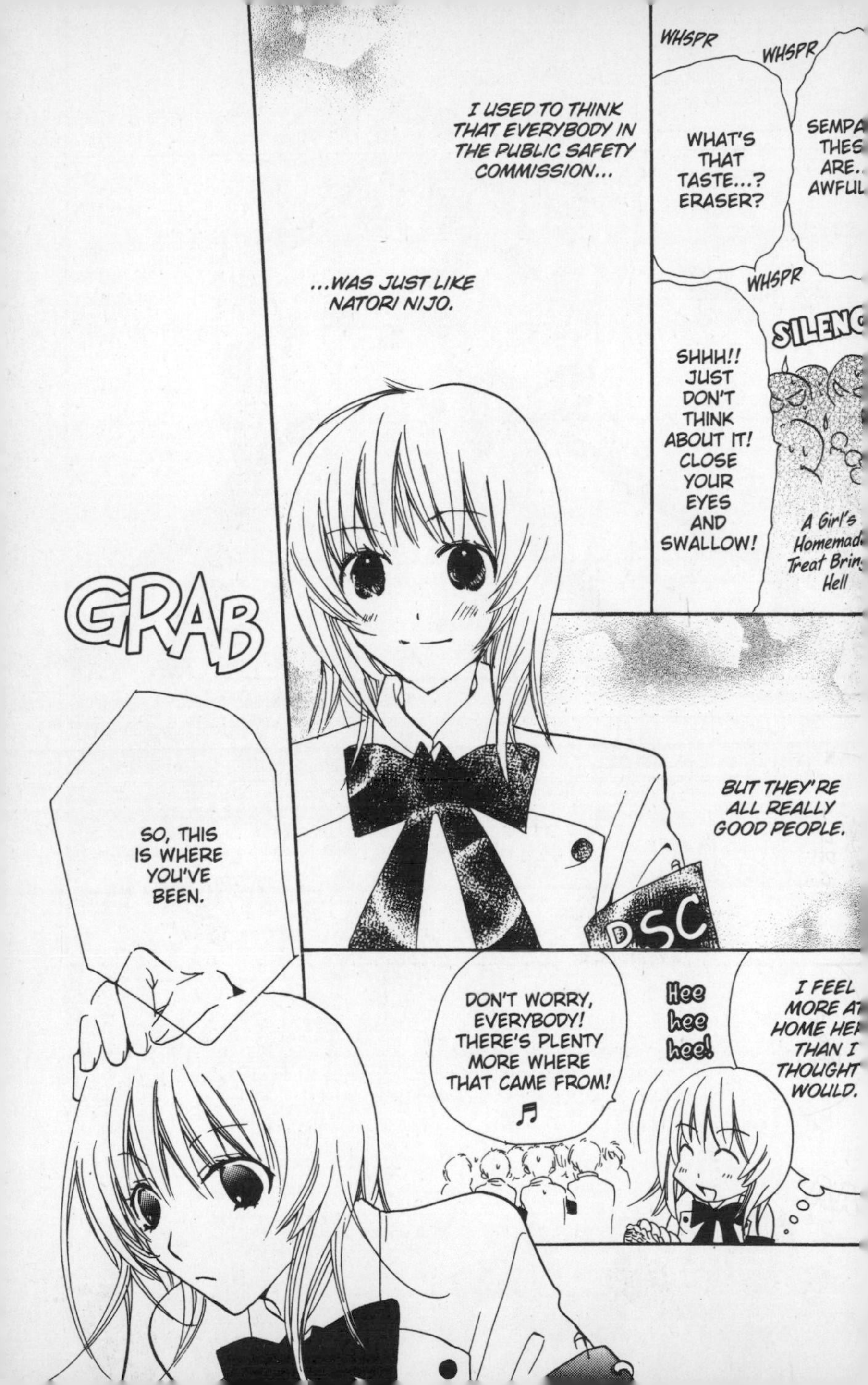
WHSPR
WHSPR
SEMPA THES ARE.. AWFUL
WHAT'S THAT TASTE...? ERASER?
WHSPR
SHHH!! JUST DON'T THINK ABOUT IT! CLOSE YOUR EYES AND SWALLOW!
SILENC
A Girl's Homemad Treat Brin Hell
I USED TO THINK THAT EVERYBODY IN THE PUBLIC SAFETY COMMISSION...
...WAS JUST LIKE NATORI NIJO.
BUT THEY'RE ALL REALLY GOOD PEOPLE.
DSC
I FEEL MORE AT HOME HEF THAN I THOUGHT WOULD.
Hee hee hee!
DON'T WORRY, EVERYBODY! THERE'S PLENTY MORE WHERE THAT CAME FROM! ♫
GRAB
SO, THIS IS WHERE YOU'VE BEEN.

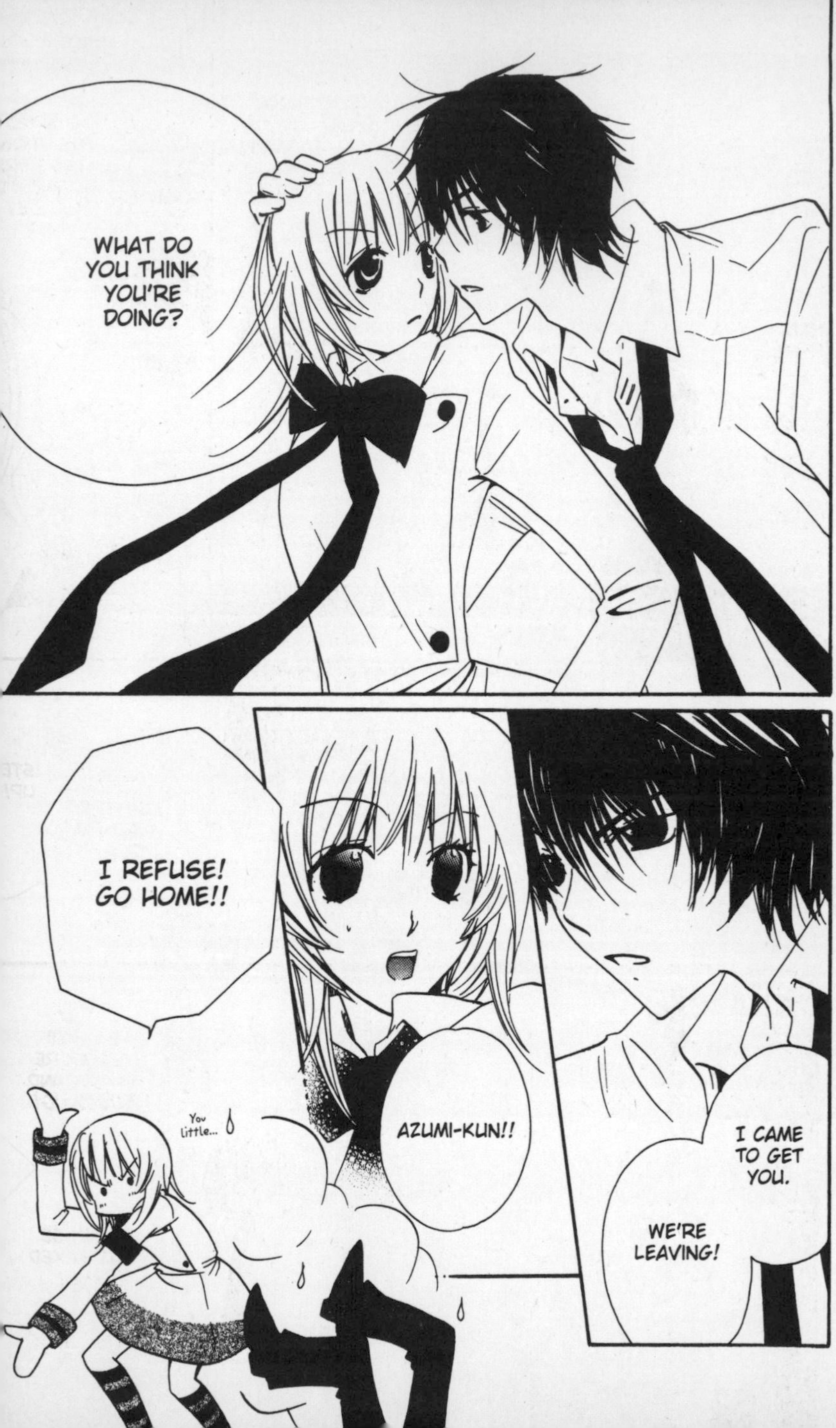
WHAT DO YOU THINK YOU'RE DOING?
I CAME TO GET YOU.
WE'RE LEAVING!
AZUMI-KUN!!
I REFUSE! GO HOME!!
You little...

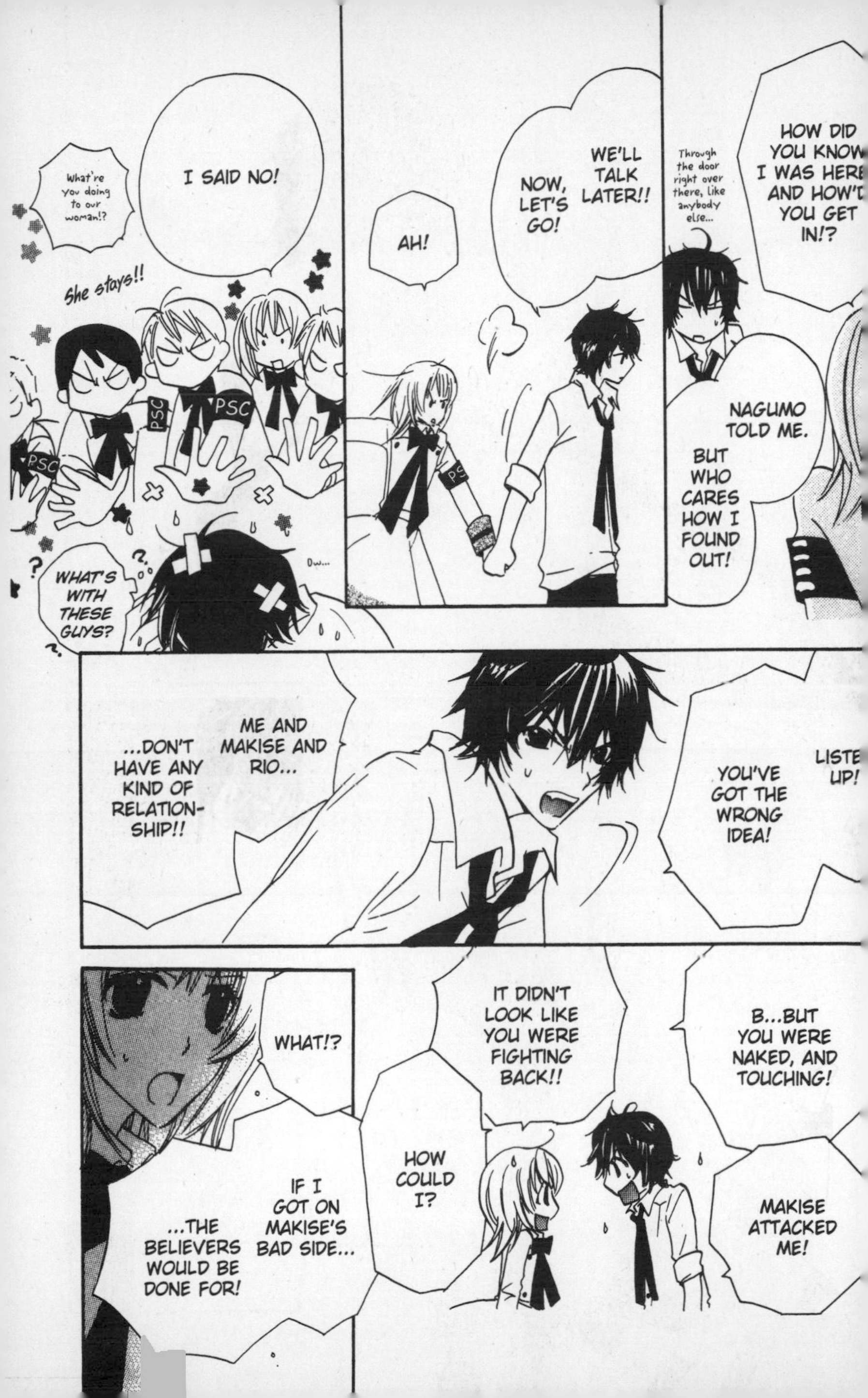
HOW DID YOU KNOW I WAS HERE AND HOW'D YOU GET IN!?
Through the door right over there, like anybody else...
NAGUMO TOLD ME.
BUT WHO CARES HOW I FOUND OUT!
WE'LL TALK LATER!!
NOW, LET'S GO!
AH!
I SAID NO!
What're you doing to our woman!?
She stays!!
Ow...
WHAT'S WITH THESE GUYS?
LISTEN UP!
YOU'VE GOT THE WRONG IDEA!
ME AND MAKISE AND RIO...
...DON'T HAVE ANY KIND OF RELATION-SHIP!!
B...BUT YOU WERE NAKED, AND TOUCHING!
MAKISE ATTACKED ME!
IT DIDN'T LOOK LIKE YOU WERE FIGHTING BACK!!
HOW COULD I?
WHAT!?
IF I GOT ON MAKISE'S BAD SIDE...
...THE BELIEVERS WOULD BE DONE FOR!

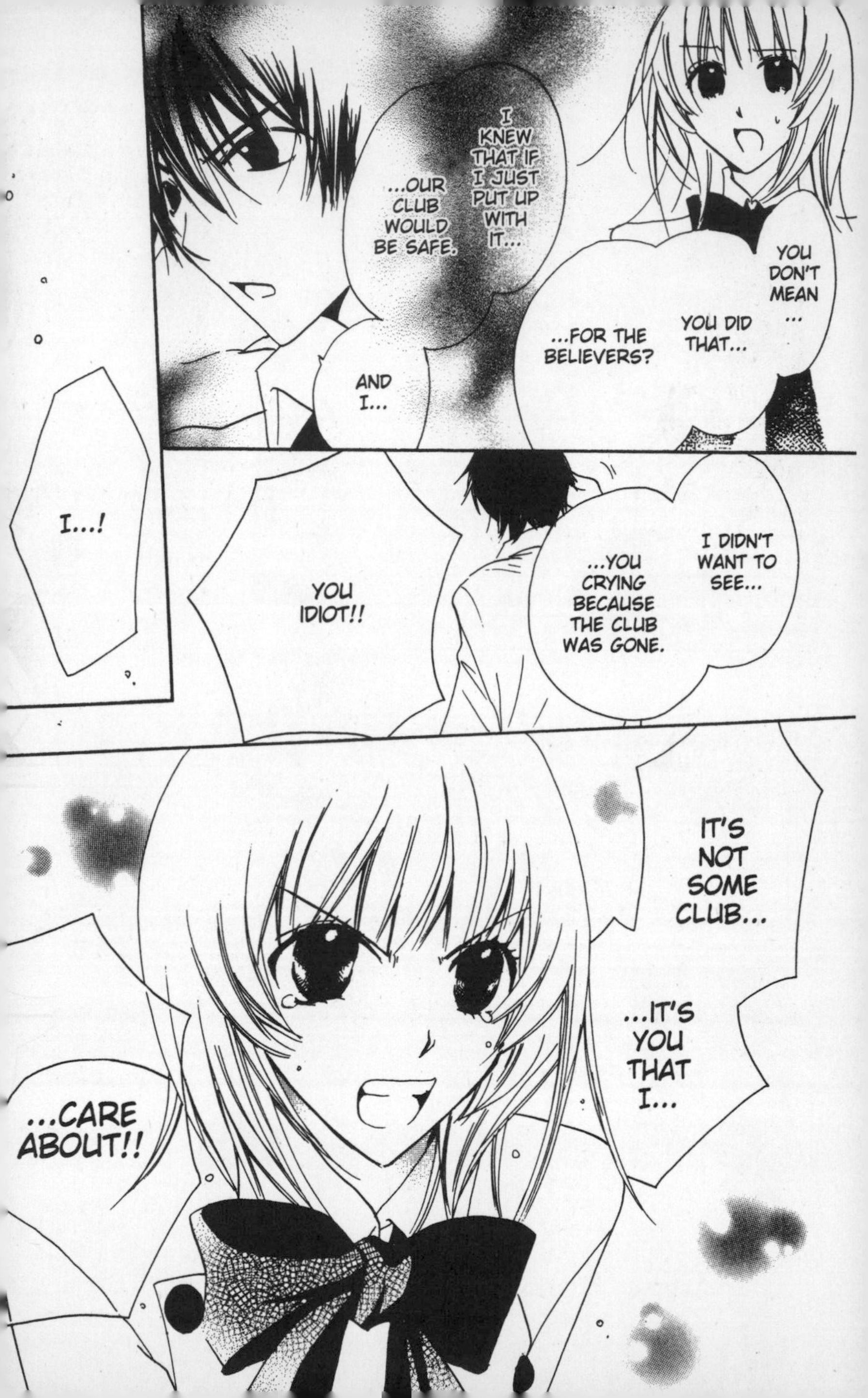
YOU DON'T MEAN ...
YOU DID THAT...
...FOR THE BELIEVERS?
I KNEW THAT IF I JUST PUT UP WITH IT...
...OUR CLUB WOULD BE SAFE.
AND I...
I DIDN'T WANT TO SEE...
...YOU CRYING BECAUSE THE CLUB WAS GONE.
YOU IDIOT!!
I...!
IT'S NOT SOME CLUB...
...IT'S YOU THAT I...
...CARE ABOUT!!

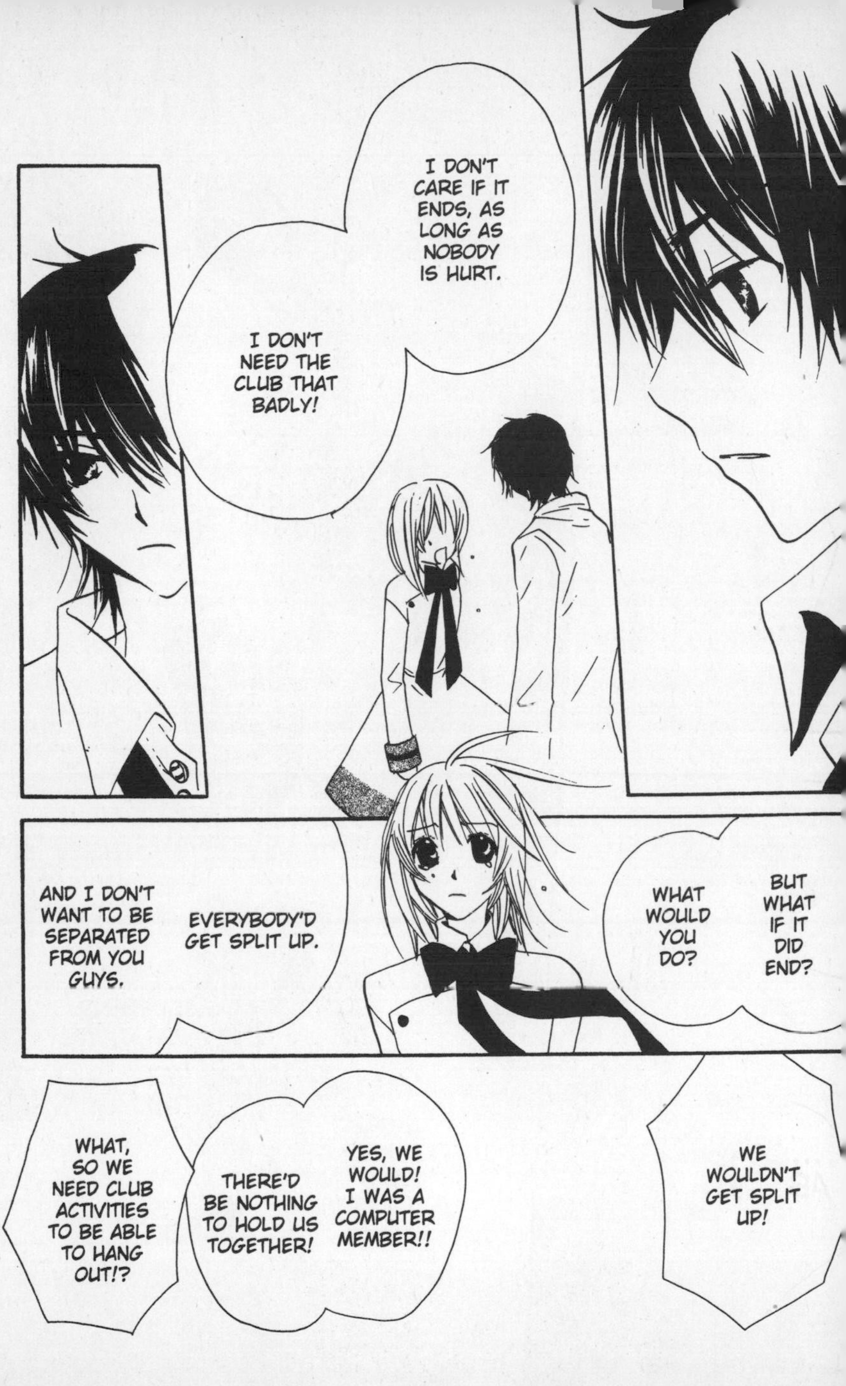
I DON'T CARE IF IT ENDS, AS LONG AS NOBODY IS HURT.
I DON'T NEED THE CLUB THAT BADLY!
BUT WHAT IF IT DID END?
WHAT WOULD YOU DO?
EVERYBODY'D GET SPLIT UP.
AND I DON'T WANT TO BE SEPARATED FROM YOU GUYS.
WE WOULDN'T GET SPLIT UP!
YES, WE WOULD! I WAS A COMPUTER MEMBER!!
THERE'D BE NOTHING TO HOLD US TOGETHER!
WHAT, SO WE NEED CLUB ACTIVITIES TO BE ABLE TO HANG OUT!?

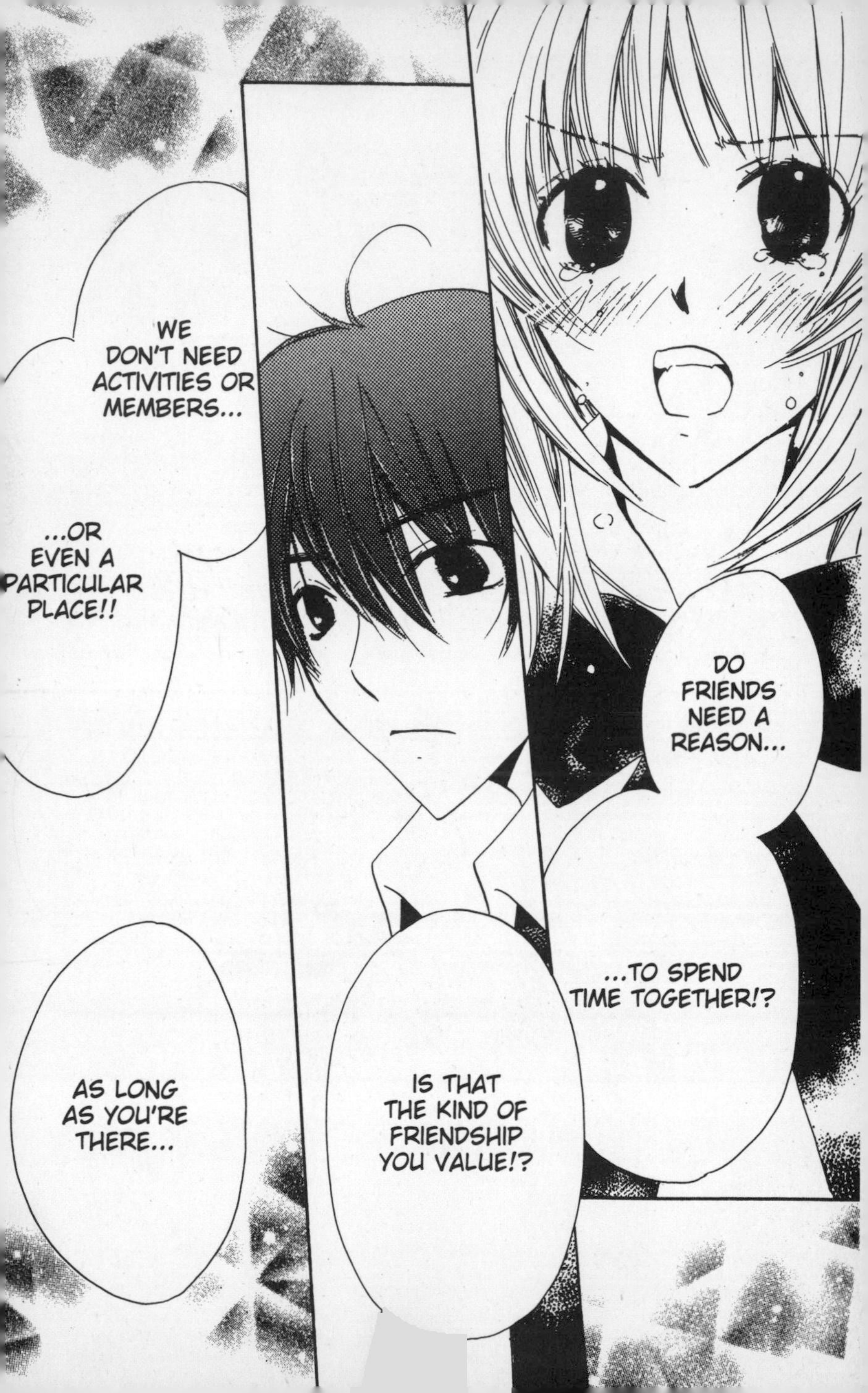
DO FRIENDS NEED A REASON...
...TO SPEND TIME TOGETHER!?
IS THAT THE KIND OF FRIENDSHIP YOU VALUE!?
WE DON'T NEED ACTIVITIES OR MEMBERS...
...OR EVEN A PARTICULAR PLACE!!
AS LONG AS YOU'RE THERE...

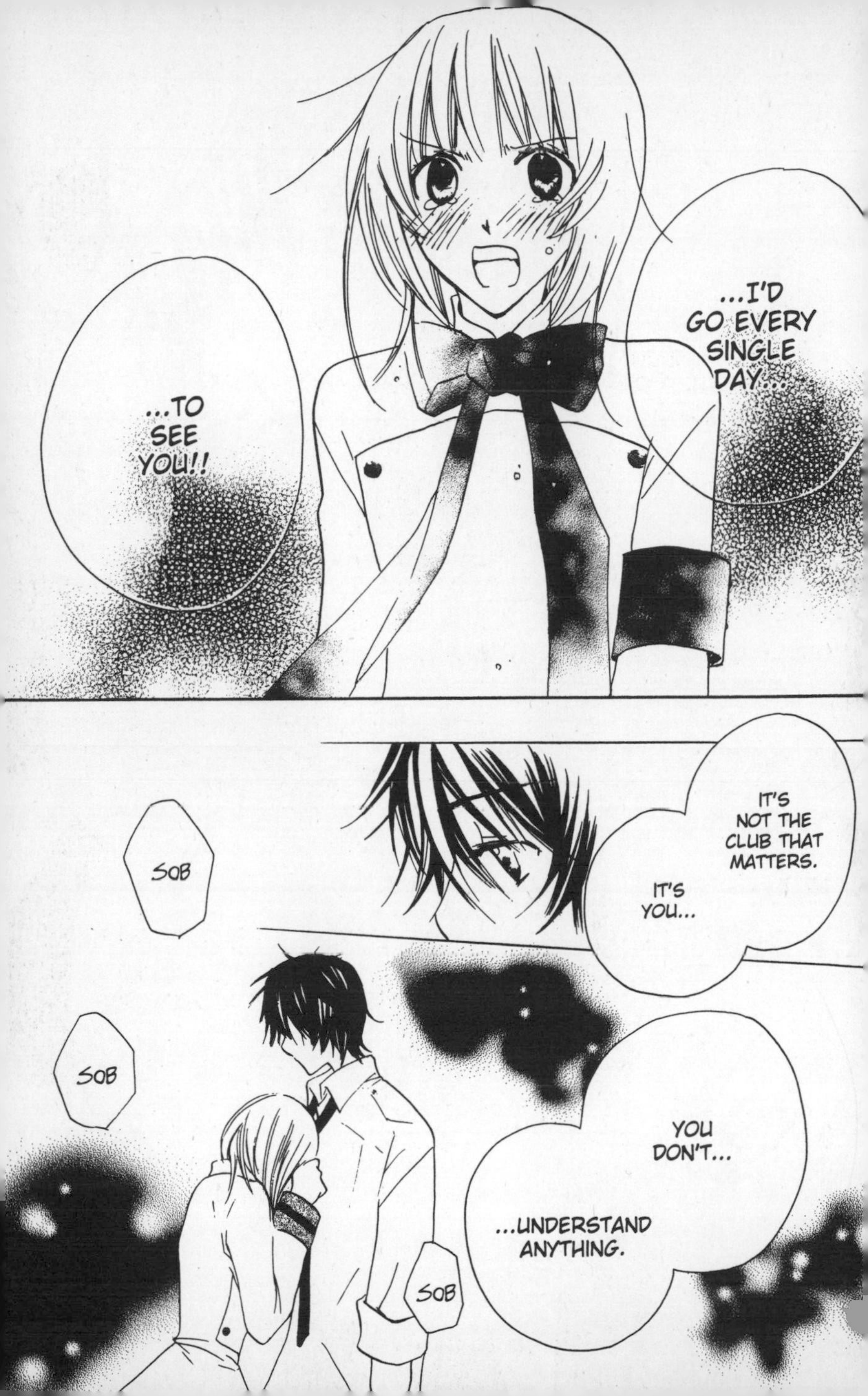
...I'D GO EVERY SINGLE DAY...
...TO SEE YOU!!
IT'S NOT THE CLUB THAT MATTERS.
IT'S YOU...
SOB
YOU DON'T...
...UNDERSTAND ANYTHING.
SOB
SOB

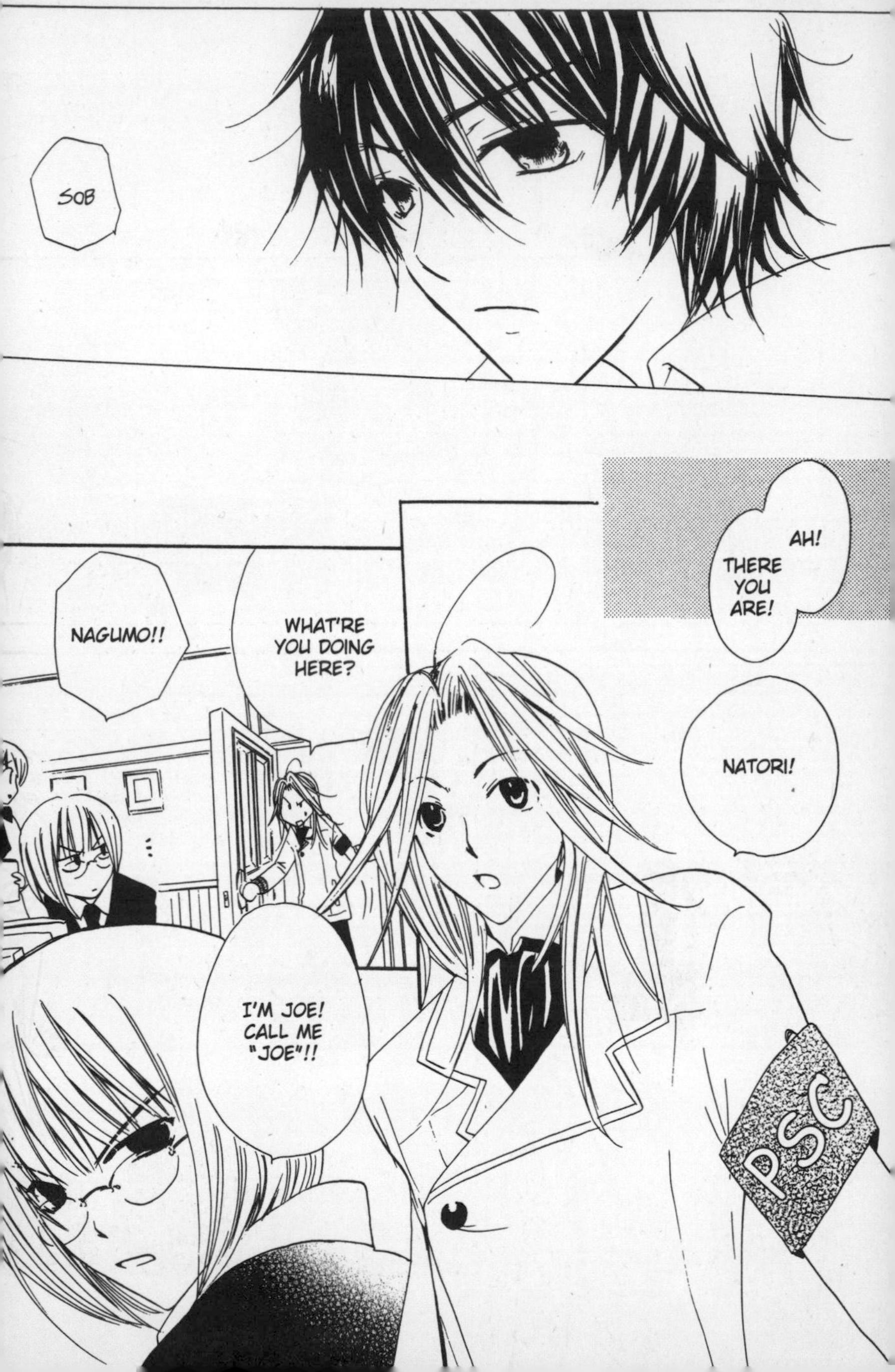
SOB
AH! THERE YOU ARE!
NATORI!
WHAT'RE YOU DOING HERE?
NAGUMO!!
I'M JOE! CALL ME "JOE"!!

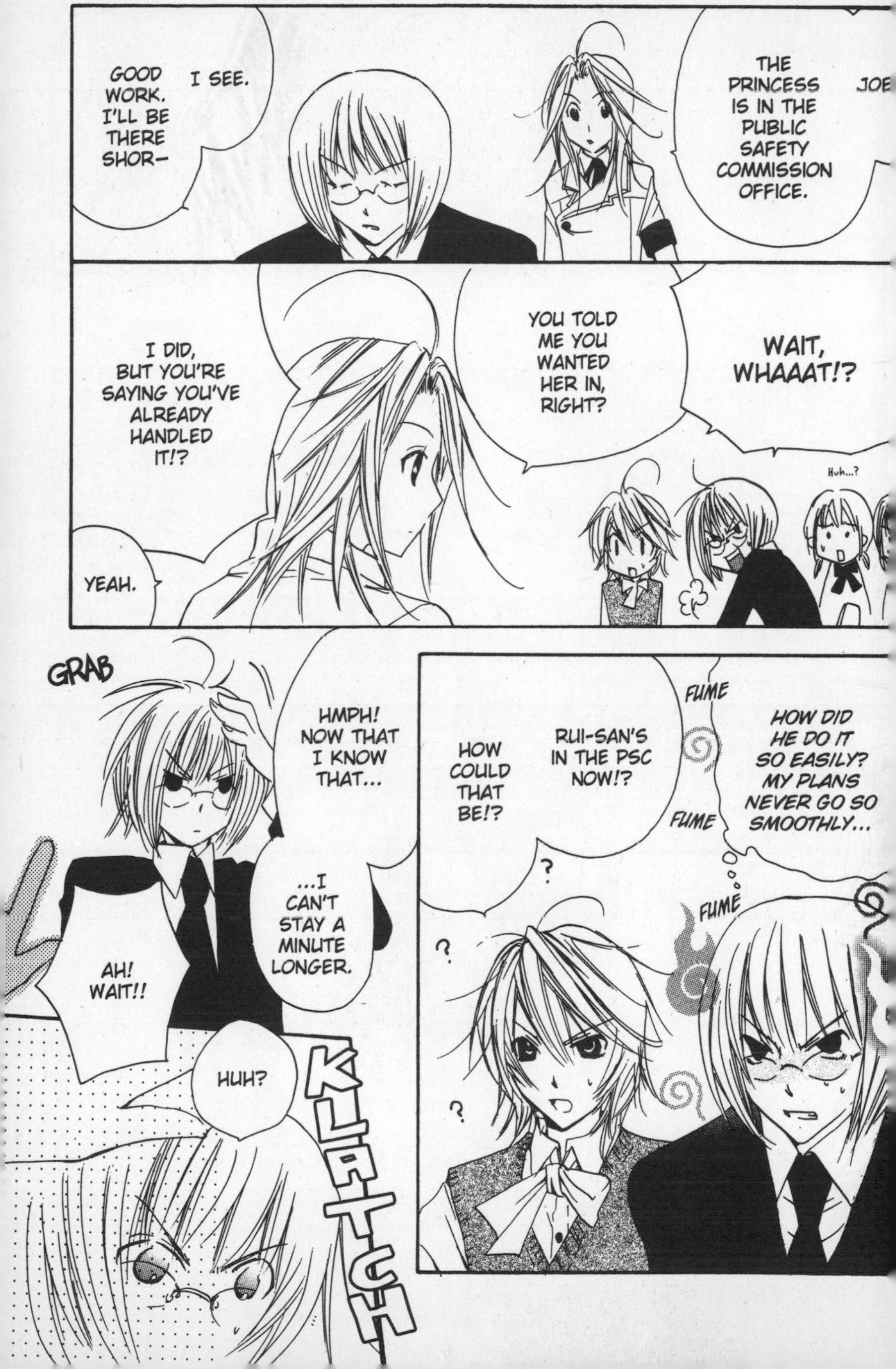
THE PRINCESS IS IN THE PUBLIC SAFETY COMMISSION OFFICE.
JOE
I SEE.
GOOD WORK. I'LL BE THERE SHOR—
WAIT, WHAAAT!?
Huh...?
YOU TOLD ME YOU WANTED HER IN, RIGHT?
I DID, BUT YOU'RE SAYING YOU'VE ALREADY HANDLED IT!?
YEAH.
HOW DID HE DO IT SO EASILY? MY PLANS NEVER GO SO SMOOTHLY...
FUME
FUME
FUME
RUI-SAN'S IN THE PSC NOW!?
HOW COULD THAT BE!?
GRAB
HMPH! NOW THAT I KNOW THAT...
...I CAN'T STAY A MINUTE LONGER.
AH! WAIT!!
HUH?
KLATCH

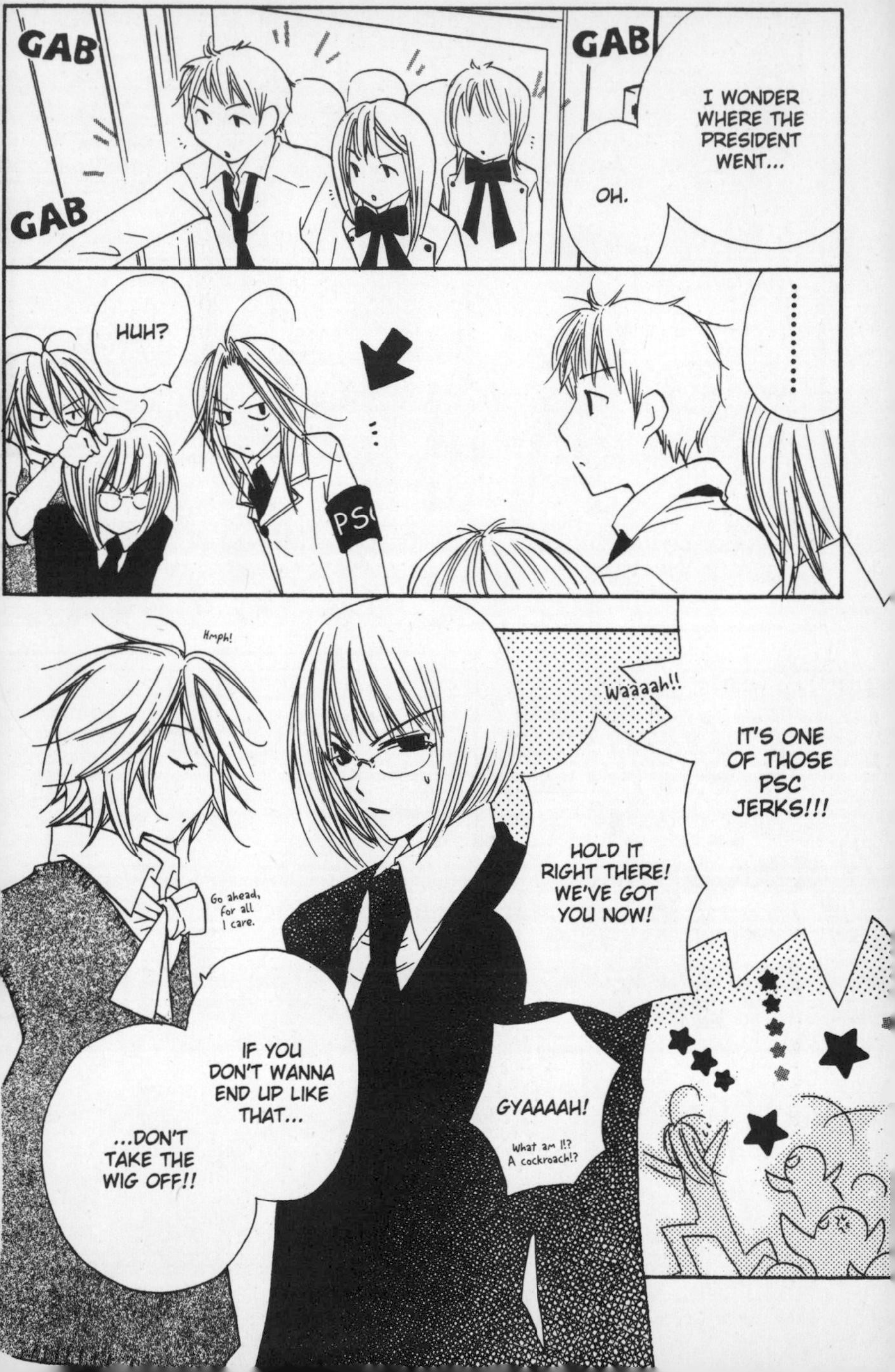
GAB
I WONDER WHERE THE PRESIDENT WENT...
OH.
GAB
GAB
......
HUH?
Waaaah!!
IT'S ONE OF THOSE PSC JERKS!!!
HOLD IT RIGHT THERE! WE'VE GOT YOU NOW!
GYAAAAH!
What am I!? A cockroach!?
Hmph!
Go ahead, for all I care.
IF YOU DON'T WANNA END UP LIKE THAT...
...DON'T TAKE THE WIG OFF!!

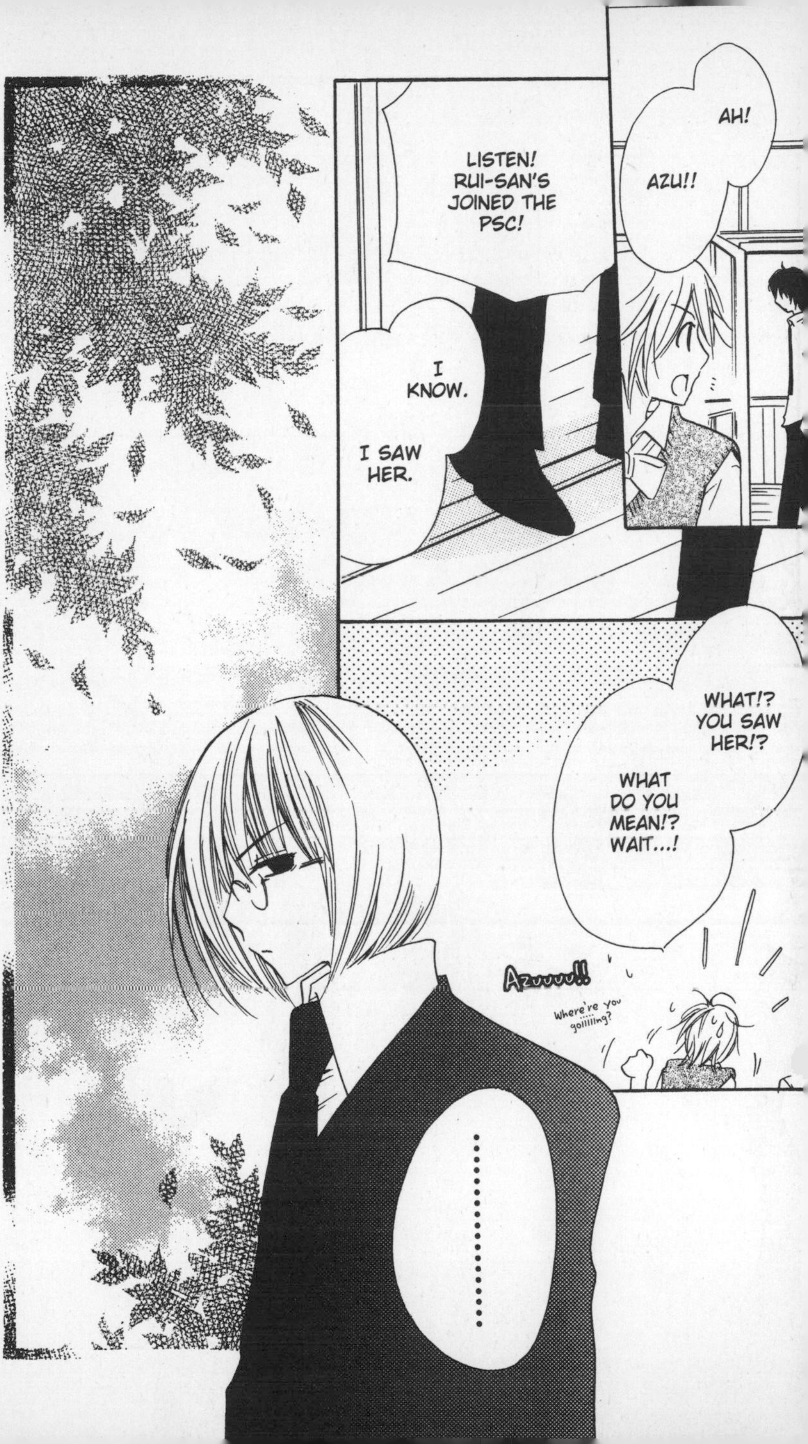
AH!
AZU!!
LISTEN! RUI-SAN'S JOINED THE PSC!
I KNOW.
I SAW HER.
WHAT!? YOU SAW HER!?
WHAT DO YOU MEAN!? WAIT...!
Azuuuu!!
Where're you goiiiiiing?
......

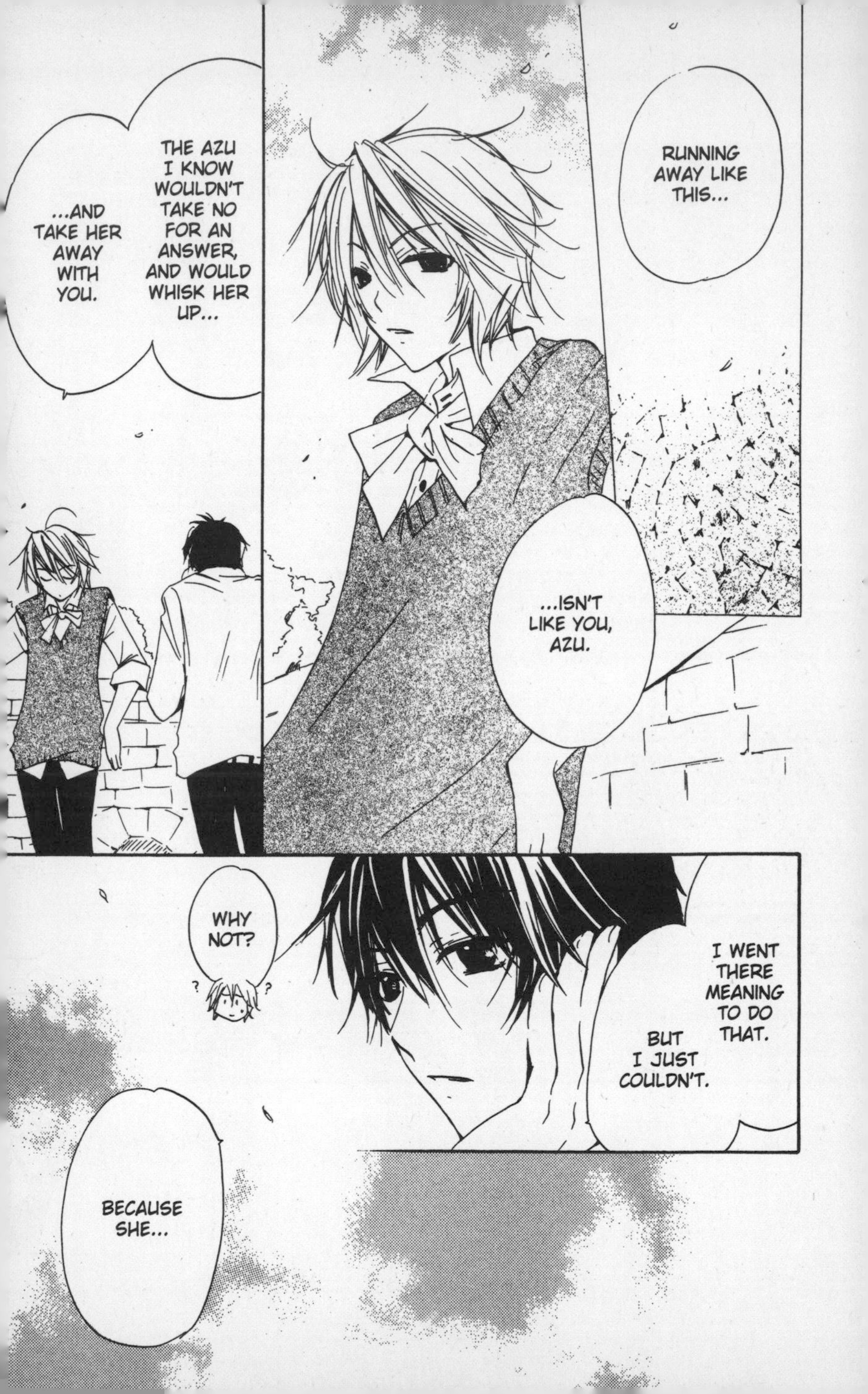
RUNNING AWAY LIKE THIS...
...ISN'T LIKE YOU, AZU.
THE AZU I KNOW WOULDN'T TAKE NO FOR AN ANSWER, AND WOULD WHISK HER UP...
...AND TAKE HER AWAY WITH YOU.
I WENT THERE MEANING TO DO THAT.
BUT I JUST COULDN'T.
WHY NOT?
?
?
BECAUSE SHE...

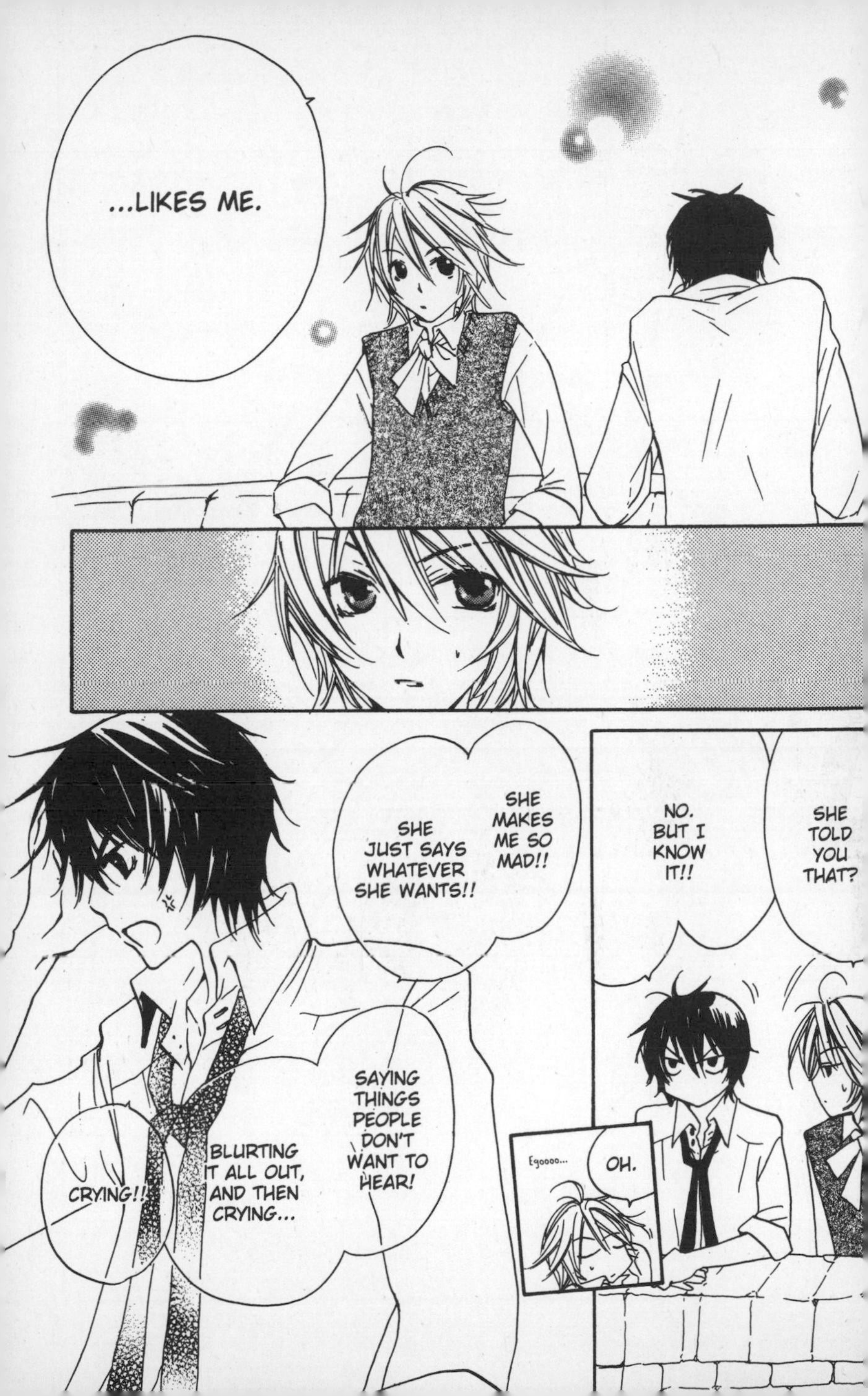
...LIKES ME.
SHE TOLD YOU THAT?
NO. BUT I KNOW IT!!
OH.
Egoooo...
SHE MAKES ME SO MAD!!
SHE JUST SAYS WHATEVER SHE WANTS!!
SAYING THINGS PEOPLE DON'T WANT TO HEAR!
BLURTING IT ALL OUT, AND THEN CRYING...
CRYING!!

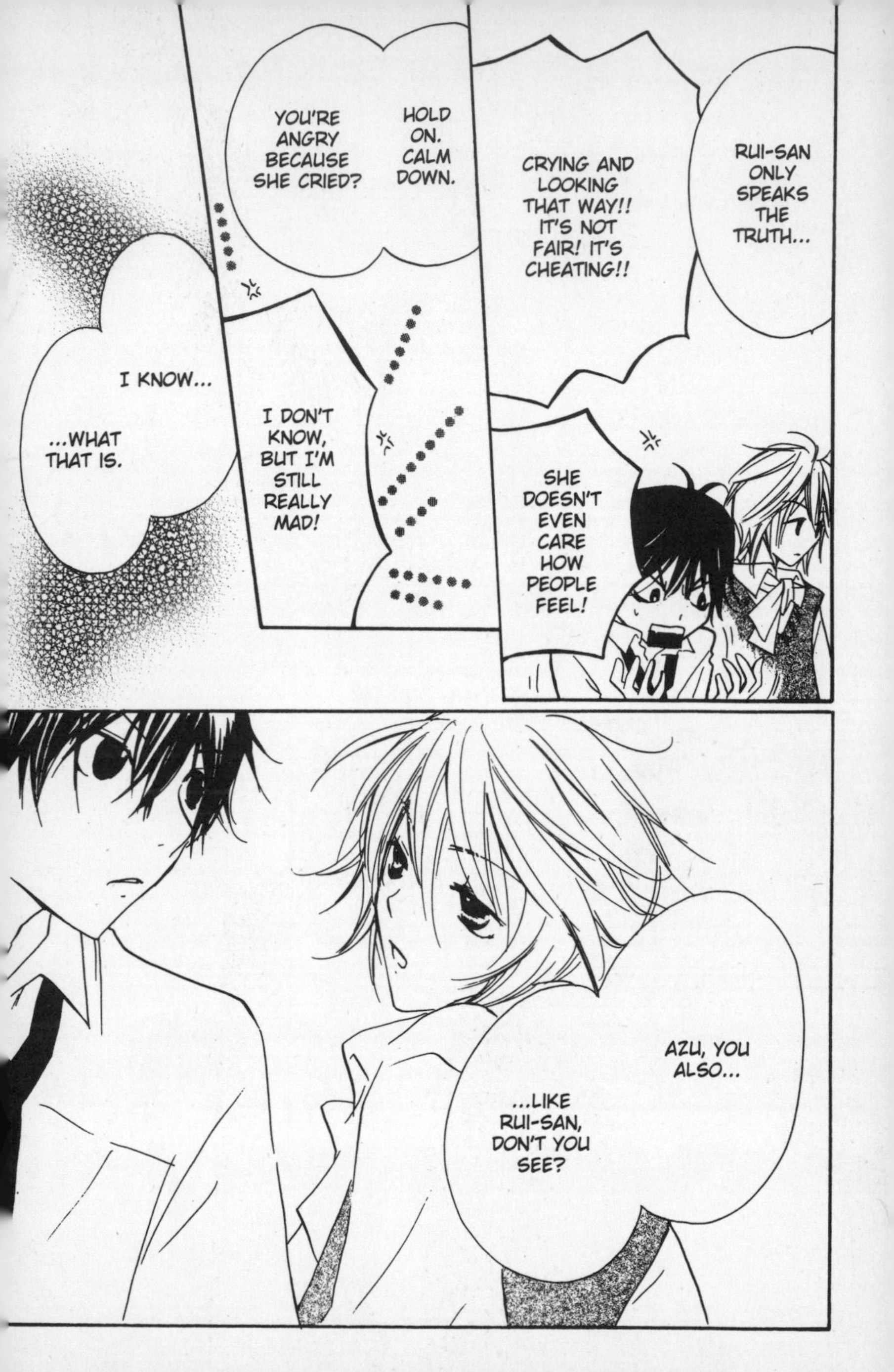
RUI-SAN ONLY SPEAKS THE TRUTH...
CRYING AND LOOKING THAT WAY!! IT'S NOT FAIR! IT'S CHEATING!!
SHE DOESN'T EVEN CARE HOW PEOPLE FEEL!
HOLD ON. CALM DOWN.
YOU'RE ANGRY BECAUSE SHE CRIED?
I DON'T KNOW, BUT I'M STILL REALLY MAD!
I KNOW...
...WHAT THAT IS.
AZU, YOU ALSO...
...LIKE RUI-SAN, DON'T YOU SEE?

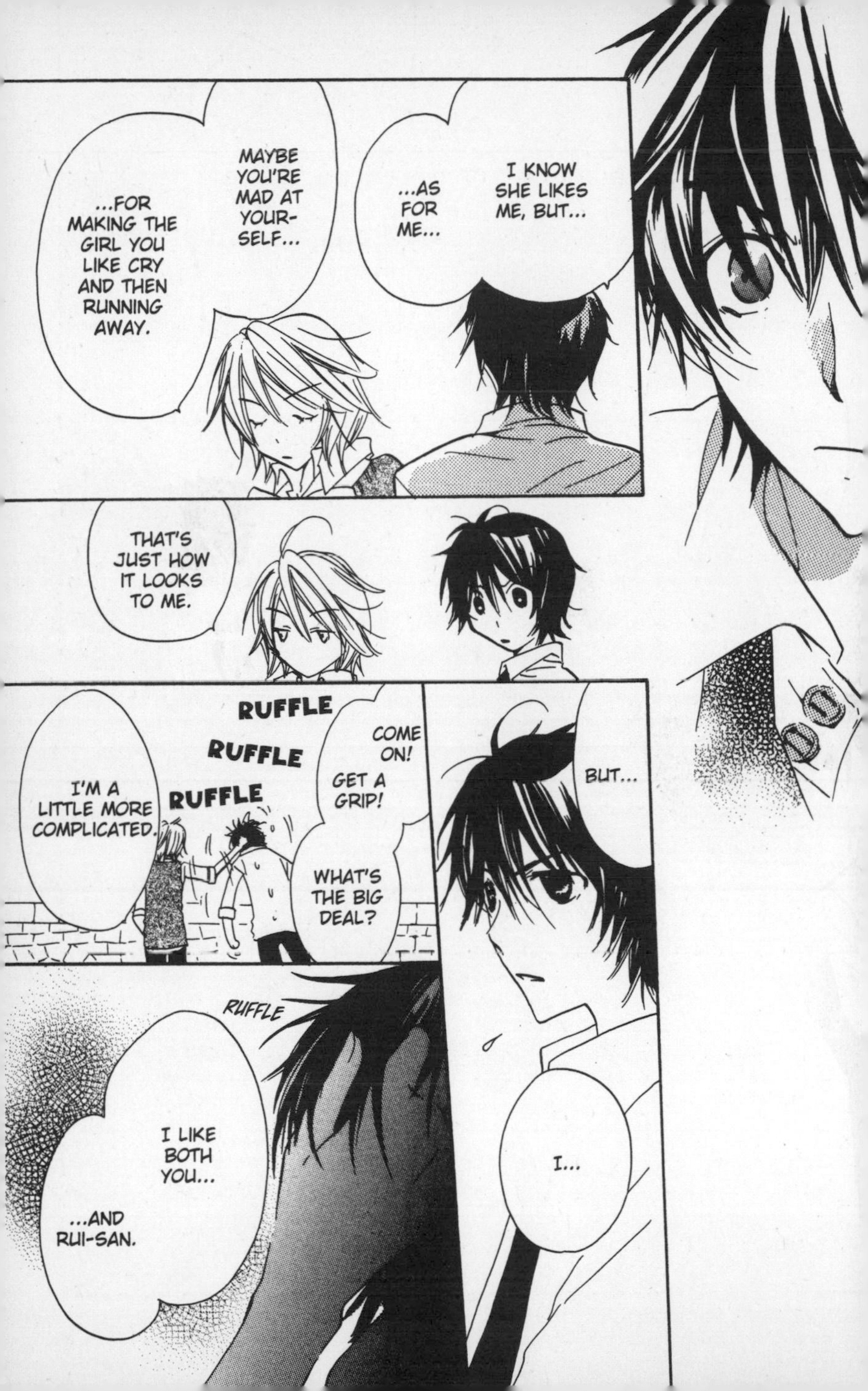
I KNOW SHE LIKES ME, BUT...
...AS FOR ME...
MAYBE YOU'RE MAD AT YOURSELF...
...FOR MAKING THE GIRL YOU LIKE CRY AND THEN RUNNING AWAY.
THAT'S JUST HOW IT LOOKS TO ME.
BUT...
I...
COME ON!
GET A GRIP!
RUFFLE
RUFFLE
RUFFLE
WHAT'S THE BIG DEAL?
I'M A LITTLE MORE COMPLICATED.
RUFFLE
I LIKE BOTH YOU...
...AND RUI-SAN.

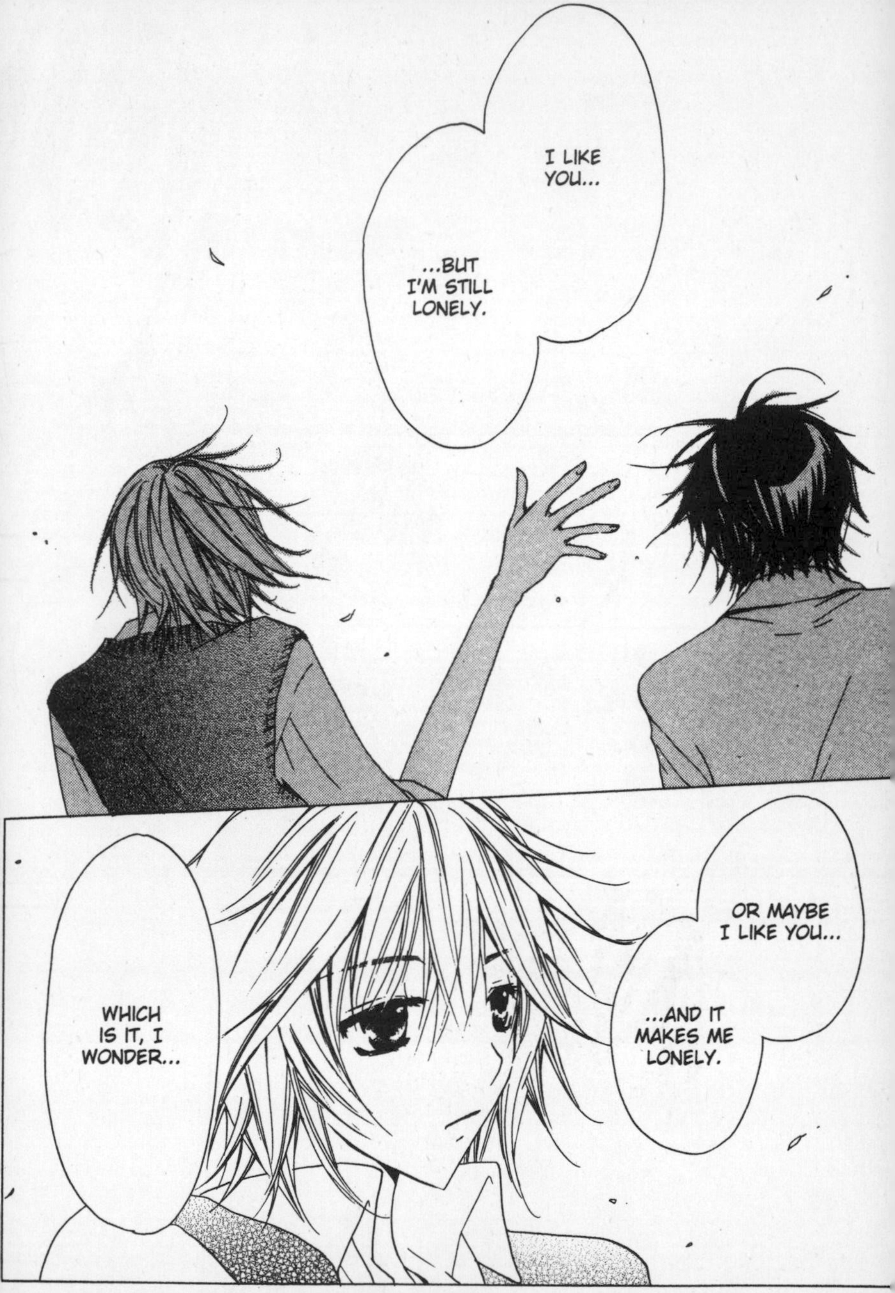
I LIKE YOU...
...BUT I'M STILL LONELY.
OR MAYBE I LIKE YOU...
...AND IT MAKES ME LONELY.
WHICH IS IT, I WONDER...

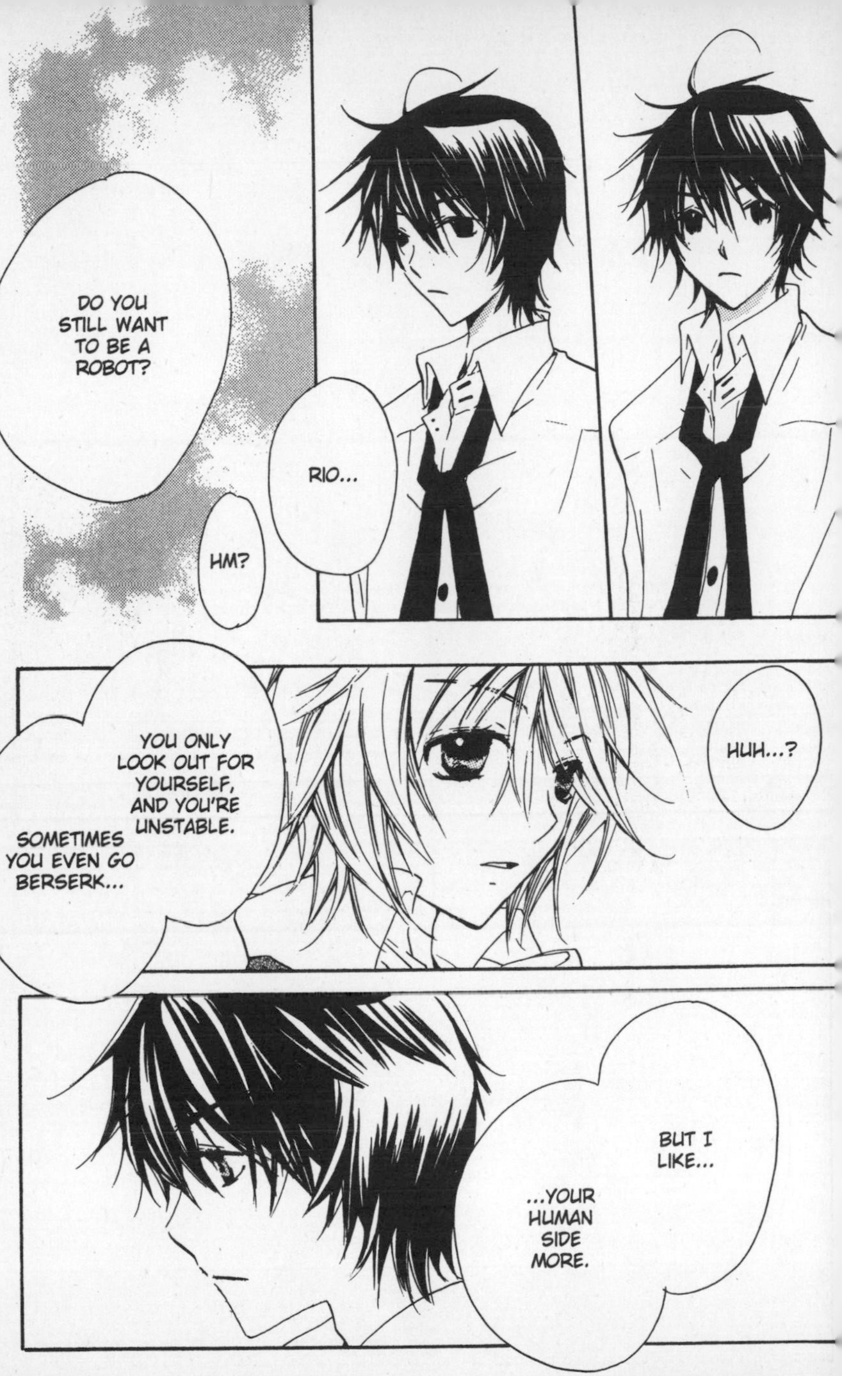
RIO...
HM?
DO YOU STILL WANT TO BE A ROBOT?
HUH...?
YOU ONLY LOOK OUT FOR YOURSELF, AND YOU'RE UNSTABLE.
SOMETIMES YOU EVEN GO BERSERK...
BUT I LIKE...
...YOUR HUMAN SIDE MORE.

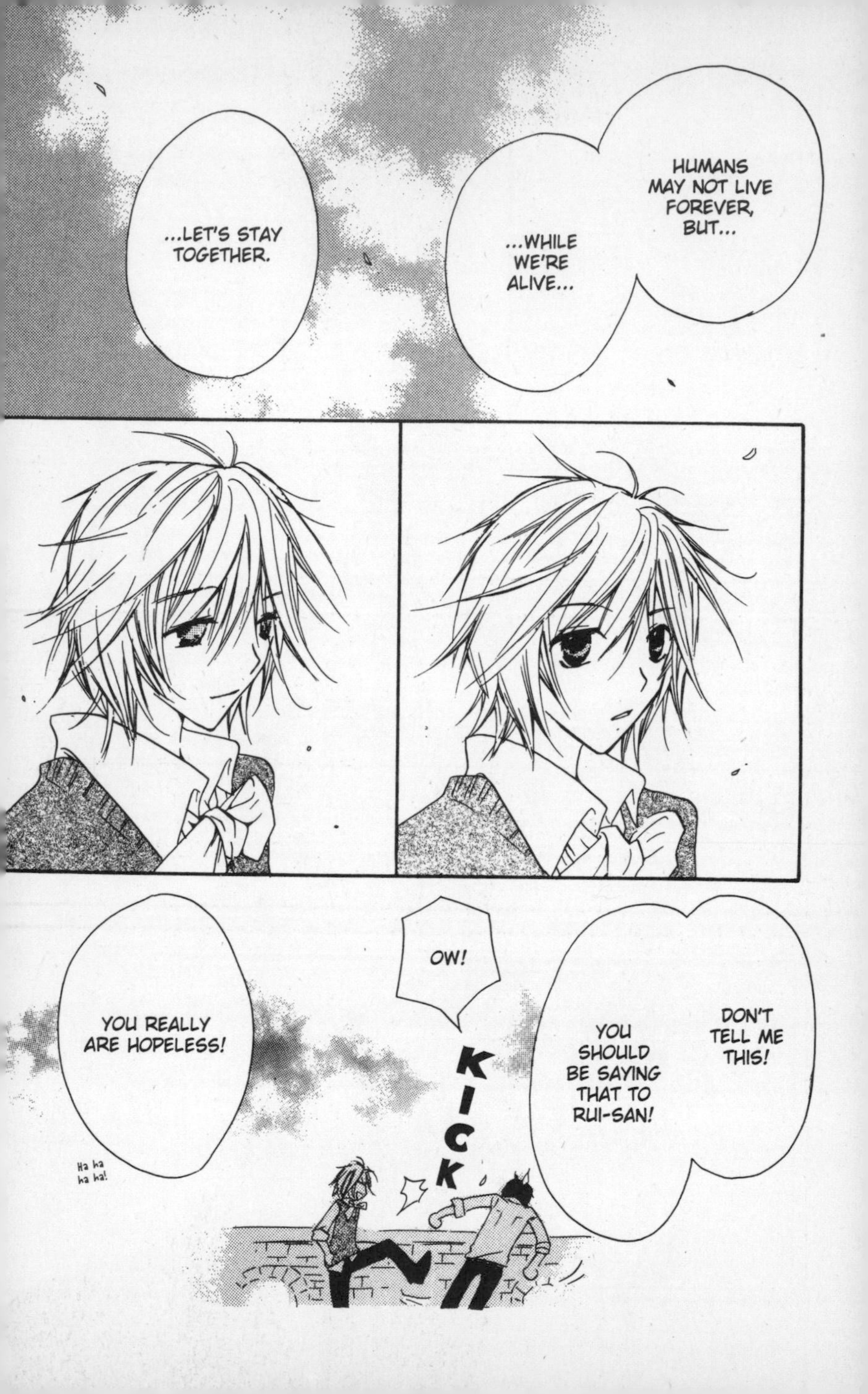
HUMANS MAY NOT LIVE FOREVER, BUT...
...WHILE WE'RE ALIVE...
...LET'S STAY TOGETHER.
DON'T TELL ME THIS!
YOU SHOULD BE SAYING THAT TO RUI-SAN!
OW!
KICK
YOU REALLY ARE HOPELESS!
Ha ha ha ha!

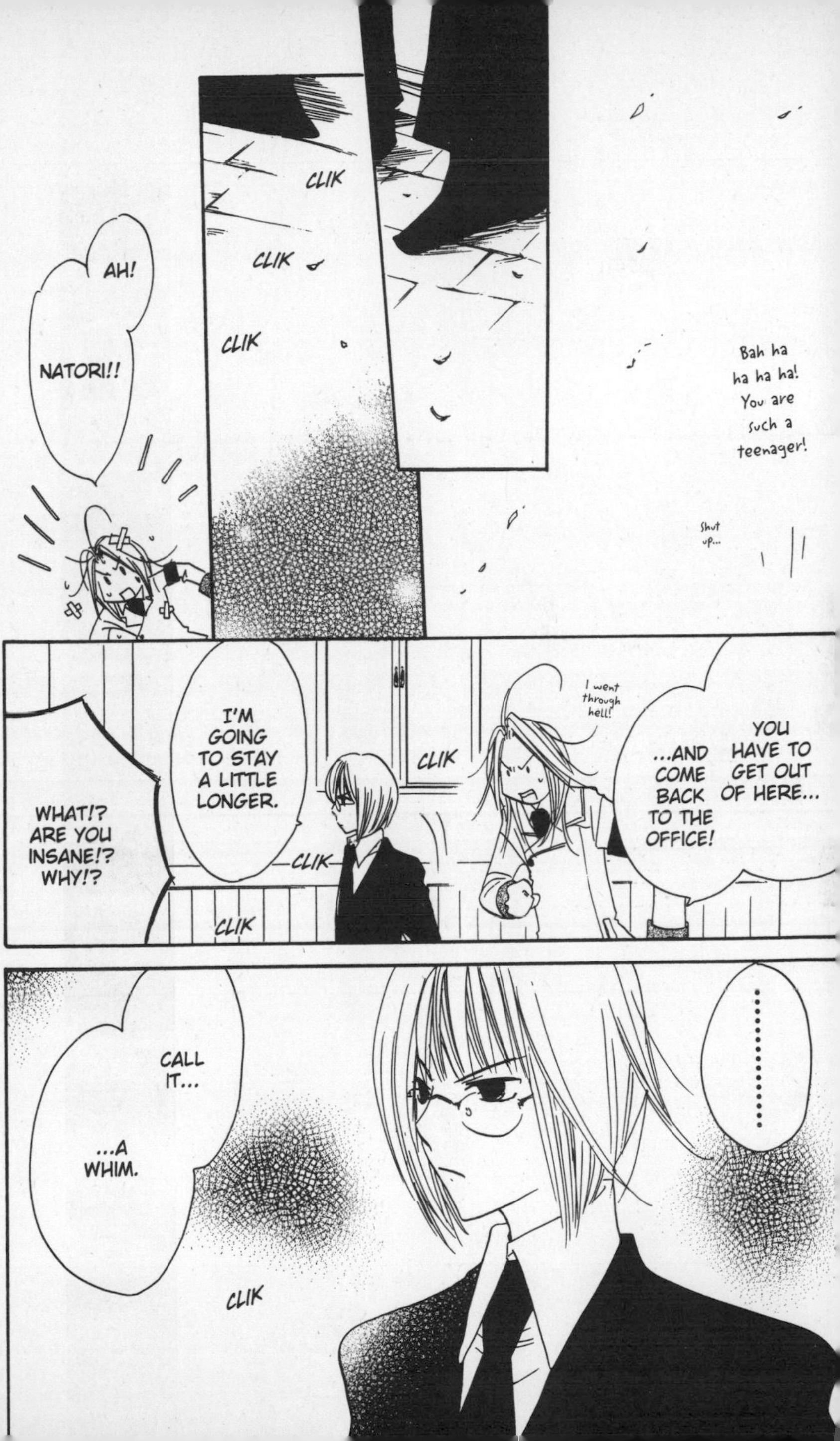
Bah ha ha ha ha! You are such a teenager!
Shut up...
CLIK
CLIK
CLIK
AH!
NATORI!!
YOU HAVE TO GET OUT OF HERE...
...AND COME BACK TO THE OFFICE!
I went through hell!
CLIK
I'M GOING TO STAY A LITTLE LONGER.
CLIK
WHAT!? ARE YOU INSANE!? WHY!?
CLIK
....
CALL IT...
...A WHIM.
CLIK

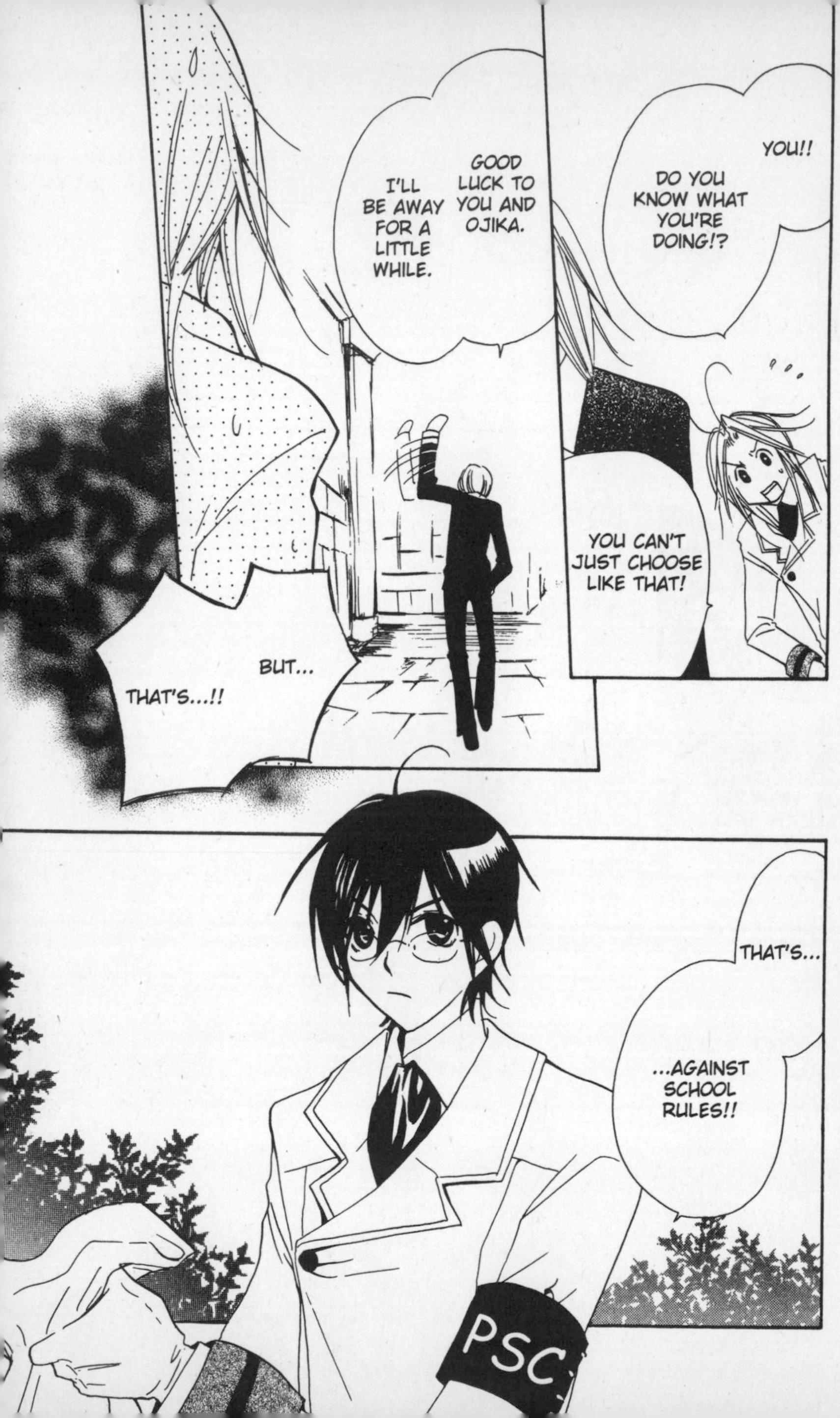
YOU!!
DO YOU KNOW WHAT YOU'RE DOING!?
YOU CAN'T JUST CHOOSE LIKE THAT!
GOOD LUCK TO YOU AND OJIKA.
I'LL BE AWAY FOR A LITTLE WHILE.
BUT...
THAT'S...!!
THAT'S...
...AGAINST SCHOOL RULES!!
PSC

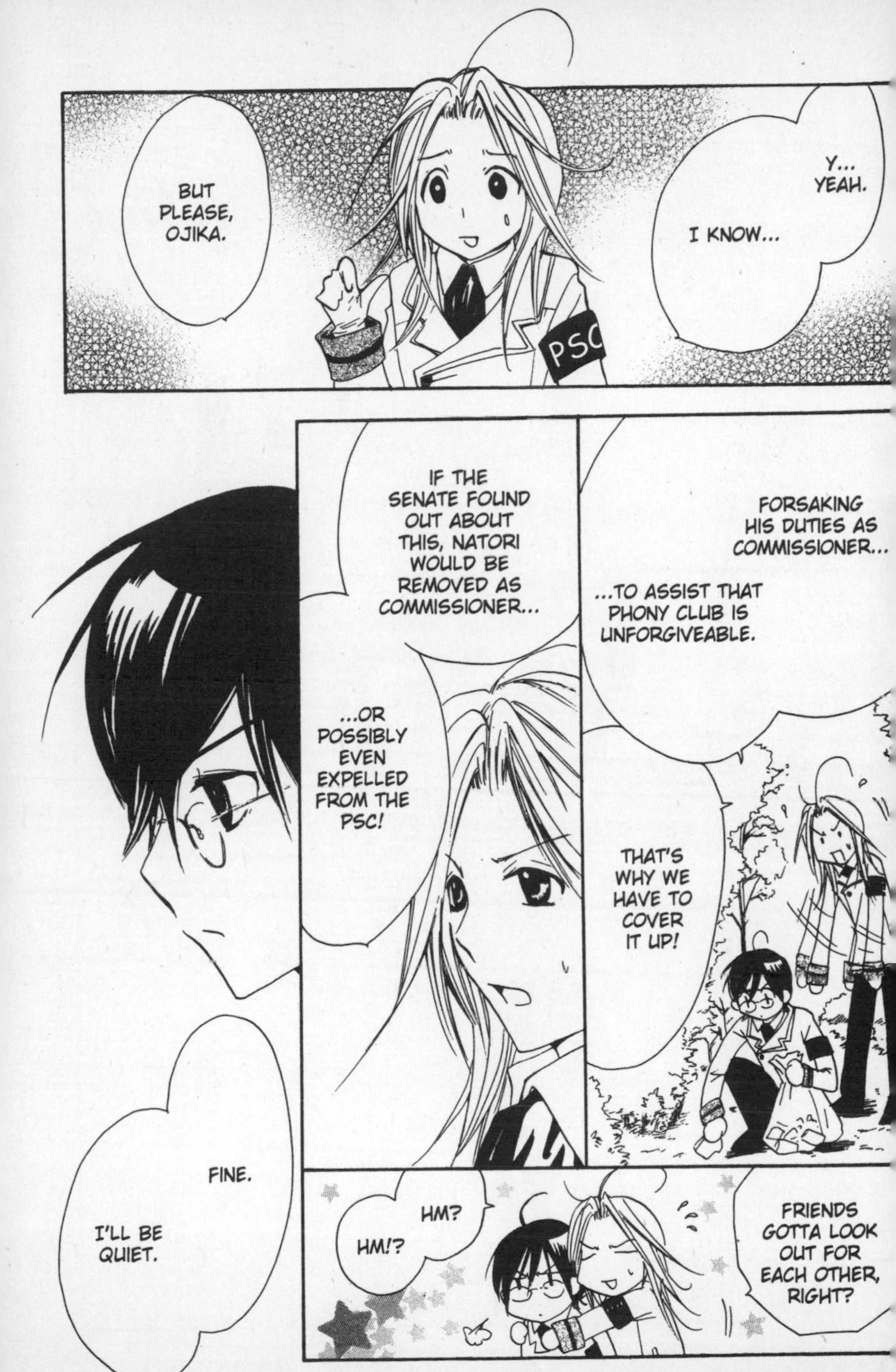
Y... YEAH.
I KNOW...
BUT PLEASE, OJIKA.
PSC
FORSAKING HIS DUTIES AS COMMISSIONER...
...TO ASSIST THAT PHONY CLUB IS UNFORGIVEABLE.
THAT'S WHY WE HAVE TO COVER IT UP!
IF THE SENATE FOUND OUT ABOUT THIS, NATORI WOULD BE REMOVED AS COMMISSIONER...
...OR POSSIBLY EVEN EXPELLED FROM THE PSC!
FRIENDS GOTTA LOOK OUT FOR EACH OTHER, RIGHT?
HM?
HM!?
FINE.
I'LL BE QUIET.

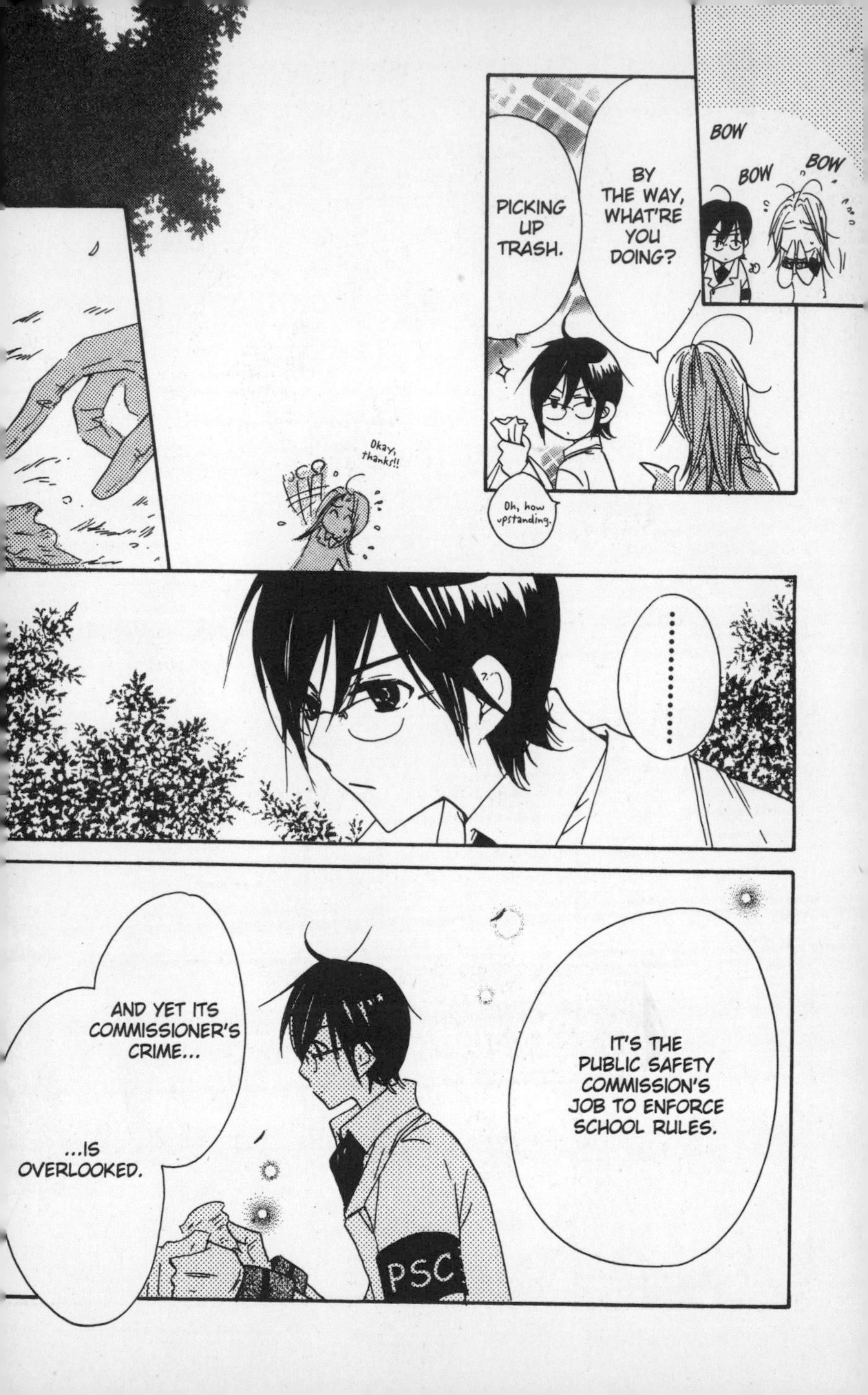
BOW
BOW
BOW
BY THE WAY, WHAT'RE YOU DOING?
PICKING UP TRASH.
Oh, how upstanding.
Okay, thanks!!
......
IT'S THE PUBLIC SAFETY COMMISSION'S JOB TO ENFORCE SCHOOL RULES.
PSC
AND YET ITS COMMISSIONER'S CRIME...
...IS OVERLOOKED.

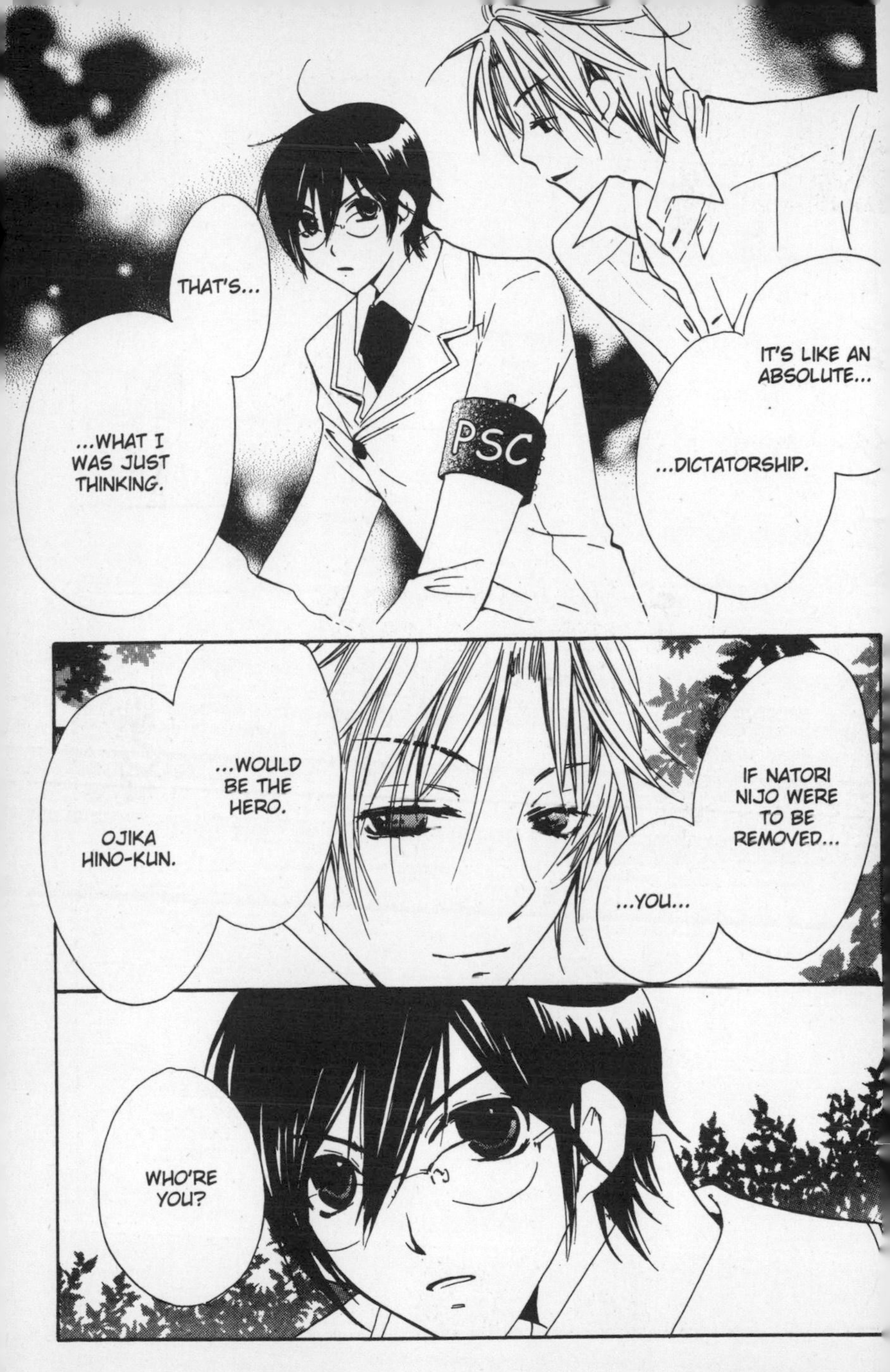
IT'S LIKE AN ABSOLUTE...
...DICTATORSHIP.
THAT'S...
...WHAT I WAS JUST THINKING.
IF NATORI NIJO WERE TO BE REMOVED...
...YOU...
...WOULD BE THE HERO.
OJIKA HINO-KUN.
WHO'RE YOU?
PSC

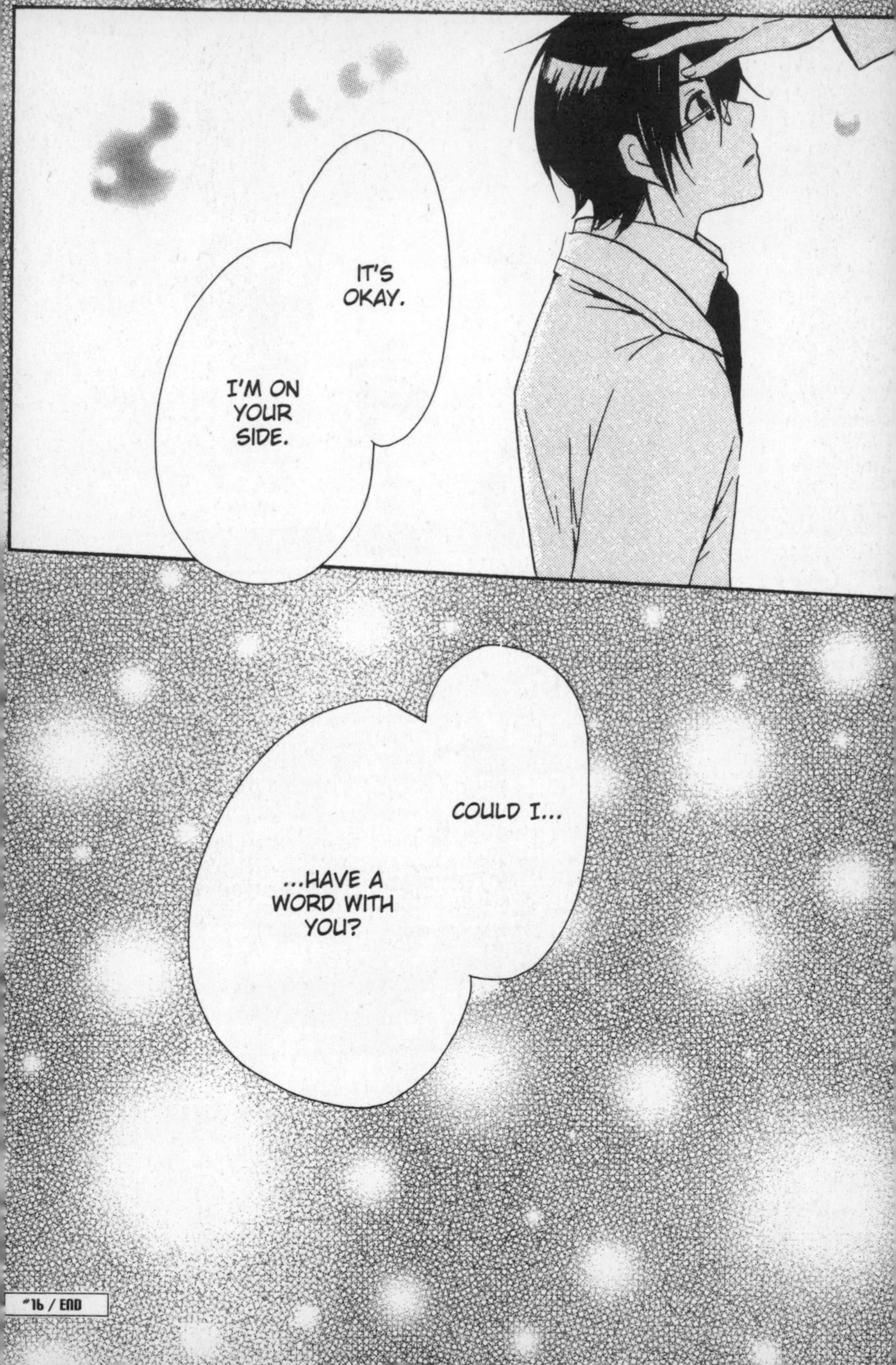
IT'S OKAY.
I'M ON YOUR SIDE.
COULD I...
...HAVE A WORD WITH YOU?
#16 / END

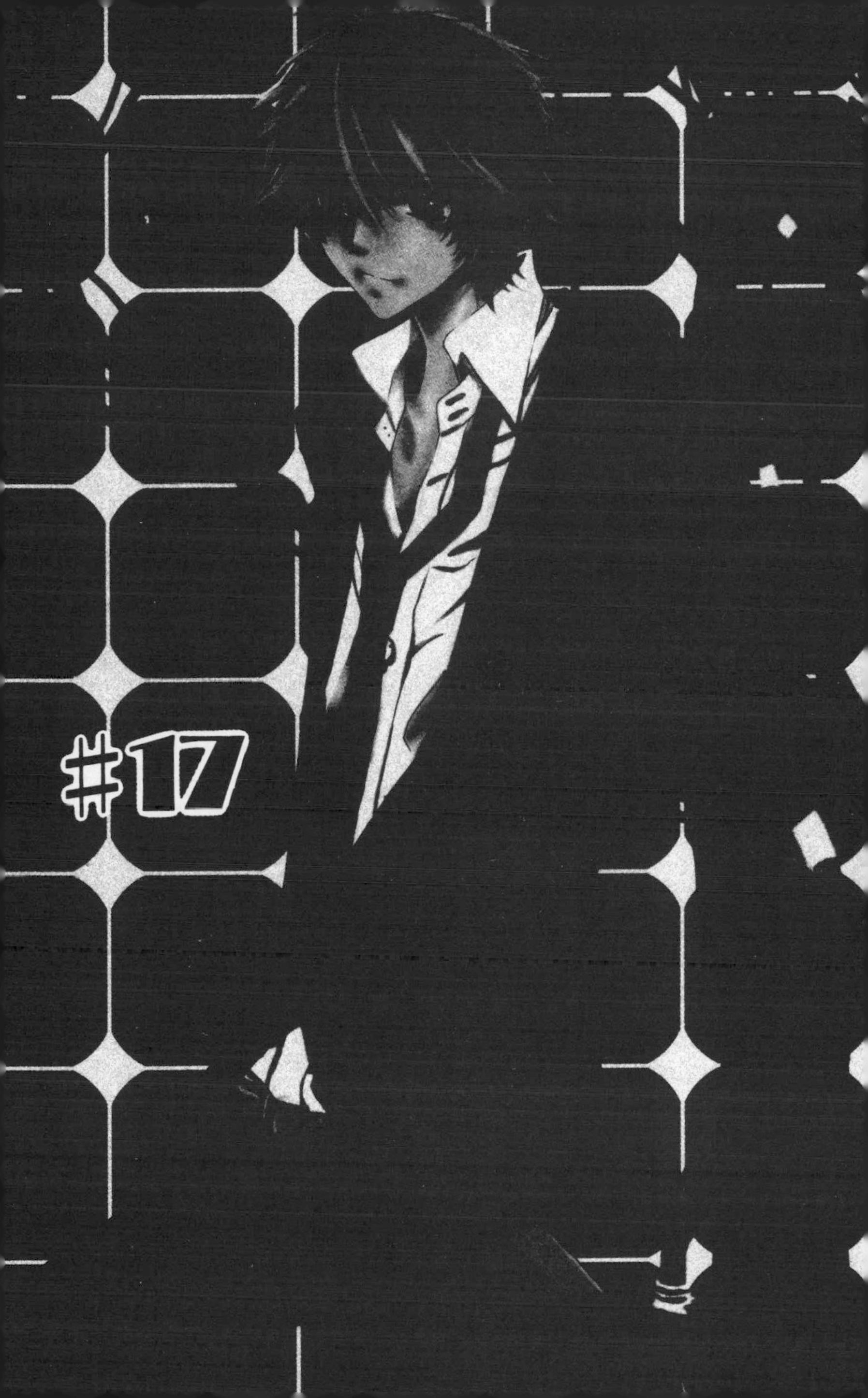
#17

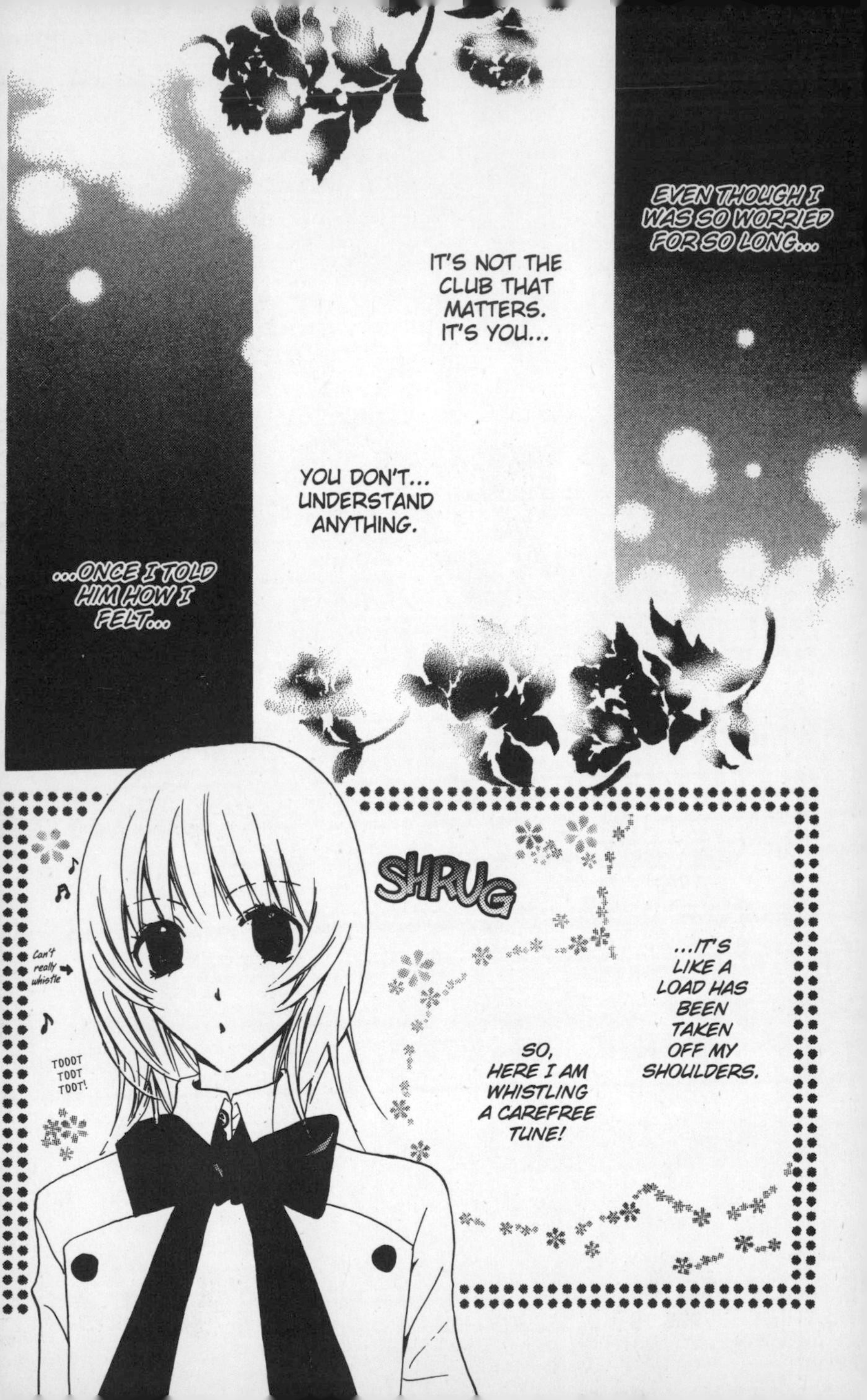
EVEN THOUGH I WAS SO WORRIED FOR SO LONG...
IT'S NOT THE CLUB THAT MATTERS. IT'S YOU...
YOU DON'T... UNDERSTAND ANYTHING.
...ONCE I TOLD HIM HOW I FELT...
SHRUG
...IT'S LIKE A LOAD HAS BEEN TAKEN OFF MY SHOULDERS.
SO, HERE I AM WHISTLING A CAREFREE TUNE!
Can't really whistle
TOOOT TOOT TOOT!

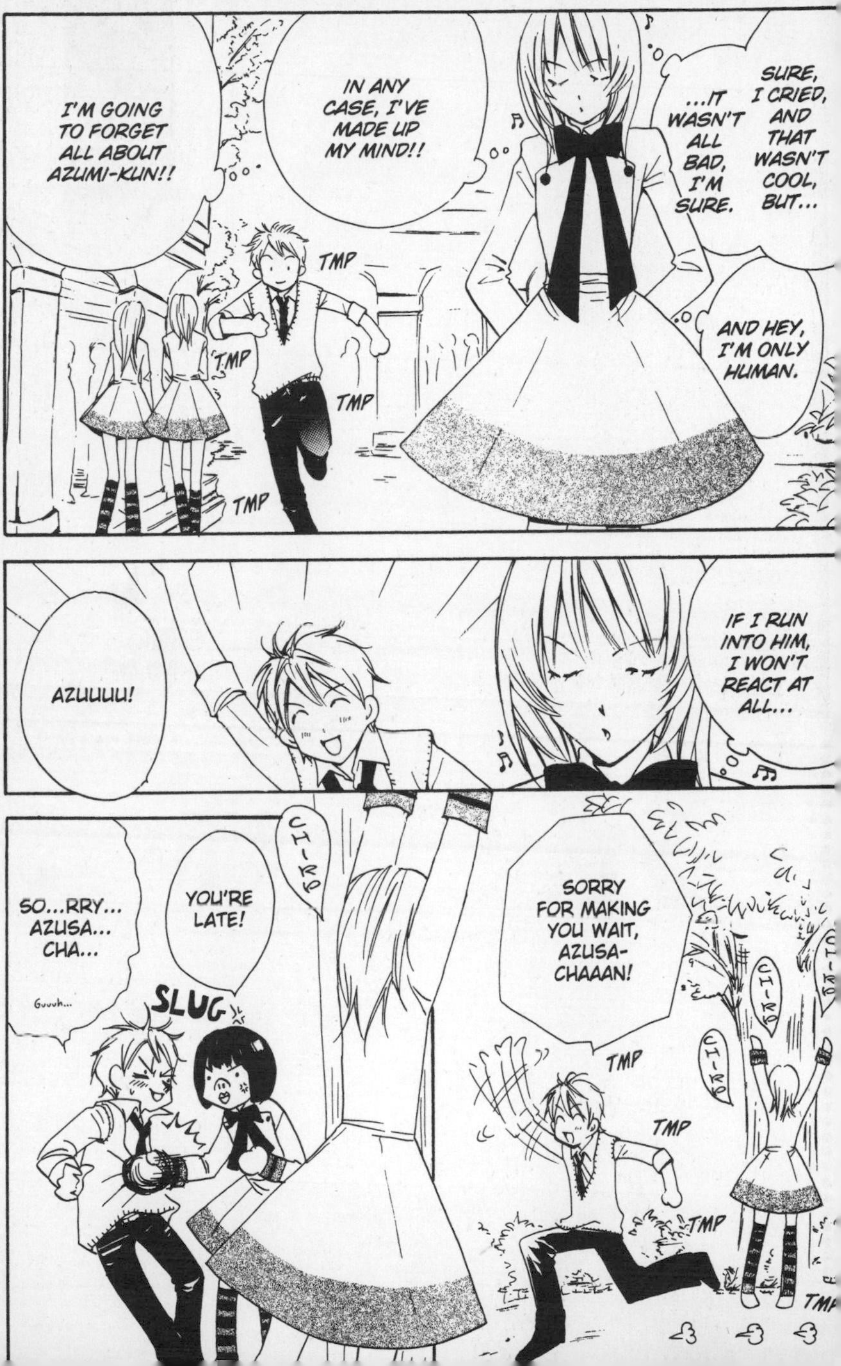
SURE, I CRIED, AND THAT WASN'T COOL, BUT...
...IT WASN'T ALL BAD, I'M SURE.
AND HEY, I'M ONLY HUMAN.
IN ANY CASE, I'VE MADE UP MY MIND!!
I'M GOING TO FORGET ALL ABOUT AZUMI-KUN!!
TMP
TMP
TMP
TMP
IF I RUN INTO HIM, I WON'T REACT AT ALL...
AZUUUU!
CHI-RO
CHI-RO
CHI-RO
TMP
TMP
TMP
SORRY FOR MAKING YOU WAIT, AZUSA-CHAAAN!
TMP
CHI-RO
YOU'RE LATE!
SLUG
SO...RRY... AZUSA... CHA...
Guuuh...

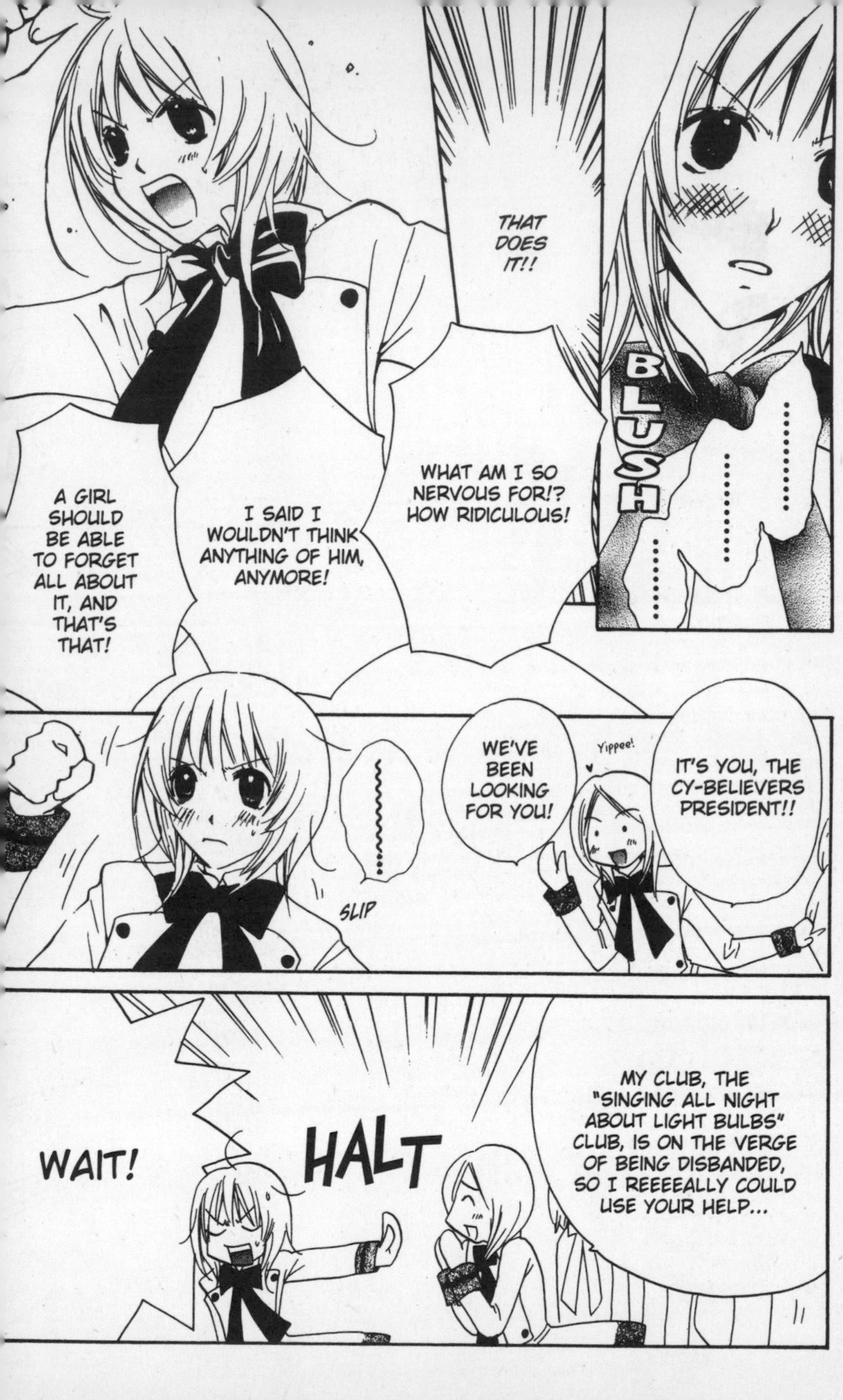
BLUSH
......
......
......
THAT DOES IT!!
WHAT AM I SO NERVOUS FOR!? HOW RIDICULOUS!
I SAID I WOULDN'T THINK ANYTHING OF HIM, ANYMORE!
A GIRL SHOULD BE ABLE TO FORGET ALL ABOUT IT, AND THAT'S THAT!
IT'S YOU, THE CY-BELIEVERS PRESIDENT!!
Yippee!
WE'VE BEEN LOOKING FOR YOU!
......
SLIP
MY CLUB, THE "SINGING ALL NIGHT ABOUT LIGHT BULBS" CLUB, IS ON THE VERGE OF BEING DISBANDED, SO I REEEEALLY COULD USE YOUR HELP...
HALT
WAIT!

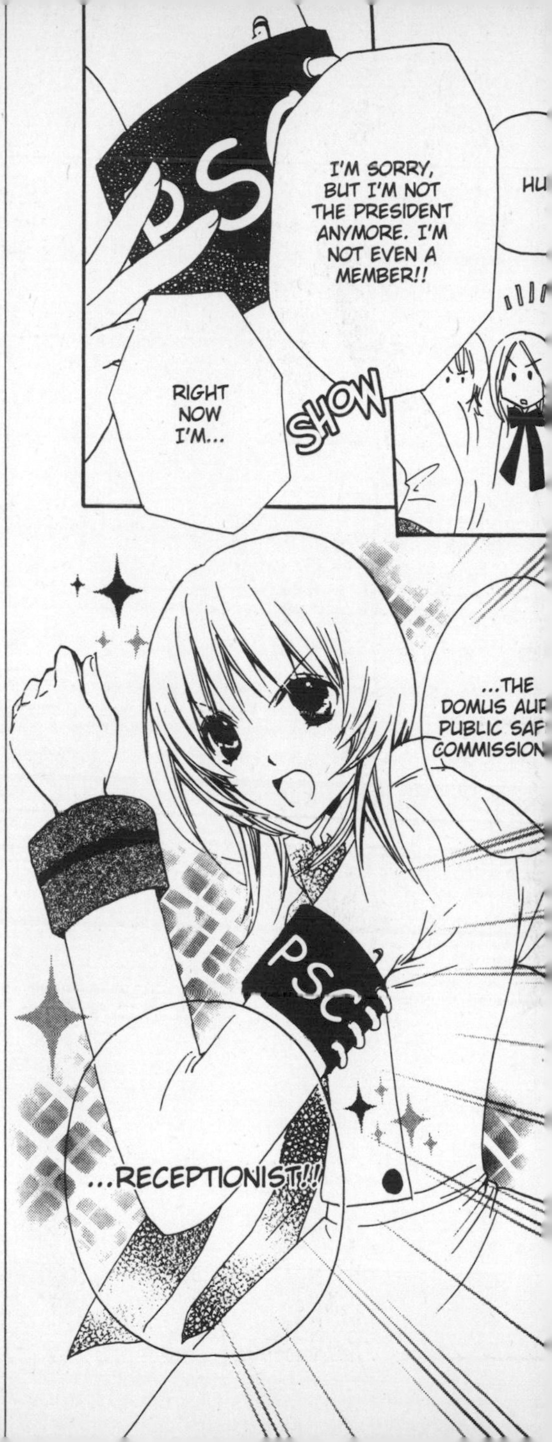
HU
I'M SORRY, BUT I'M NOT THE PRESIDENT ANYMORE. I'M NOT EVEN A MEMBER!!
PSC
SHOW
RIGHT NOW I'M...
...THE DOMUS AUR
PUBLIC SAF
COMMISSION
PSC
...RECEPTIONIST!!

About the Domus Aurea School Public Safety Commission

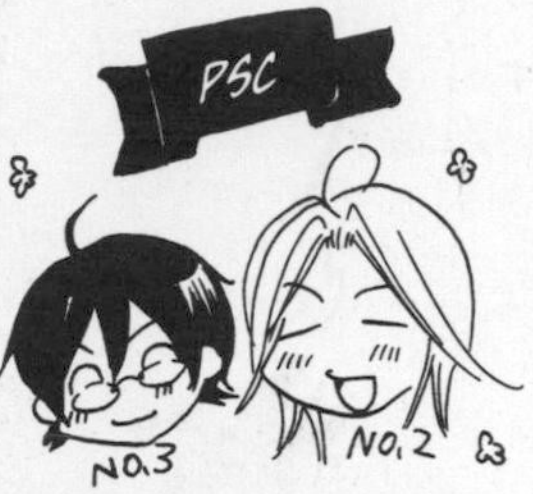
PSC
No.3
No.2

The primary job of the Public Safety Commission is to supervise the countless clubs and social circles. They really have no jurisdiction over individual students' decisions when it comes to other things (like being late, following the dress code, etc). For example, they make sure clubs are paying their dues, check to make sure there aren't any made-up clubs or made-up invoices for budgets, stop strikes and demonstrations before they happen, etc. Stuff like that.

Since they're so busy, they have some branch offices ("side offices") and besides Natori and company who stand out quite a bit, there are also a number of Commission members busily working in the background. No. 3 Ojika represents that group, and he's the righteous, gentle, and capable brain of the group. So, with the charismatic leadership of Natori, the attentive No. 2 Nagumo, and the quiet and intelligent No. 3 Ojika, the three make for a diligent group of pals, and overall a fantastic working team. Though with a leader like that...you know how it can get sometimes...

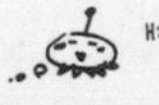
Ha ha ha...

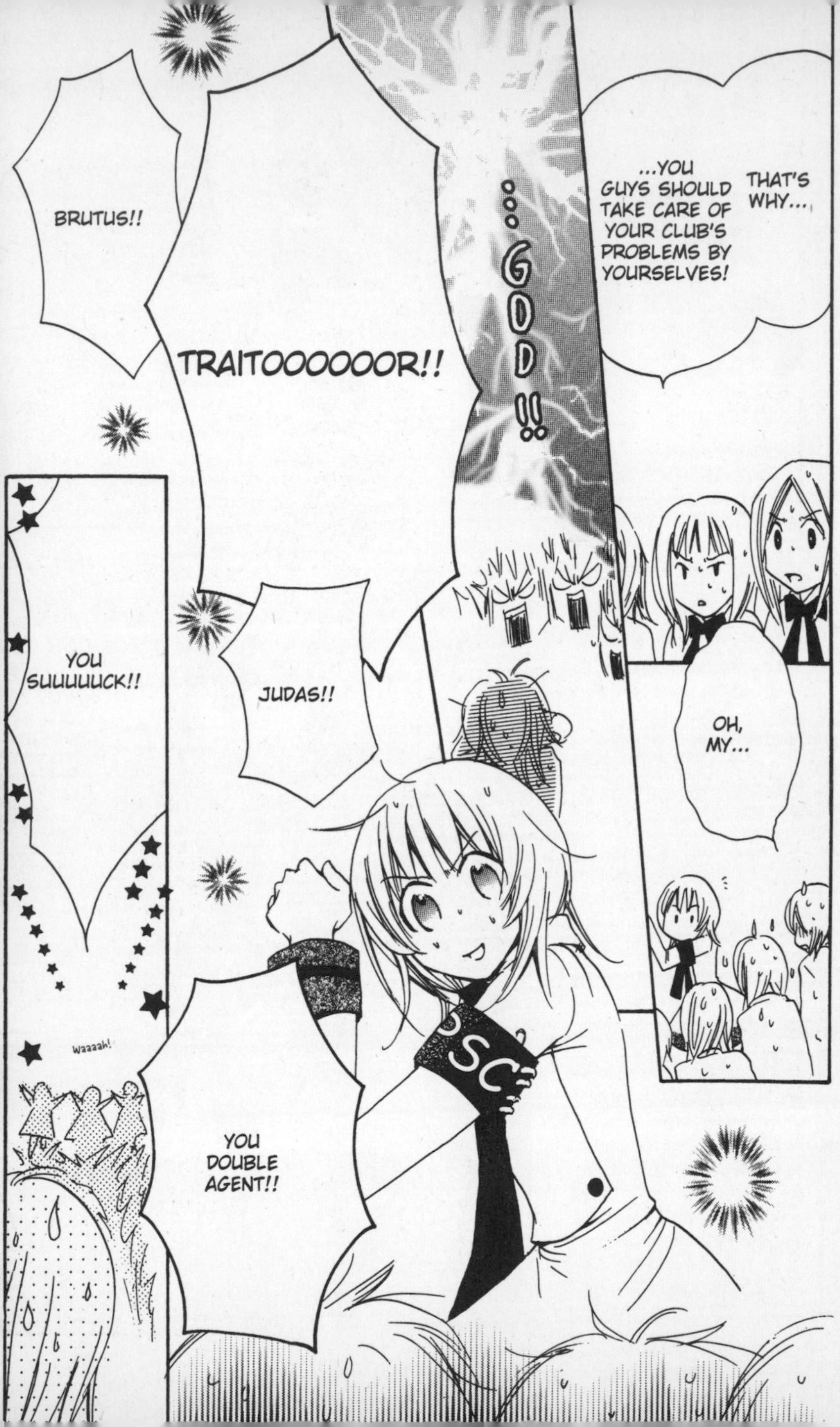
THAT'S WHY...,
...YOU GUYS SHOULD TAKE CARE OF YOUR CLUB'S PROBLEMS BY YOURSELVES!
...GOD!!
OH, MY...
TRAITOOOOOOR!!
BRUTUS!!
JUDAS!!
YOU SUUUUUCK!!
Waaaah!
YOU DOUBLE AGENT!!

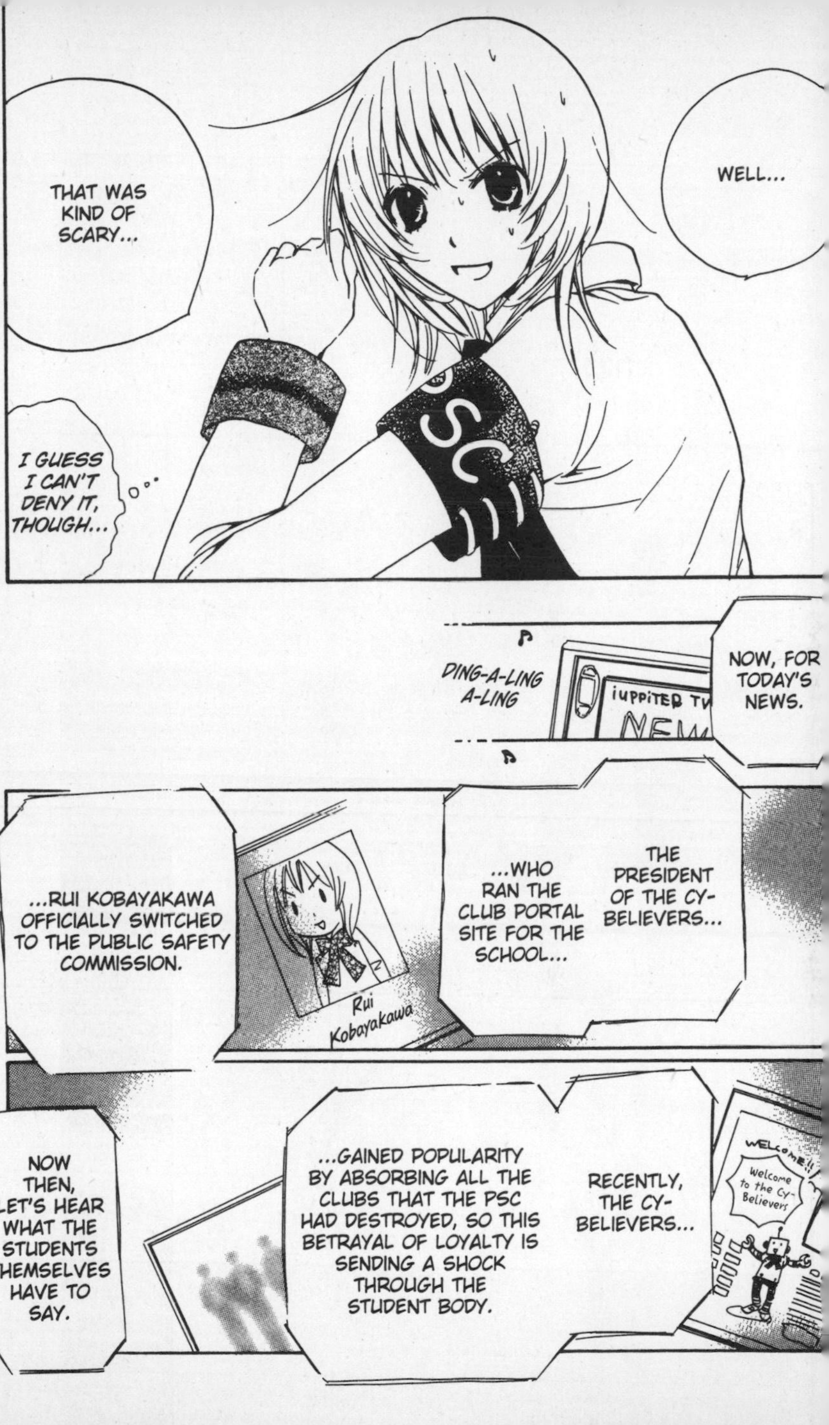
WELL...
THAT WAS KIND OF SCARY...
I GUESS I CAN'T DENY IT, THOUGH...
NOW, FOR TODAY'S NEWS.
DING-A-LING A-LING
THE PRESIDENT OF THE CY-BELIEVERS...
...WHO RAN THE CLUB PORTAL SITE FOR THE SCHOOL...
...RUI KOBAYAKAWA OFFICIALLY SWITCHED TO THE PUBLIC SAFETY COMMISSION.
Rui Kobayakawa
WELCOME!!
Welcome to the Cy-Believers
RECENTLY, THE CY-BELIEVERS...
...GAINED POPULARITY BY ABSORBING ALL THE CLUBS THAT THE PSC HAD DESTROYED, SO THIS BETRAYAL OF LOYALTY IS SENDING A SHOCK THROUGH THE STUDENT BODY.
NOW THEN, LET'S HEAR WHAT THE STUDENTS THEMSELVES HAVE TO SAY.

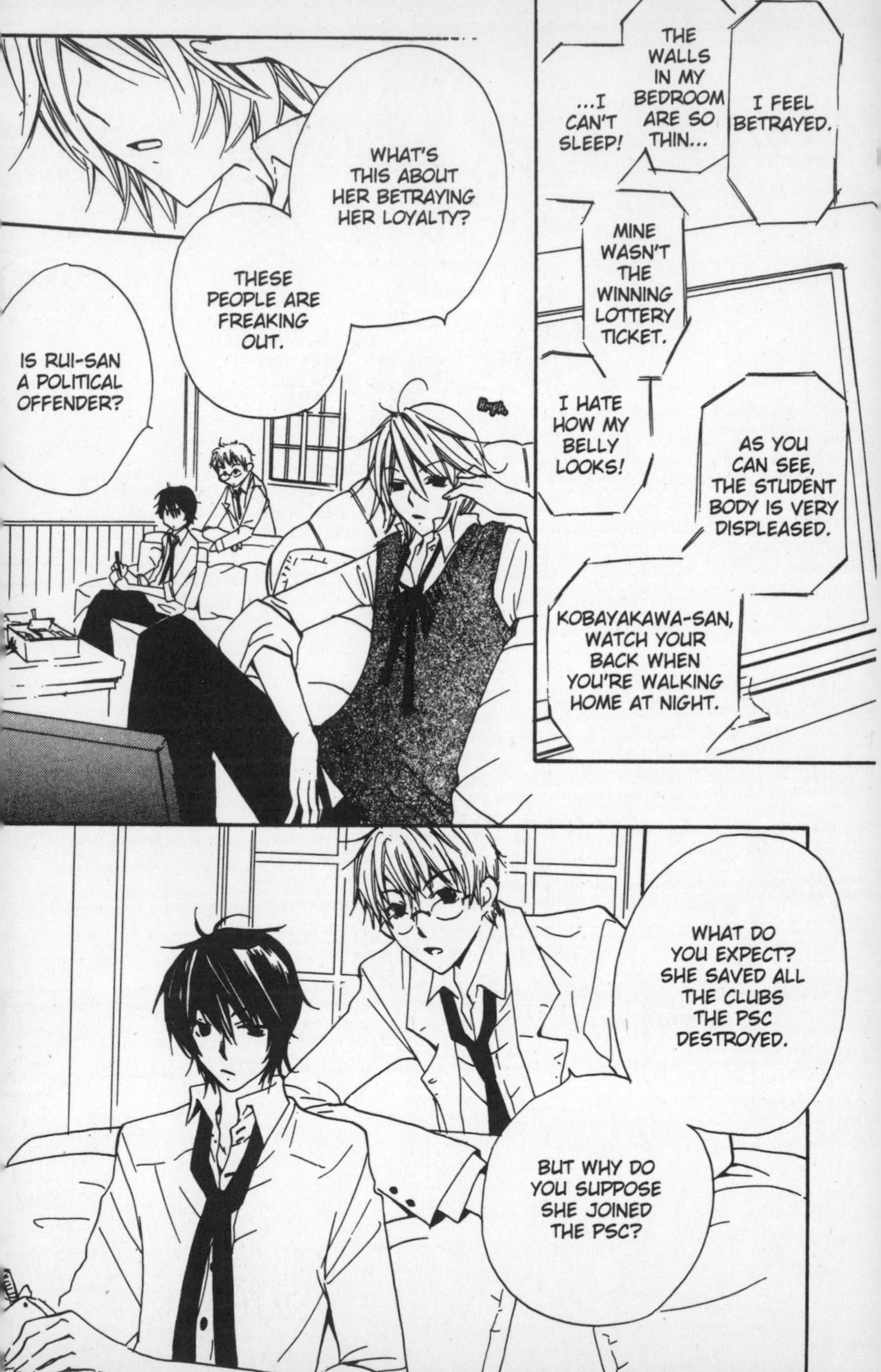
I FEEL BETRAYED.
THE WALLS IN MY BEDROOM ARE SO THIN...
...I CAN'T SLEEP!
MINE WASN'T THE WINNING LOTTERY TICKET.
AS YOU CAN SEE, THE STUDENT BODY IS VERY DISPLEASED.
I HATE HOW MY BELLY LOOKS!
KOBAYAKAWA-SAN, WATCH YOUR BACK WHEN YOU'RE WALKING HOME AT NIGHT.
WHAT'S THIS ABOUT HER BETRAYING HER LOYALTY?
Hrmph.
THESE PEOPLE ARE FREAKING OUT.
IS RUI-SAN A POLITICAL OFFENDER?
WHAT DO YOU EXPECT? SHE SAVED ALL THE CLUBS THE PSC DESTROYED.
BUT WHY DO YOU SUPPOSE SHE JOINED THE PSC?

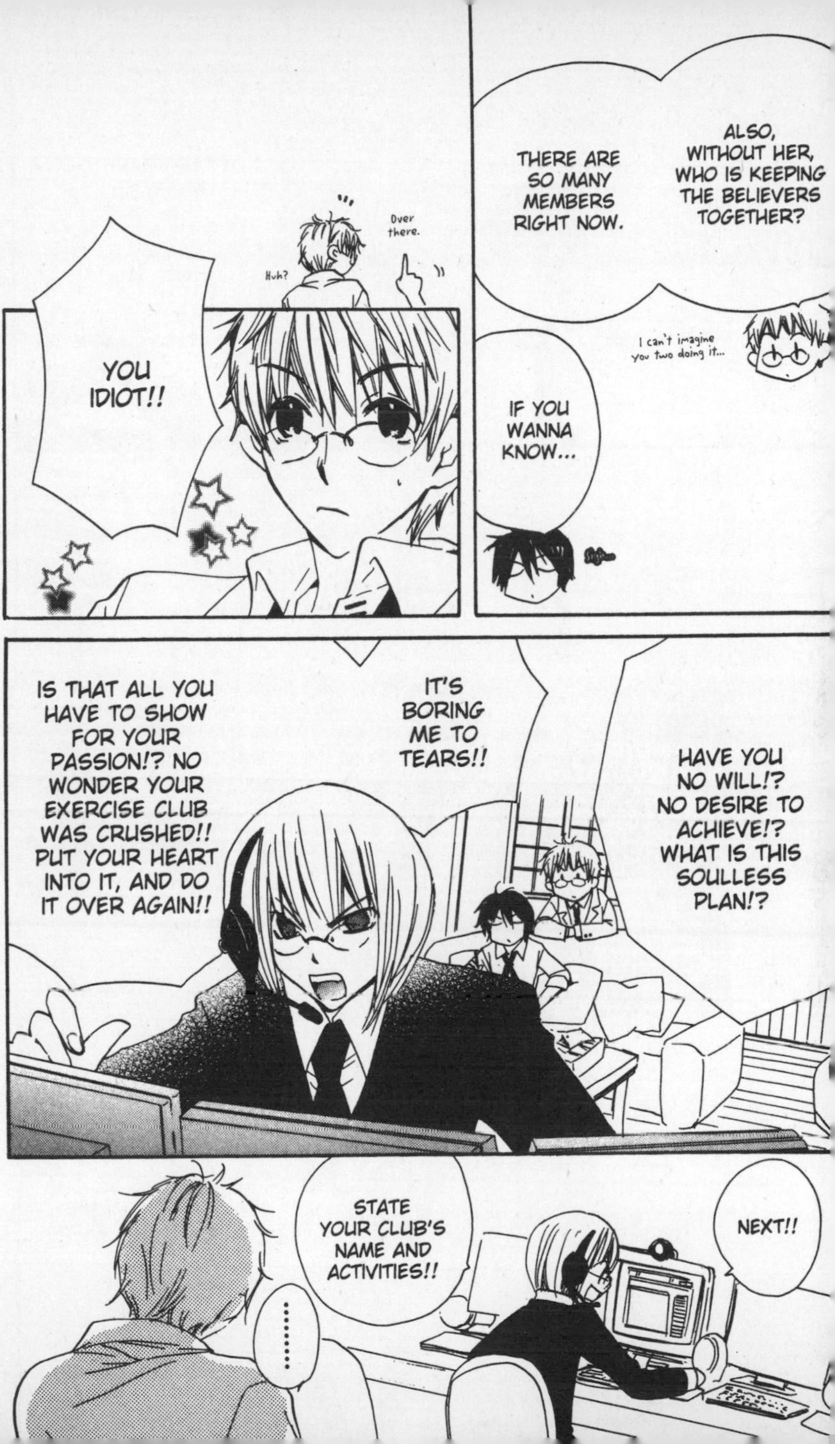
ALSO, WITHOUT HER, WHO IS KEEPING THE BELIEVERS TOGETHER?
THERE ARE SO MANY MEMBERS RIGHT NOW.
I can't imagine you two doing it...
IF YOU WANNA KNOW...
Over there.
Huh?
YOU IDIOT!!
HAVE YOU NO WILL!? NO DESIRE TO ACHIEVE!? WHAT IS THIS SOULLESS PLAN!?
IT'S BORING ME TO TEARS!!
IS THAT ALL YOU HAVE TO SHOW FOR YOUR PASSION!? NO WONDER YOUR EXERCISE CLUB WAS CRUSHED!! PUT YOUR HEART INTO IT, AND DO IT OVER AGAIN!!
NEXT!!
STATE YOUR CLUB'S NAME AND ACTIVITIES!!
....

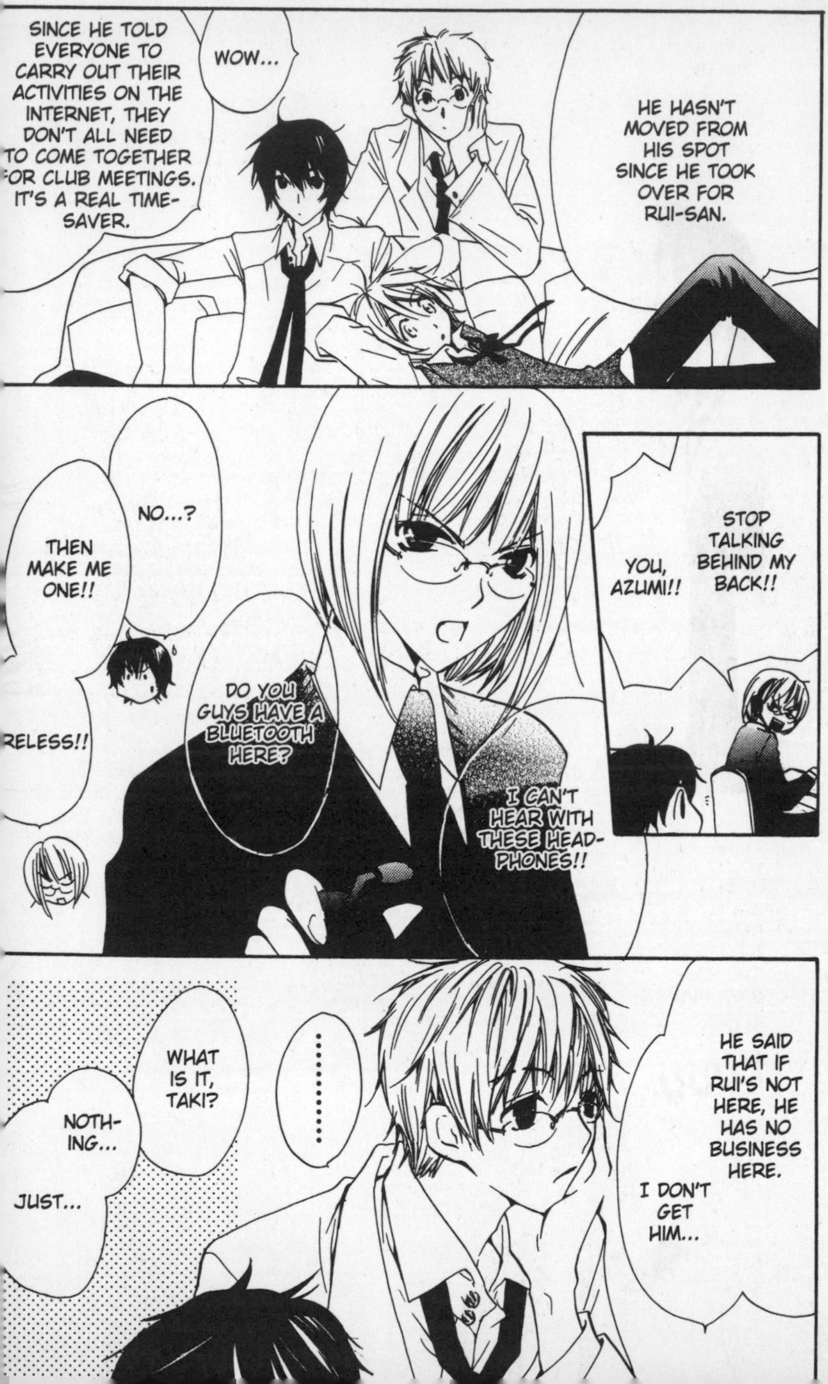
HE HASN'T MOVED FROM HIS SPOT SINCE HE TOOK OVER FOR RUI-SAN.
WOW...
SINCE HE TOLD EVERYONE TO CARRY OUT THEIR ACTIVITIES ON THE INTERNET, THEY DON'T ALL NEED TO COME TOGETHER FOR CLUB MEETINGS. IT'S A REAL TIME-SAVER.
STOP TALKING BEHIND MY BACK!!
YOU, AZUMI!!
I CAN'T HEAR WITH THESE HEADPHONES!!
DO YOU GUYS HAVE A BLUETOOTH HERE?
NO...?
THEN MAKE ME ONE!!
RELESS!!
HE SAID THAT IF RUI'S NOT HERE, HE HAS NO BUSINESS HERE.
I DON'T GET HIM...
....
WHAT IS IT, TAKI?
NOTHING...
JUST...

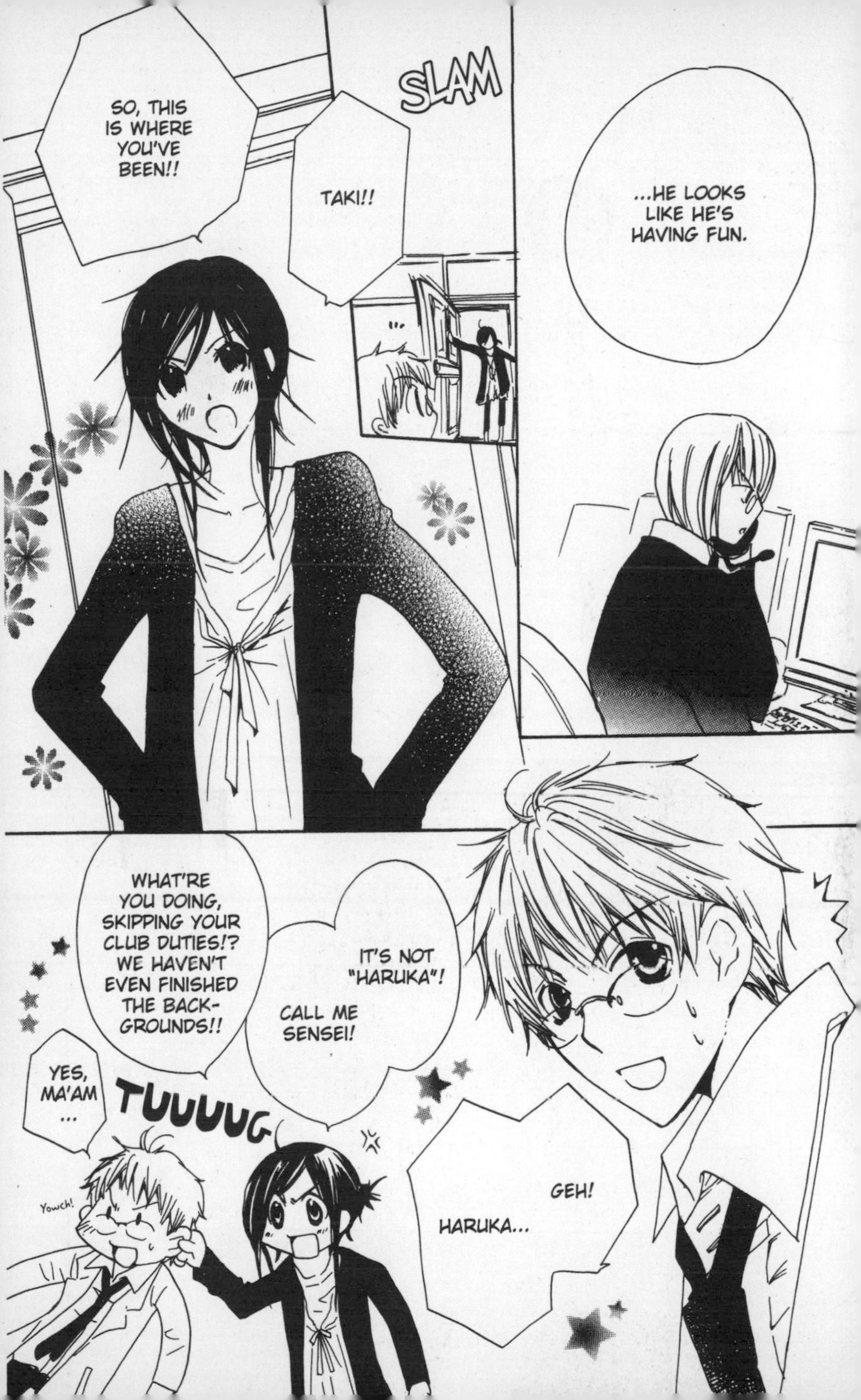
...HE LOOKS LIKE HE'S HAVING FUN.
SLAM
...
TAKI!!
SO, THIS IS WHERE YOU'VE BEEN!!
GEH!
HARUKA...
IT'S NOT "HARUKA"!
CALL ME SENSEI!
WHAT'RE YOU DOING, SKIPPING YOUR CLUB DUTIES!? WE HAVEN'T EVEN FINISHED THE BACK-GROUNDS!!
TUUUUG
YES, MA'AM ...
Yowch!

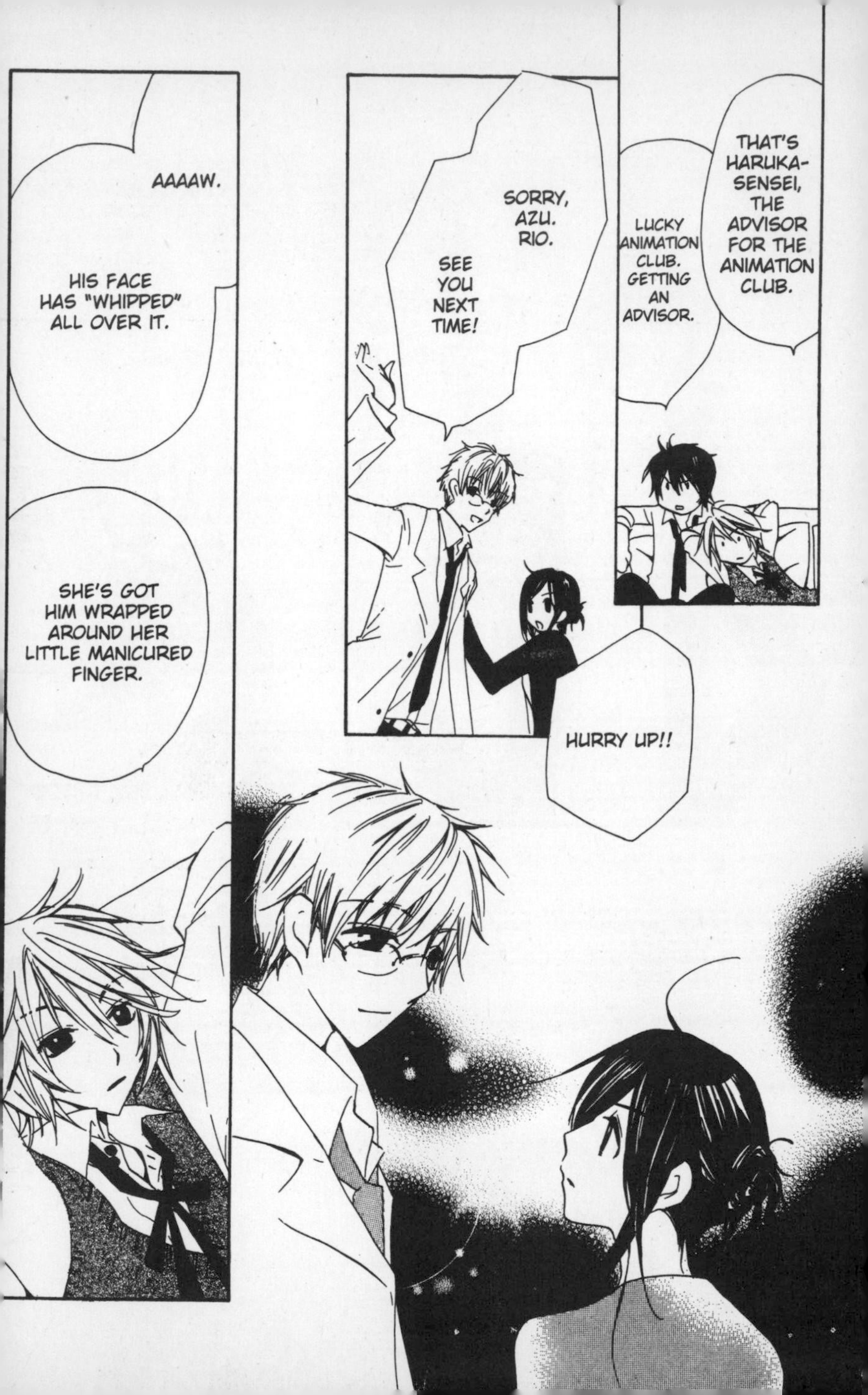
THAT'S HARUKA-SENSEI, THE ADVISOR FOR THE ANIMATION CLUB.
LUCKY ANIMATION CLUB. GETTING AN ADVISOR.
SORRY, AZU. RIO.
SEE YOU NEXT TIME!
HURRY UP!!
AAAAW.
HIS FACE HAS "WHIPPED" ALL OVER IT.
SHE'S GOT HIM WRAPPED AROUND HER LITTLE MANICURED FINGER.

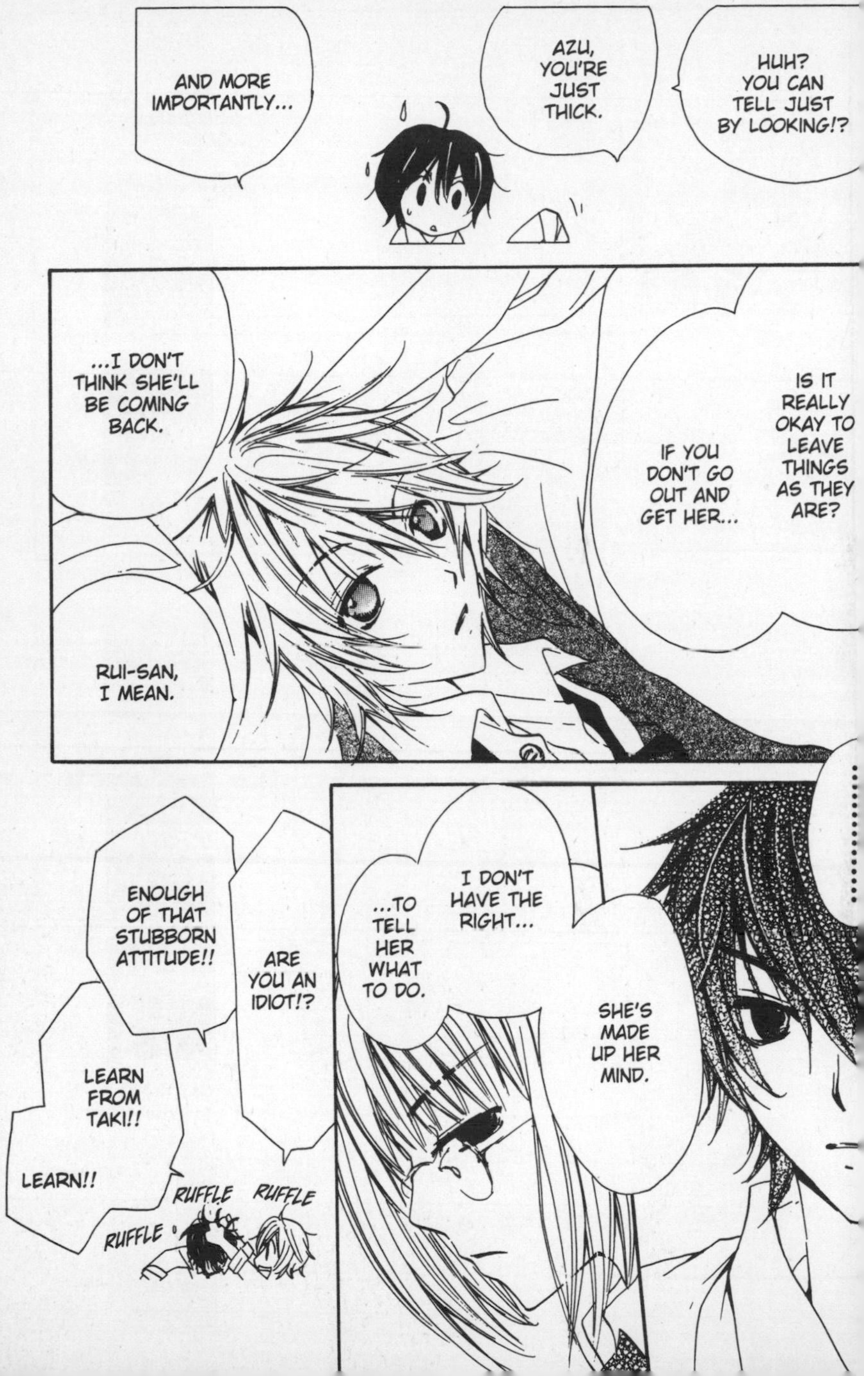
HUH? YOU CAN TELL JUST BY LOOKING!?
AZU, YOU'RE JUST THICK.
AND MORE IMPORTANTLY...
IS IT REALLY OKAY TO LEAVE THINGS AS THEY ARE?
IF YOU DON'T GO OUT AND GET HER...
...I DON'T THINK SHE'LL BE COMING BACK.
RUI-SAN, I MEAN.
I DON'T HAVE THE RIGHT...
...TO TELL HER WHAT TO DO.
SHE'S MADE UP HER MIND.
ARE YOU AN IDIOT!?
ENOUGH OF THAT STUBBORN ATTITUDE!!
LEARN FROM TAKI!!
LEARN!!
RUFFLE
RUFFLE
RUFFLE

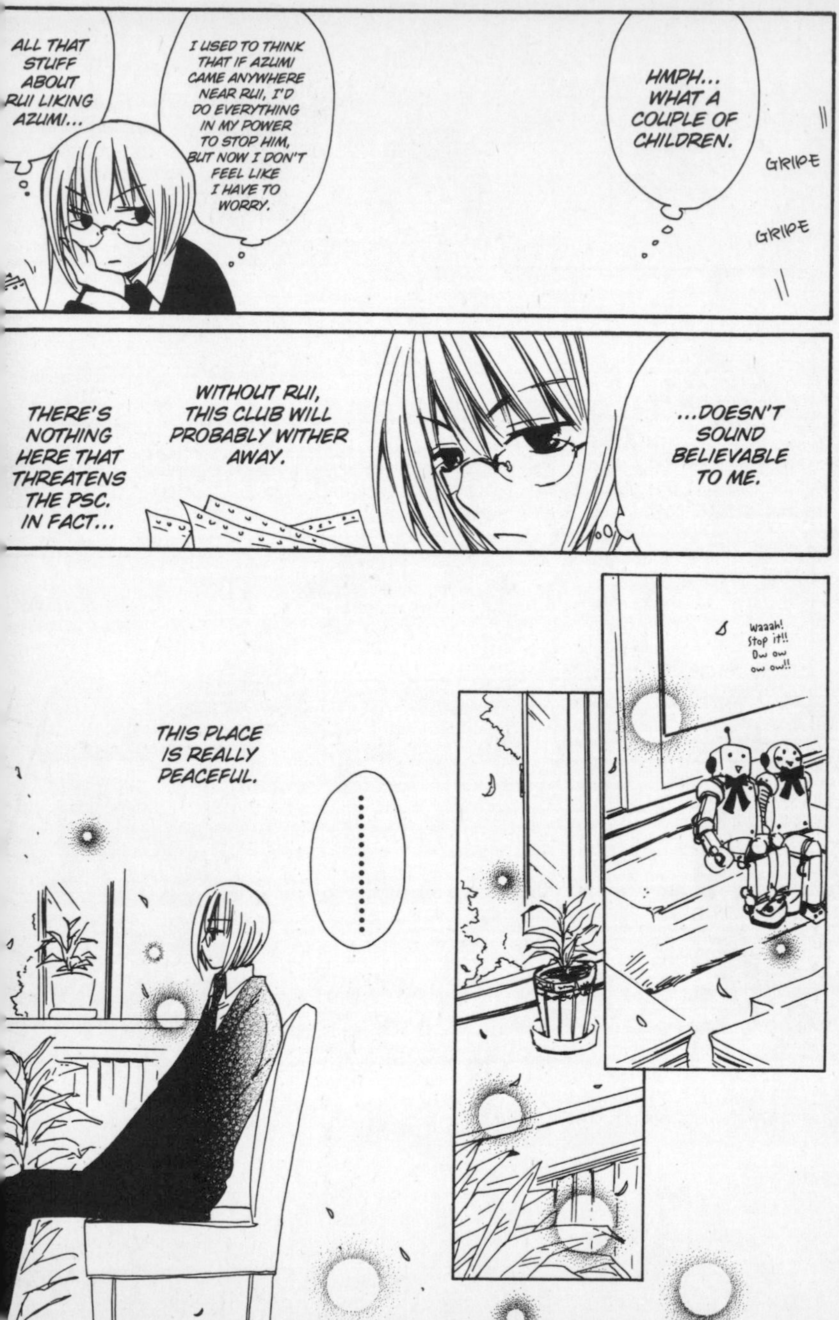
HMPH... WHAT A COUPLE OF CHILDREN.
GRIPE
GRIPE
I USED TO THINK THAT IF AZUMI CAME ANYWHERE NEAR RUI, I'D DO EVERYTHING IN MY POWER TO STOP HIM, BUT NOW I DON'T FEEL LIKE I HAVE TO WORRY.
ALL THAT STUFF ABOUT RUI LIKING AZUMI...
...DOESN'T SOUND BELIEVABLE TO ME.
WITHOUT RUI, THIS CLUB WILL PROBABLY WITHER AWAY.
THERE'S NOTHING HERE THAT THREATENS THE PSC. IN FACT...
Waaah! Stop it!! Ow ow ow ow!!
....
THIS PLACE IS REALLY PEACEFUL.

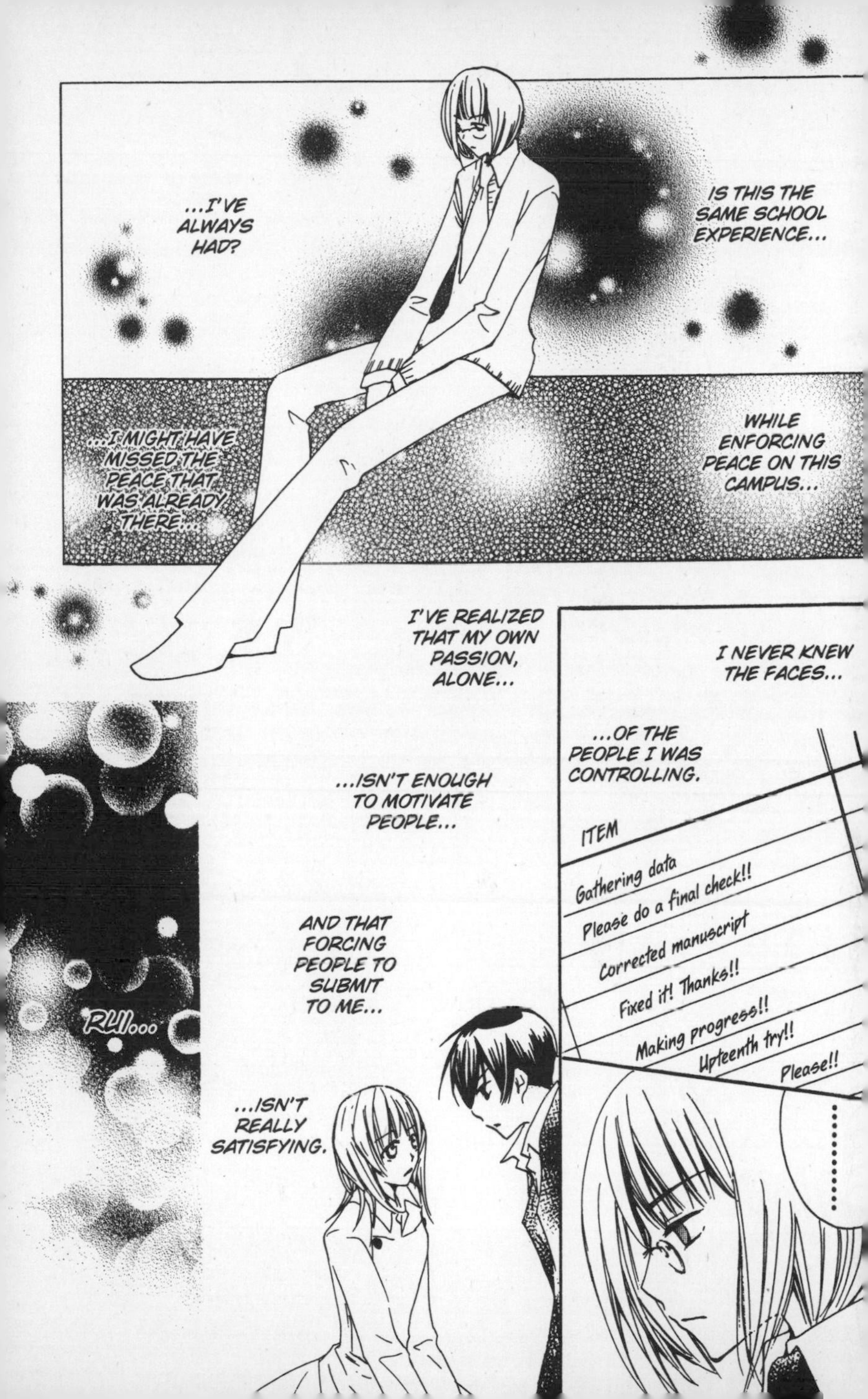
IS THIS THE SAME SCHOOL EXPERIENCE...
...I'VE ALWAYS HAD?
WHILE ENFORCING PEACE ON THIS CAMPUS...
...I MIGHT HAVE MISSED THE PEACE THAT WAS ALREADY THERE...
I NEVER KNEW THE FACES...
...OF THE PEOPLE I WAS CONTROLLING.
ITEM
Gathering data
Please do a final check!!
Corrected manuscript
Fixed it! Thanks!!
Making progress!!
Upteenth try!!
Please!!
......
I'VE REALIZED THAT MY OWN PASSION, ALONE...
...ISN'T ENOUGH TO MOTIVATE PEOPLE...
AND THAT FORCING PEOPLE TO SUBMIT TO ME...
...ISN'T REALLY SATISFYING.
RUI...

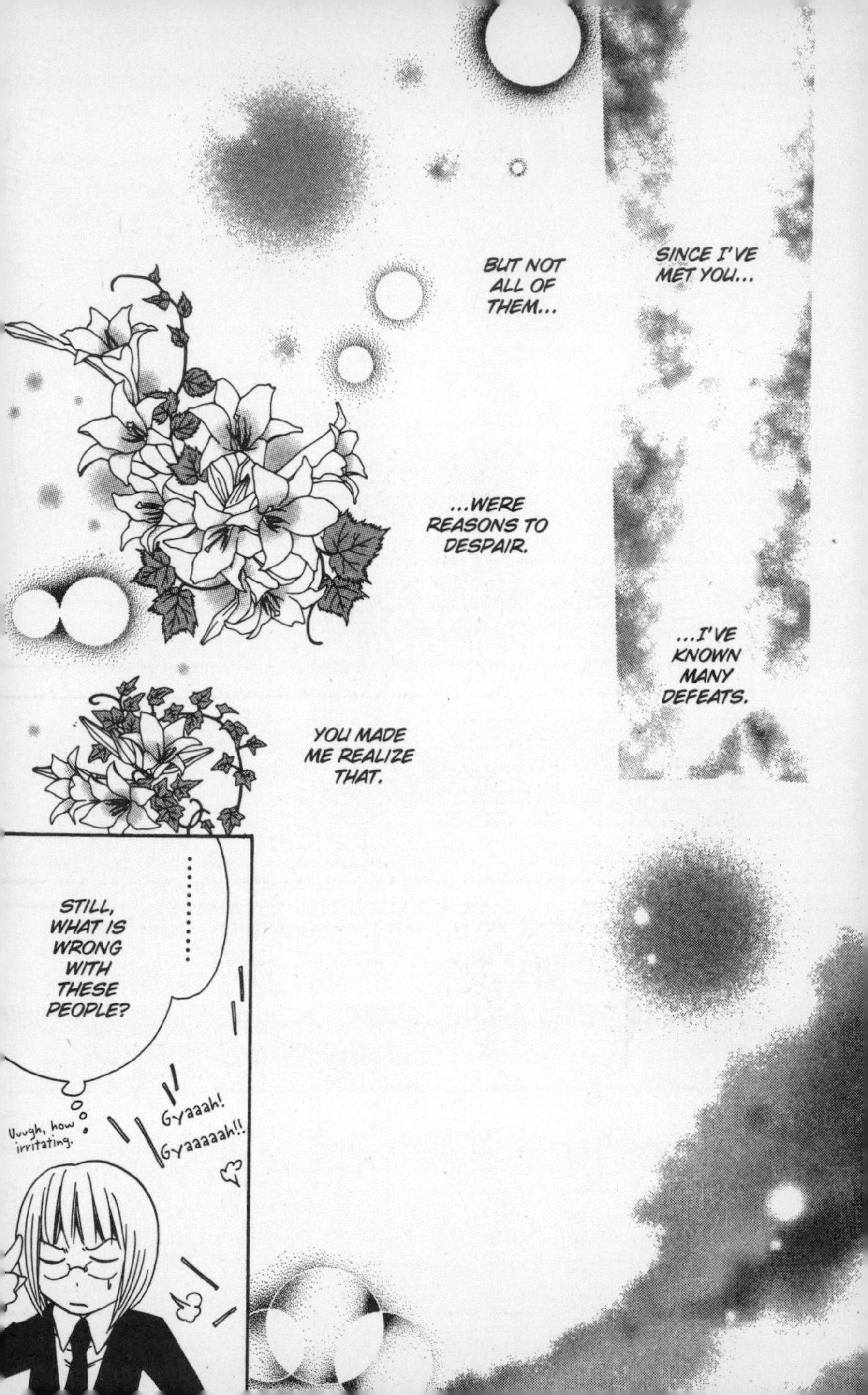
SINCE I'VE MET YOU...
...I'VE KNOWN MANY DEFEATS.
BUT NOT ALL OF THEM...
...WERE REASONS TO DESPAIR.
YOU MADE ME REALIZE THAT.
......
STILL, WHAT IS WRONG WITH THESE PEOPLE?
Gyaaah! Gyaaaaah!!
Uuugh, how irritating.

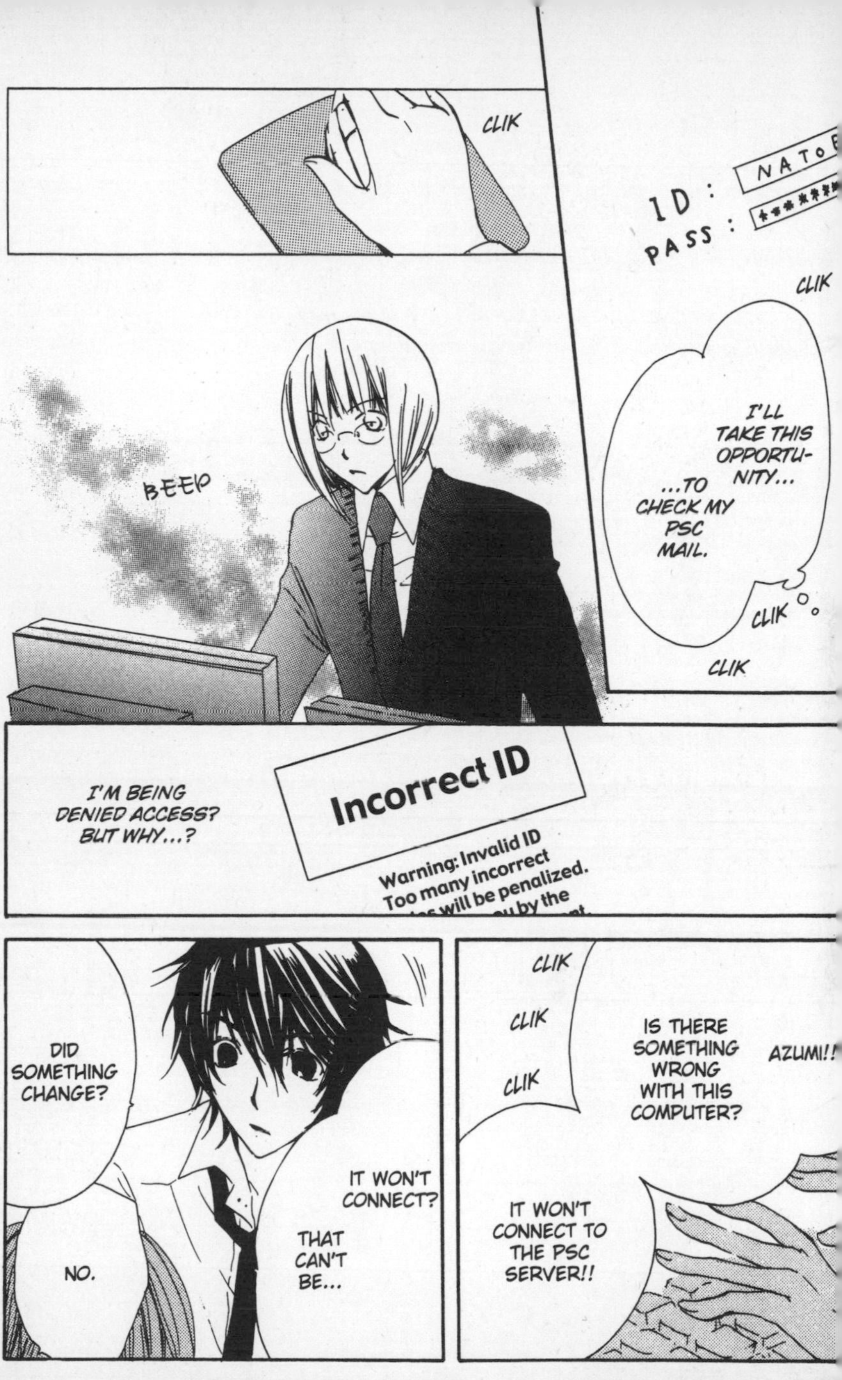
ID : NATO
PASS : ********
CLIK
I'LL TAKE THIS OPPORTUNITY...
...TO CHECK MY PSC MAIL.
CLIK
CLIK
CLIK
BEEP
I'M BEING DENIED ACCESS? BUT WHY...?
Incorrect ID
Warning: Invalid ID
Too many incorrect
will be penalized.
by the
AZUMI!!
IS THERE SOMETHING WRONG WITH THIS COMPUTER?
CLIK
CLIK
CLIK
IT WON'T CONNECT TO THE PSC SERVER!!
DID SOMETHING CHANGE?
IT WON'T CONNECT?
THAT CAN'T BE...
NO.

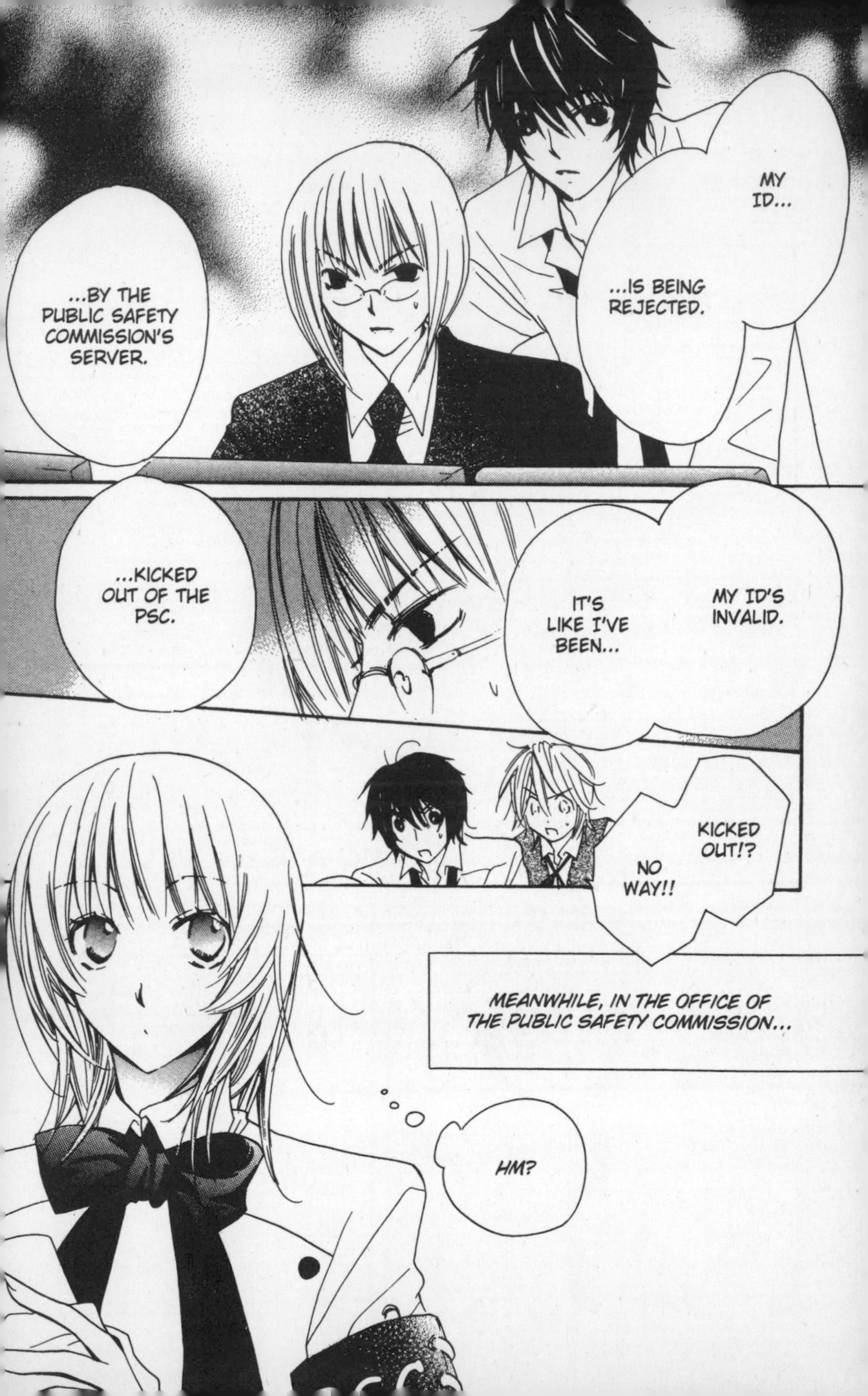
MY ID...
...IS BEING REJECTED.
...BY THE PUBLIC SAFETY COMMISSION'S SERVER.
MY ID'S INVALID.
IT'S LIKE I'VE BEEN...
...KICKED OUT OF THE PSC.
KICKED OUT!?
NO WAY!!
MEANWHILE, IN THE OFFICE OF THE PUBLIC SAFETY COMMISSION...
HM?

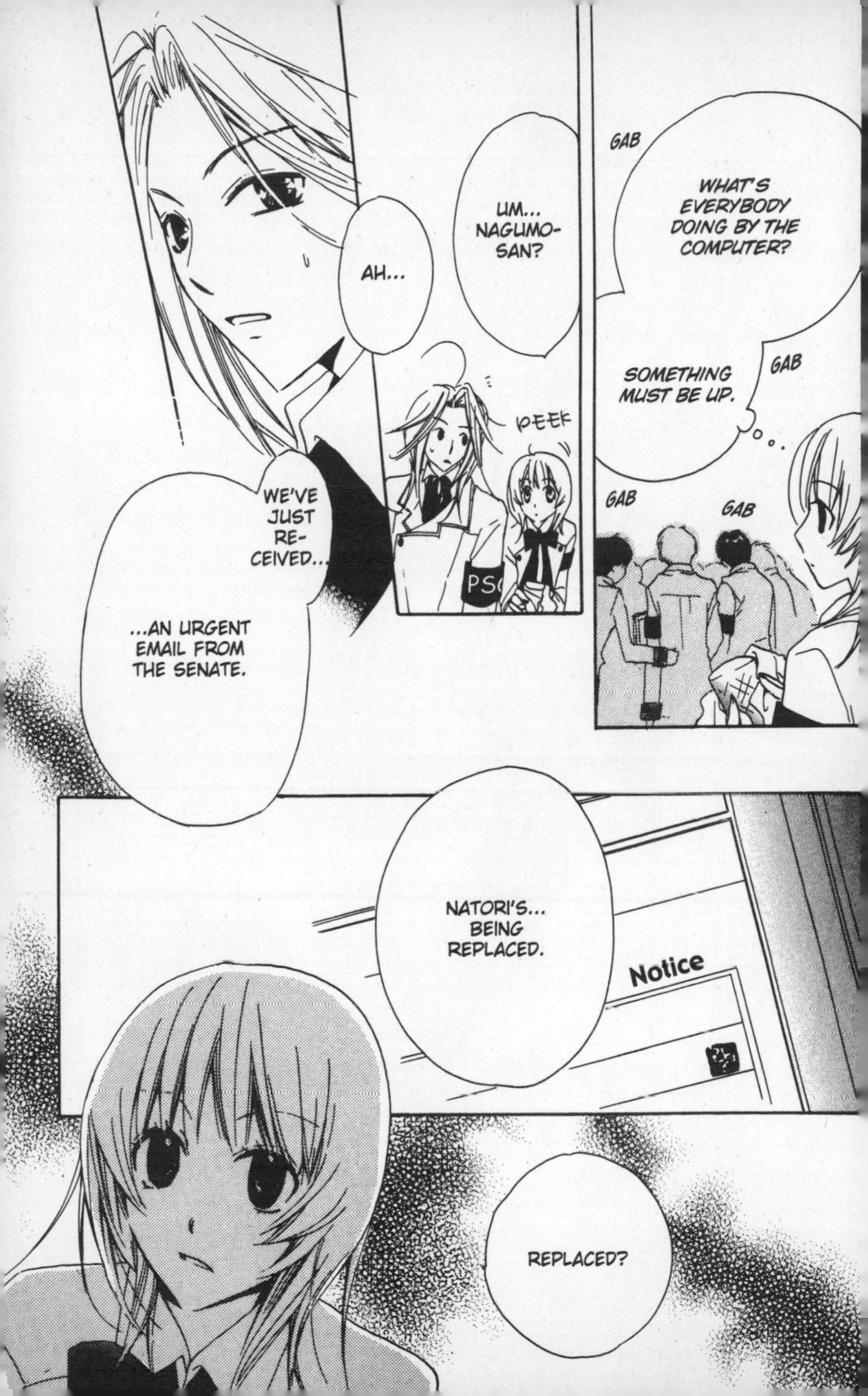
GAB
WHAT'S EVERYBODY DOING BY THE COMPUTER?
SOMETHING MUST BE UP.
GAB
GAB
GAB
UM... NAGUMO-SAN?
PEEK
PSC
AH...
WE'VE JUST RE-CEIVED...
...AN URGENT EMAIL FROM THE SENATE.
NATORI'S... BEING REPLACED.
Notice
REPLACED?

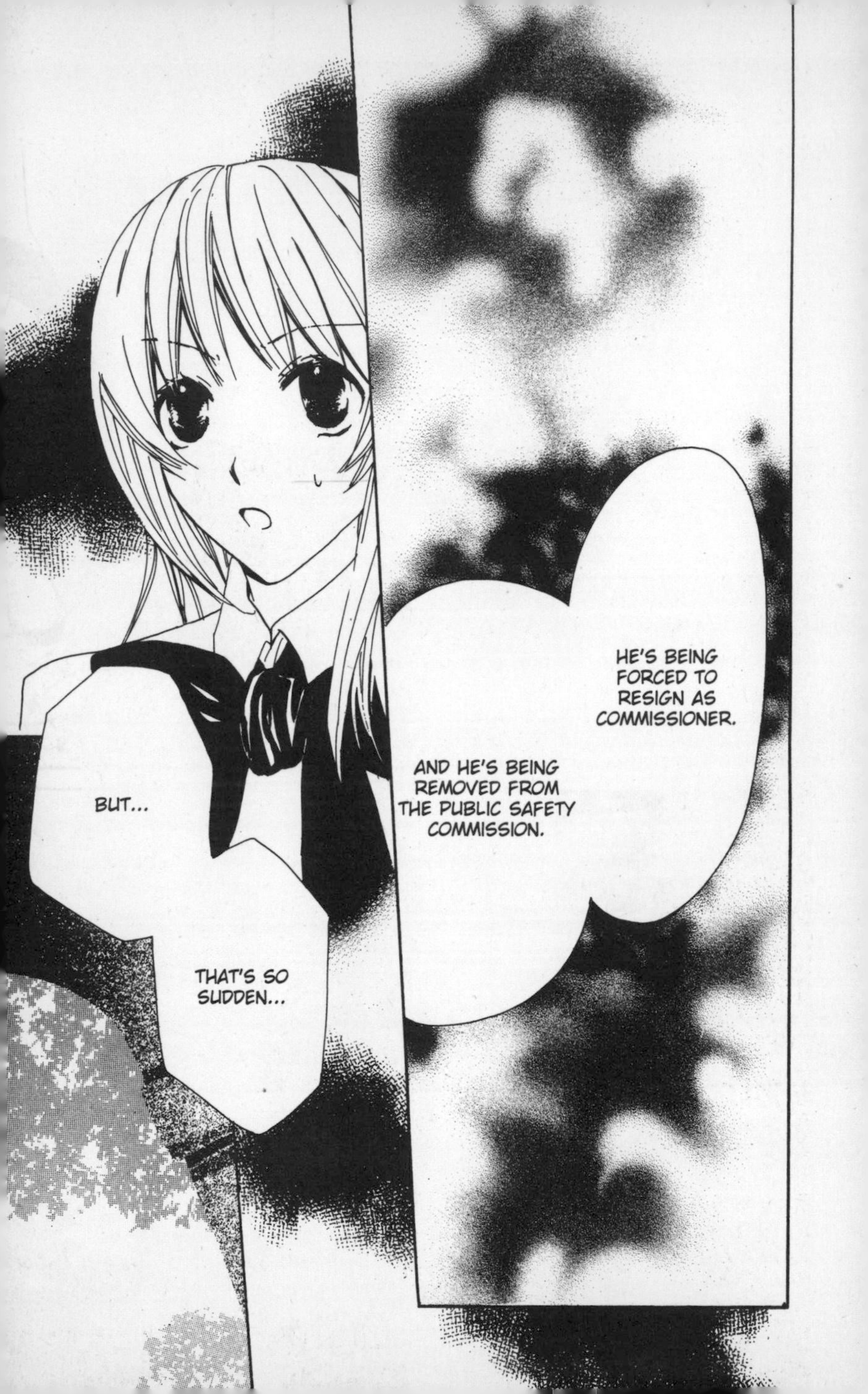
HE'S BEING FORCED TO RESIGN AS COMMISSIONER.
AND HE'S BEING REMOVED FROM THE PUBLIC SAFETY COMMISSION.
BUT...
THAT'S SO SUDDEN...

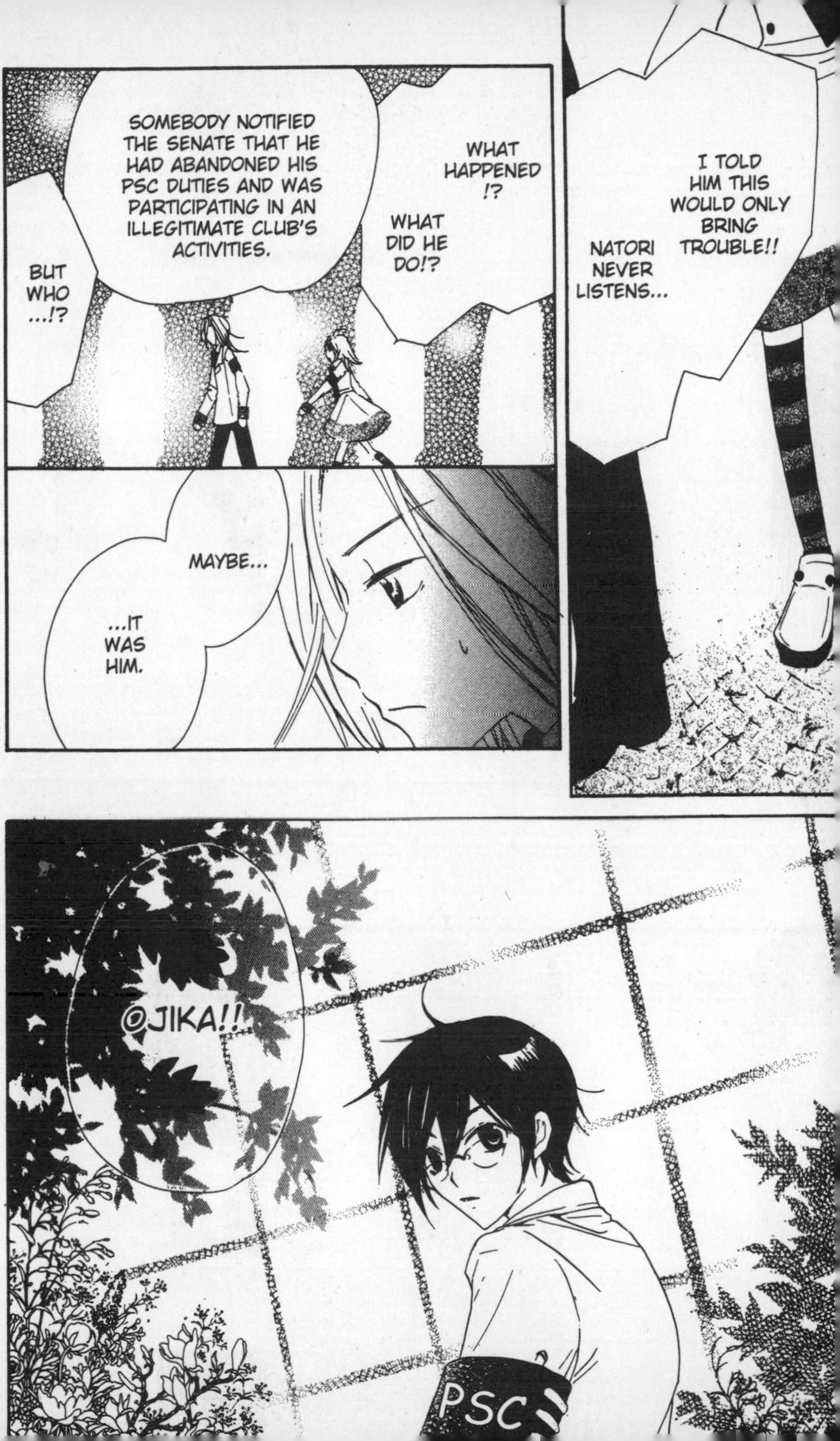
I TOLD HIM THIS WOULD ONLY BRING TROUBLE!!
NATORI NEVER LISTENS...
WHAT HAPPENED!?
WHAT DID HE DO!?
SOMEBODY NOTIFIED THE SENATE THAT HE HAD ABANDONED HIS PSC DUTIES AND WAS PARTICIPATING IN AN ILLEGITIMATE CLUB'S ACTIVITIES.
BUT WHO...!?
MAYBE...
...IT WAS HIM.
OJIKA!!
PSC

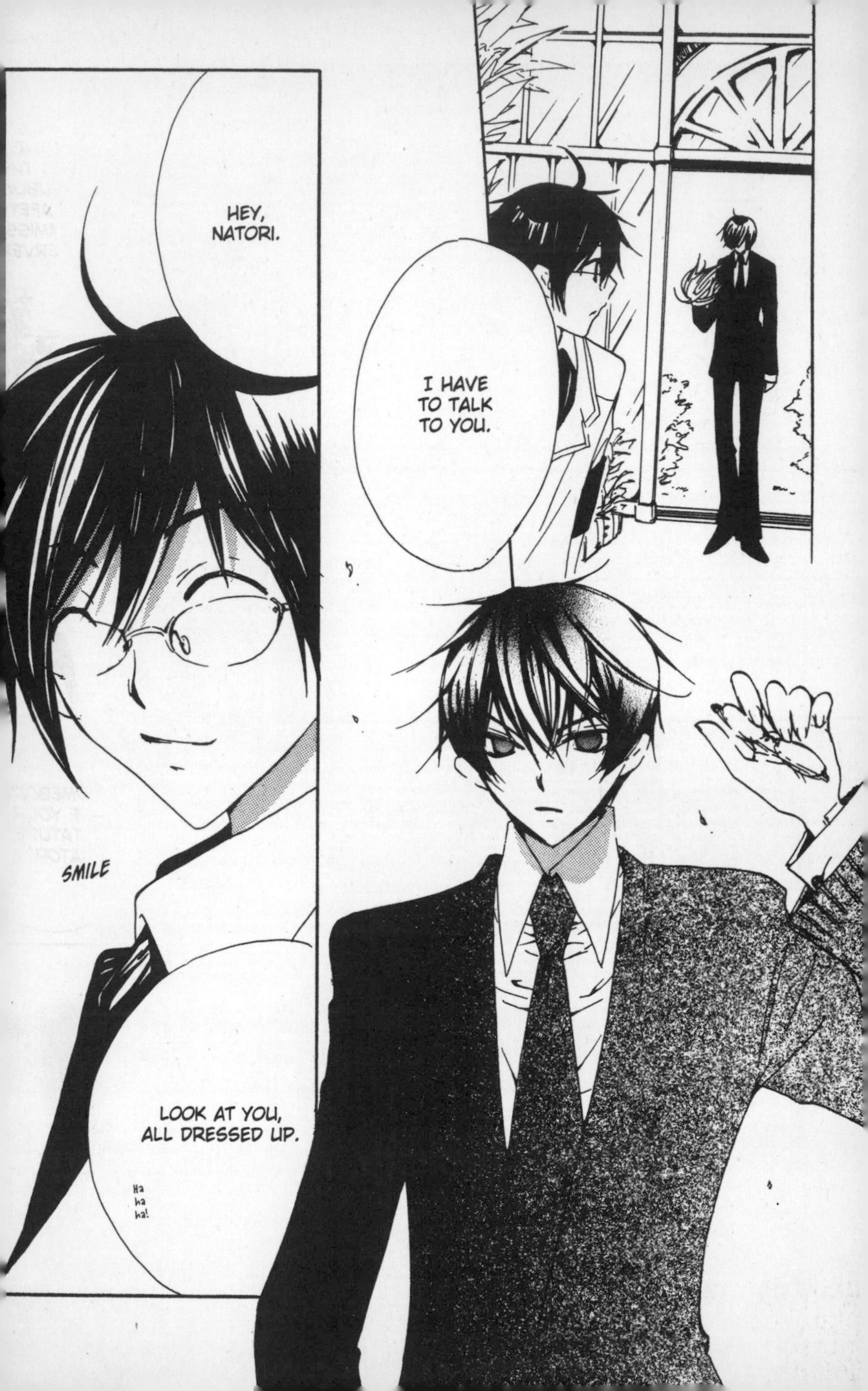
I HAVE TO TALK TO YOU.
HEY, NATORI.
SMILE
LOOK AT YOU, ALL DRESSED UP.
Ha ha ha!

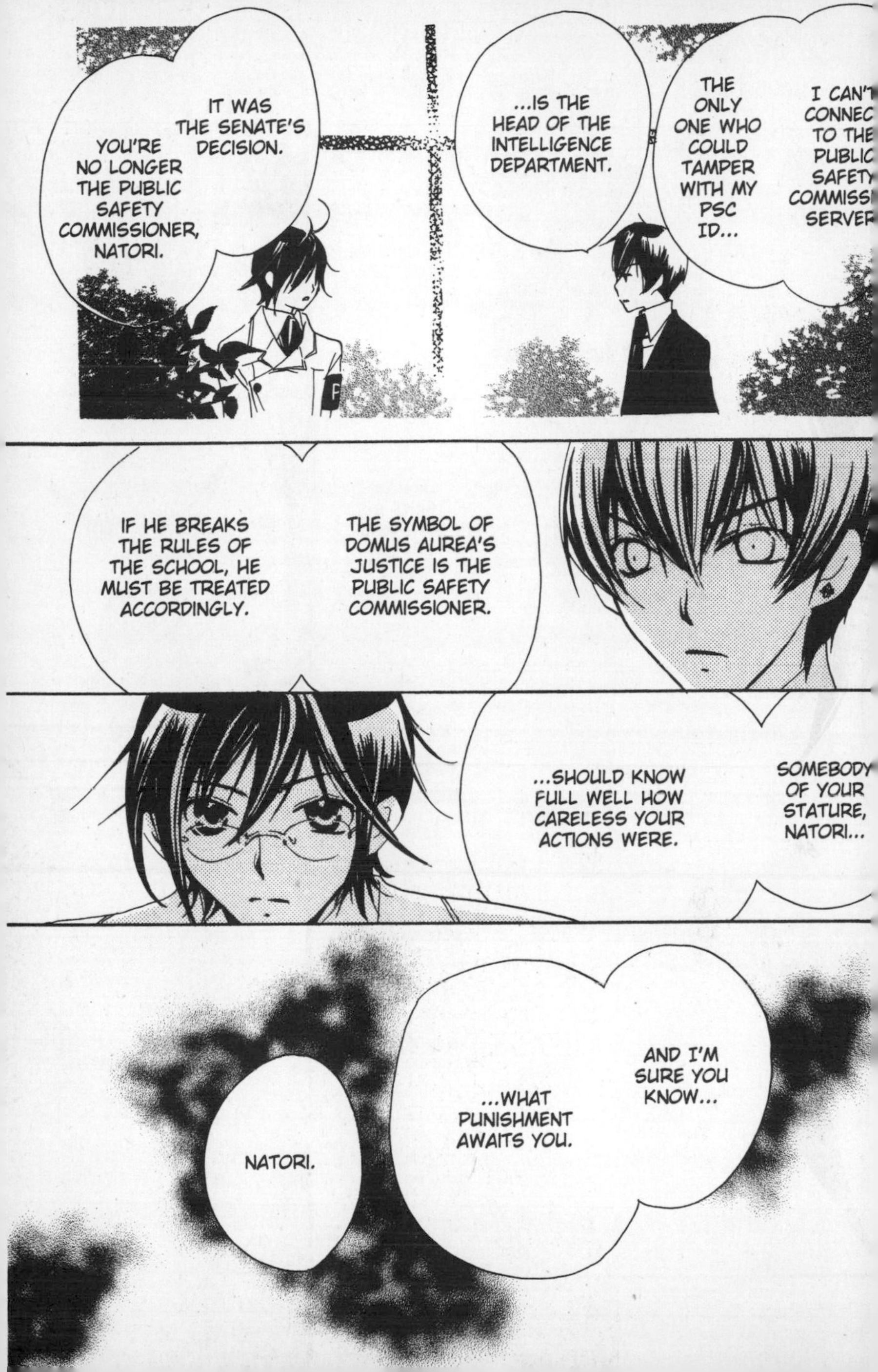
I CAN'T CONNEC TO THE PUBLIC SAFETY COMMISS SERVER
THE ONLY ONE WHO COULD TAMPER WITH MY PSC ID...
...IS THE HEAD OF THE INTELLIGENCE DEPARTMENT.
IT WAS THE SENATE'S DECISION.
YOU'RE NO LONGER THE PUBLIC SAFETY COMMISSIONER, NATORI.
THE SYMBOL OF DOMUS AUREA'S JUSTICE IS THE PUBLIC SAFETY COMMISSIONER.
IF HE BREAKS THE RULES OF THE SCHOOL, HE MUST BE TREATED ACCORDINGLY.
SOMEBODY OF YOUR STATURE, NATORI...
...SHOULD KNOW FULL WELL HOW CARELESS YOUR ACTIONS WERE.
AND I'M SURE YOU KNOW...
...WHAT PUNISHMENT AWAITS YOU.
NATORI.

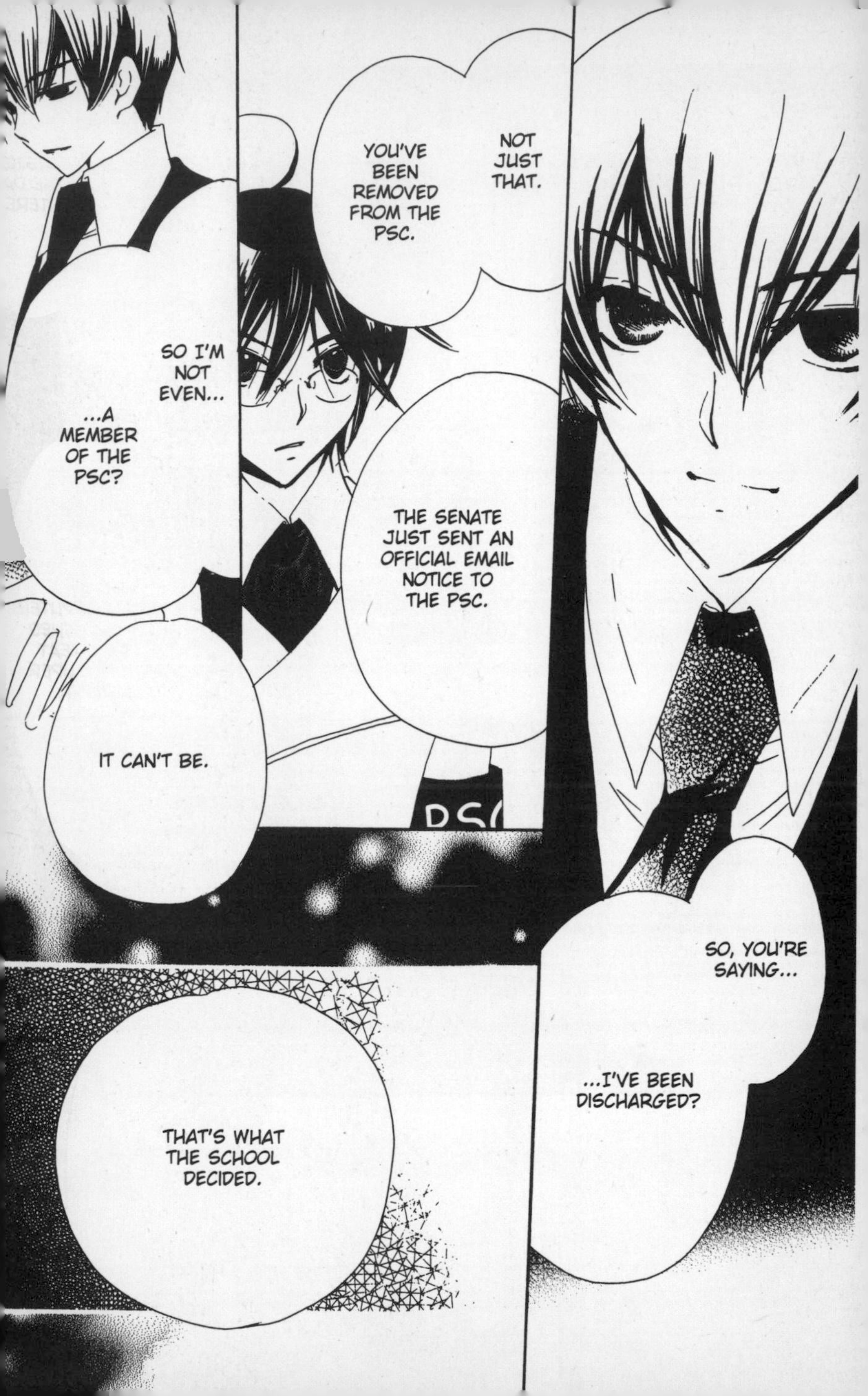
SO, YOU'RE SAYING...
...I'VE BEEN DISCHARGED?
NOT JUST THAT.
YOU'VE BEEN REMOVED FROM THE PSC.
THE SENATE JUST SENT AN OFFICIAL EMAIL NOTICE TO THE PSC.
SO I'M NOT EVEN...
...A MEMBER OF THE PSC?
IT CAN'T BE.
THAT'S WHAT THE SCHOOL DECIDED.

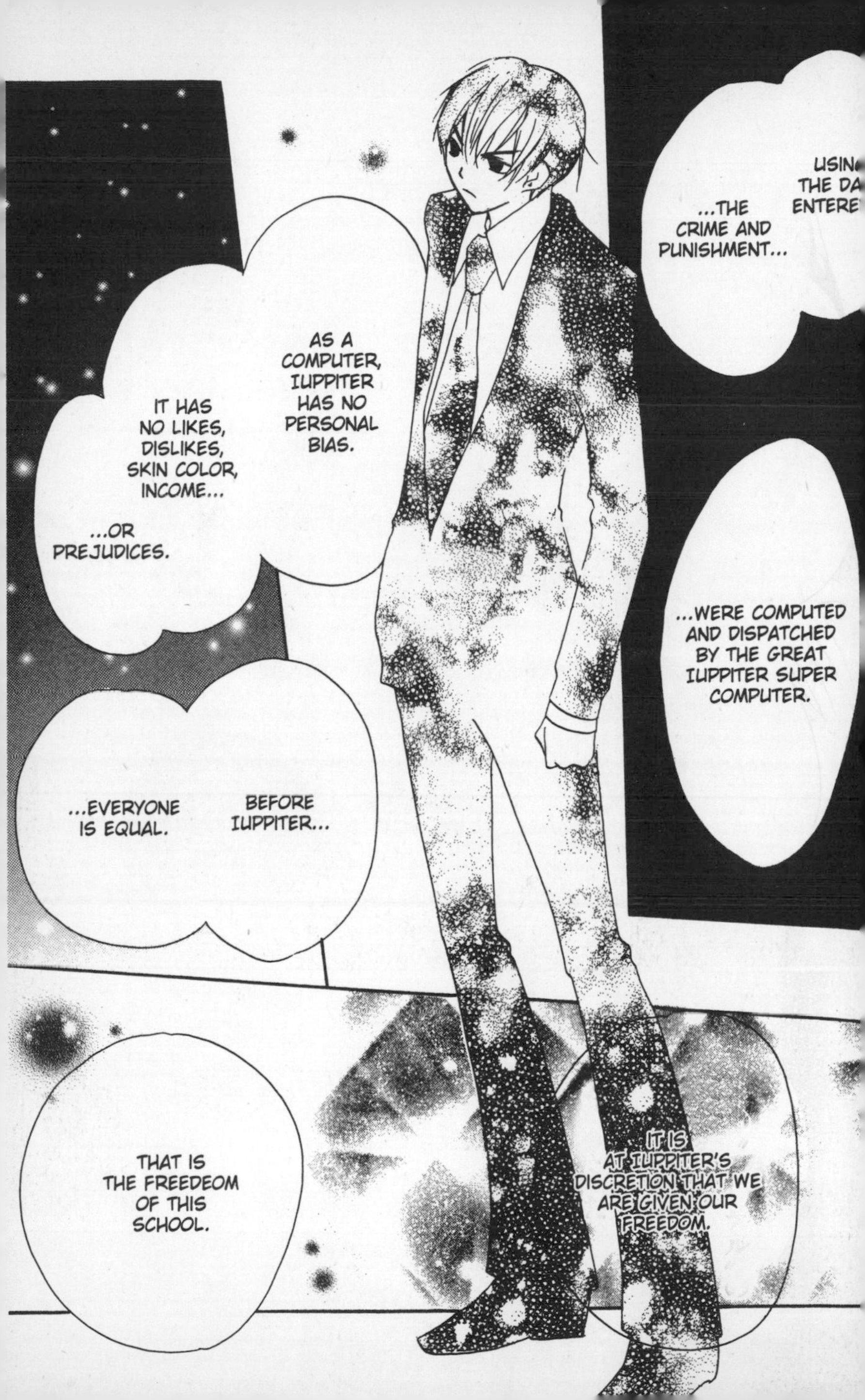
...THE CRIME AND PUNISHMENT...
...WERE COMPUTED AND DISPATCHED BY THE GREAT IUPPITER SUPER COMPUTER.
AS A COMPUTER, IUPPITER HAS NO PERSONAL BIAS.
IT HAS NO LIKES, DISLIKES, SKIN COLOR, INCOME...
...OR PREJUDICES.
BEFORE IUPPITER...
...EVERYONE IS EQUAL.
IT IS AT IUPPITER'S DISCRETION THAT WE ARE GIVEN OUR FREEDOM.
THAT IS THE FREEDEOM OF THIS SCHOOL.

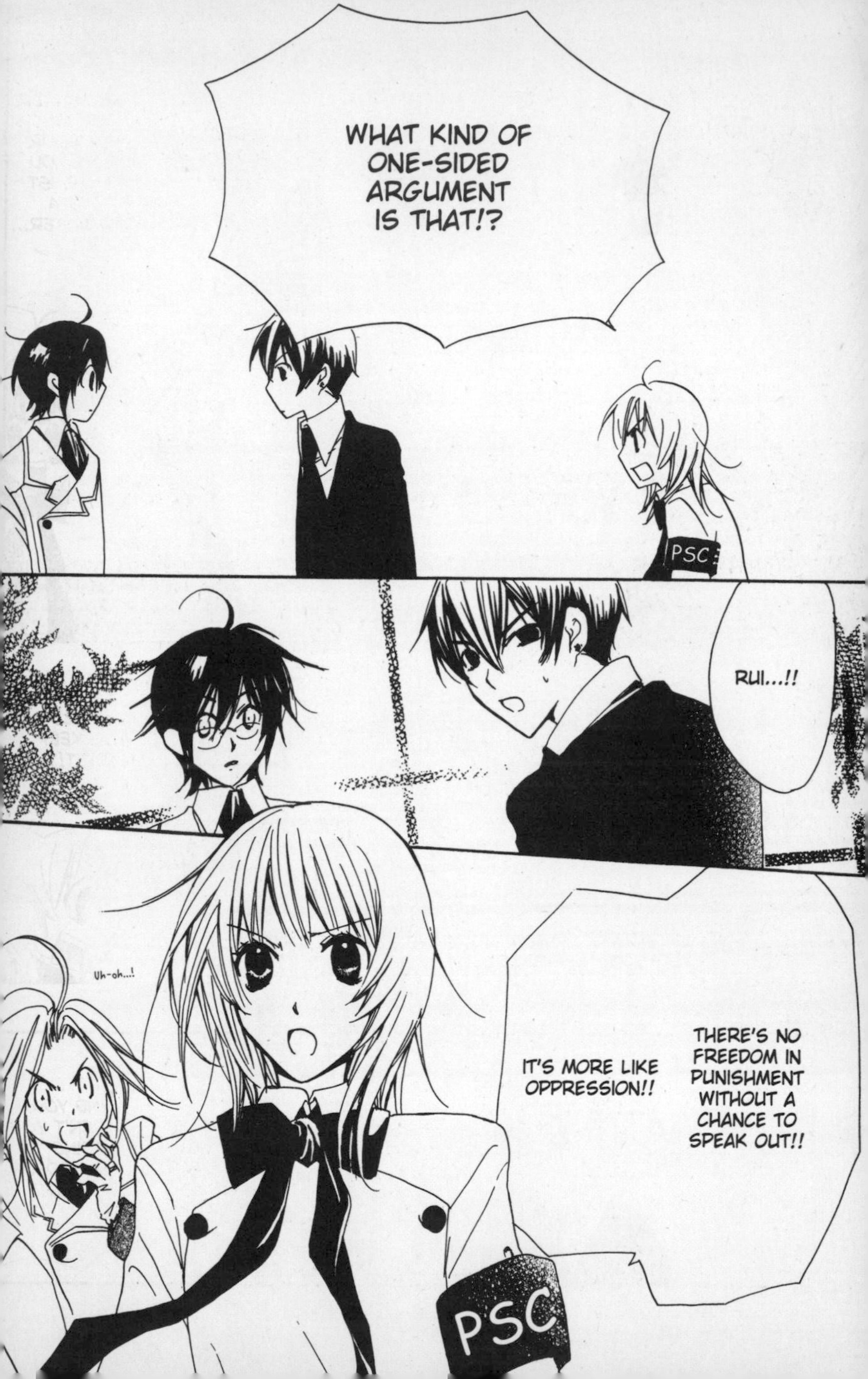
WHAT KIND OF ONE-SIDED ARGUMENT IS THAT!?
PSC
RUI...!!
THERE'S NO FREEDOM IN PUNISHMENT WITHOUT A CHANCE TO SPEAK OUT!!
IT'S MORE LIKE OPPRESSION!!
Uh-oh...!
PSC

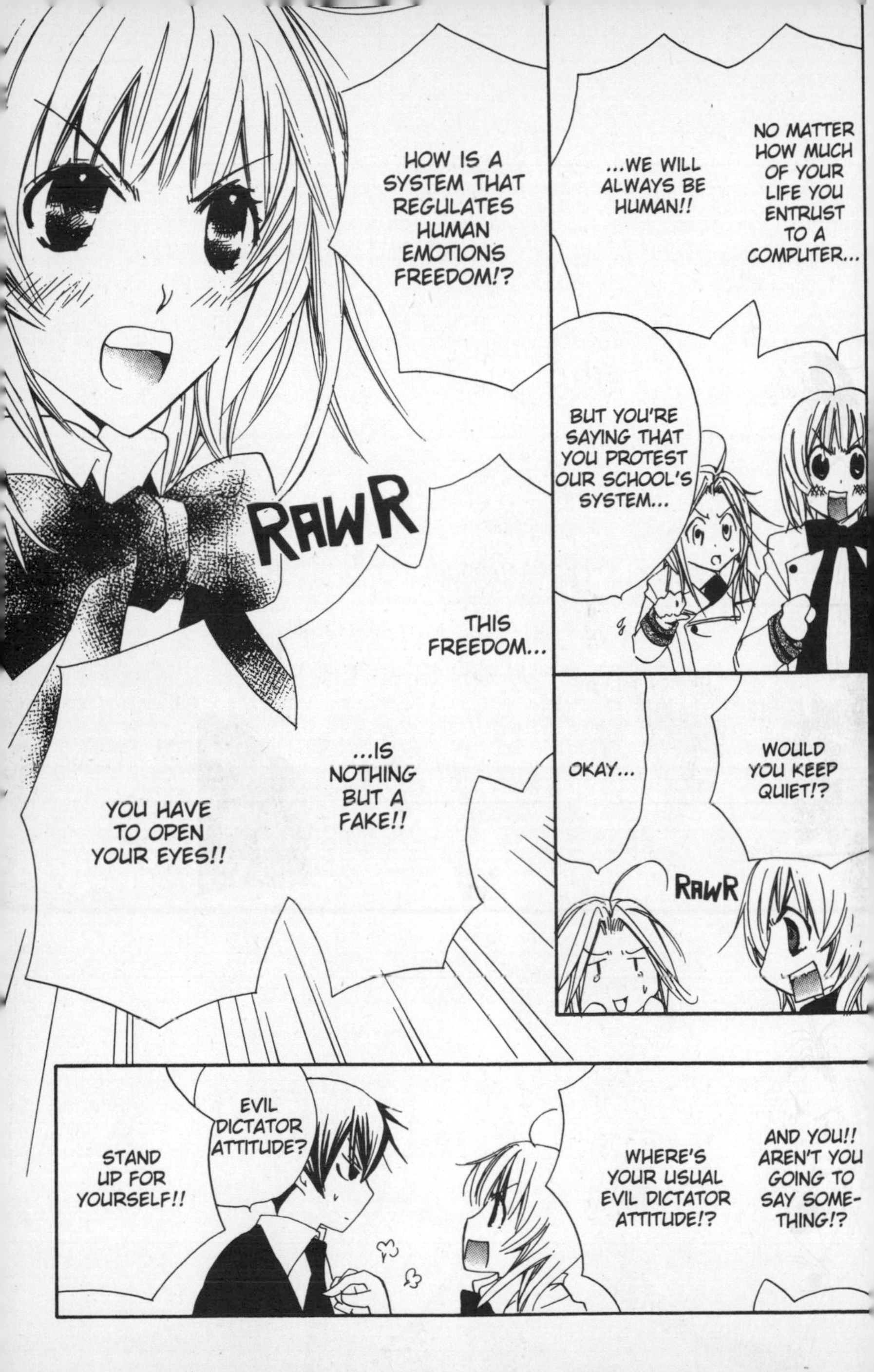
NO MATTER HOW MUCH OF YOUR LIFE YOU ENTRUST TO A COMPUTER...
...WE WILL ALWAYS BE HUMAN!!
BUT YOU'RE SAYING THAT YOU PROTEST OUR SCHOOL'S SYSTEM...
WOULD YOU KEEP QUIET!?
OKAY...
RAWR
HOW IS A SYSTEM THAT REGULATES HUMAN EMOTIONS FREEDOM!?
RAWR
THIS FREEDOM...
...IS NOTHING BUT A FAKE!!
YOU HAVE TO OPEN YOUR EYES!!
AND YOU!! AREN'T YOU GOING TO SAY SOME-THING!?
WHERE'S YOUR USUAL EVIL DICTATOR ATTITUDE!?
EVIL DICTATOR ATTITUDE?
STAND UP FOR YOURSELF!!

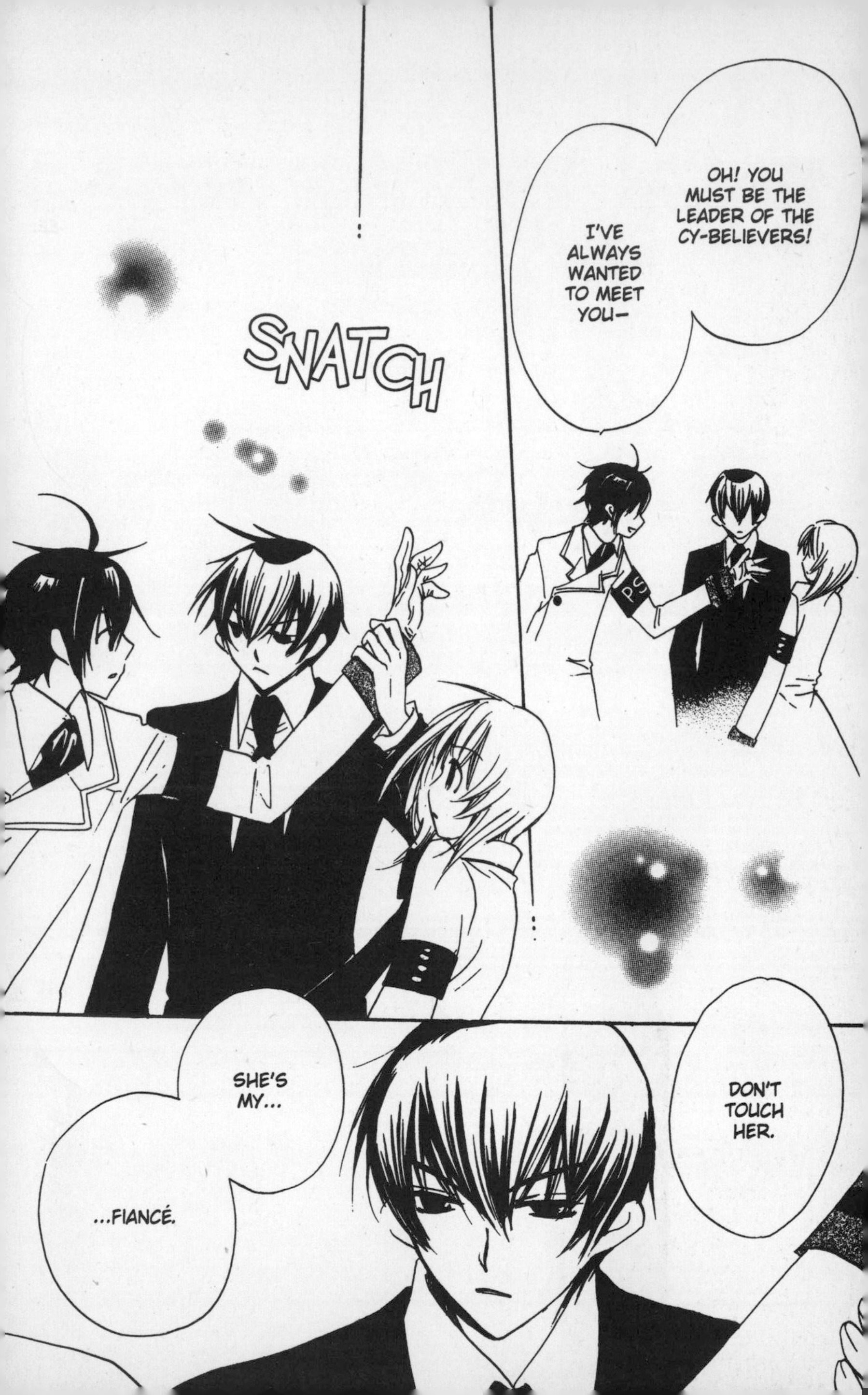
OH! YOU MUST BE THE LEADER OF THE CY-BELIEVERS!
I'VE ALWAYS WANTED TO MEET YOU–
SNATCH
DON'T TOUCH HER.
SHE'S MY...
...FIANCÉ.

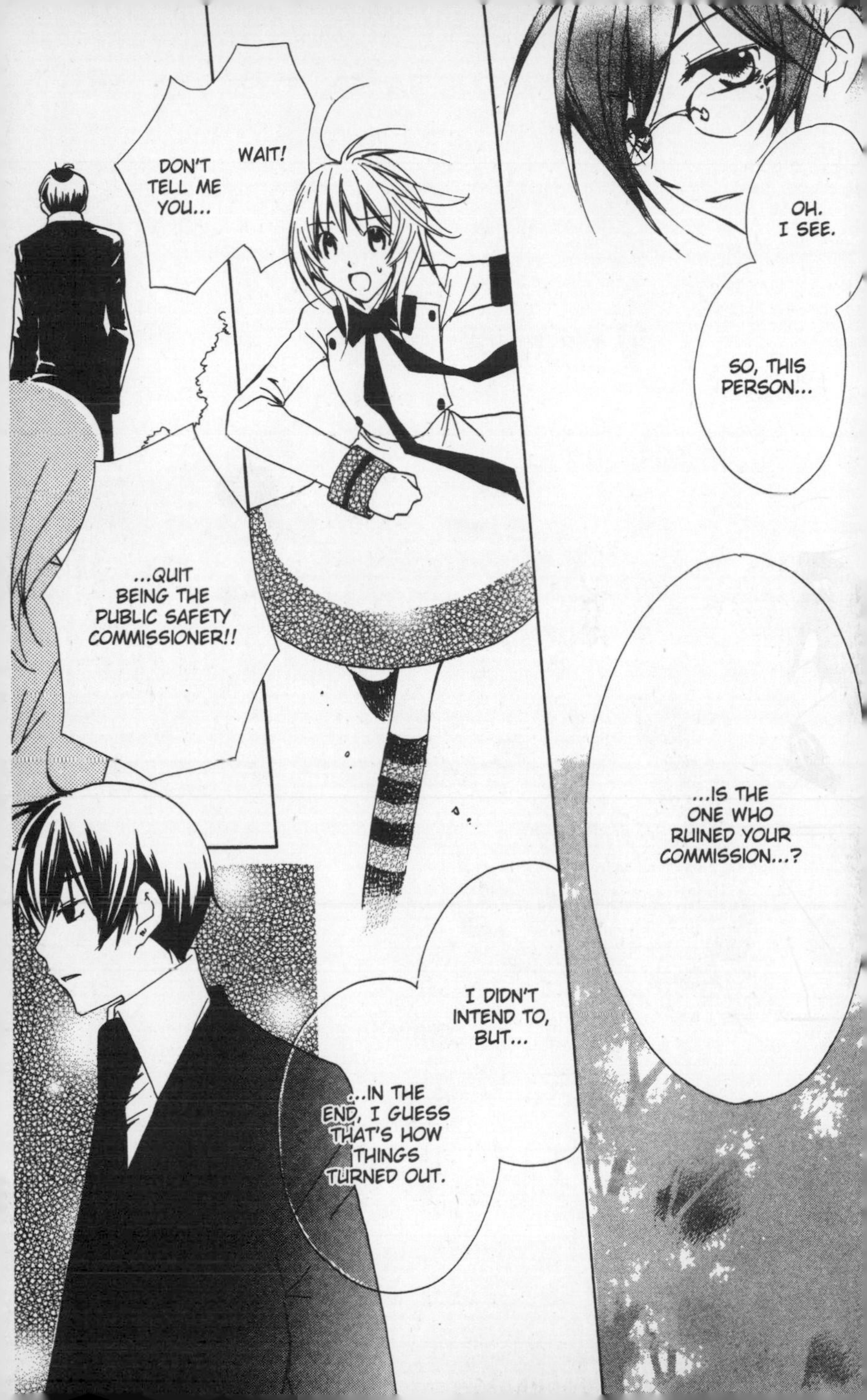
OH. I SEE.
SO, THIS PERSON...
...IS THE ONE WHO RUINED YOUR COMMISSION...?
WAIT!
DON'T TELL ME YOU...
...QUIT BEING THE PUBLIC SAFETY COMMISSIONER!!
I DIDN'T INTEND TO, BUT...
...IN THE END, I GUESS THAT'S HOW THINGS TURNED OUT.

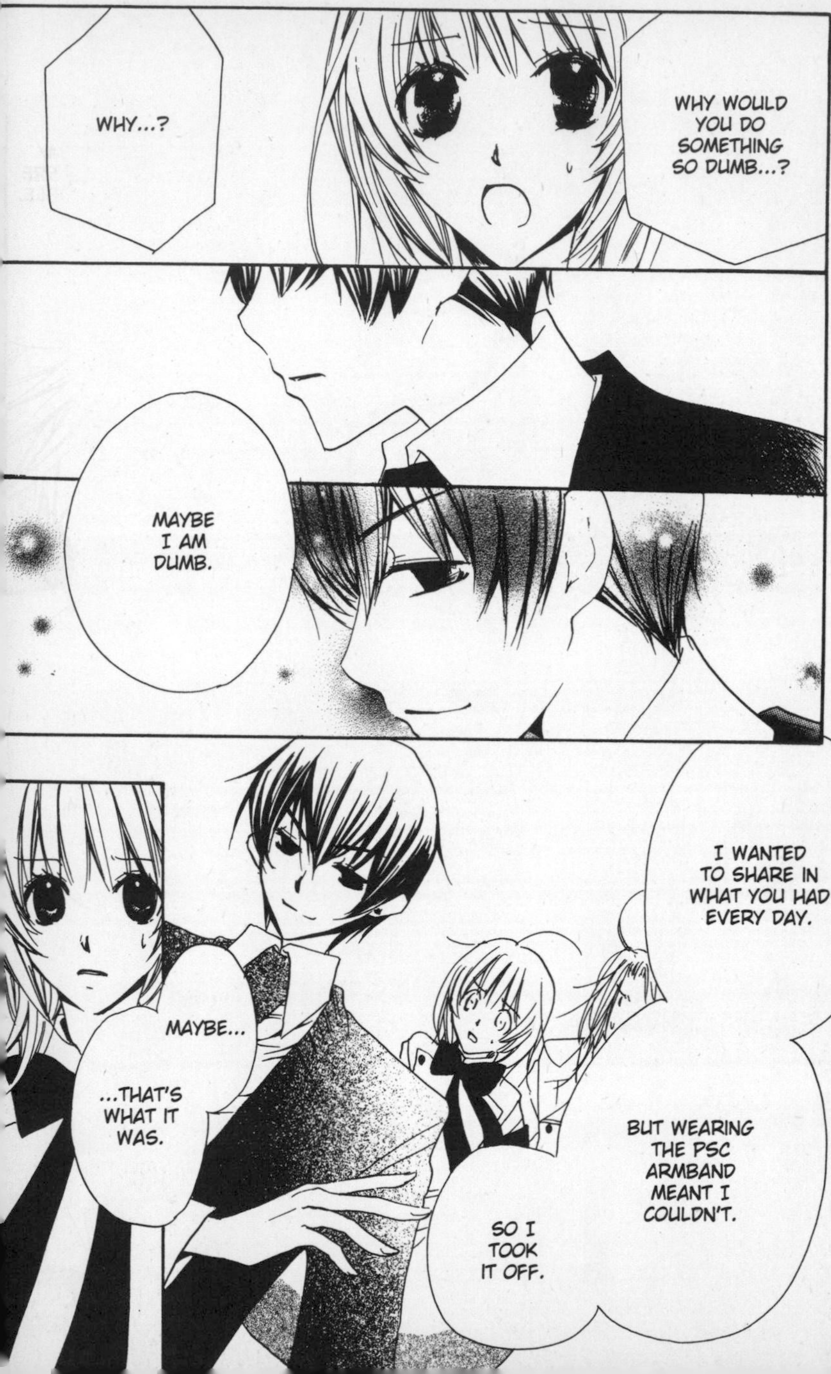
WHY WOULD YOU DO SOMETHING SO DUMB...?
WHY...?
MAYBE I AM DUMB.
I WANTED TO SHARE IN WHAT YOU HAD EVERY DAY.
BUT WEARING THE PSC ARMBAND MEANT I COULDN'T.
SO I TOOK IT OFF.
MAYBE...
...THAT'S WHAT IT WAS.

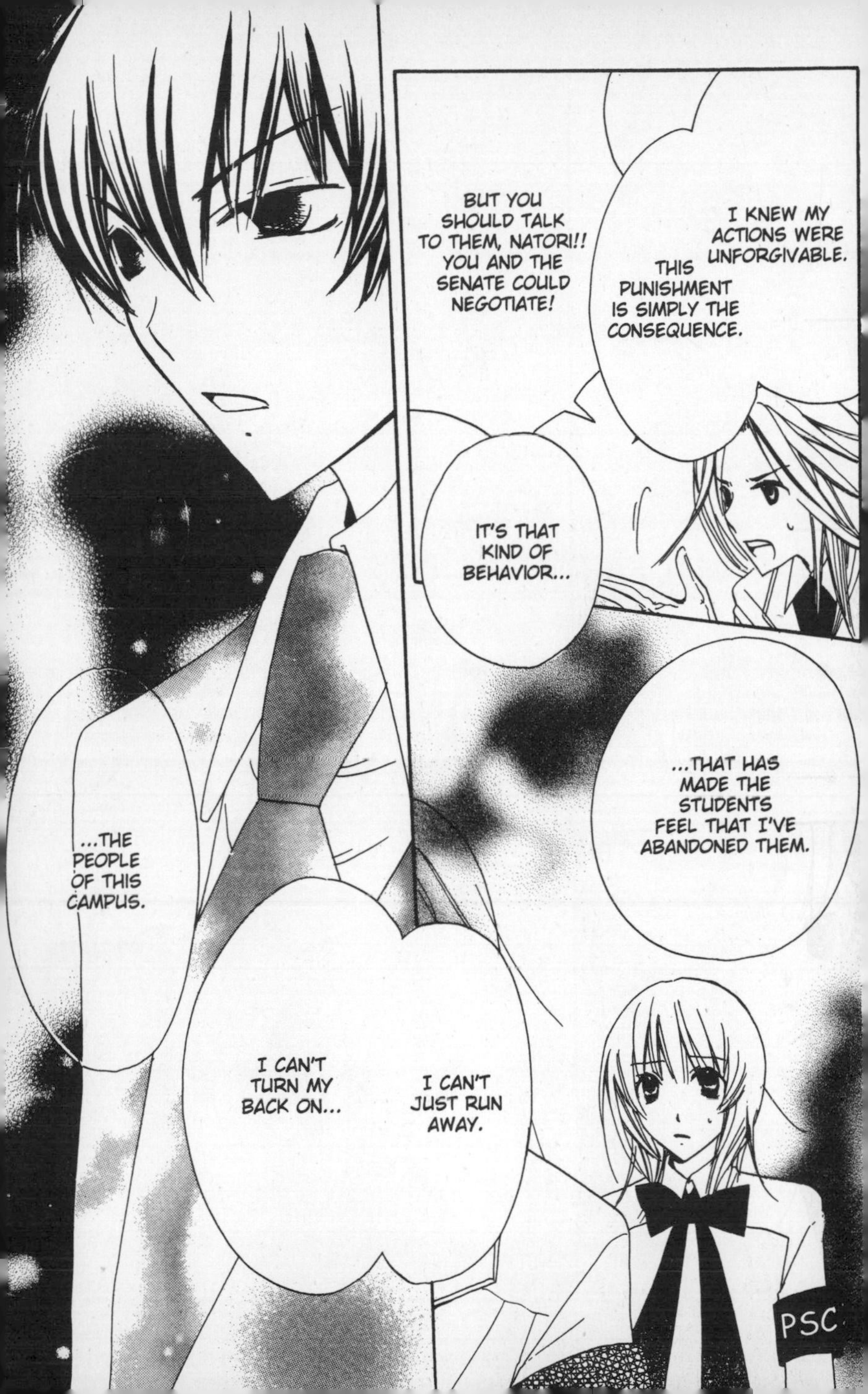
I KNEW MY ACTIONS WERE UNFORGIVABLE.
THIS PUNISHMENT IS SIMPLY THE CONSEQUENCE.
BUT YOU SHOULD TALK TO THEM, NATORI!! YOU AND THE SENATE COULD NEGOTIATE!
IT'S THAT KIND OF BEHAVIOR...
...THAT HAS MADE THE STUDENTS FEEL THAT I'VE ABANDONED THEM.
I CAN'T JUST RUN AWAY.
I CAN'T TURN MY BACK ON...
...THE PEOPLE OF THIS CAMPUS.
PSC

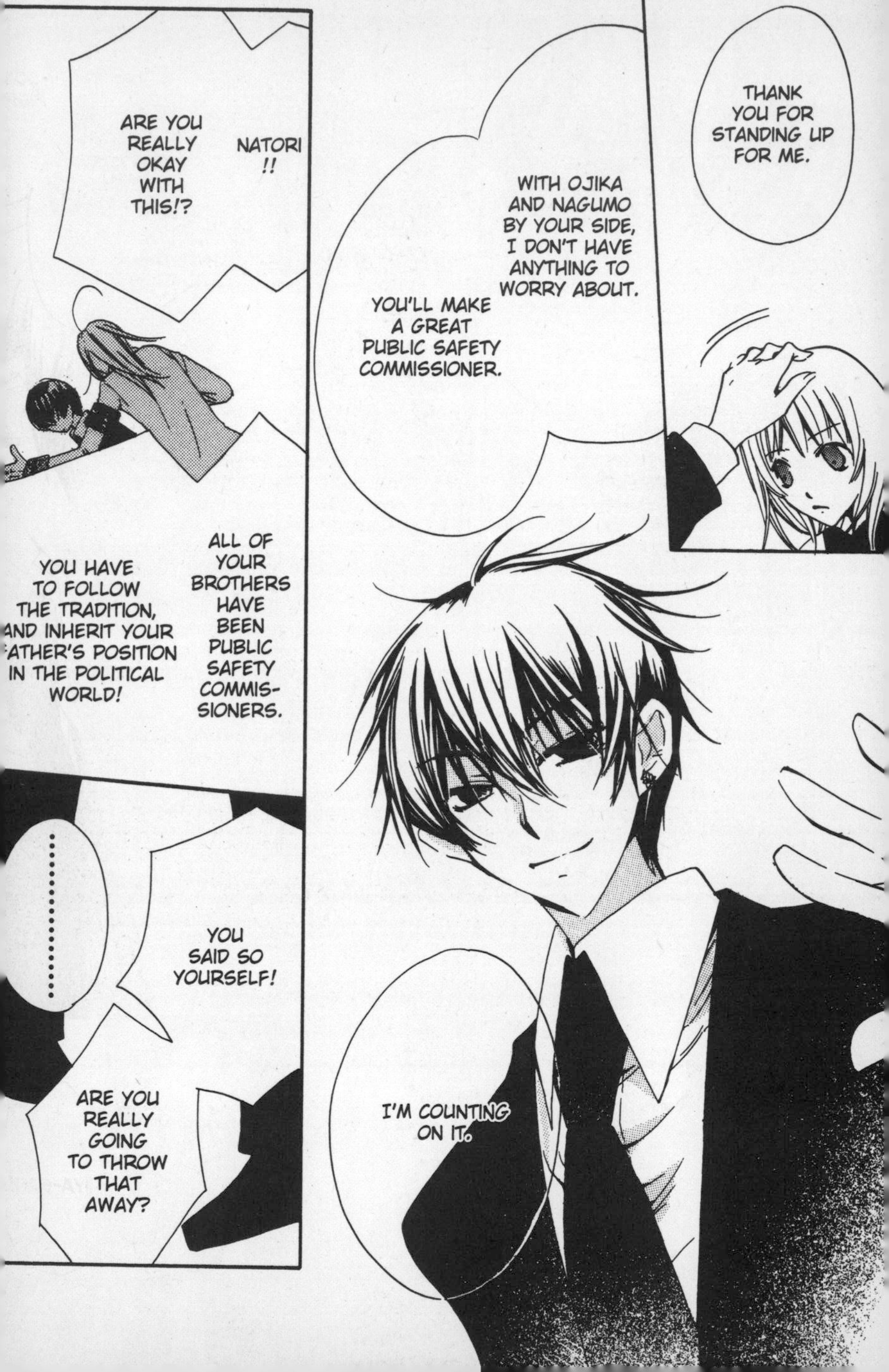
THANK YOU FOR STANDING UP FOR ME.
WITH OJIKA AND NAGUMO BY YOUR SIDE, I DON'T HAVE ANYTHING TO WORRY ABOUT.
YOU'LL MAKE A GREAT PUBLIC SAFETY COMMISSIONER.
I'M COUNTING ON IT.
NATORI!!
ARE YOU REALLY OKAY WITH THIS!?
ALL OF YOUR BROTHERS HAVE BEEN PUBLIC SAFETY COMMISSIONERS.
YOU HAVE TO FOLLOW THE TRADITION, AND INHERIT YOUR FATHER'S POSITION IN THE POLITICAL WORLD!
YOU SAID SO YOURSELF!
ARE YOU REALLY GOING TO THROW THAT AWAY?
……

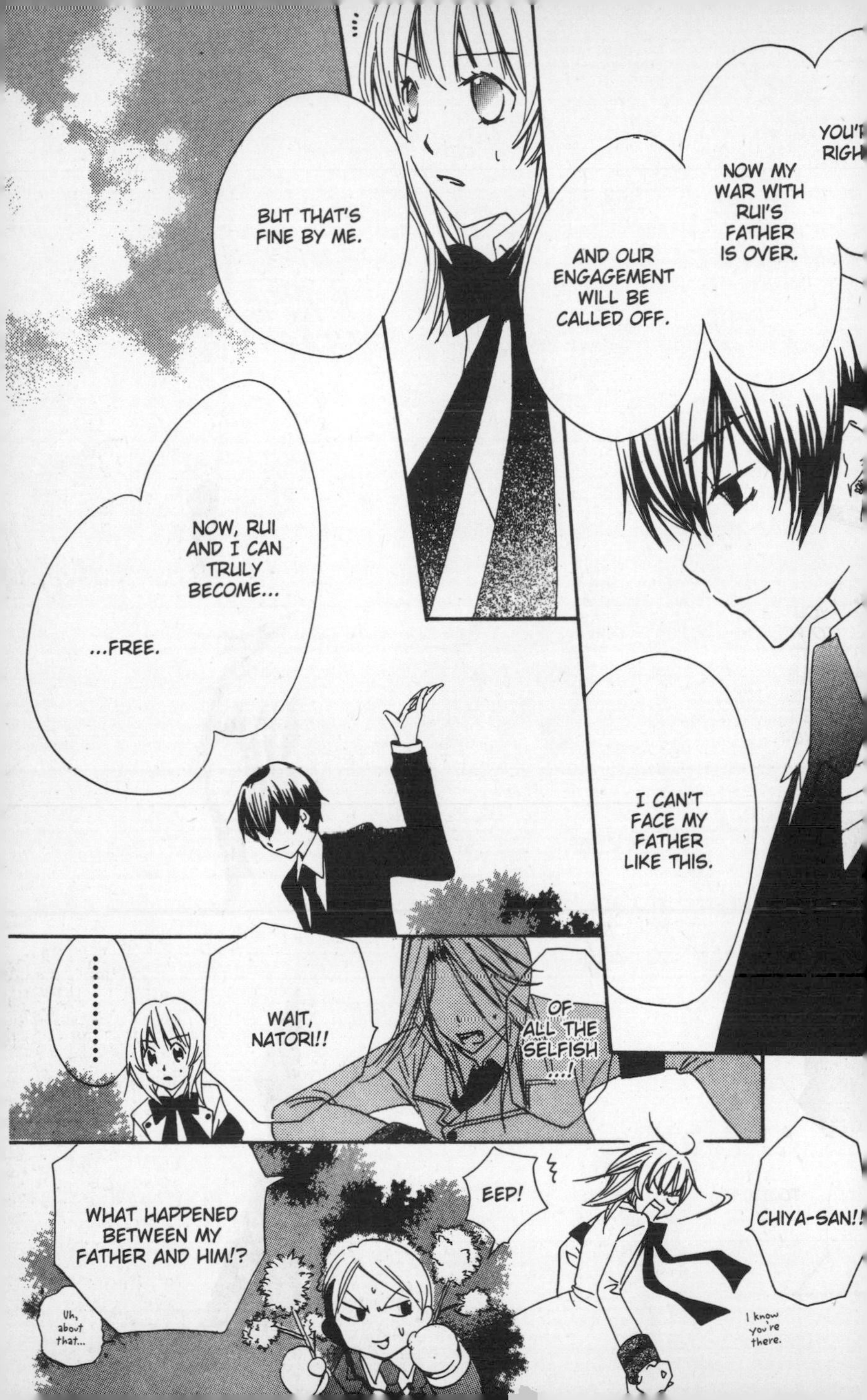

YOU'
RIGH
NOW MY WAR WITH RUI'S FATHER IS OVER.
AND OUR ENGAGEMENT WILL BE CALLED OFF.
I CAN'T FACE MY FATHER LIKE THIS.
....
BUT THAT'S FINE BY ME.
NOW, RUI AND I CAN TRULY BECOME...
...FREE.
OF ALL THE SELFISH...!
WAIT, NATORI!!
......
CHIYA-SAN!!
I know you're there.
EEP!
WHAT HAPPENED BETWEEN MY FATHER AND HIM!?
Uh, about that...

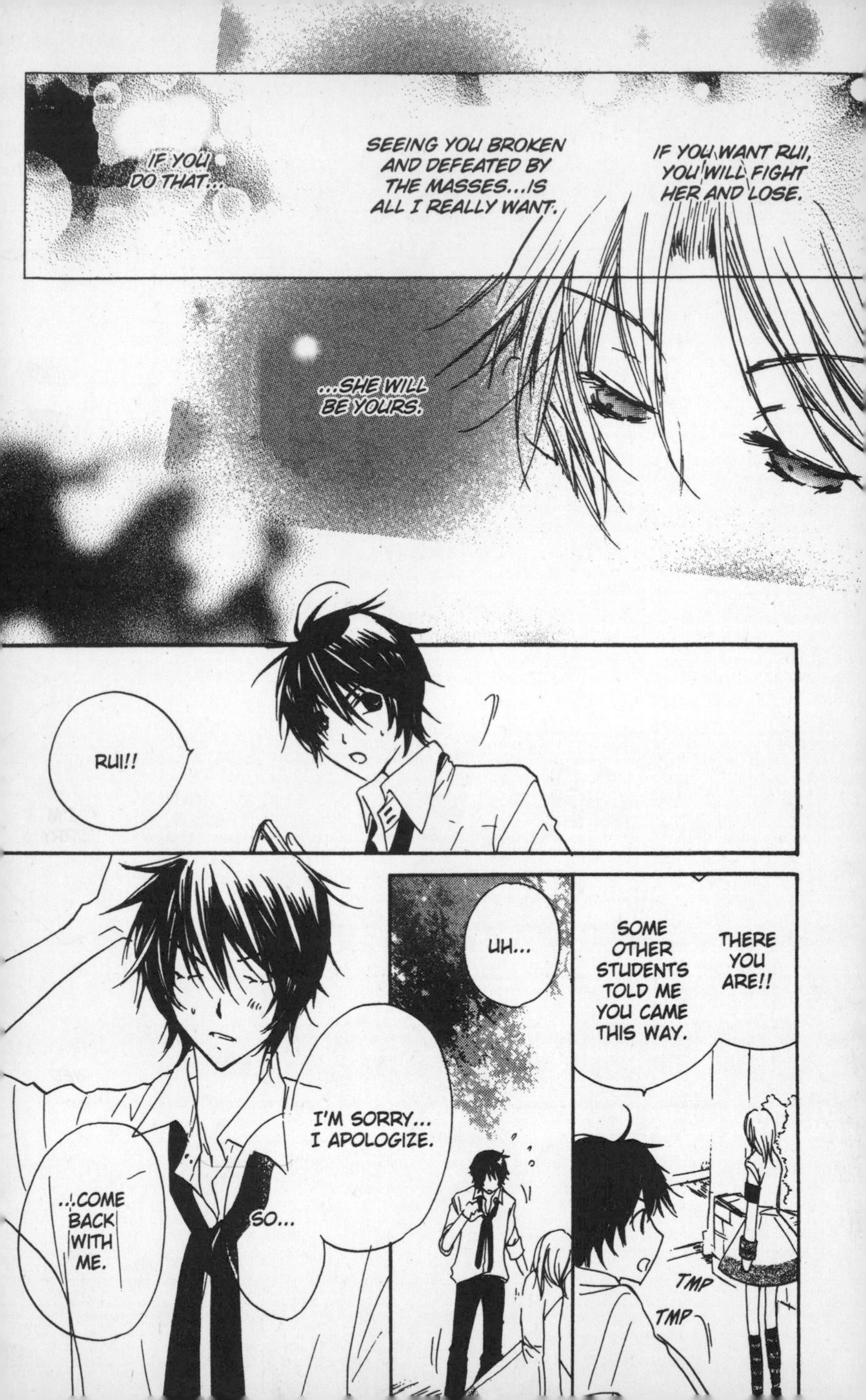
IF YOU WANT RUI, YOU WILL FIGHT HER AND LOSE.
SEEING YOU BROKEN AND DEFEATED BY THE MASSES...IS ALL I REALLY WANT.
IF YOU DO THAT...
...SHE WILL BE YOURS.
RUI!!
THERE YOU ARE!!
SOME OTHER STUDENTS TOLD ME YOU CAME THIS WAY.
TMP
TMP
UH...
I'M SORRY... I APOLOGIZE.
SO...
...COME BACK WITH ME.

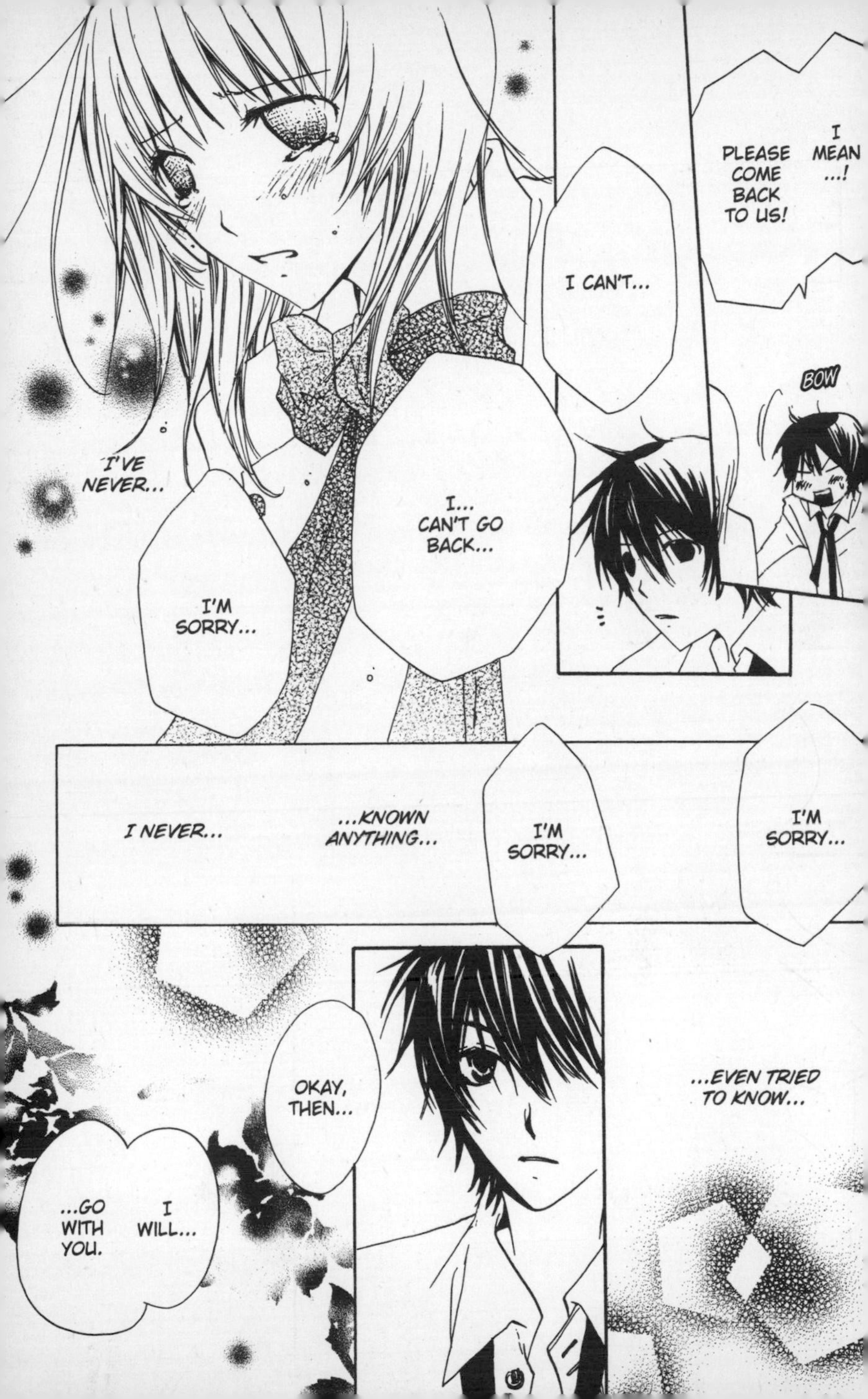
I MEAN ...! PLEASE COME BACK TO US!
BOW
I CAN'T...
I... CAN'T GO BACK...
I'M SORRY...
I'VE NEVER...
I'M SORRY...
I'M SORRY...
...KNOWN ANYTHING...
I NEVER...
...EVEN TRIED TO KNOW...
OKAY, THEN...
I WILL... ...GO WITH YOU.

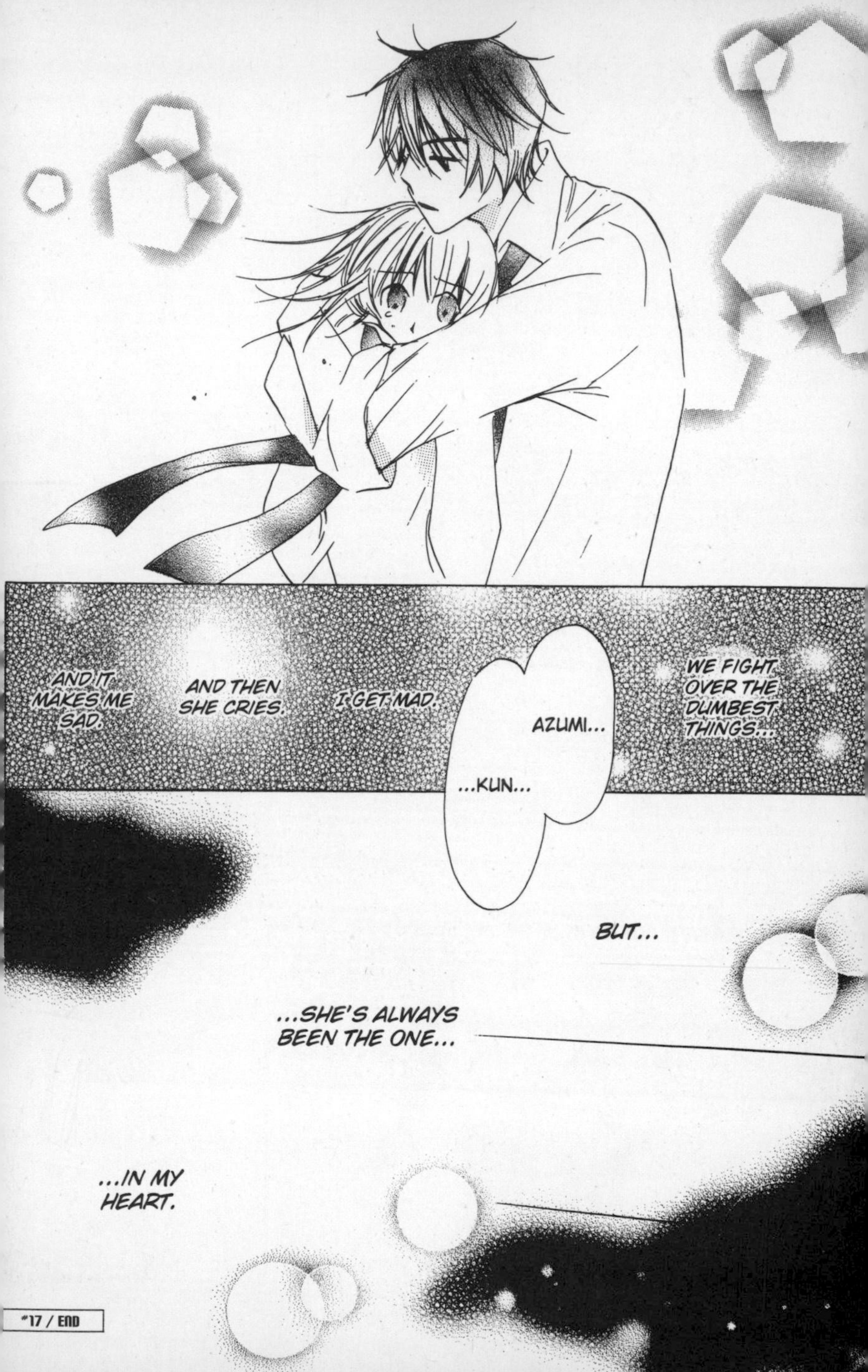
WE FIGHT OVER THE DUMBEST THINGS...
AZUMI... ...KUN...
I GET MAD.
AND THEN SHE CRIES.
AND IT MAKES ME SAD.
BUT...
...SHE'S ALWAYS BEEN THE ONE...
...IN MY HEART.
#17 / END

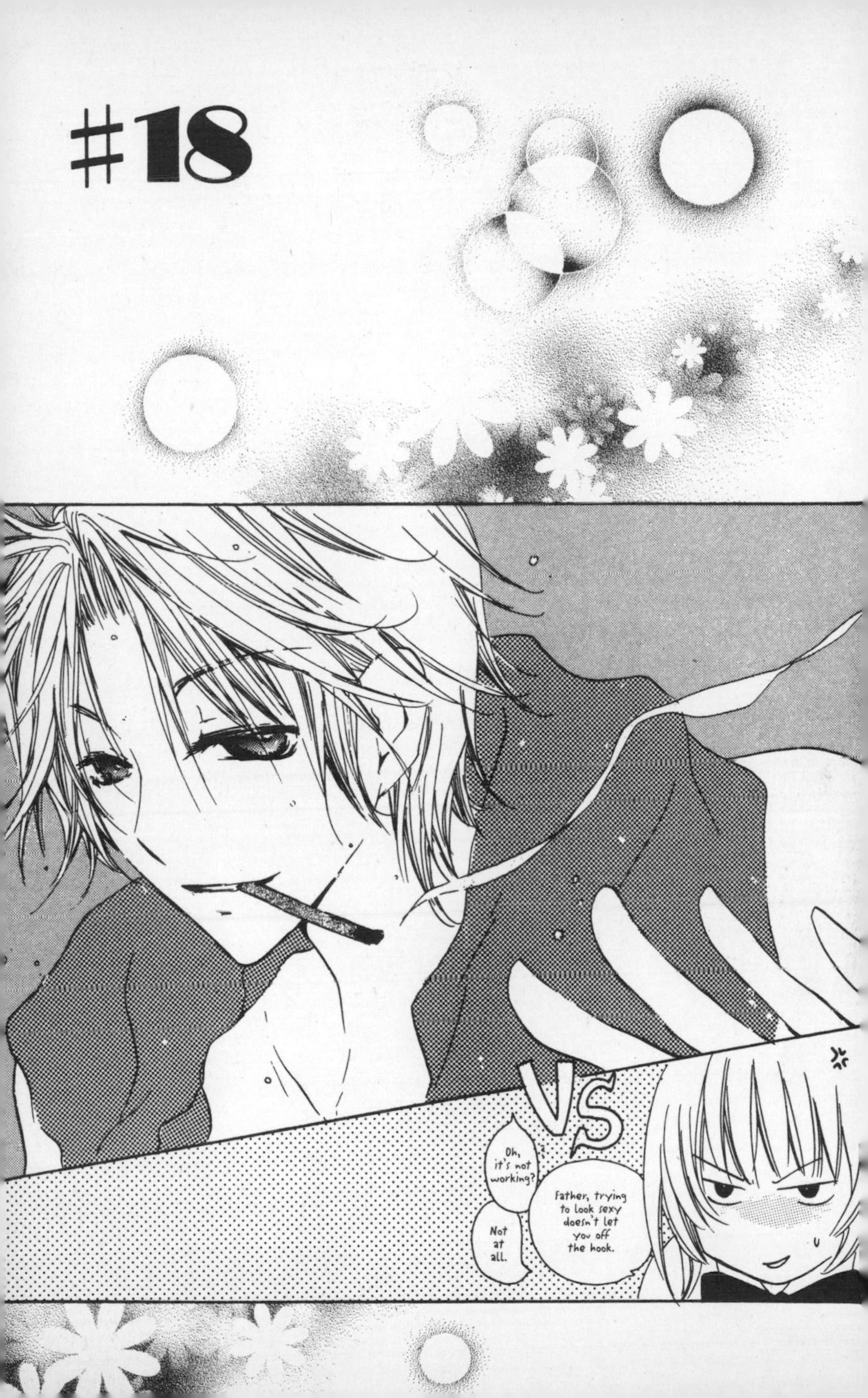
#18
VS
Father, trying to look sexy doesn't let you off the hook.
Oh, it's not working?
Not at all.

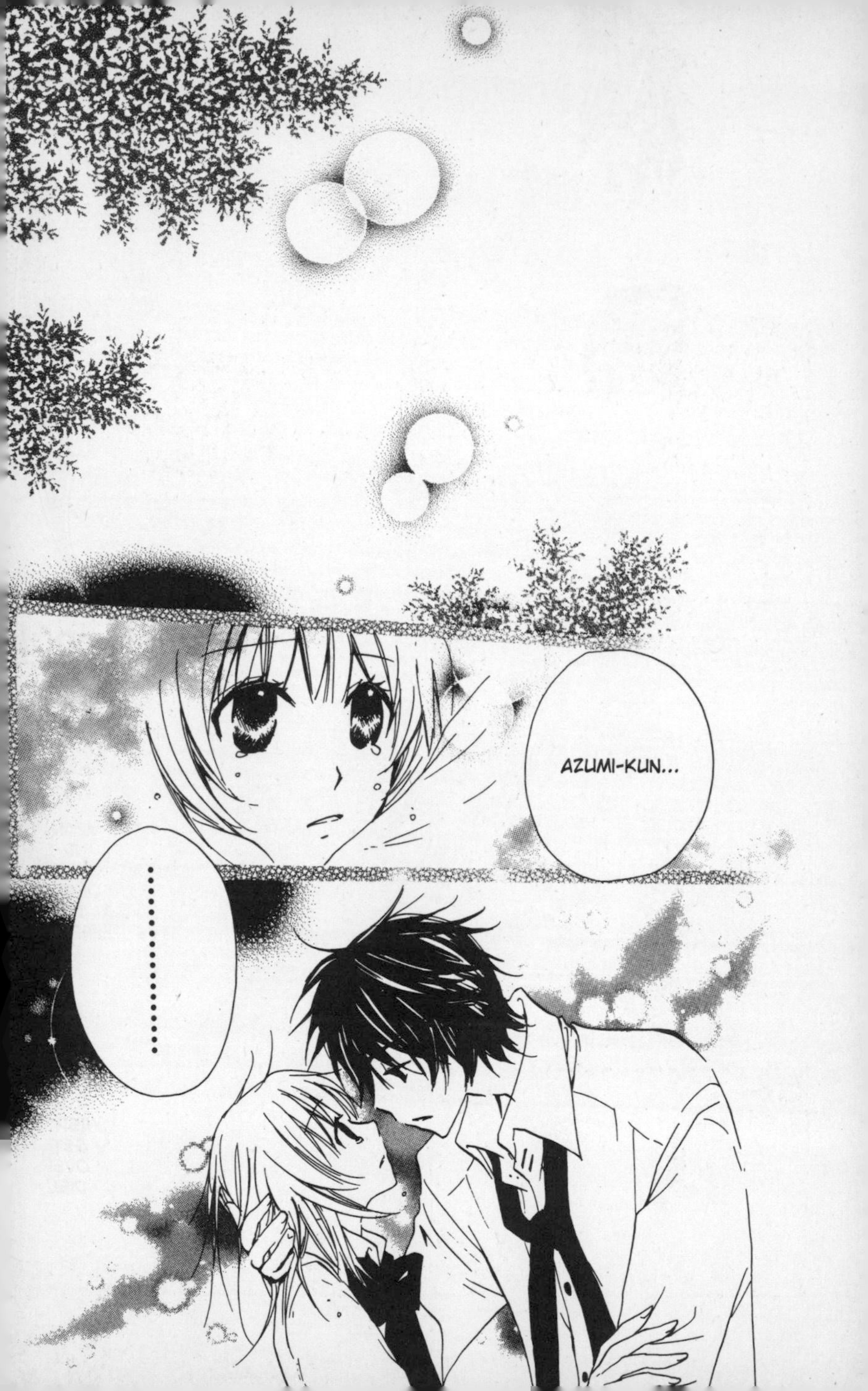
AZUMI-KUN...
....

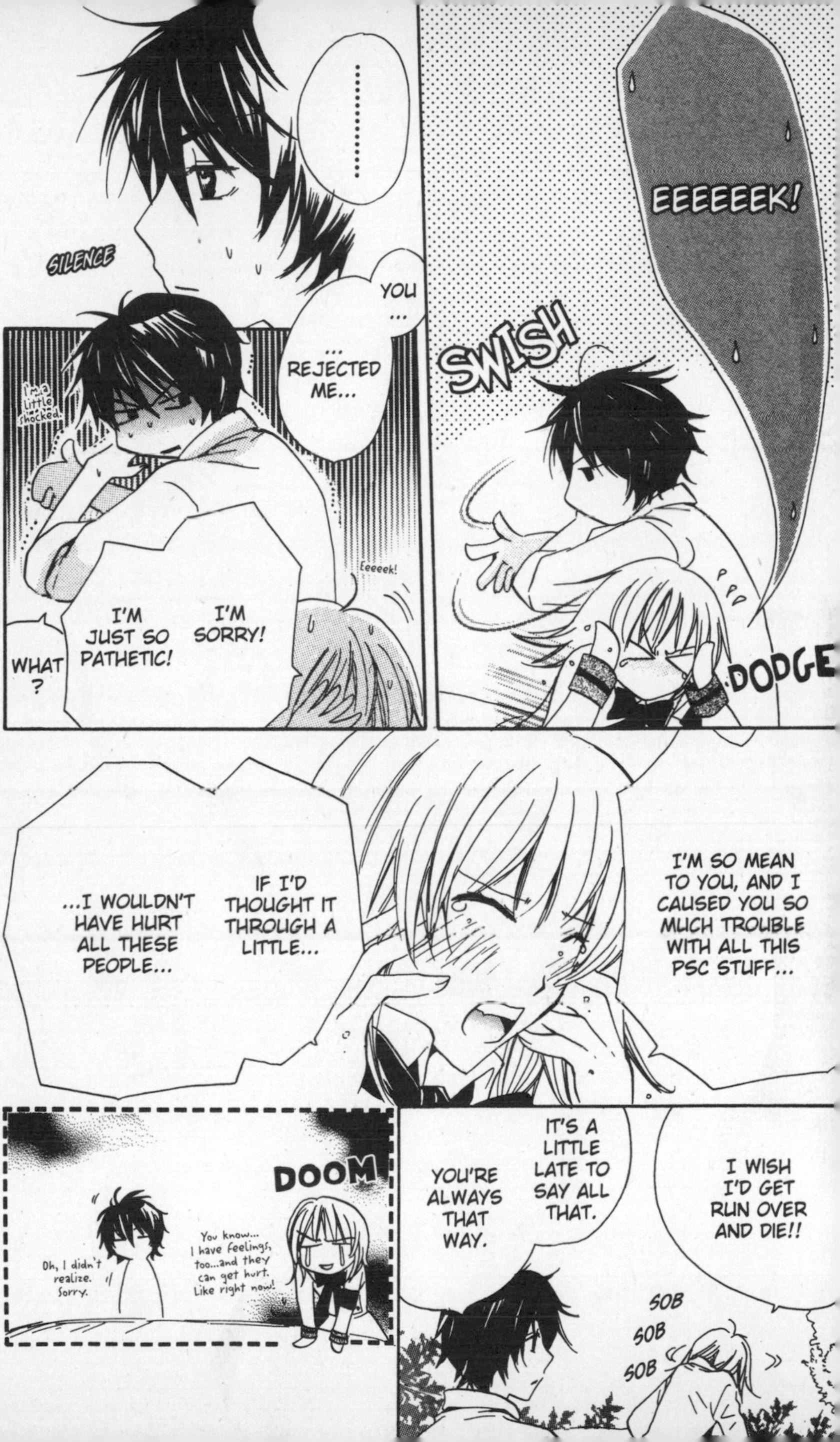
EEEEEEK!
SWISH
DODGE
......
SILENCE
YOU...
...REJECTED ME...
I'm a little shocked.
Eeeeek!
I'M SORRY!
I'M JUST SO PATHETIC!
WHAT?
I'M SO MEAN TO YOU, AND I CAUSED YOU SO MUCH TROUBLE WITH ALL THIS PSC STUFF...
IF I'D THOUGHT IT THROUGH A LITTLE...
...I WOULDN'T HAVE HURT ALL THESE PEOPLE...
I WISH I'D GET RUN OVER AND DIE!!
IT'S A LITTLE LATE TO SAY ALL THAT.
YOU'RE ALWAYS THAT WAY.
SOB
SOB
SOB
DOOM
You know... I have feelings, too...and they can get hurt. Like right now!
Oh, I didn't realize. Sorry.

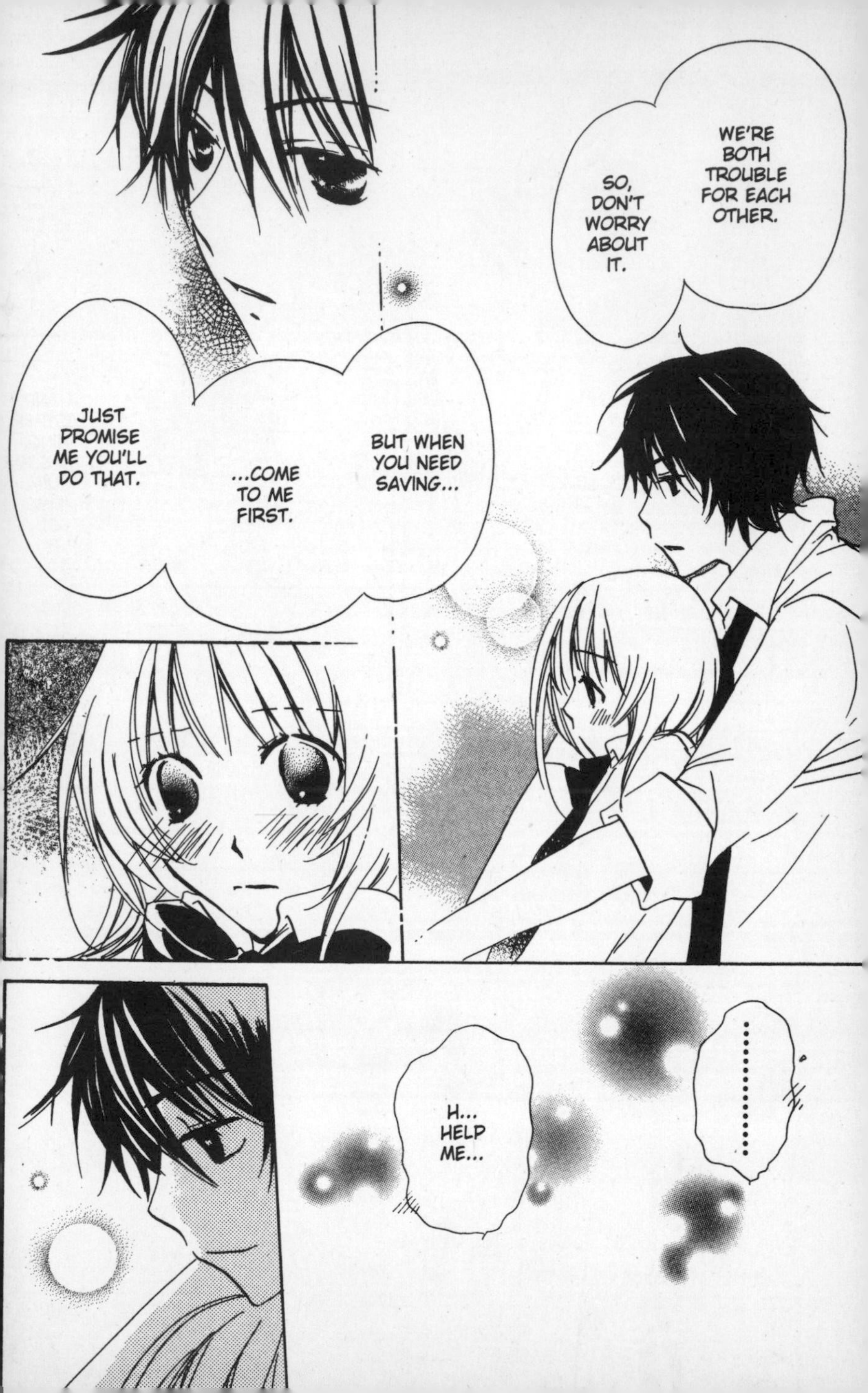
WE'RE BOTH TROUBLE FOR EACH OTHER.
SO, DON'T WORRY ABOUT IT.
BUT WHEN YOU NEED SAVING...
...COME TO ME FIRST.
JUST PROMISE ME YOU'LL DO THAT.
......
H... HELP ME...

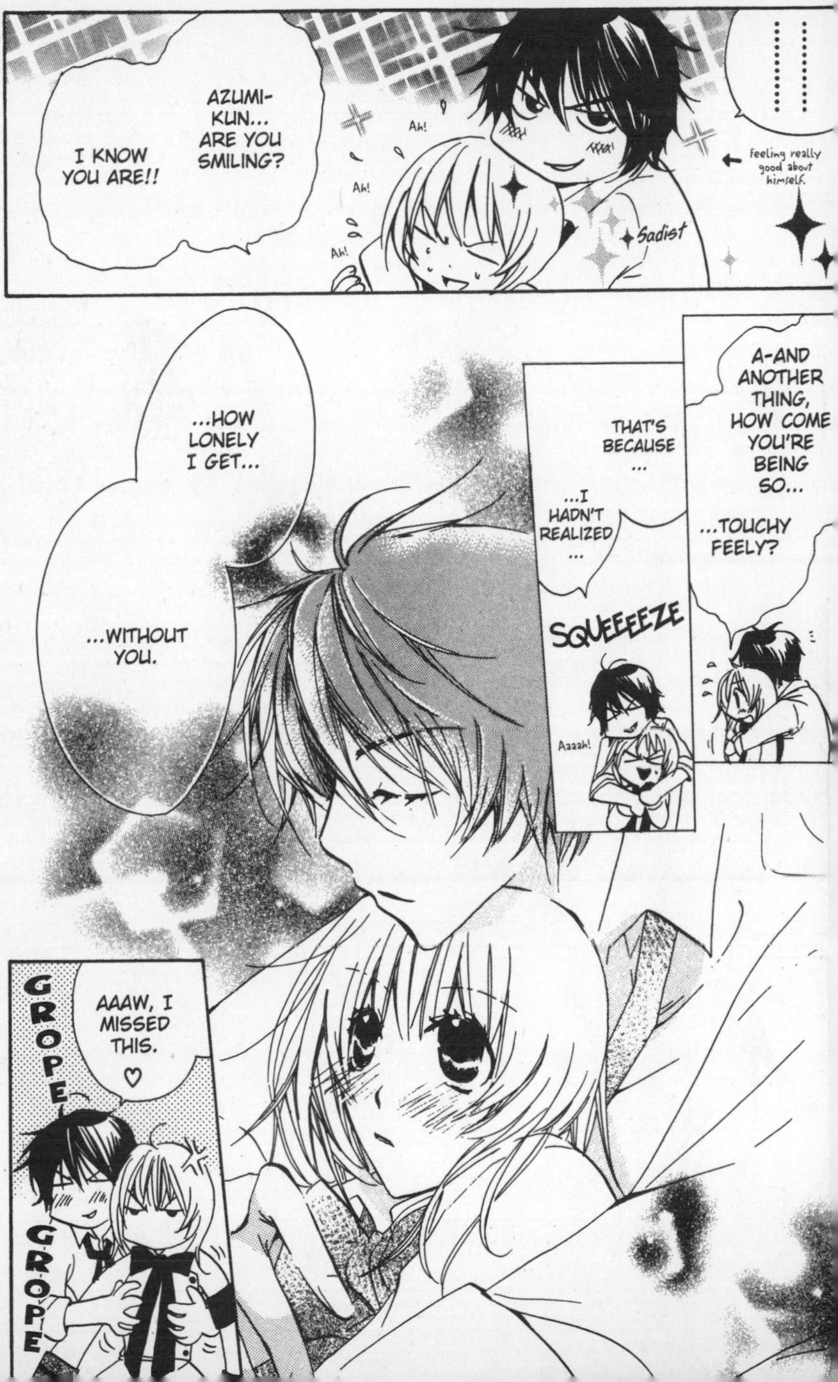
......
feeling really good about himself.
Sadist
Ah!
Ah!
Ah!
AZUMI-KUN... ARE YOU SMILING?
I KNOW YOU ARE!!
A-AND ANOTHER THING, HOW COME YOU'RE BEING SO...
...TOUCHY FEELY?
THAT'S BECAUSE...
...I HADN'T REALIZED...
SQUEEEEEZE
Aaaah!
...HOW LONELY I GET...
...WITHOUT YOU.
AAAW, I MISSED THIS. ♡
GROPE
GROPE

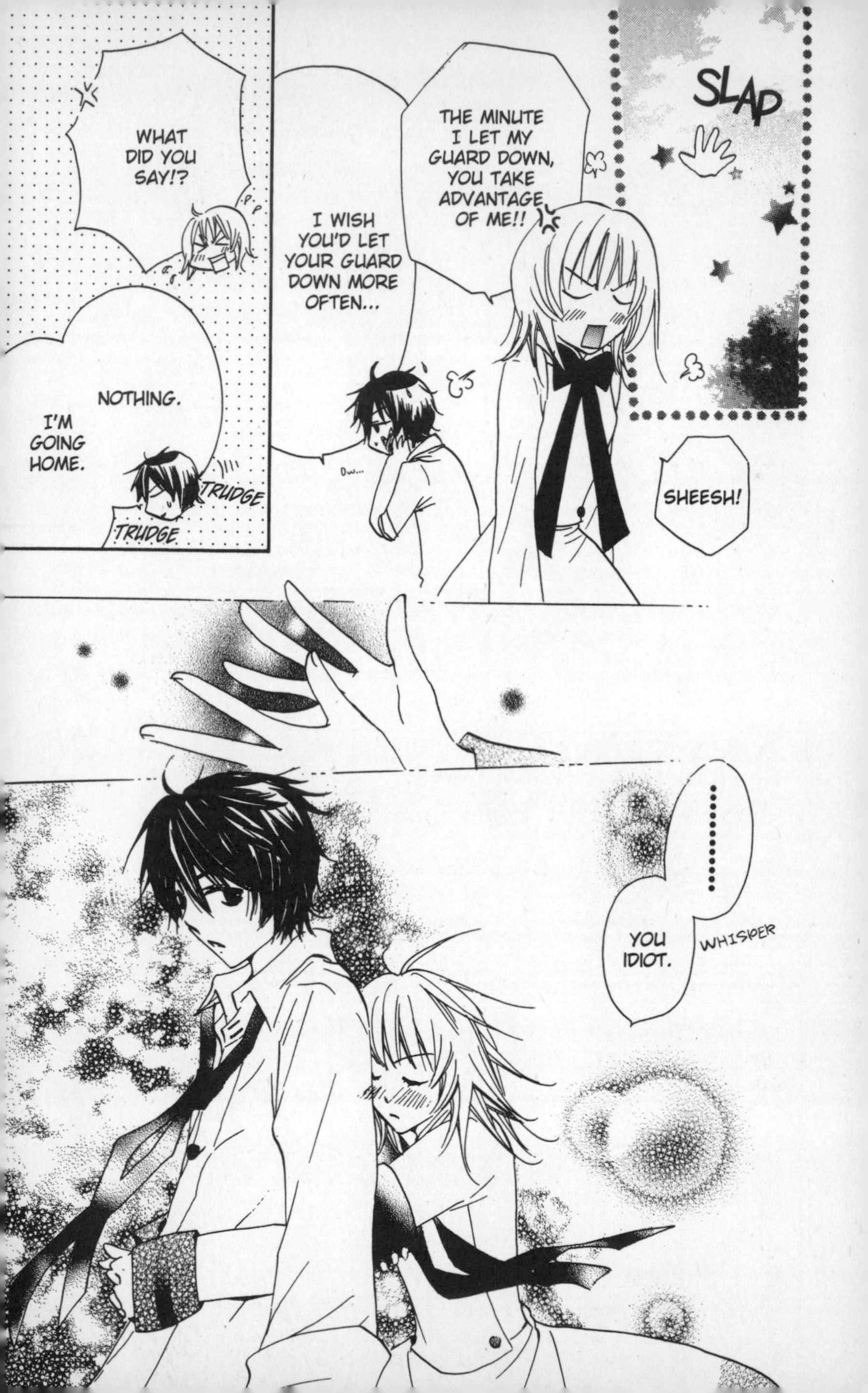
SLAP
THE MINUTE I LET MY GUARD DOWN, YOU TAKE ADVANTAGE OF ME!!
I WISH YOU'D LET YOUR GUARD DOWN MORE OFTEN...
SHEESH!
Ow...
WHAT DID YOU SAY!?
NOTHING.
I'M GOING HOME.
TRUDGE
TRUDGE
......
WHISPER
YOU IDIOT.

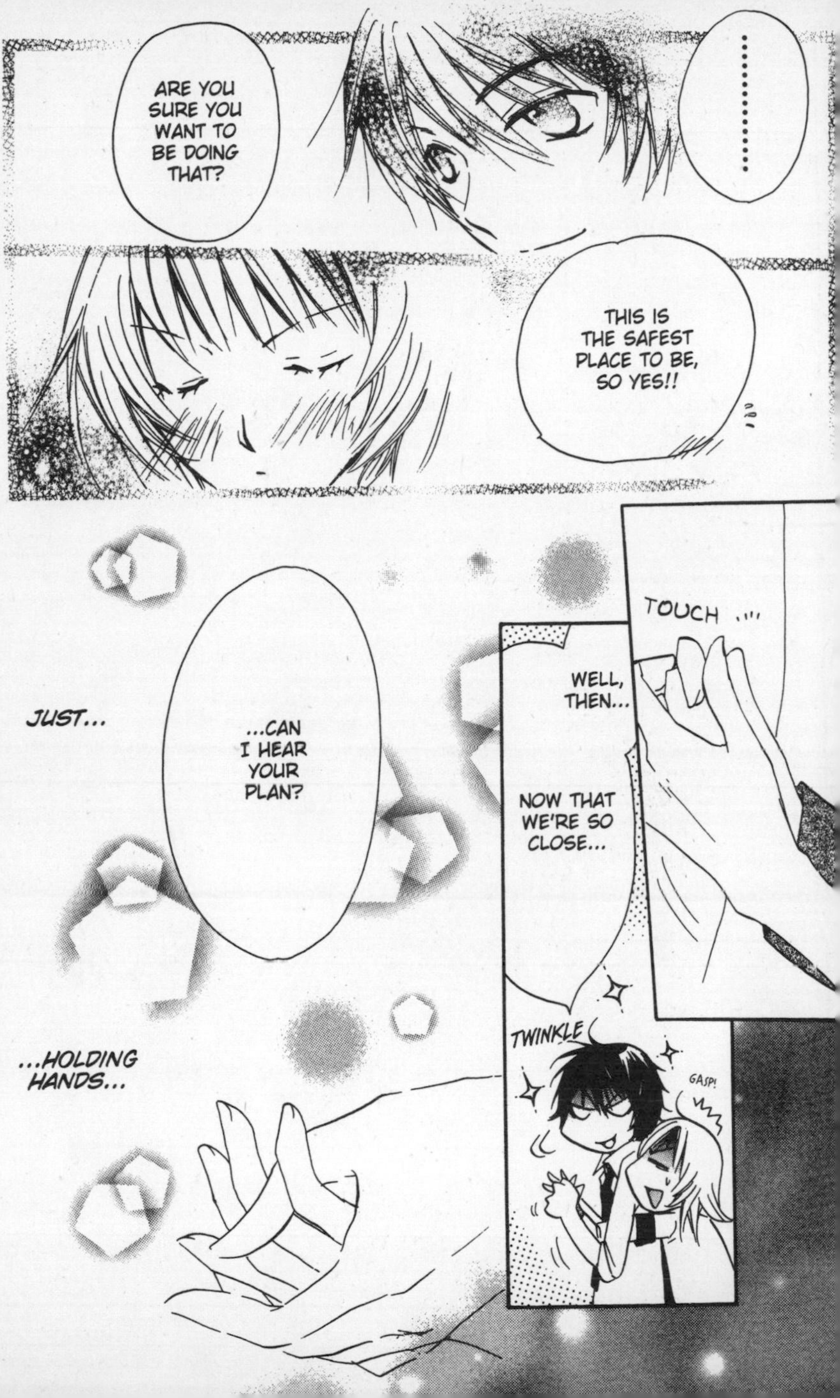
......
ARE YOU SURE YOU WANT TO BE DOING THAT?
THIS IS THE SAFEST PLACE TO BE, SO YES!!
TOUCH ...
WELL, THEN...
NOW THAT WE'RE SO CLOSE...
TWINKLE
GASP!
...CAN I HEAR YOUR PLAN?
JUST...
...HOLDING HANDS...

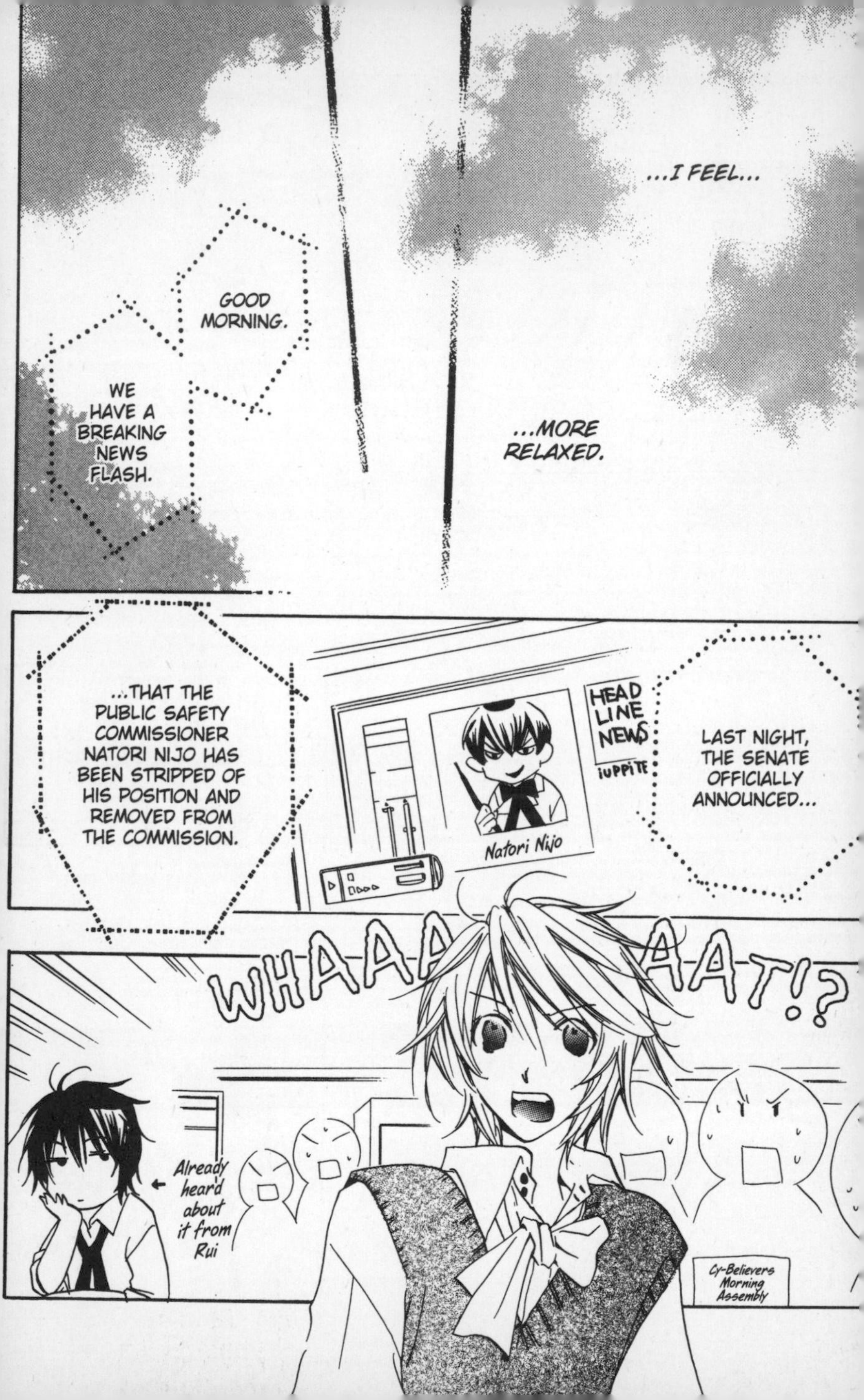

...I FEEL...
...MORE RELAXED.
GOOD MORNING.
WE HAVE A BREAKING NEWS FLASH.
LAST NIGHT, THE SENATE OFFICIALLY ANNOUNCED...
HEAD LINE NEWS
iUPPITE
Natori Nijo
...THAT THE PUBLIC SAFETY COMMISSIONER NATORI NIJO HAS BEEN STRIPPED OF HIS POSITION AND REMOVED FROM THE COMMISSION.
WHAAA AAT!?
Cy-Believers Morning Assembly
Already heard about it from Rui

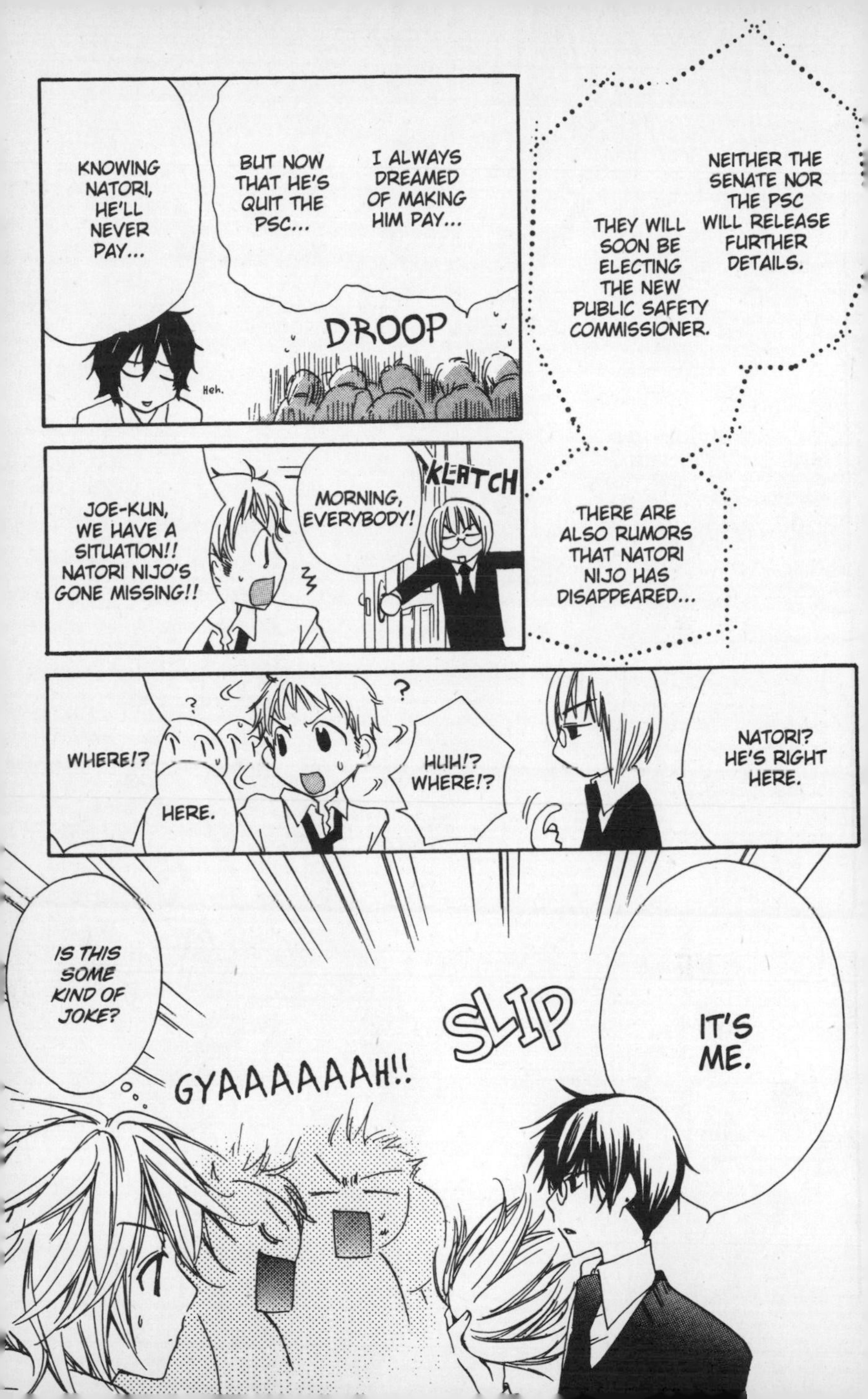
NEITHER THE SENATE NOR THE PSC WILL RELEASE FURTHER DETAILS.
THEY WILL SOON BE ELECTING THE NEW PUBLIC SAFETY COMMISSIONER.
THERE ARE ALSO RUMORS THAT NATORI NIJO HAS DISAPPEARED...
I ALWAYS DREAMED OF MAKING HIM PAY...
BUT NOW THAT HE'S QUIT THE PSC...
DROOP
KNOWING NATORI, HE'LL NEVER PAY...
Heh.
KLATCH
MORNING, EVERYBODY!
JOE-KUN, WE HAVE A SITUATION!! NATORI NIJO'S GONE MISSING!!
NATORI? HE'S RIGHT HERE.
HUH!? WHERE!?
WHERE!?
HERE.
IT'S ME.
SLIP
GYAAAAAAH!!
IS THIS SOME KIND OF JOKE?

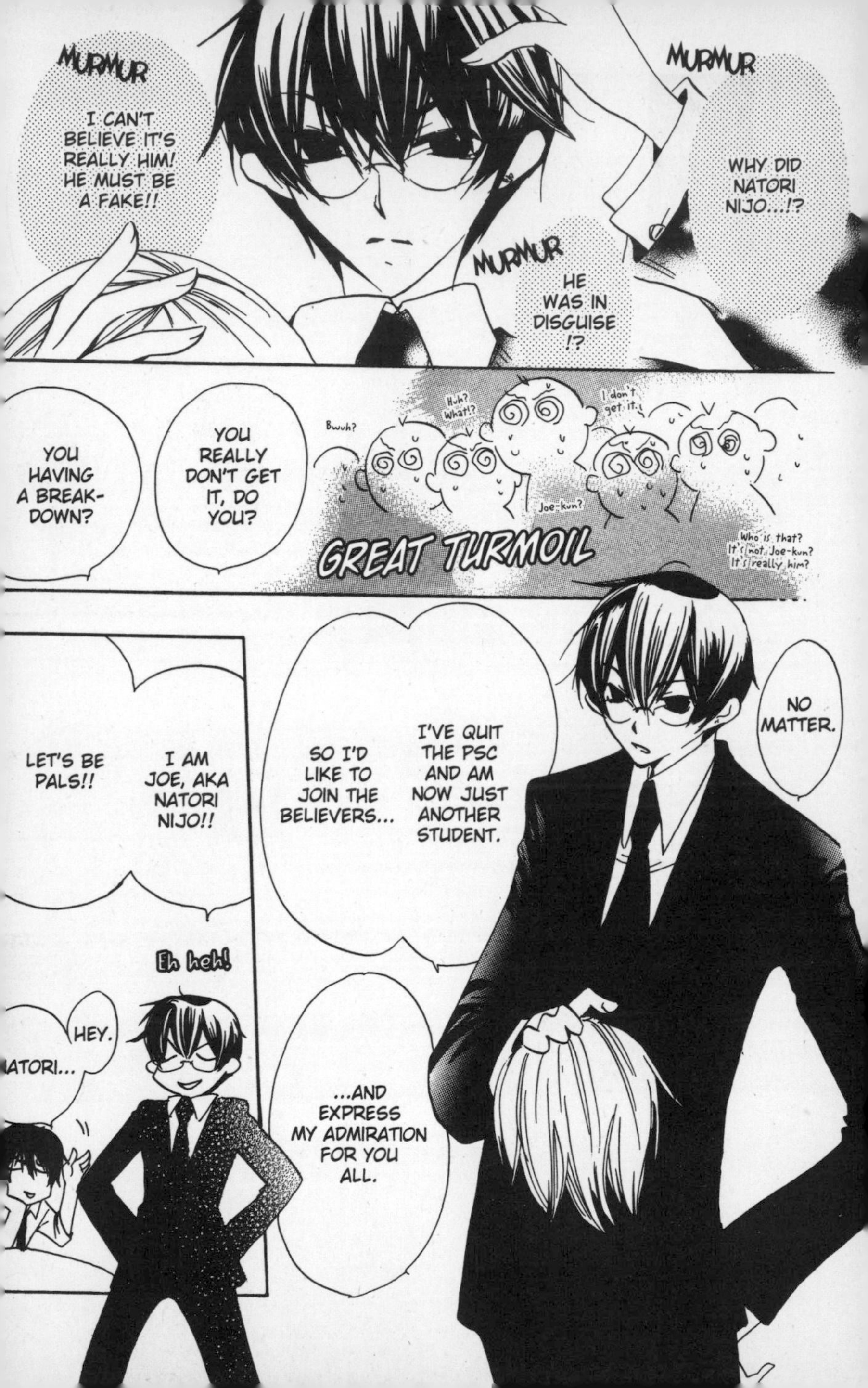
MURMUR
WHY DID NATORI NIJO...!?
MURMUR
HE WAS IN DISGUISE !?
MURMUR
I CAN'T BELIEVE IT'S REALLY HIM! HE MUST BE A FAKE!!
Who is that? It's not Joe-kun? It's really him?
I don't get it.
Huh? What!?
Bwuh?
Joe-kun?
GREAT TURMOIL
YOU REALLY DON'T GET IT, DO YOU?
YOU HAVING A BREAK-DOWN?
NO MATTER.
I'VE QUIT THE PSC AND AM NOW JUST ANOTHER STUDENT.
SO I'D LIKE TO JOIN THE BELIEVERS...
...AND EXPRESS MY ADMIRATION FOR YOU ALL.
I AM JOE, AKA NATORI NIJO!!
LET'S BE PALS!!
Eh heh!
HEY.
ATORI...

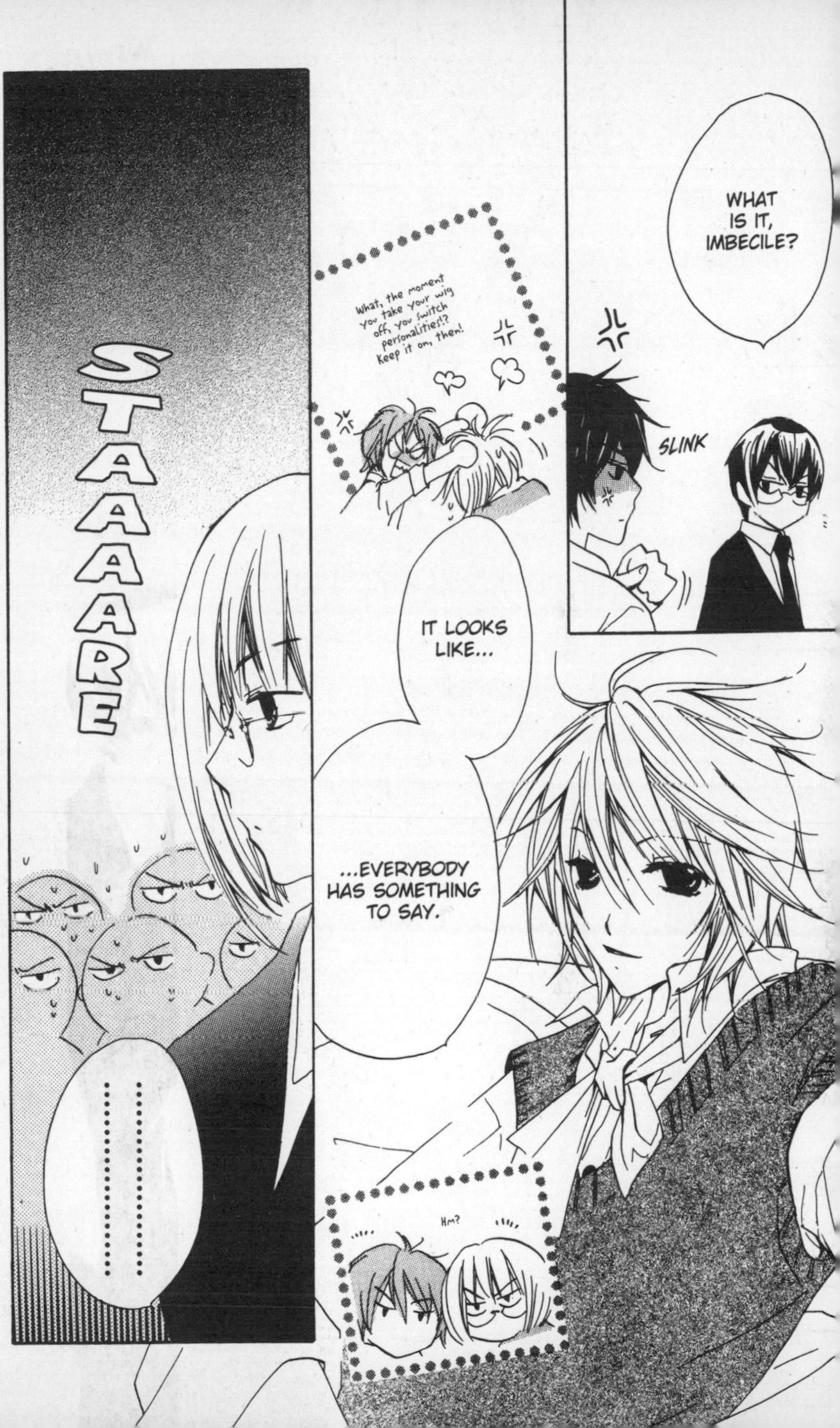
WHAT IS IT, IMBECILE?
SLINK
What, the moment you take your wig off, you switch personalities!? Keep it on, then!
IT LOOKS LIKE...
...EVERYBODY HAS SOMETHING TO SAY.
Hm?
STAAAARE
......

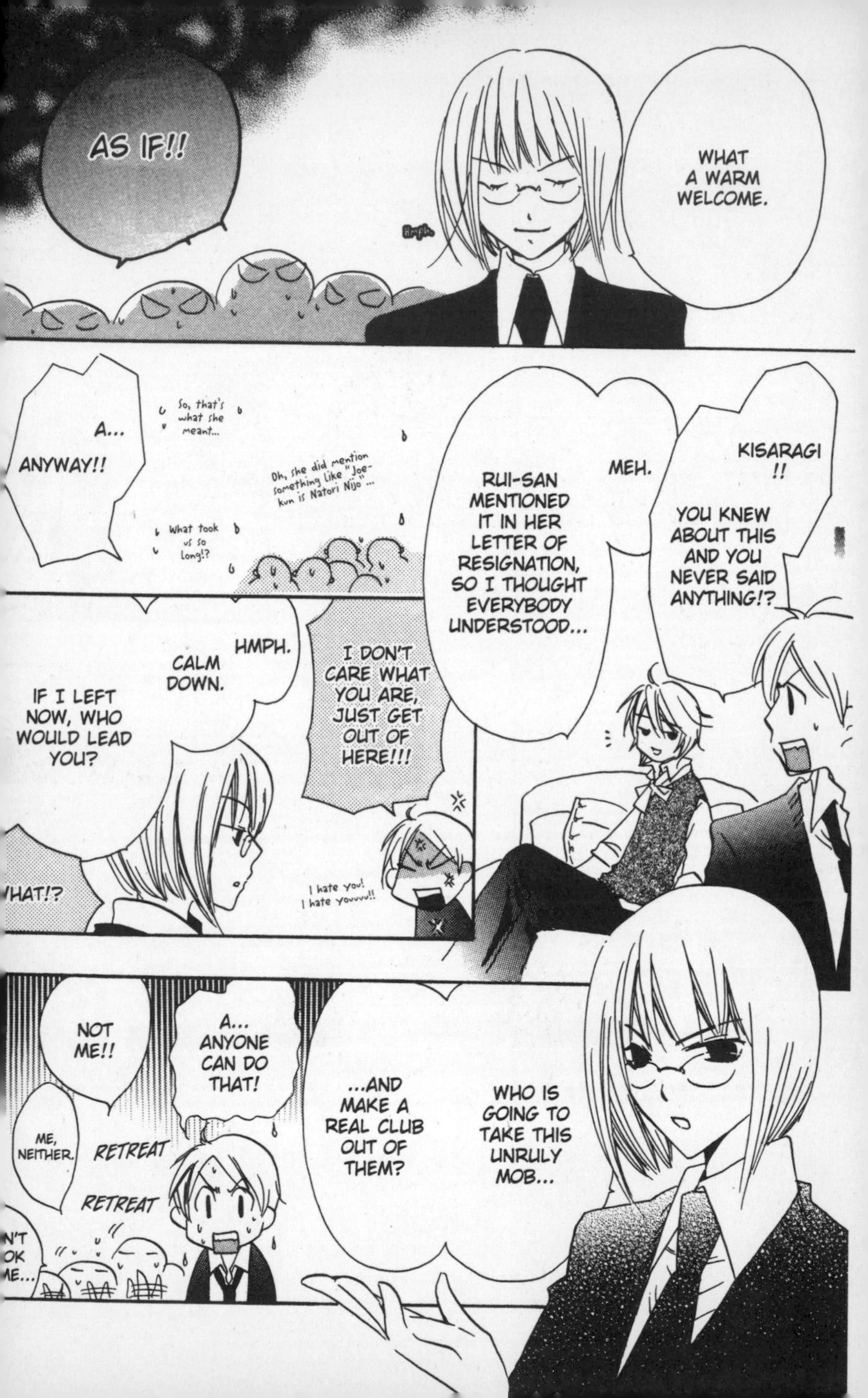
WHAT A WARM WELCOME.
Hmph.
AS IF!!
KISARAGI!!
YOU KNEW ABOUT THIS AND YOU NEVER SAID ANYTHING!?
MEH.
RUI-SAN MENTIONED IT IN HER LETTER OF RESIGNATION, SO I THOUGHT EVERYBODY UNDERSTOOD...
Oh, she did mention something like "Joe-kun is Natori Nijo"...
So, that's what she meant...
What took us so long!?
A... ANYWAY!!
I DON'T CARE WHAT YOU ARE, JUST GET OUT OF HERE!!!
I hate you! I hate youuuu!!
HMPH.
CALM DOWN.
IF I LEFT NOW, WHO WOULD LEAD YOU?
HAT!?
WHO IS GOING TO TAKE THIS UNRULY MOB...
...AND MAKE A REAL CLUB OUT OF THEM?
A... ANYONE CAN DO THAT!
NOT ME!!
ME, NEITHER.
RETREAT
RETREAT
N'T OK ME...

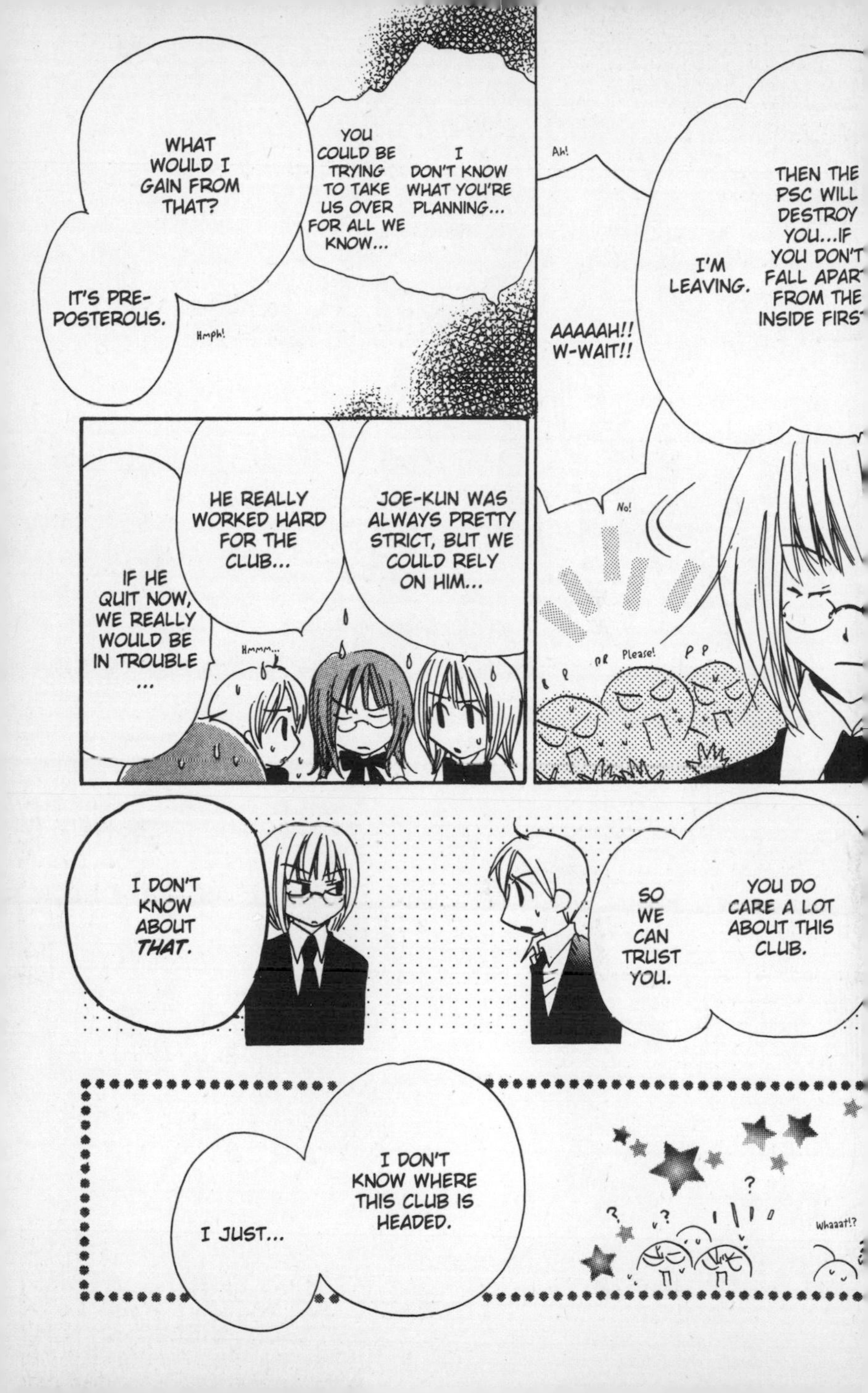
THEN THE PSC WILL DESTROY YOU...IF YOU DON'T FALL APART FROM THE INSIDE FIRST
I'M LEAVING.
Ah!
AAAAAH!! W-WAIT!!
No!
Please!
I DON'T KNOW WHAT YOU'RE PLANNING...
YOU COULD BE TRYING TO TAKE US OVER FOR ALL WE KNOW...
WHAT WOULD I GAIN FROM THAT?
IT'S PRE-POSTEROUS.
Hmph!
JOE-KUN WAS ALWAYS PRETTY STRICT, BUT WE COULD RELY ON HIM...
HE REALLY WORKED HARD FOR THE CLUB...
IF HE QUIT NOW, WE REALLY WOULD BE IN TROUBLE ...
Hmmm...
YOU DO CARE A LOT ABOUT THIS CLUB.
SO WE CAN TRUST YOU.
I DON'T KNOW ABOUT *THAT*.
Whaaat!?
I DON'T KNOW WHERE THIS CLUB IS HEADED.
I JUST...

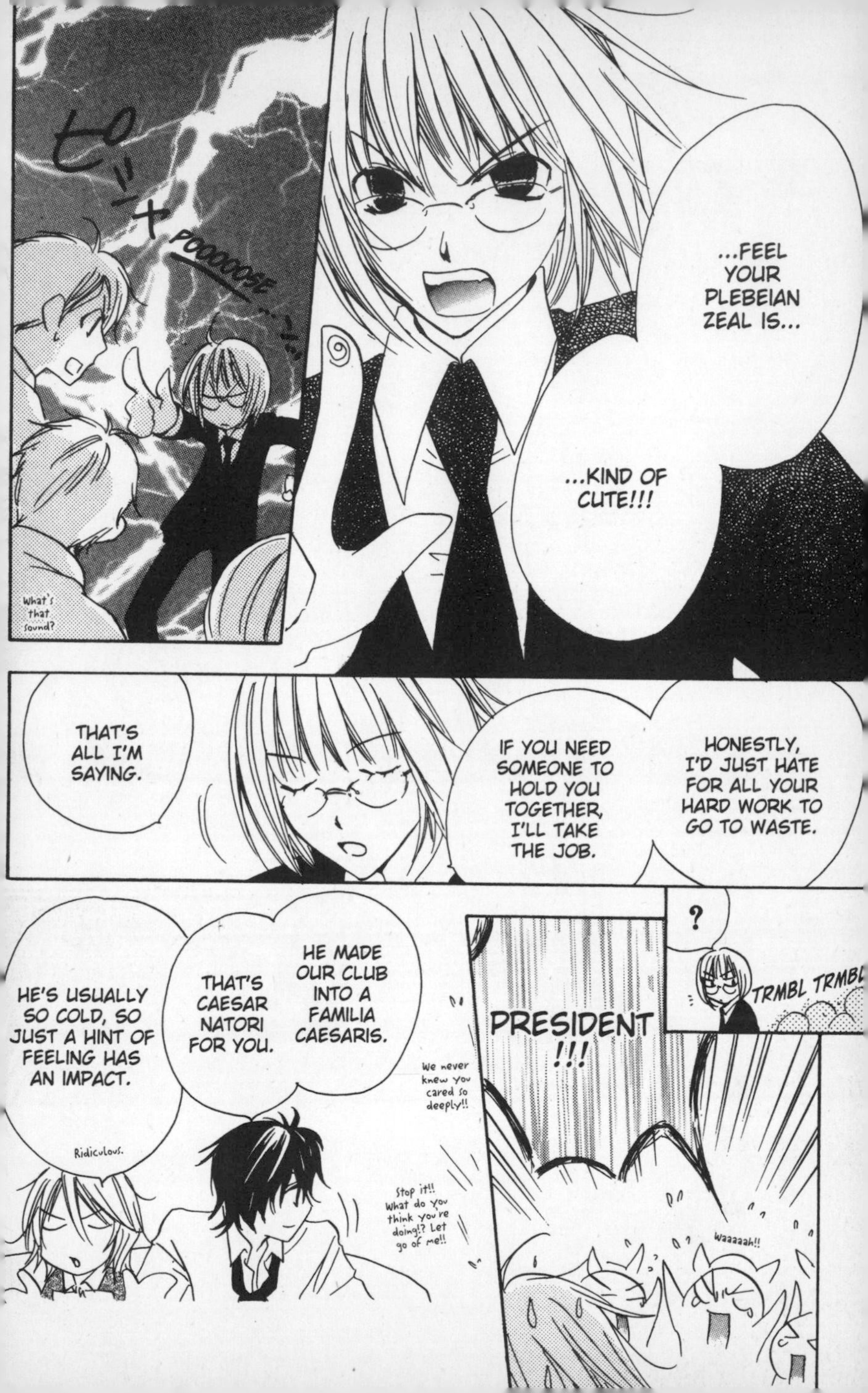
...FEEL YOUR PLEBEIAN ZEAL IS...
...KIND OF CUTE!!!
POOOOOOSE
What's that sound?
HONESTLY, I'D JUST HATE FOR ALL YOUR HARD WORK TO GO TO WASTE.
IF YOU NEED SOMEONE TO HOLD YOU TOGETHER, I'LL TAKE THE JOB.
THAT'S ALL I'M SAYING.
?
TRMBL TRMBL
PRESIDENT!!!
We never knew you cared so deeply!!
Stop it!! What do you think you're doing!? Let go of me!!
Waaaaah!!
HE MADE OUR CLUB INTO A FAMILIA CAESARIS.
THAT'S CAESAR NATORI FOR YOU.
HE'S USUALLY SO COLD, SO JUST A HINT OF FEELING HAS AN IMPACT.
Ridiculous.

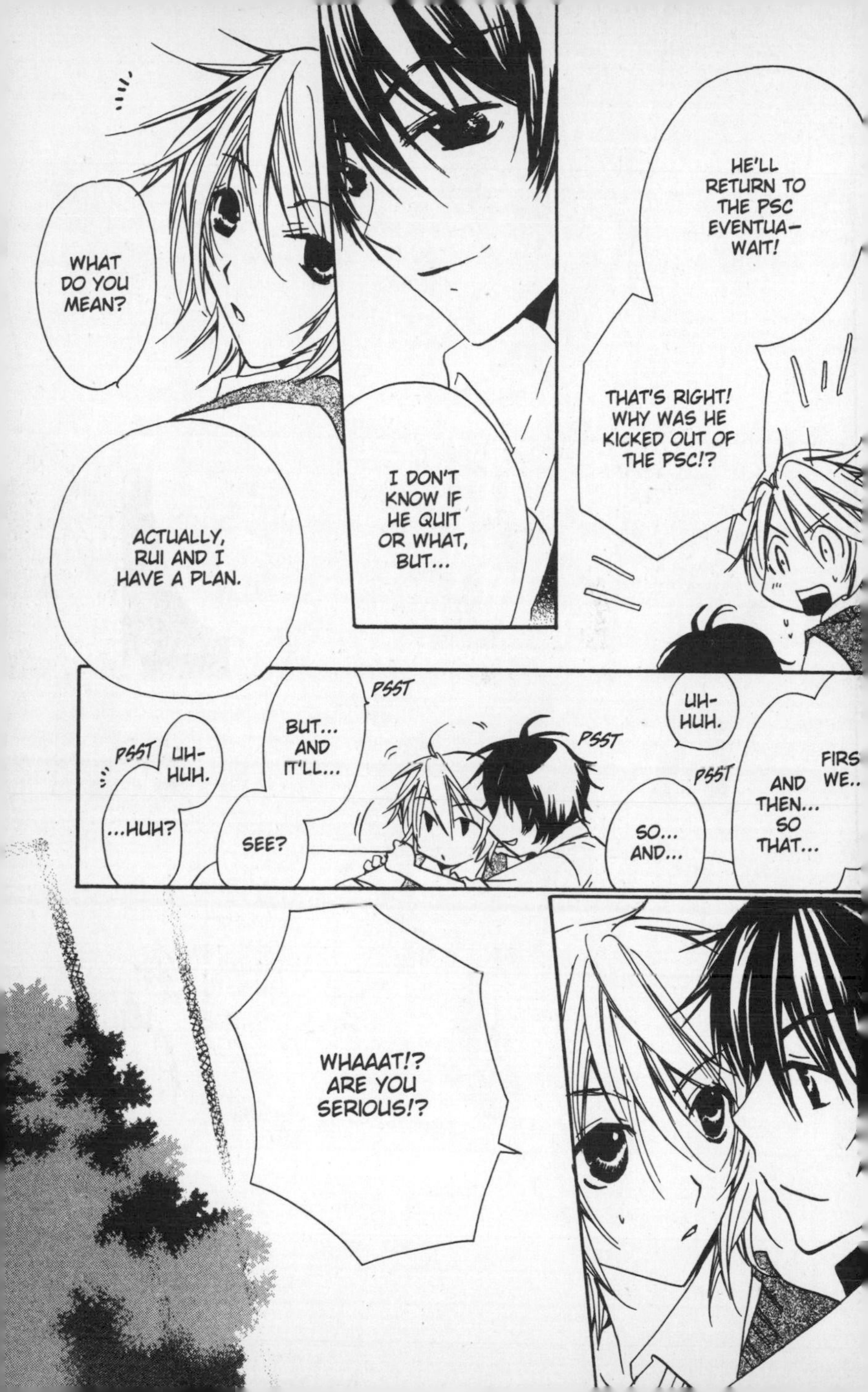
HE'LL RETURN TO THE PSC EVENTUA- WAIT!
THAT'S RIGHT! WHY WAS HE KICKED OUT OF THE PSC!?
I DON'T KNOW IF HE QUIT OR WHAT, BUT...
WHAT DO YOU MEAN?
ACTUALLY, RUI AND I HAVE A PLAN.
FIRS WE..
AND THEN... SO THAT...
UH-HUH.
PSST
SO... AND...
PSST
PSST
BUT... AND IT'LL...
SEE?
PSST
UH-HUH.
...HUH?
WHAAAT!? ARE YOU SERIOUS!?

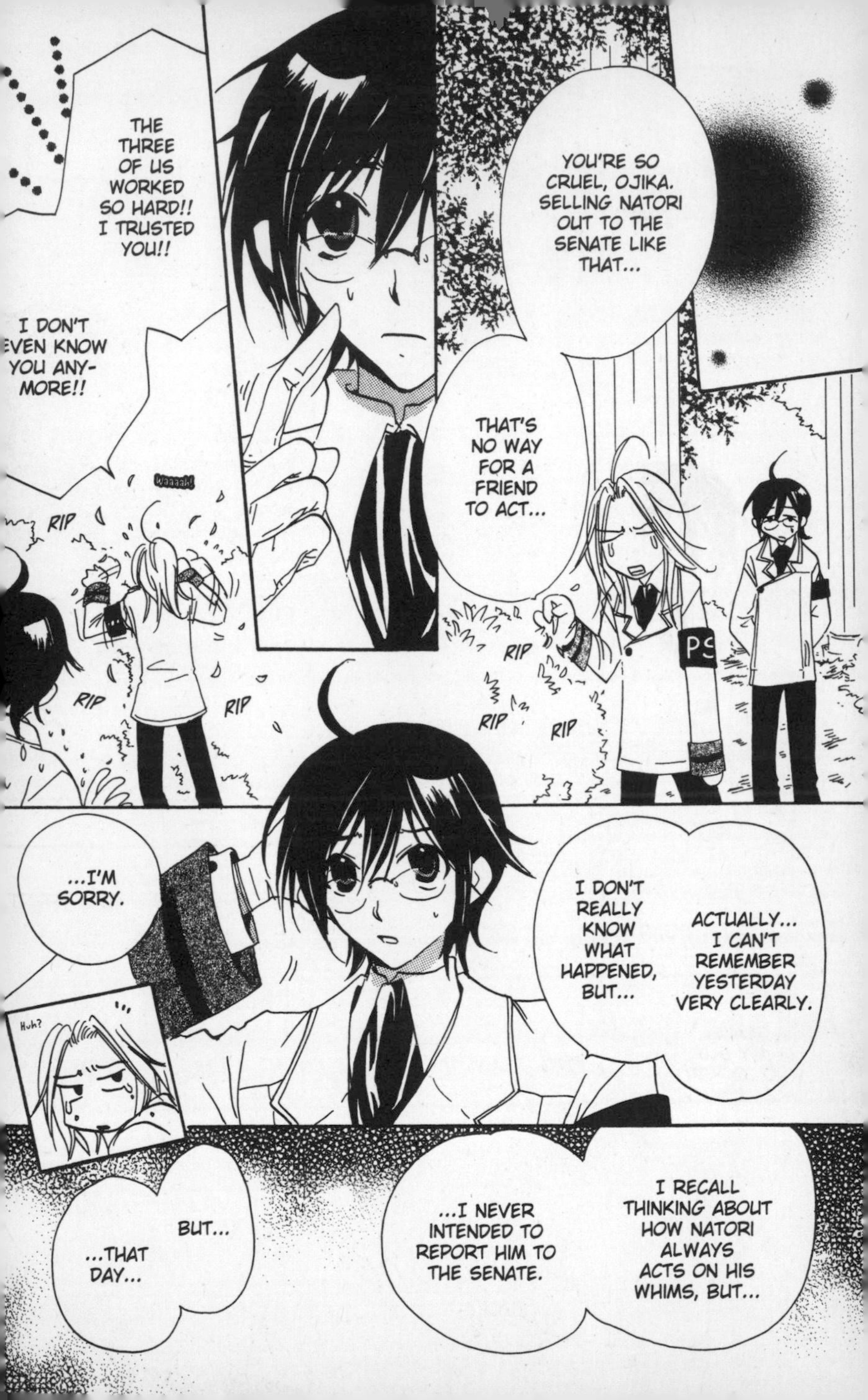

YOU'RE SO CRUEL, OJIKA. SELLING NATORI OUT TO THE SENATE LIKE THAT...
THAT'S NO WAY FOR A FRIEND TO ACT...
RIP
RIP
RIP
THE THREE OF US WORKED SO HARD!! I TRUSTED YOU!!
I DON'T EVEN KNOW YOU ANY-MORE!!
Waaaah!
RIP
RIP
RIP
ACTUALLY... I CAN'T REMEMBER YESTERDAY VERY CLEARLY.
I DON'T REALLY KNOW WHAT HAPPENED, BUT...
...I'M SORRY.
Huh?
...
I RECALL THINKING ABOUT HOW NATORI ALWAYS ACTS ON HIS WHIMS, BUT...
...I NEVER INTENDED TO REPORT HIM TO THE SENATE.
BUT...
...THAT DAY...

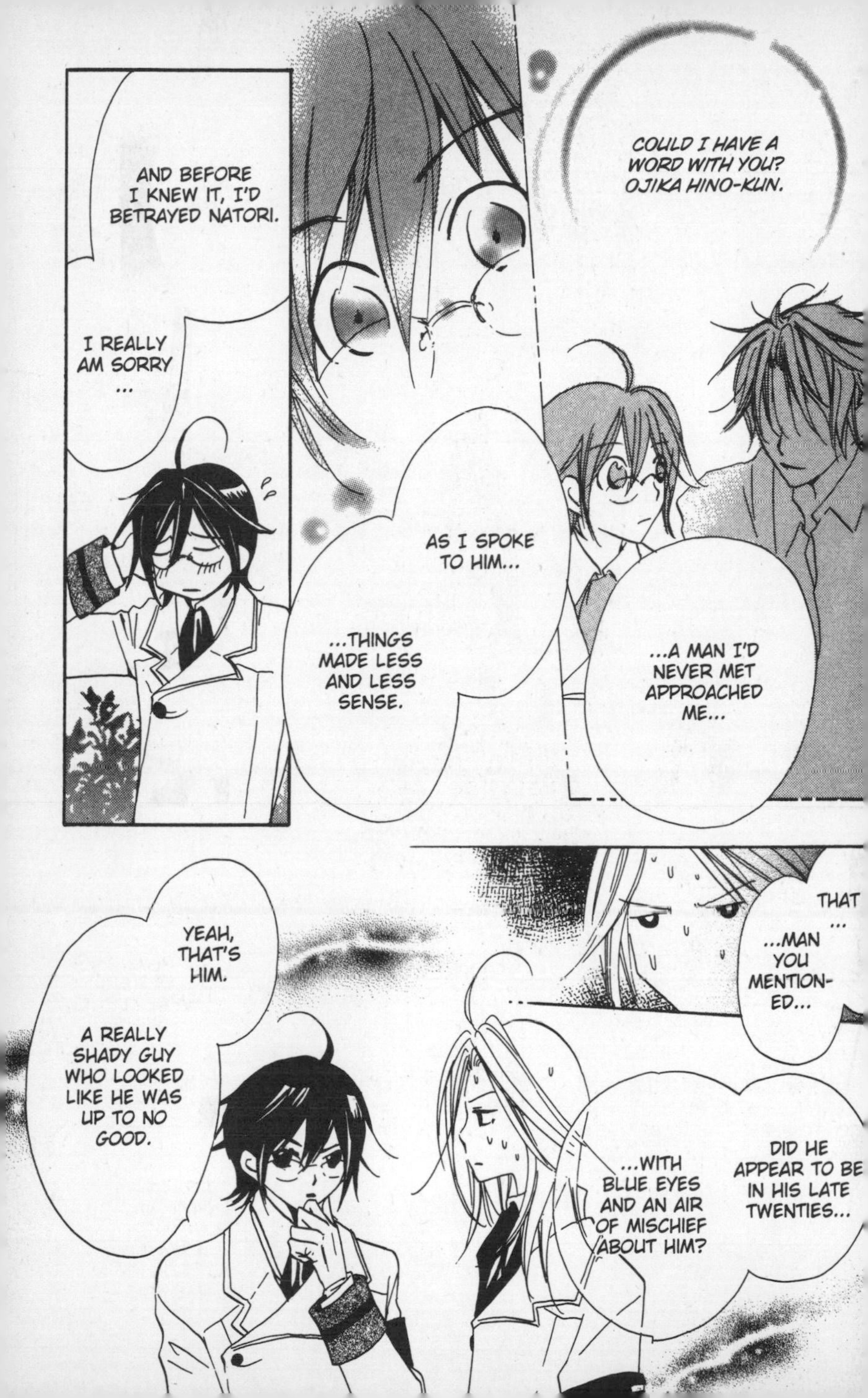
COULD I HAVE A WORD WITH YOU? OJIKA HINO-KUN.
...A MAN I'D NEVER MET APPROACHED ME...
AS I SPOKE TO HIM...
...THINGS MADE LESS AND LESS SENSE.
AND BEFORE I KNEW IT, I'D BETRAYED NATORI.
I REALLY AM SORRY...
THAT... ...MAN YOU MENTIONED...
DID HE APPEAR TO BE IN HIS LATE TWENTIES...
...WITH BLUE EYES AND AN AIR OF MISCHIEF ABOUT HIM?
YEAH, THAT'S HIM.
A REALLY SHADY GUY WHO LOOKED LIKE HE WAS UP TO NO GOOD.

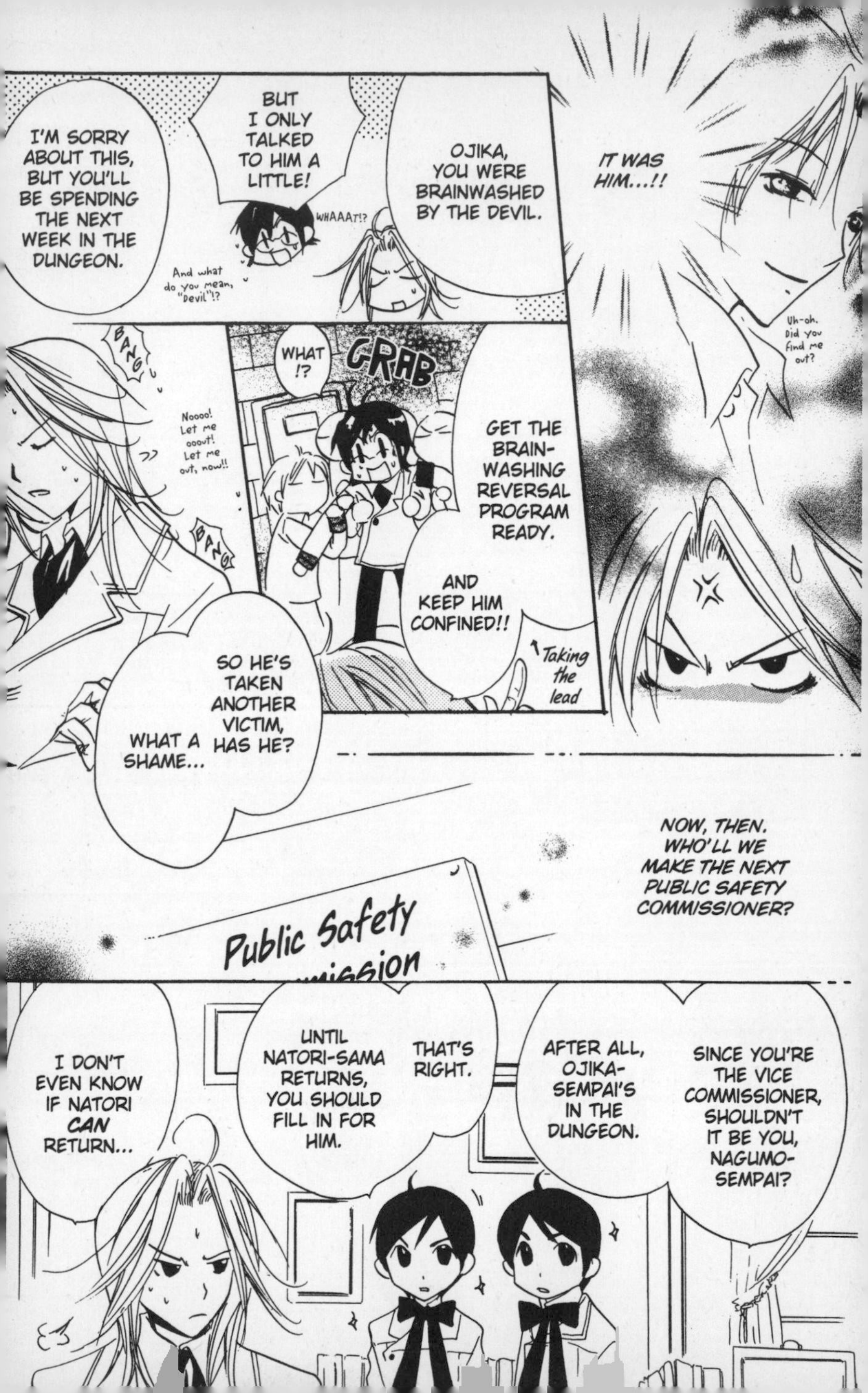
IT WAS HIM...!!
Uh-oh. Did you find me out?
OJIKA, YOU WERE BRAINWASHED BY THE DEVIL.
BUT I ONLY TALKED TO HIM A LITTLE!
WHAAAT!?
I'M SORRY ABOUT THIS, BUT YOU'LL BE SPENDING THE NEXT WEEK IN THE DUNGEON.
And what do you mean, "Devil"!?
GET THE BRAIN-WASHING REVERSAL PROGRAM READY.
GRAB
WHAT !?
AND KEEP HIM CONFINED!!
Taking the lead
BANG
Noooo! Let me ooout! Let me out, now!!
BANG
SO HE'S TAKEN ANOTHER VICTIM, HAS HE?
WHAT A SHAME...
NOW, THEN. WHO'LL WE MAKE THE NEXT PUBLIC SAFETY COMMISSIONER?
Public Safety
SINCE YOU'RE THE VICE COMMISSIONER, SHOULDN'T IT BE YOU, NAGUMO-SEMPAI?
AFTER ALL, OJIKA-SEMPAI'S IN THE DUNGEON.
THAT'S RIGHT.
UNTIL NATORI-SAMA RETURNS, YOU SHOULD FILL IN FOR HIM.
I DON'T EVEN KNOW IF NATORI CAN RETURN...

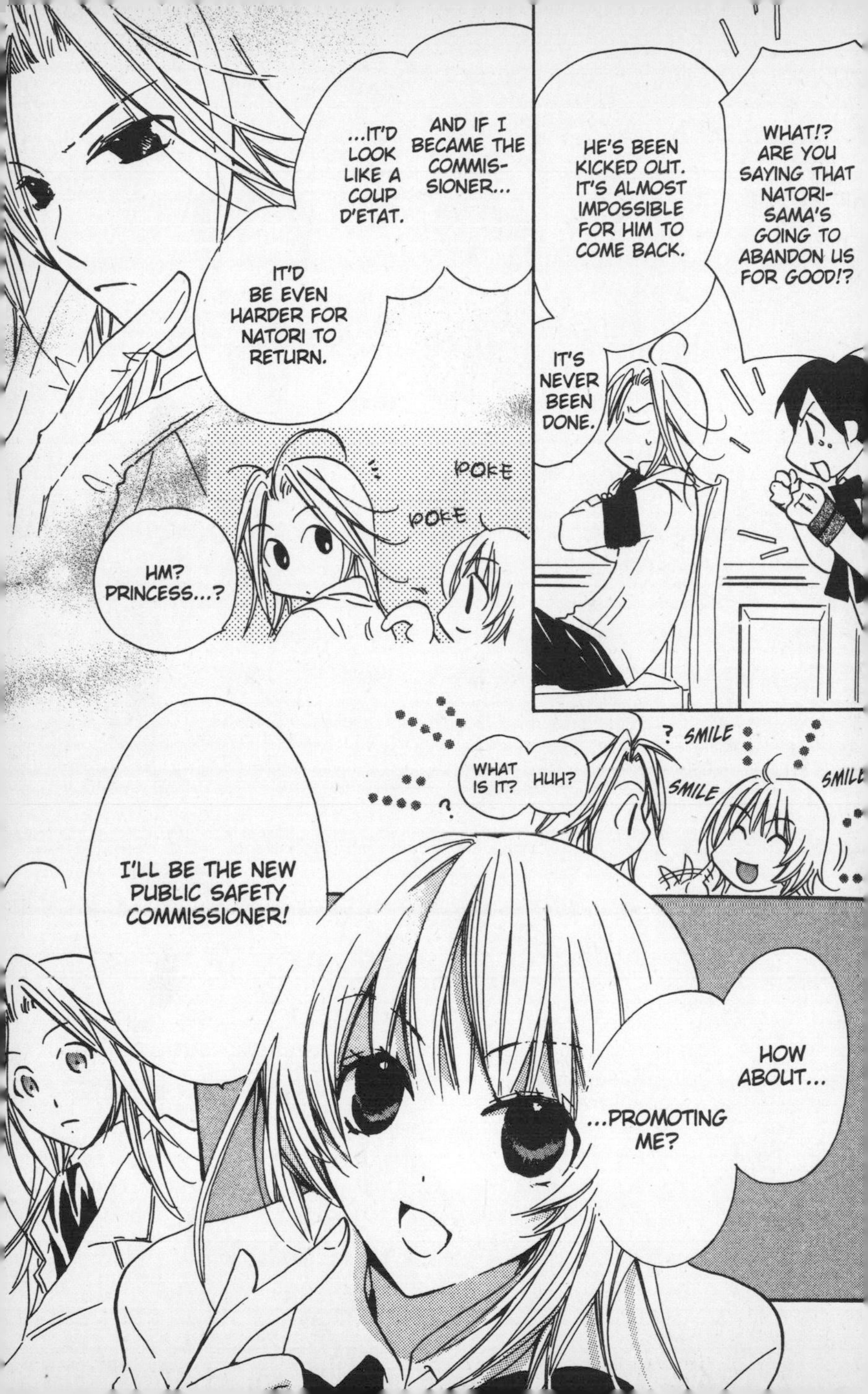
WHAT!? ARE YOU SAYING THAT NATORI-SAMA'S GOING TO ABANDON US FOR GOOD!?
HE'S BEEN KICKED OUT. IT'S ALMOST IMPOSSIBLE FOR HIM TO COME BACK.
IT'S NEVER BEEN DONE.
AND IF I BECAME THE COMMIS-SIONER...
...IT'D LOOK LIKE A COUP D'ETAT.
IT'D BE EVEN HARDER FOR NATORI TO RETURN.
POKE
POKE
HM? PRINCESS...?
SMILE
SMILE
?
HUH?
WHAT IS IT?
?
HOW ABOUT...
...PROMOTING ME?
I'LL BE THE NEW PUBLIC SAFETY COMMISSIONER!

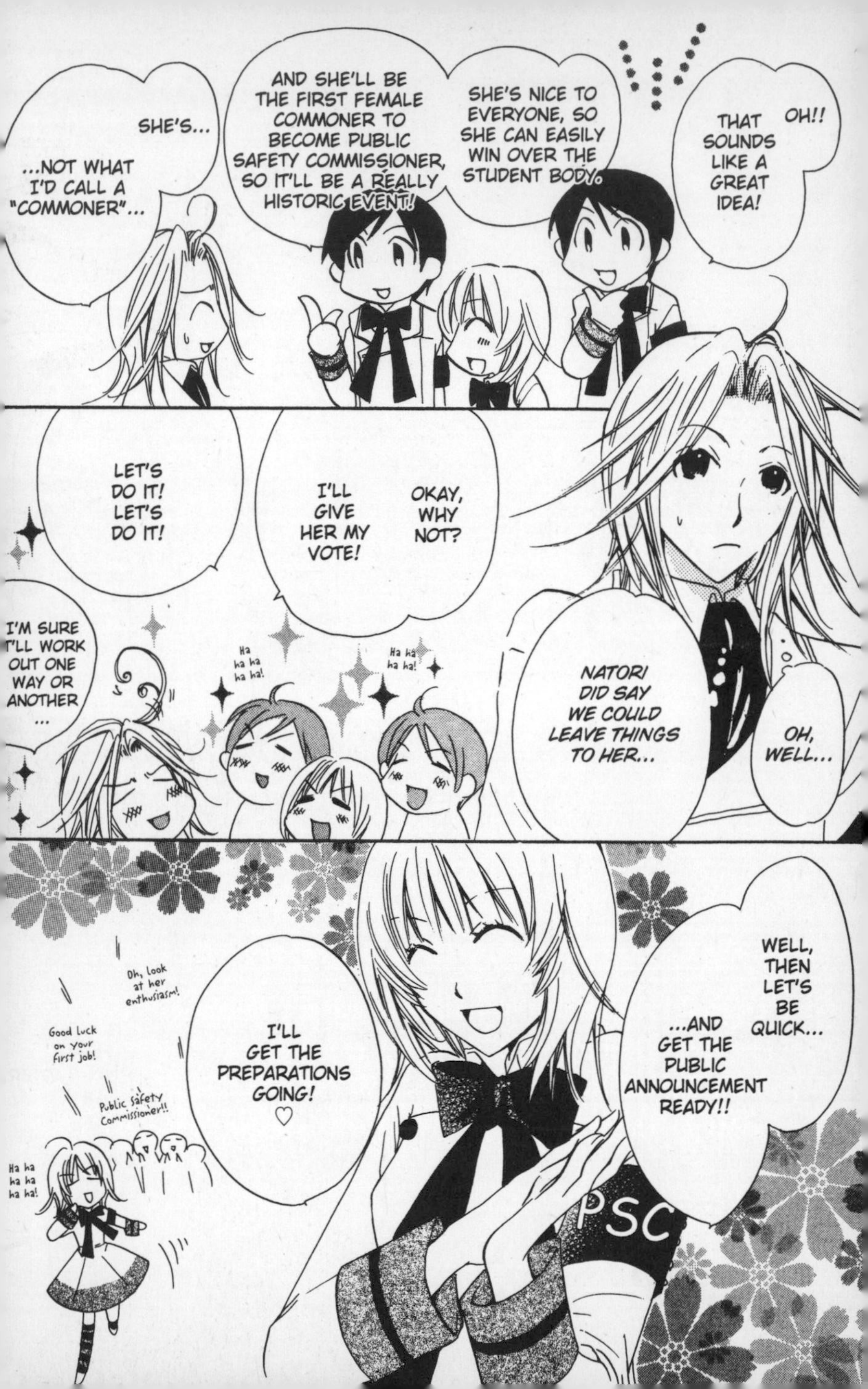
OH!!
THAT SOUNDS LIKE A GREAT IDEA!
SHE'S NICE TO EVERYONE, SO SHE CAN EASILY WIN OVER THE STUDENT BODY.
AND SHE'LL BE THE FIRST FEMALE COMMONER TO BECOME PUBLIC SAFETY COMMISSIONER, SO IT'LL BE A REALLY HISTORIC EVENT!
SHE'S...
...NOT WHAT I'D CALL A "COMMONER"...
NATORI DID SAY WE COULD LEAVE THINGS TO HER...
OH, WELL...
OKAY, WHY NOT?
I'LL GIVE HER MY VOTE!
LET'S DO IT! LET'S DO IT!
Ha ha ha ha!
Ha ha ha ha!
I'M SURE T'LL WORK OUT ONE WAY OR ANOTHER...
WELL, THEN LET'S BE QUICK...
...AND GET THE PUBLIC ANNOUNCEMENT READY!!
I'LL GET THE PREPARATIONS GOING! ♡
PSC
Oh, look at her enthusiasm!
Good luck on your first job!
Public Safety Commissioner!!
Ha ha ha ha ha ha!

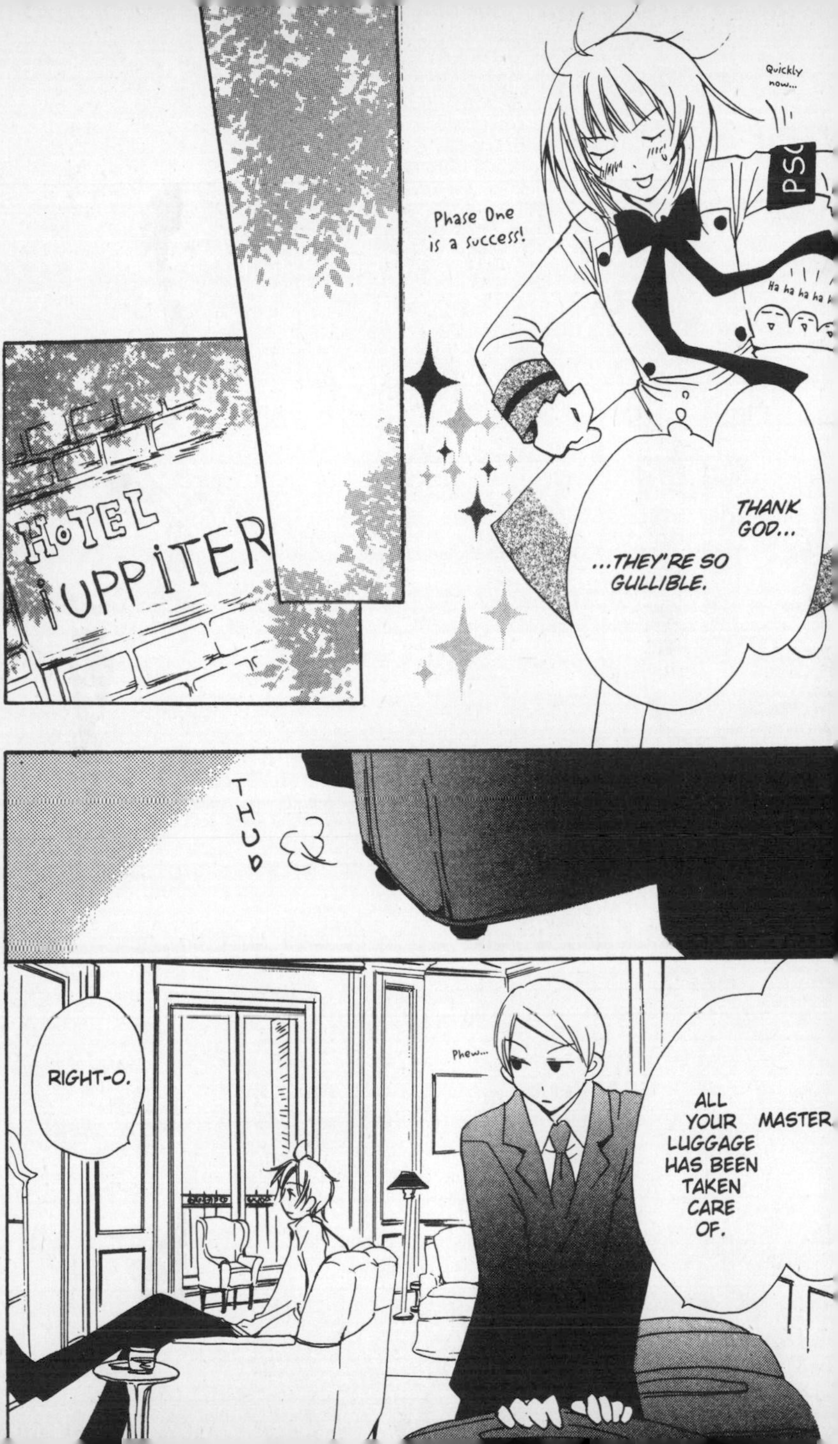
Quickly now...
Phase One is a success!
Ha ha ha ha
THANK GOD...
...THEY'RE SO GULLIBLE.
HOTEL JUPPITER
THUD
MASTER
ALL YOUR LUGGAGE HAS BEEN TAKEN CARE OF.
Phew...
RIGHT-O.

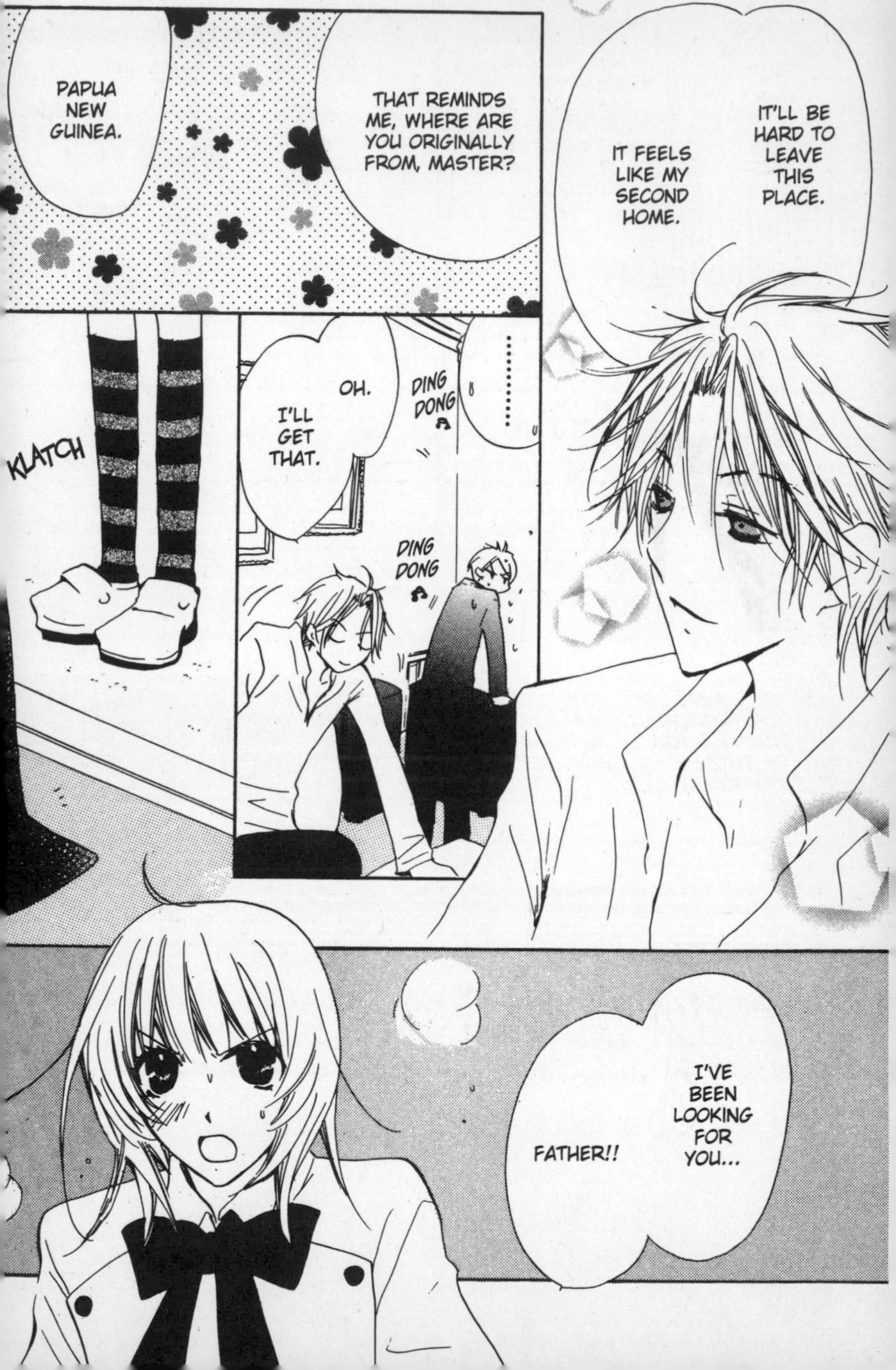
IT'LL BE HARD TO LEAVE THIS PLACE.
IT FEELS LIKE MY SECOND HOME.
THAT REMINDS ME, WHERE ARE YOU ORIGINALLY FROM, MASTER?
PAPUA NEW GUINEA.
......
DING DONG
OH.
I'LL GET THAT.
DING DONG
KLATCH
I'VE BEEN LOOKING FOR YOU...
FATHER!!

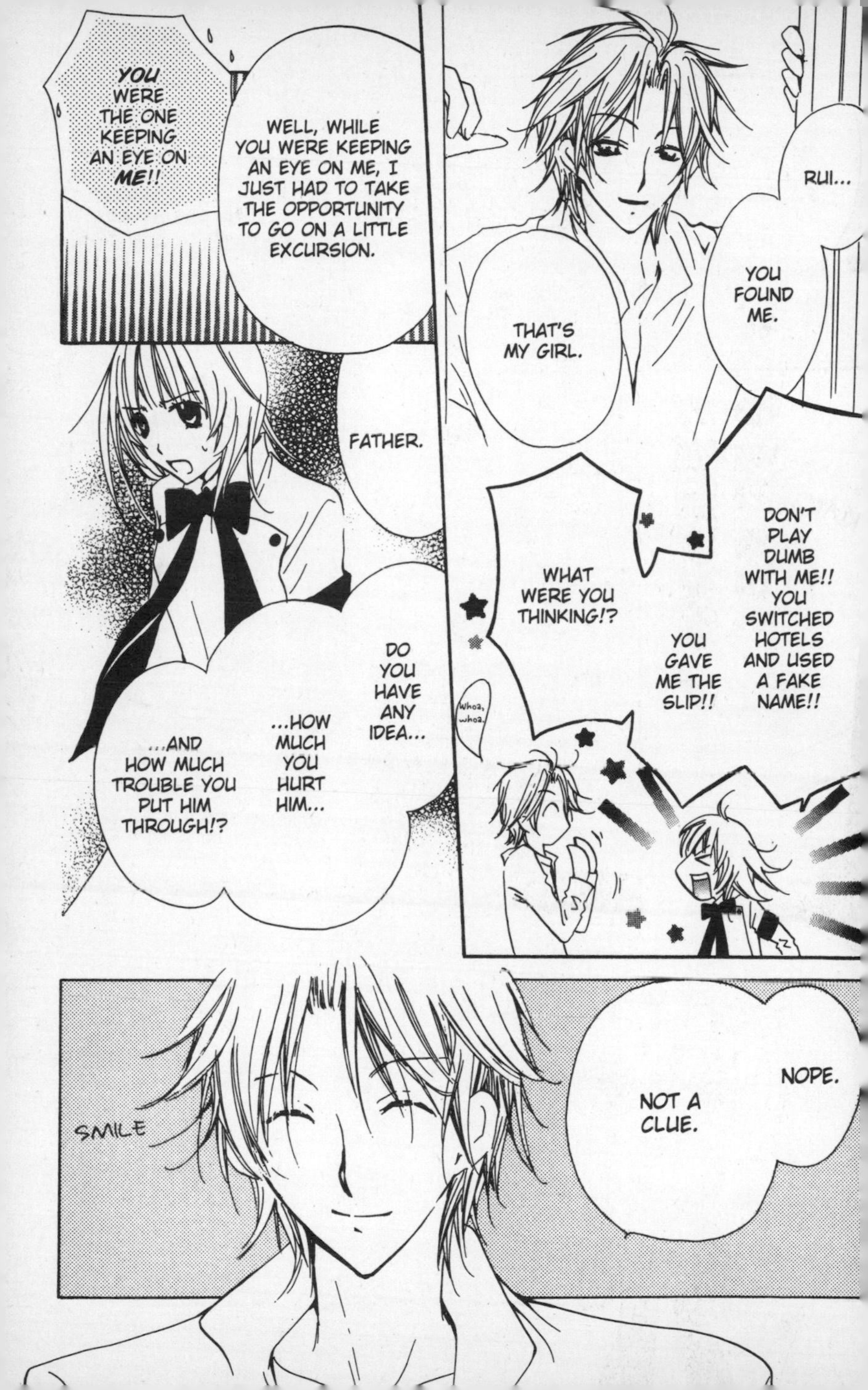
RUI...
YOU FOUND ME.
THAT'S MY GIRL.
WELL, WHILE YOU WERE KEEPING AN EYE ON ME, I JUST HAD TO TAKE THE OPPORTUNITY TO GO ON A LITTLE EXCURSION.
YOU WERE THE ONE KEEPING AN EYE ON ME!!
DON'T PLAY DUMB WITH ME!! YOU SWITCHED HOTELS AND USED A FAKE NAME!!
YOU GAVE ME THE SLIP!!
WHAT WERE YOU THINKING!?
Whoa, whoa.
FATHER.
DO YOU HAVE ANY IDEA...
...HOW MUCH YOU HURT HIM...
...AND HOW MUCH TROUBLE YOU PUT HIM THROUGH!?
NOPE.
NOT A CLUE.
SMILE

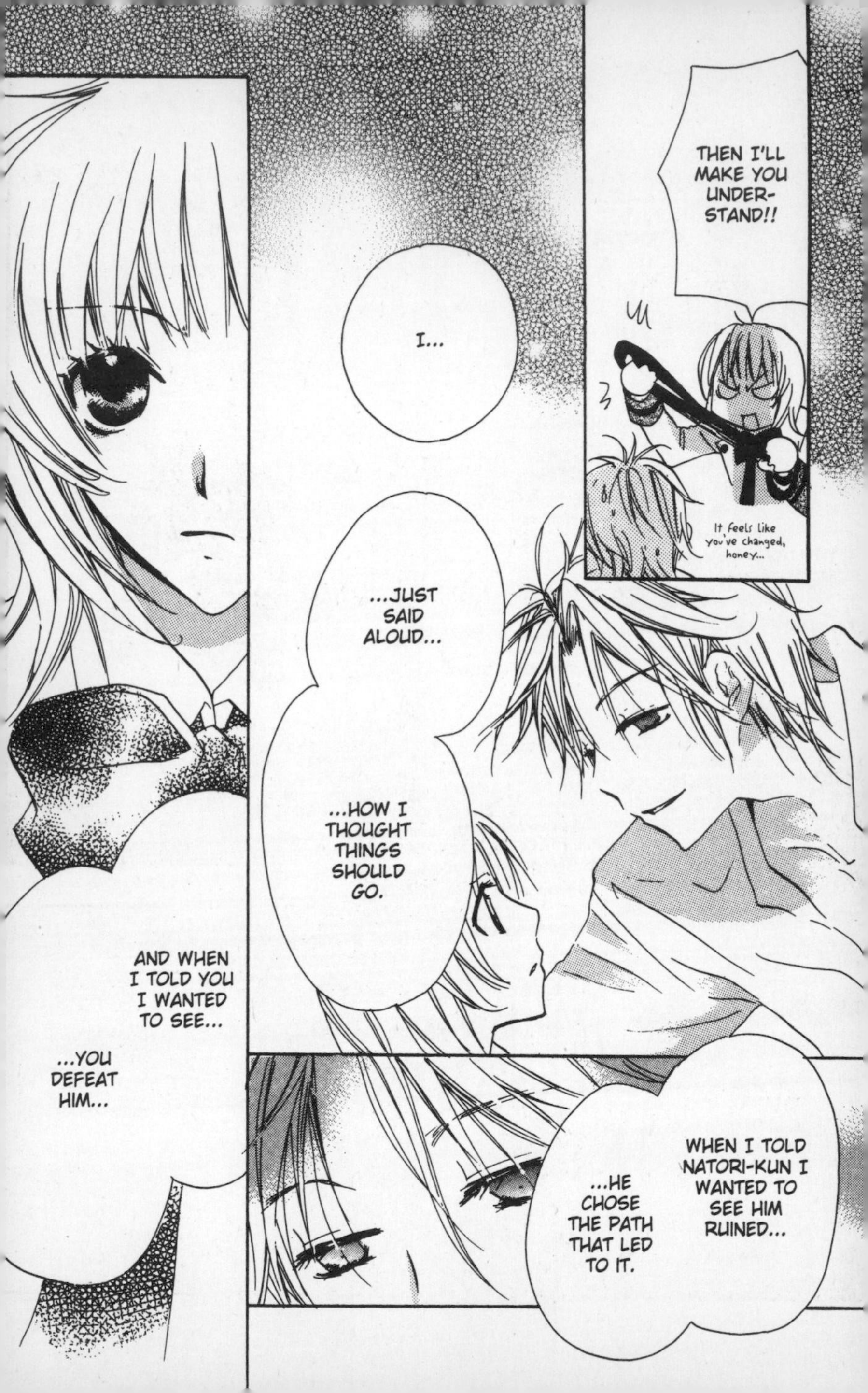
THEN I'LL MAKE YOU UNDER-STAND!!
It feels like you've changed, honey...
I...
...JUST SAID ALOUD...
...HOW I THOUGHT THINGS SHOULD GO.
WHEN I TOLD NATORI-KUN I WANTED TO SEE HIM RUINED...
...HE CHOSE THE PATH THAT LED TO IT.
AND WHEN I TOLD YOU I WANTED TO SEE...
...YOU DEFEAT HIM...

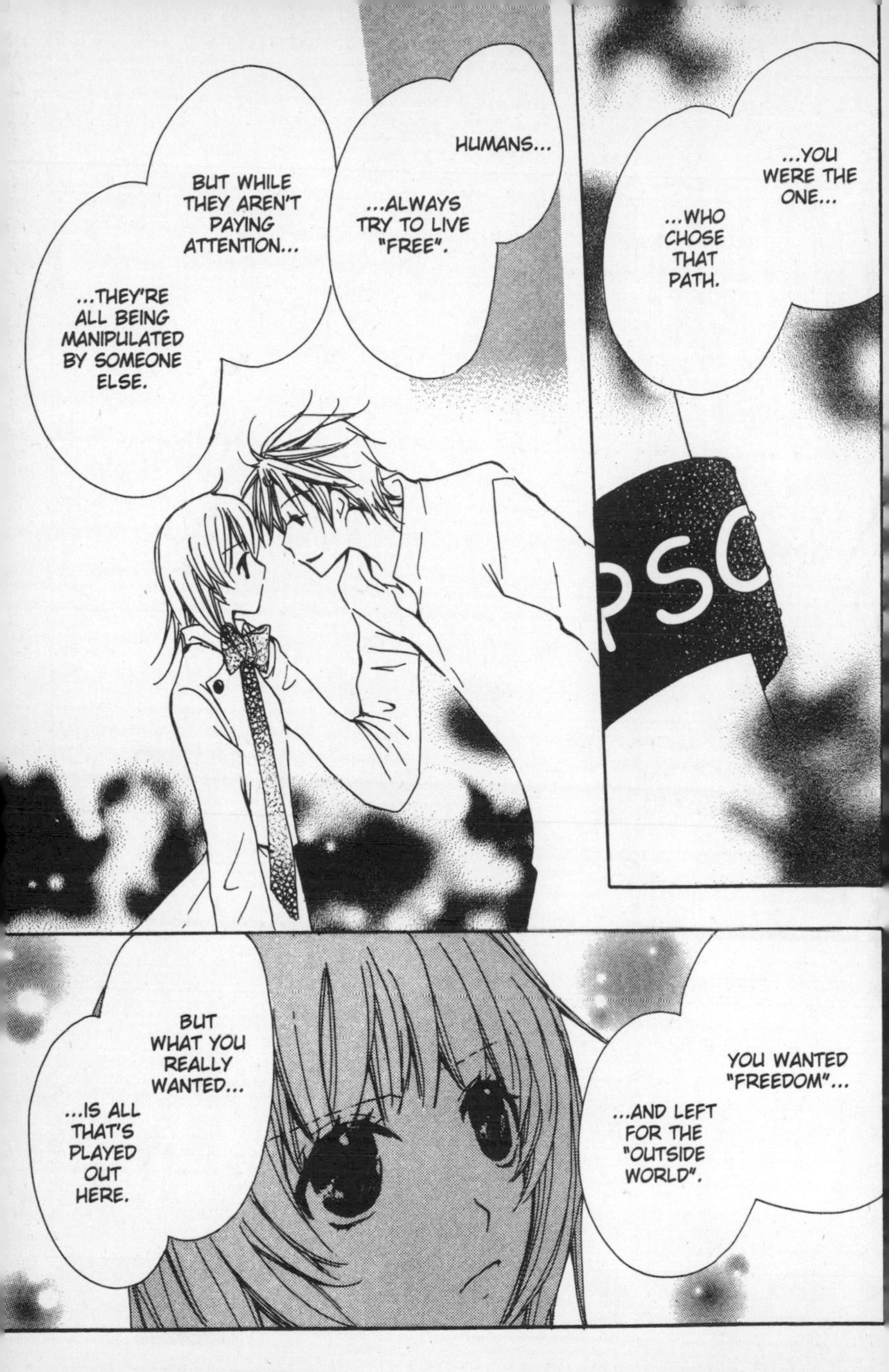
...YOU WERE THE ONE...
...WHO CHOSE THAT PATH.
PSC
HUMANS...
...ALWAYS TRY TO LIVE "FREE".
BUT WHILE THEY AREN'T PAYING ATTENTION...
...THEY'RE ALL BEING MANIPULATED BY SOMEONE ELSE.
YOU WANTED "FREEDOM"...
...AND LEFT FOR THE "OUTSIDE WORLD".
BUT WHAT YOU REALLY WANTED...
...IS ALL THAT'S PLAYED OUT HERE.

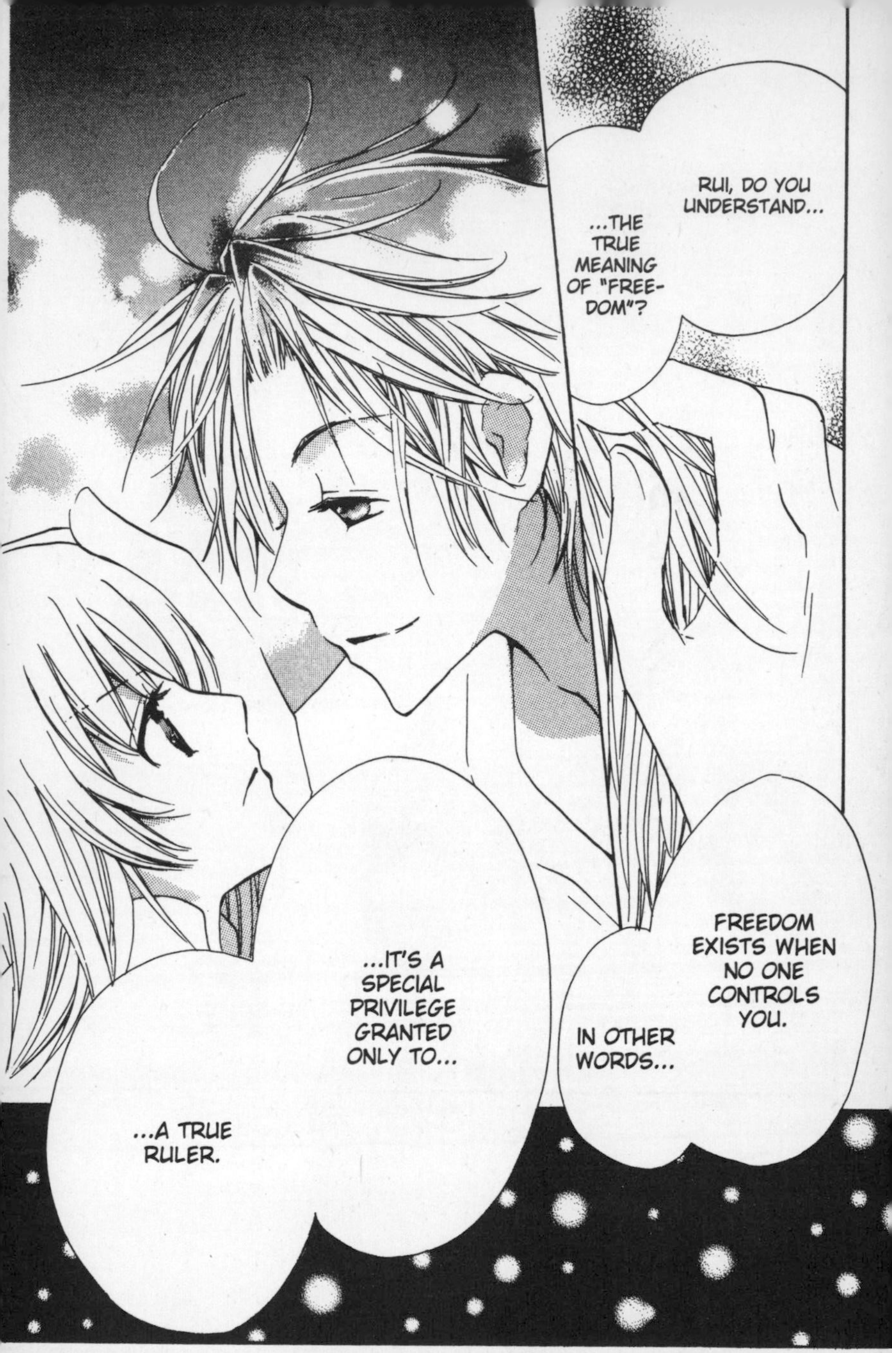
RUI, DO YOU UNDERSTAND...
...THE TRUE MEANING OF "FREE-DOM"?
FREEDOM EXISTS WHEN NO ONE CONTROLS YOU.
IN OTHER WORDS...
...IT'S A SPECIAL PRIVILEGE GRANTED ONLY TO...
...A TRUE RULER.

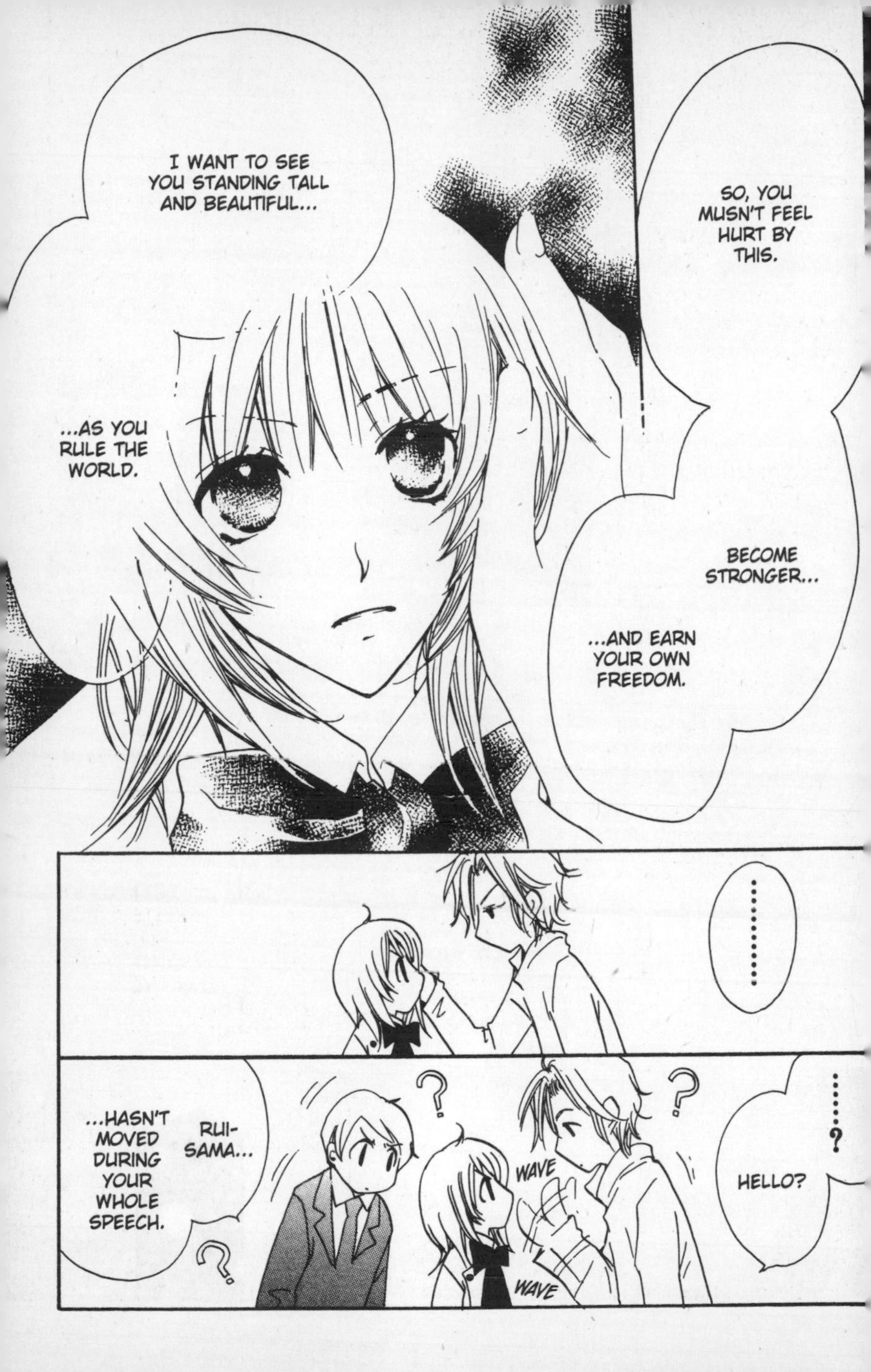
SO, YOU MUSN'T FEEL HURT BY THIS.
I WANT TO SEE YOU STANDING TALL AND BEAUTIFUL...
...AS YOU RULE THE WORLD.
BECOME STRONGER...
...AND EARN YOUR OWN FREEDOM.
......
......?
HELLO?
WAVE
WAVE
RUI-SAMA...
...HASN'T MOVED DURING YOUR WHOLE SPEECH.

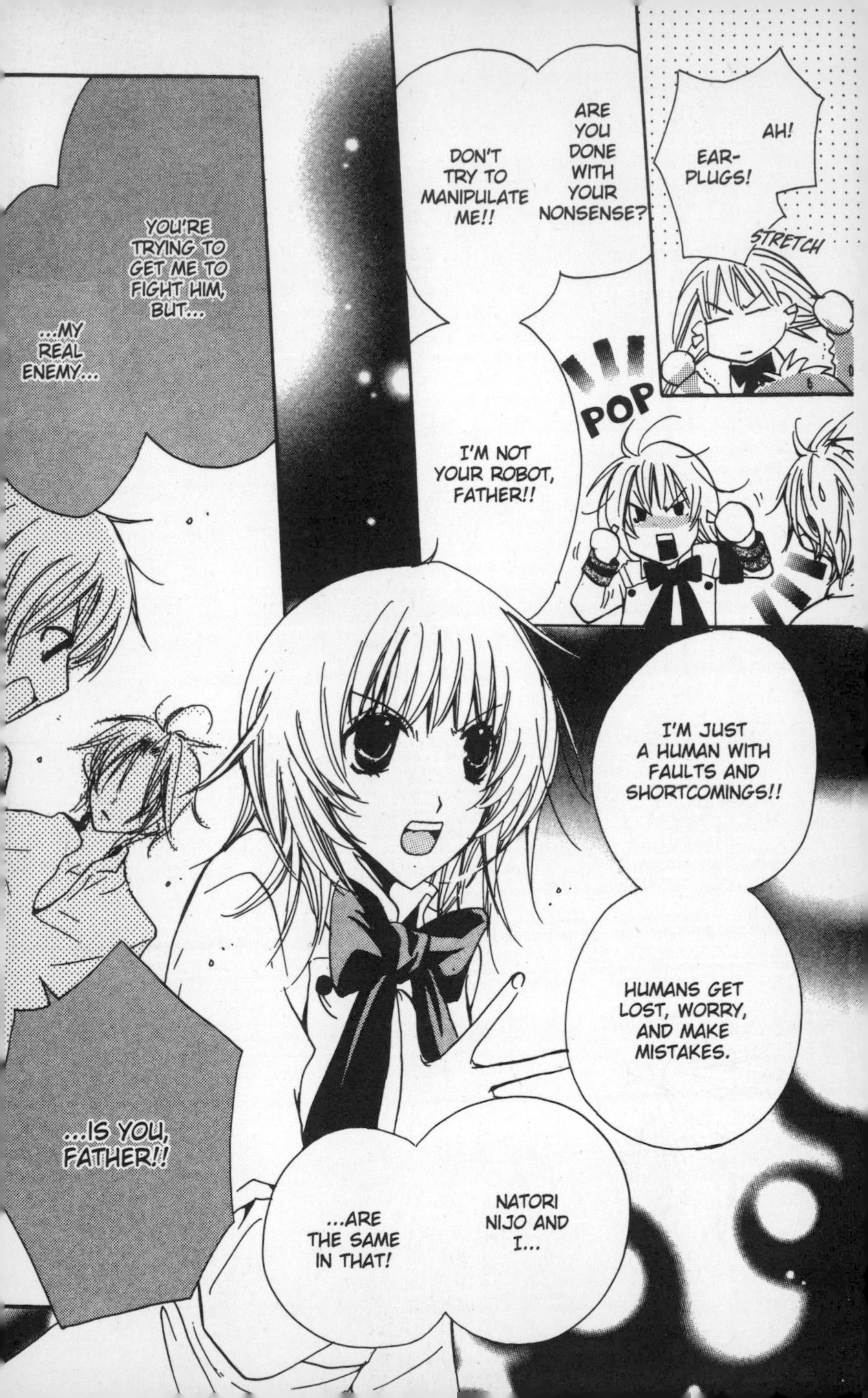
AH!
EAR-PLUGS!
STRETCH
POP
ARE YOU DONE WITH YOUR NONSENSE?
DON'T TRY TO MANIPULATE ME!!
I'M NOT YOUR ROBOT, FATHER!!
YOU'RE TRYING TO GET ME TO FIGHT HIM, BUT...
...MY REAL ENEMY...
...IS YOU, FATHER!!
I'M JUST A HUMAN WITH FAULTS AND SHORTCOMINGS!!
HUMANS GET LOST, WORRY, AND MAKE MISTAKES.
NATORI NIJO AND I...
...ARE THE SAME IN THAT!

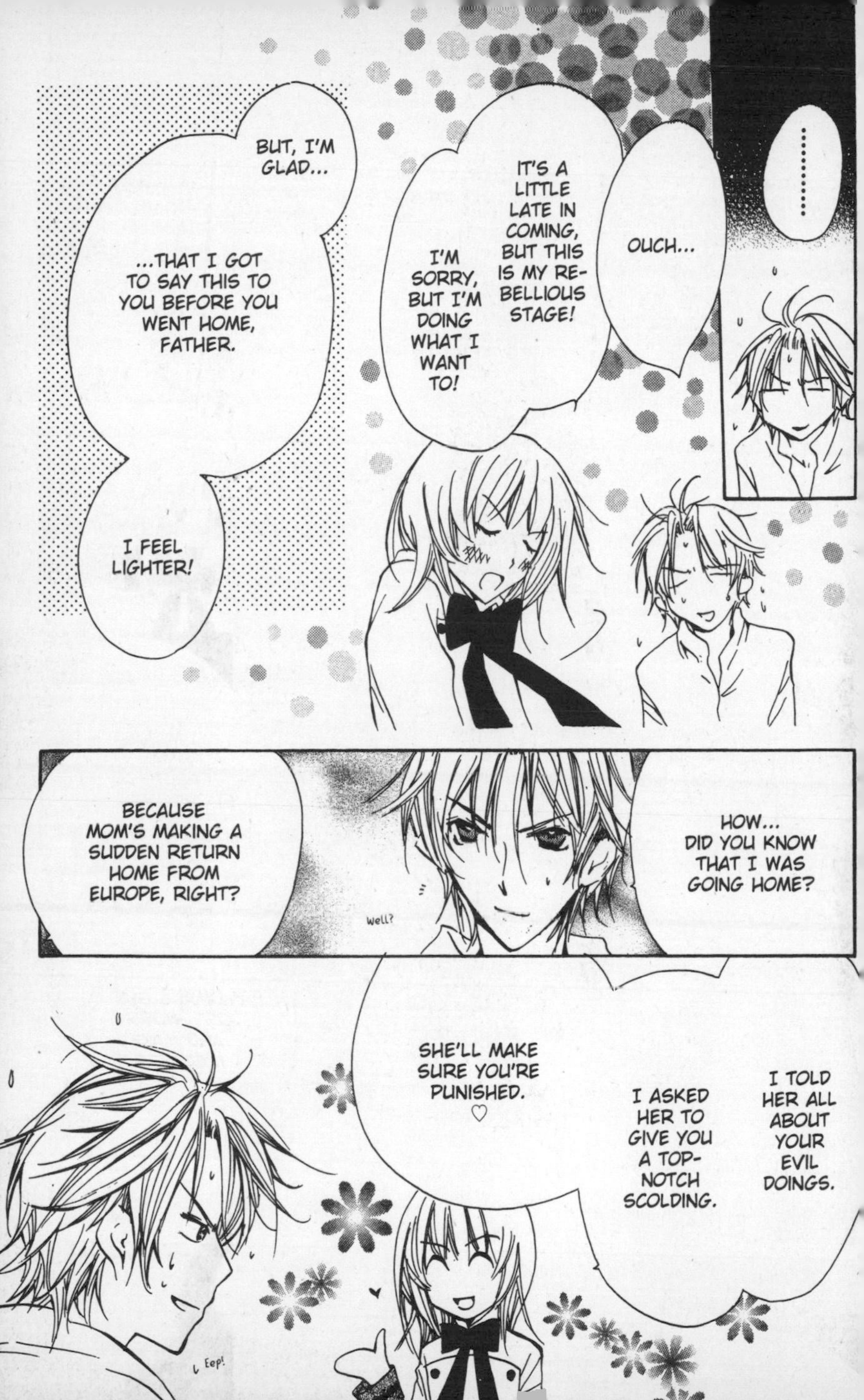
......
OUCH...
IT'S A LITTLE LATE IN COMING, BUT THIS IS MY RE-BELLIOUS STAGE!
I'M SORRY, BUT I'M DOING WHAT I WANT TO!
BUT, I'M GLAD...
...THAT I GOT TO SAY THIS TO YOU BEFORE YOU WENT HOME, FATHER.
I FEEL LIGHTER!
HOW... DID YOU KNOW THAT I WAS GOING HOME?
Well?
BECAUSE MOM'S MAKING A SUDDEN RETURN HOME FROM EUROPE, RIGHT?
I TOLD HER ALL ABOUT YOUR EVIL DOINGS.
I ASKED HER TO GIVE YOU A TOP-NOTCH SCOLDING.
SHE'LL MAKE SURE YOU'RE PUNISHED. ♡
Eep!

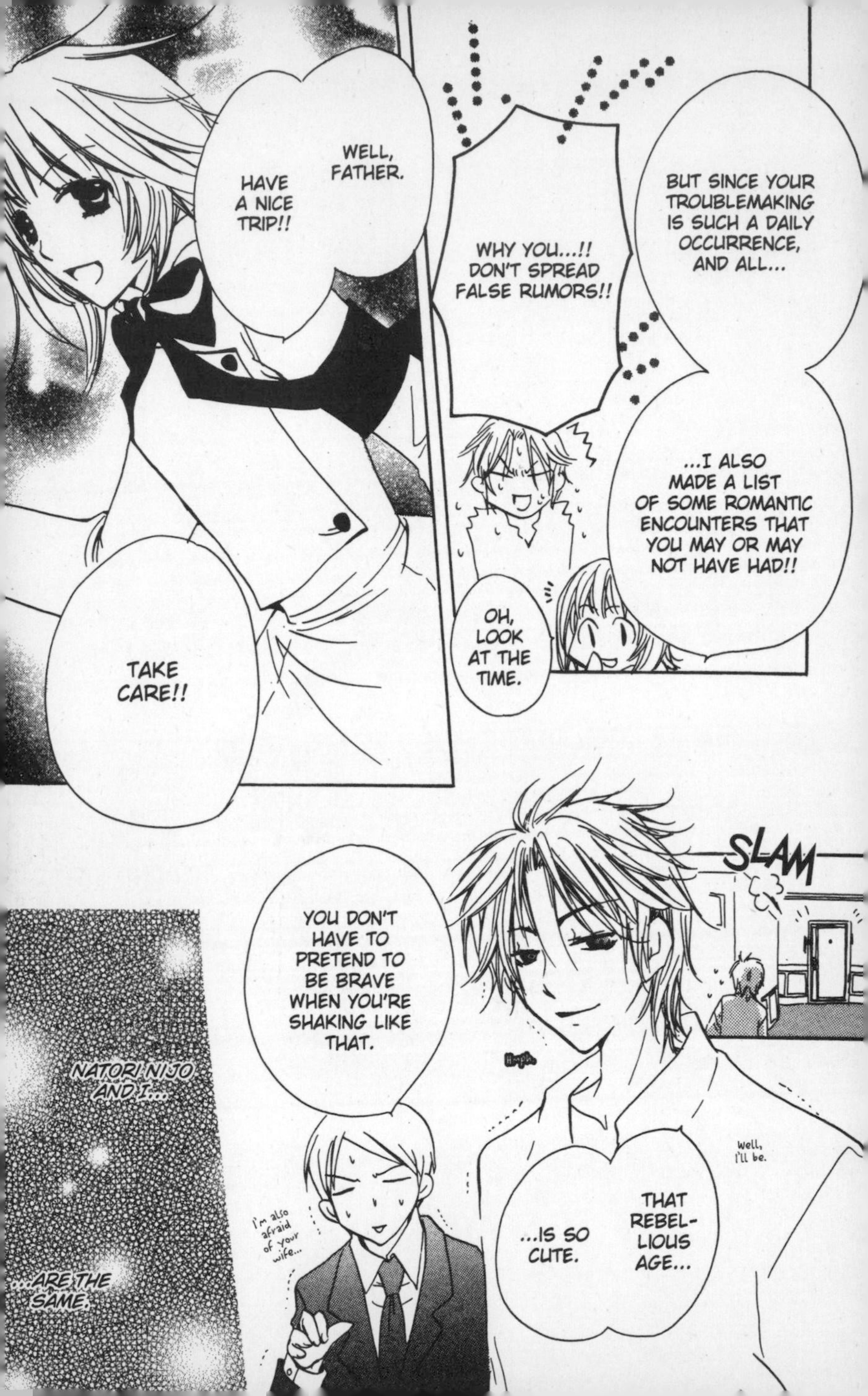
BUT SINCE YOUR TROUBLEMAKING IS SUCH A DAILY OCCURRENCE, AND ALL...
WHY YOU...!! DON'T SPREAD FALSE RUMORS!!
...I ALSO MADE A LIST OF SOME ROMANTIC ENCOUNTERS THAT YOU MAY OR MAY NOT HAVE HAD!!
OH, LOOK AT THE TIME.
WELL, FATHER.
HAVE A NICE TRIP!!
TAKE CARE!!
SLAM
Well, I'll be.
THAT REBELLIOUS AGE...
...IS SO CUTE.
Hmph.
YOU DON'T HAVE TO PRETEND TO BE BRAVE WHEN YOU'RE SHAKING LIKE THAT.
I'm also afraid of your wife...
NATORI NIJO AND I...
...ARE THE SAME.

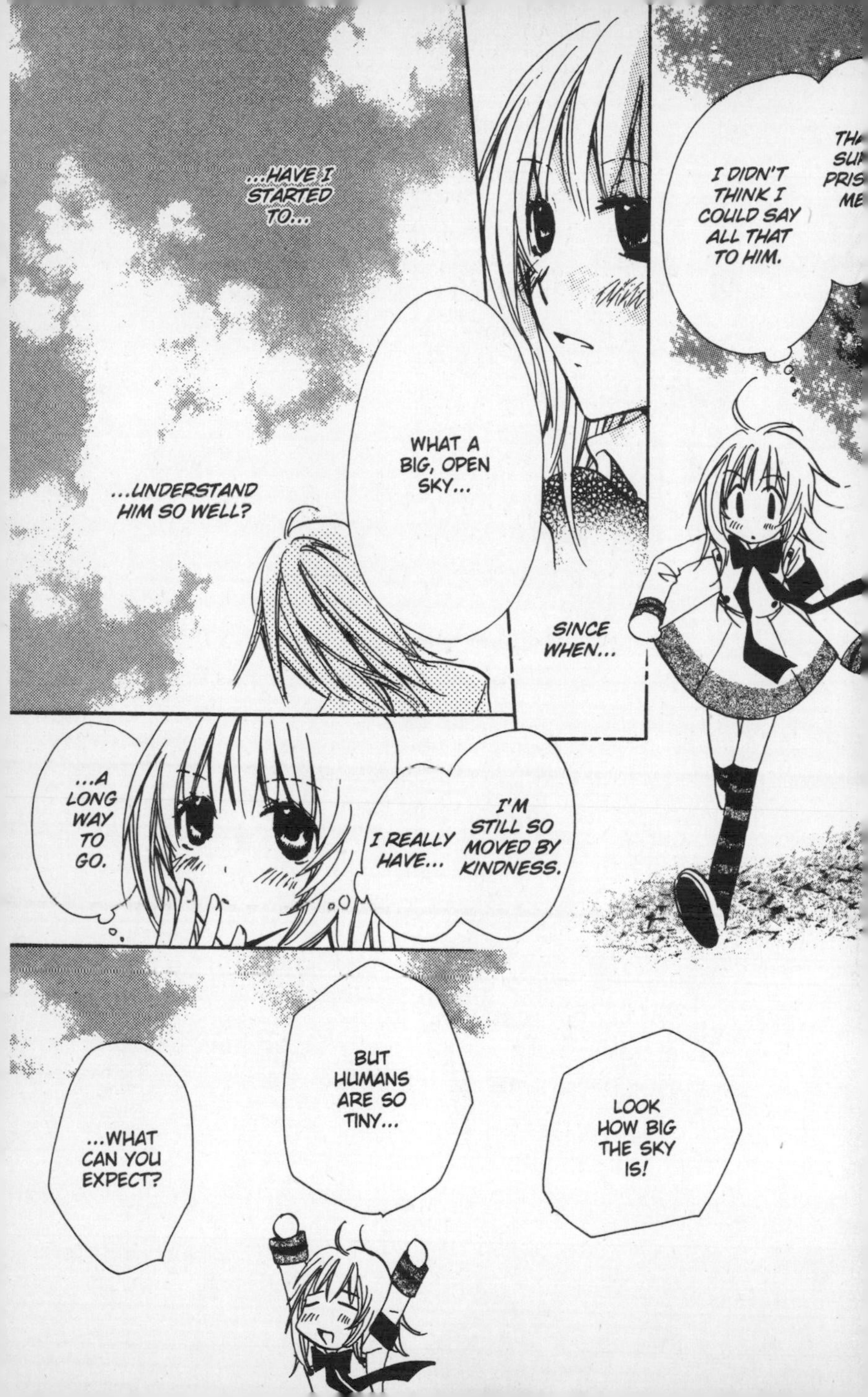
I DIDN'T THINK I COULD SAY ALL THAT TO HIM.
WHAT A BIG, OPEN SKY...
SINCE WHEN...
...HAVE I STARTED TO...
...UNDERSTAND HIM SO WELL?
I'M STILL SO MOVED BY KINDNESS.
I REALLY HAVE...
...A LONG WAY TO GO.
LOOK HOW BIG THE SKY IS!
BUT HUMANS ARE SO TINY...
...WHAT CAN YOU EXPECT?

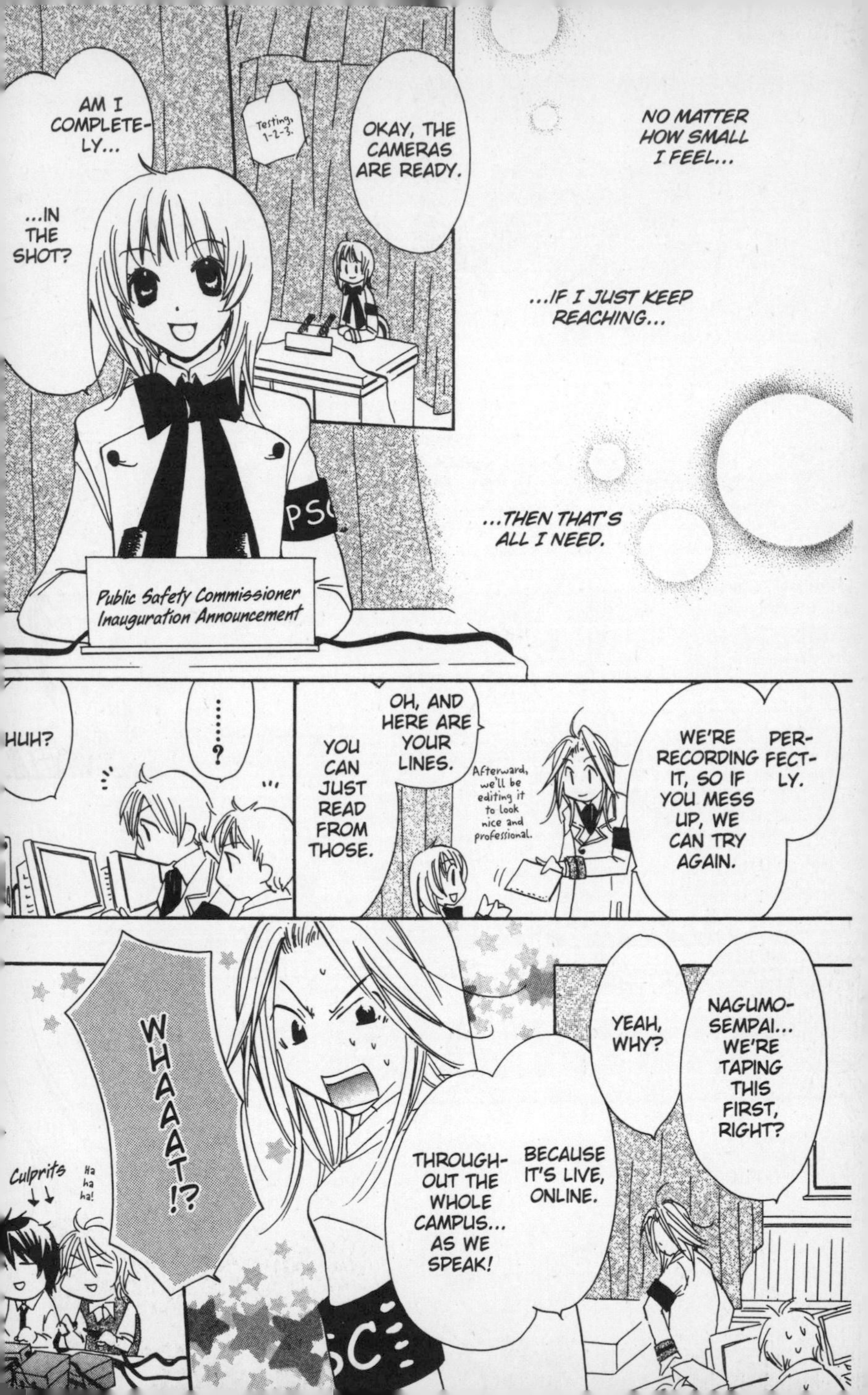
NO MATTER HOW SMALL I FEEL...
...IF I JUST KEEP REACHING...
...THEN THAT'S ALL I NEED.
OKAY, THE CAMERAS ARE READY.
Testing, 1-2-3.
AM I COMPLETELY...
...IN THE SHOT?
Public Safety Commissioner Inauguration Announcement
PSC
PERFECTLY.
WE'RE RECORDING IT, SO IF YOU MESS UP, WE CAN TRY AGAIN.
Afterward, we'll be editing it to look nice and professional.
OH, AND HERE ARE YOUR LINES.
YOU CAN JUST READ FROM THOSE.
......?
HUH?
NAGUMO-SEMPAI... WE'RE TAPING THIS FIRST, RIGHT?
YEAH, WHY?
BECAUSE IT'S LIVE, ONLINE.
THROUGHOUT THE WHOLE CAMPUS... AS WE SPEAK!
WHAAAT!?
Culprits
Ha ha ha!

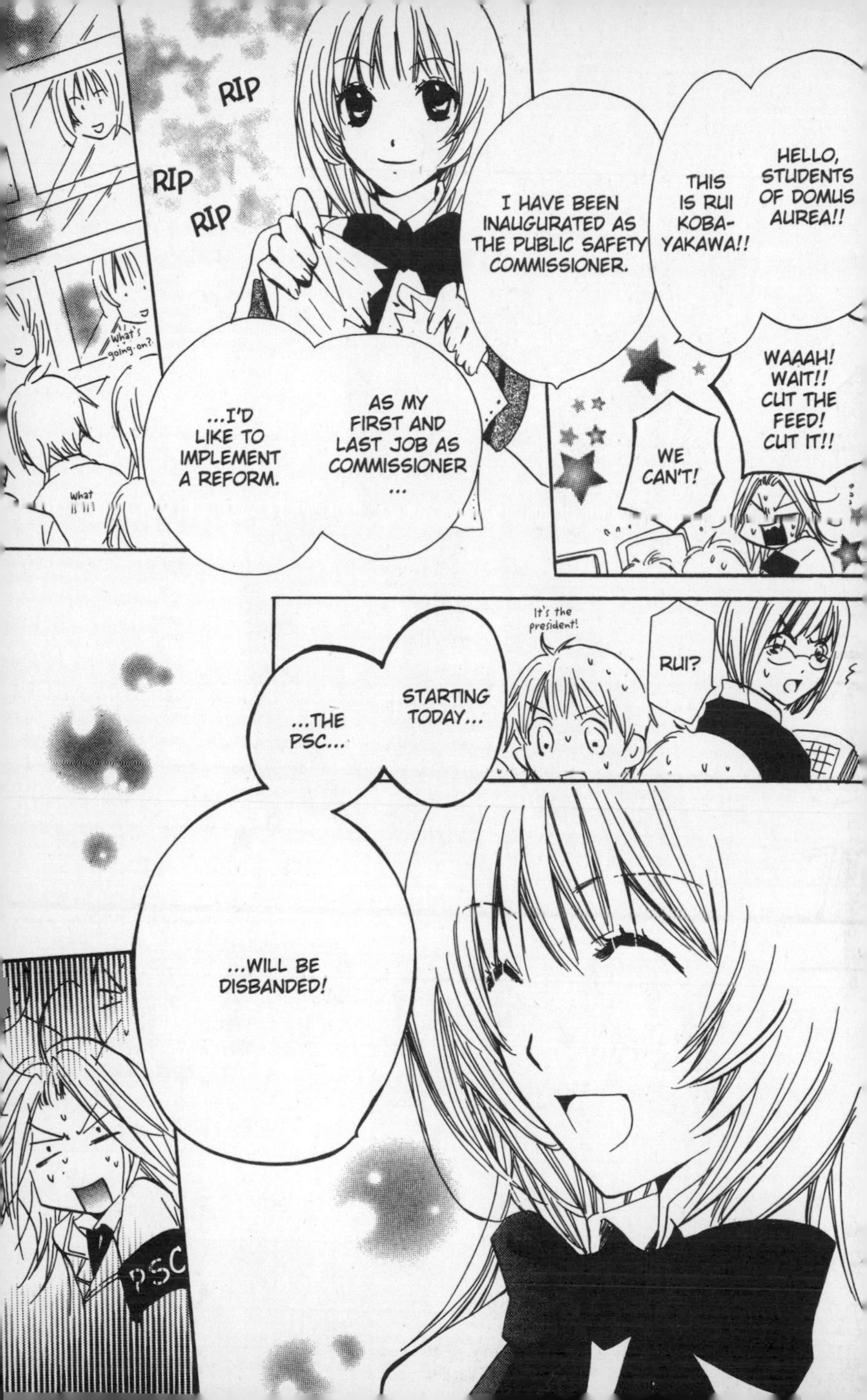
HELLO, STUDENTS OF DOMUS AUREA!!
THIS IS RUI KOBA-YAKAWA!!
I HAVE BEEN INAUGURATED AS THE PUBLIC SAFETY COMMISSIONER.
RIP
RIP
RIP
WAAAH! WAIT!! CUT THE FEED! CUT IT!!
WE CAN'T!
AS MY FIRST AND LAST JOB AS COMMISSIONER ...
...I'D LIKE TO IMPLEMENT A REFORM.
What's going on?
What
RUI?
It's the president!
STARTING TODAY...
...THE PSC...
...WILL BE DISBANDED!
PSC

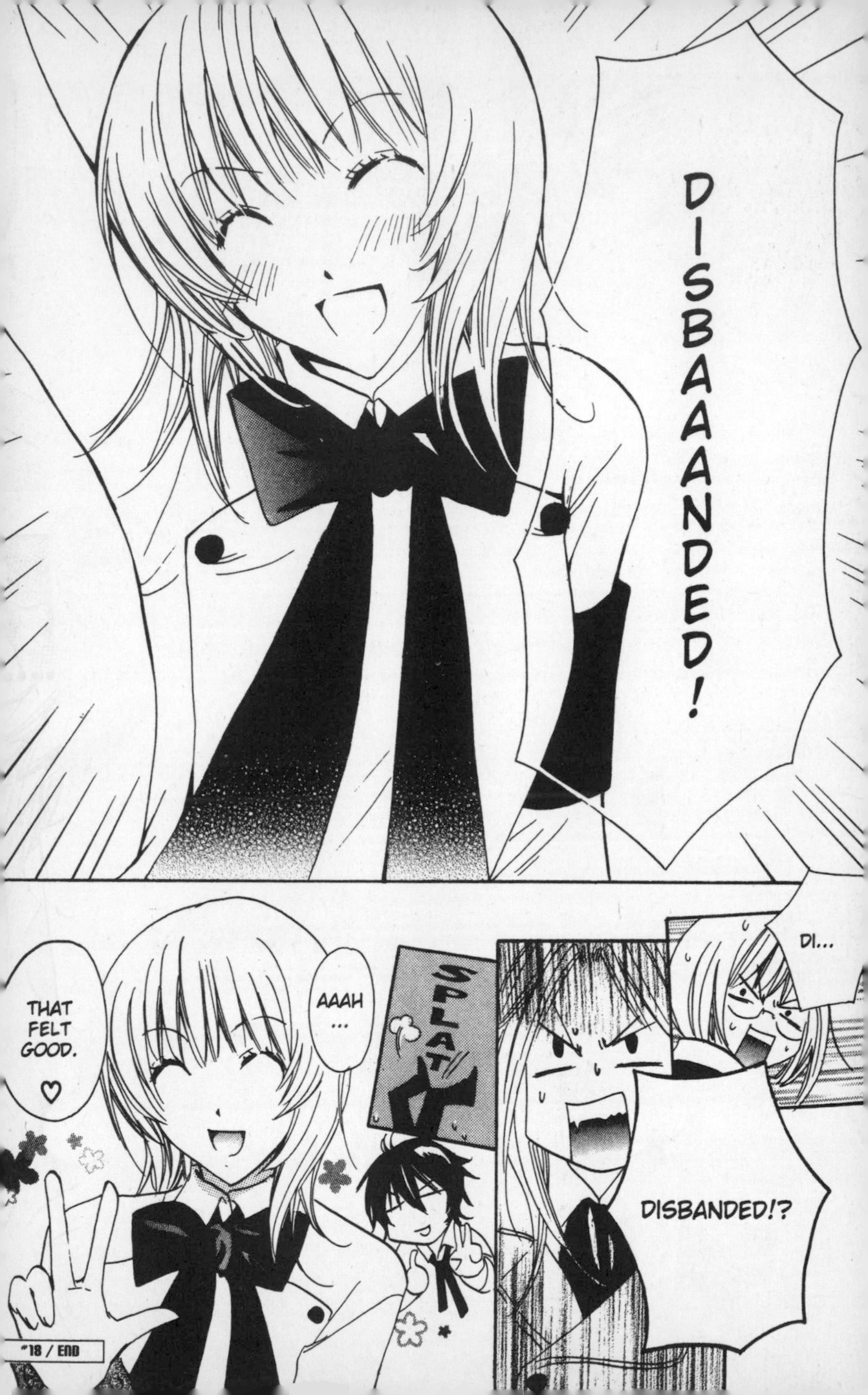

DISBAAAANDED!
DI...
DISBANDED!?
SPLAT
AAAH ...
THAT FELT GOOD. ♥
#18 / END

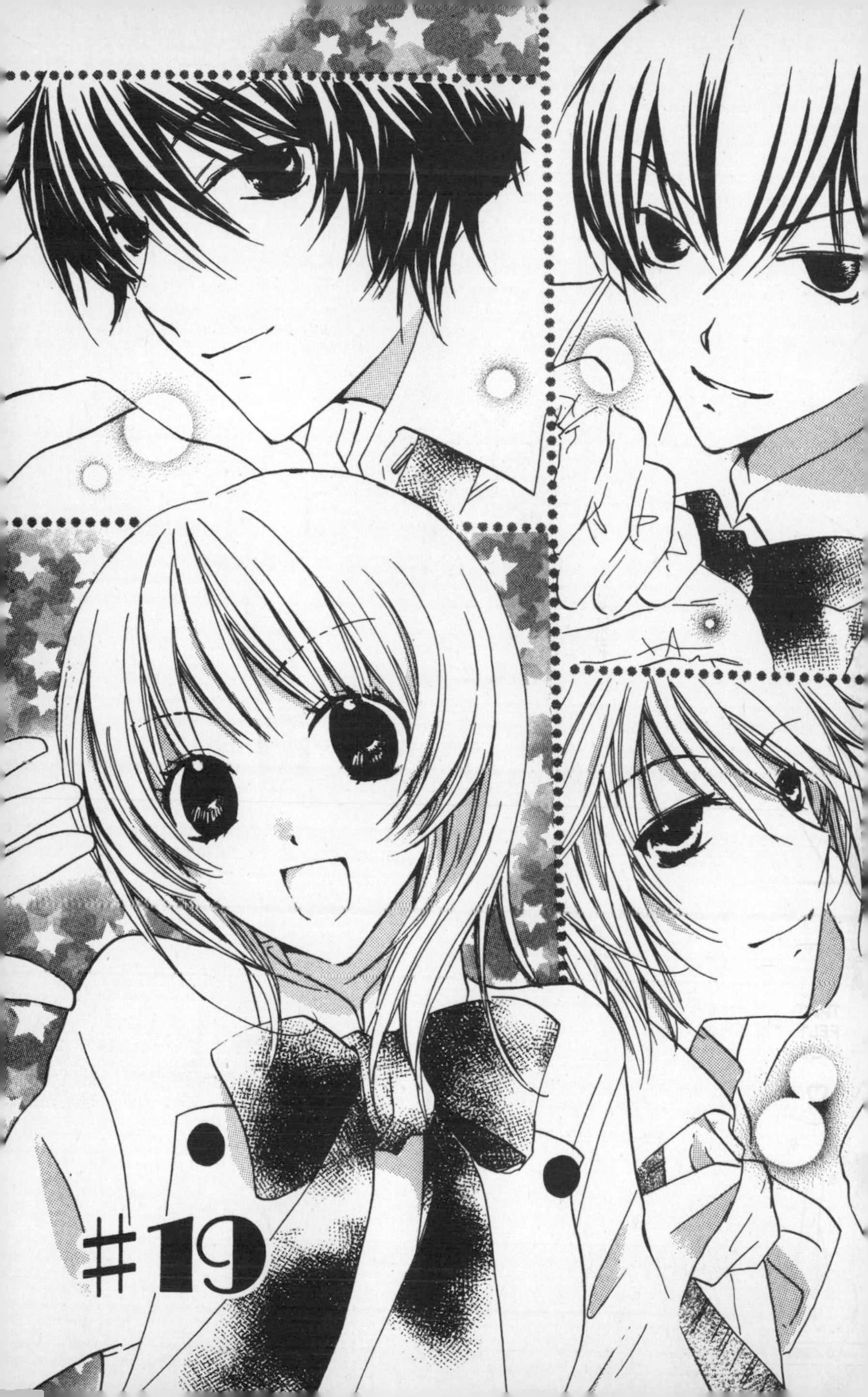
#19

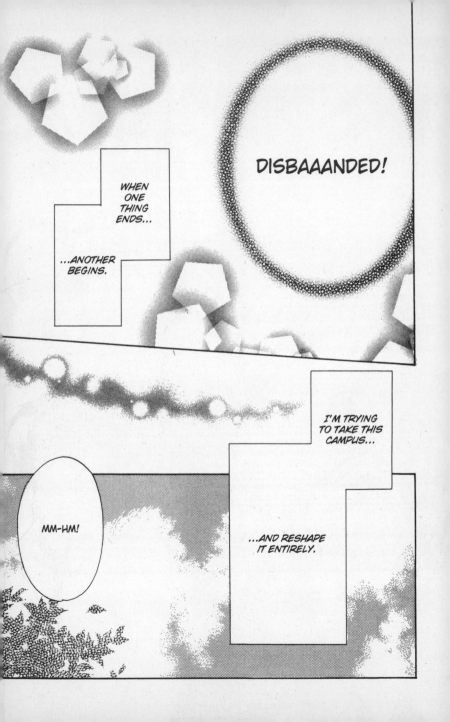

DISBAAANDED!

WHEN ONE THING ENDS...

...ANOTHER BEGINS.

I'M TRYING TO TAKE THIS CAMPUS...

MM-HM!

...AND RESHAPE IT ENTIRELY.

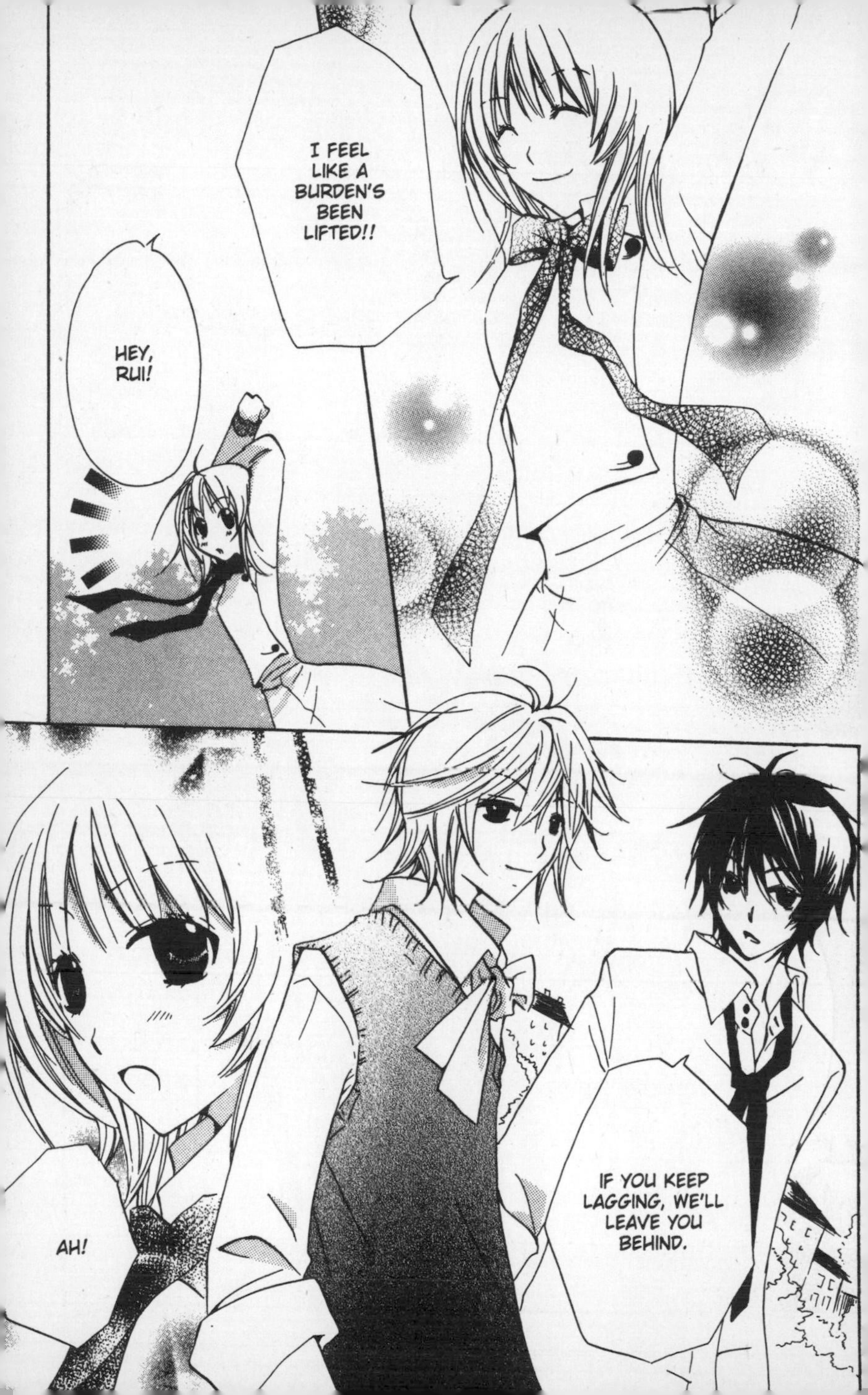
I FEEL LIKE A BURDEN'S BEEN LIFTED!!
HEY, RUI!
IF YOU KEEP LAGGING, WE'LL LEAVE YOU BEHIND.
AH!

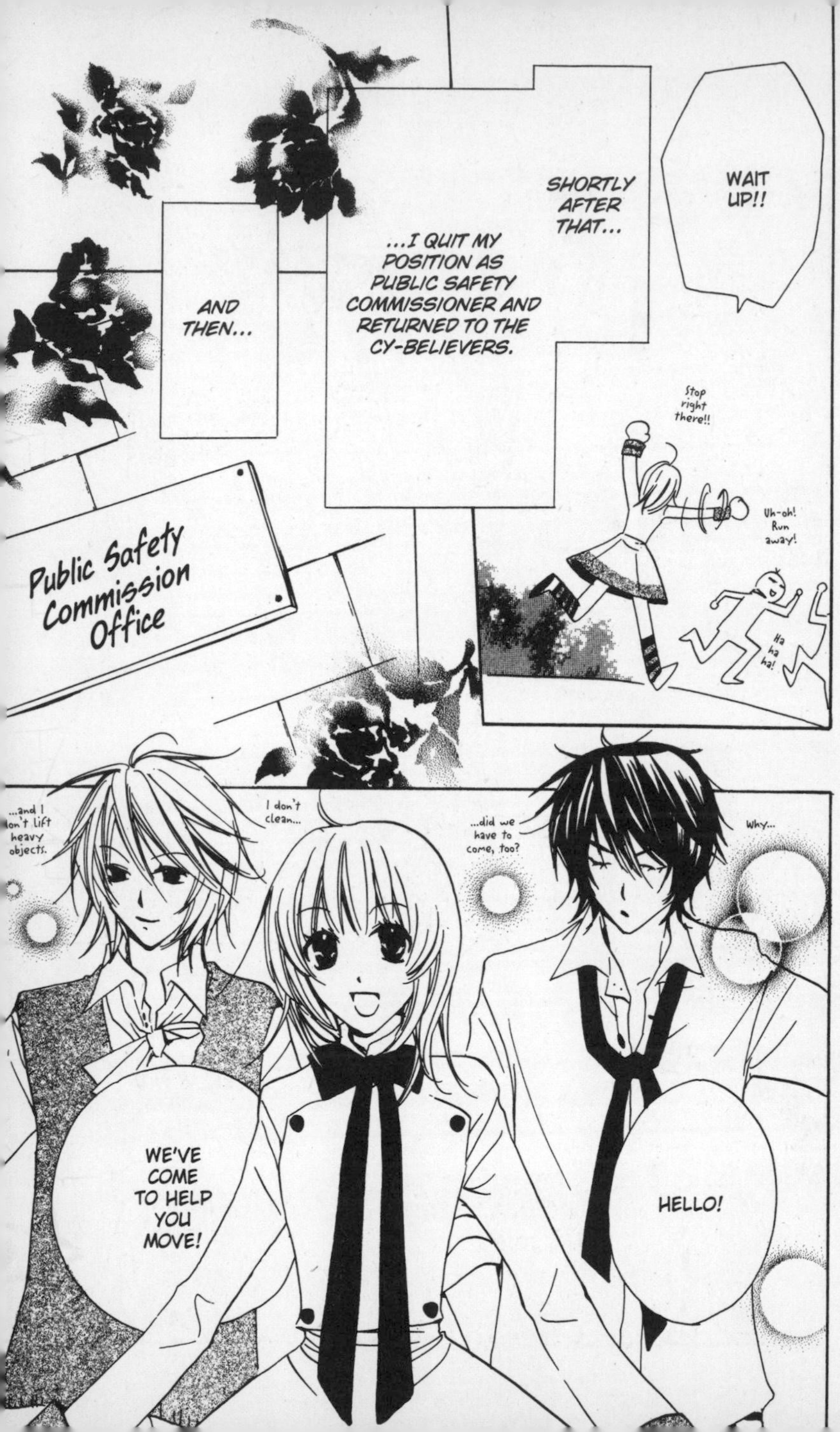

SHORTLY AFTER THAT...
...I QUIT MY POSITION AS PUBLIC SAFETY COMMISSIONER AND RETURNED TO THE CY-BELIEVERS.
AND THEN...
Public Safety Commission Office
WAIT UP!!
Stop right there!!
Uh-oh! Run away!
Ha ha ha!
Why...
HELLO!
...did we have to come, too?
I don't clean...
...and I on't lift heavy objects.
WE'VE COME TO HELP YOU MOVE!

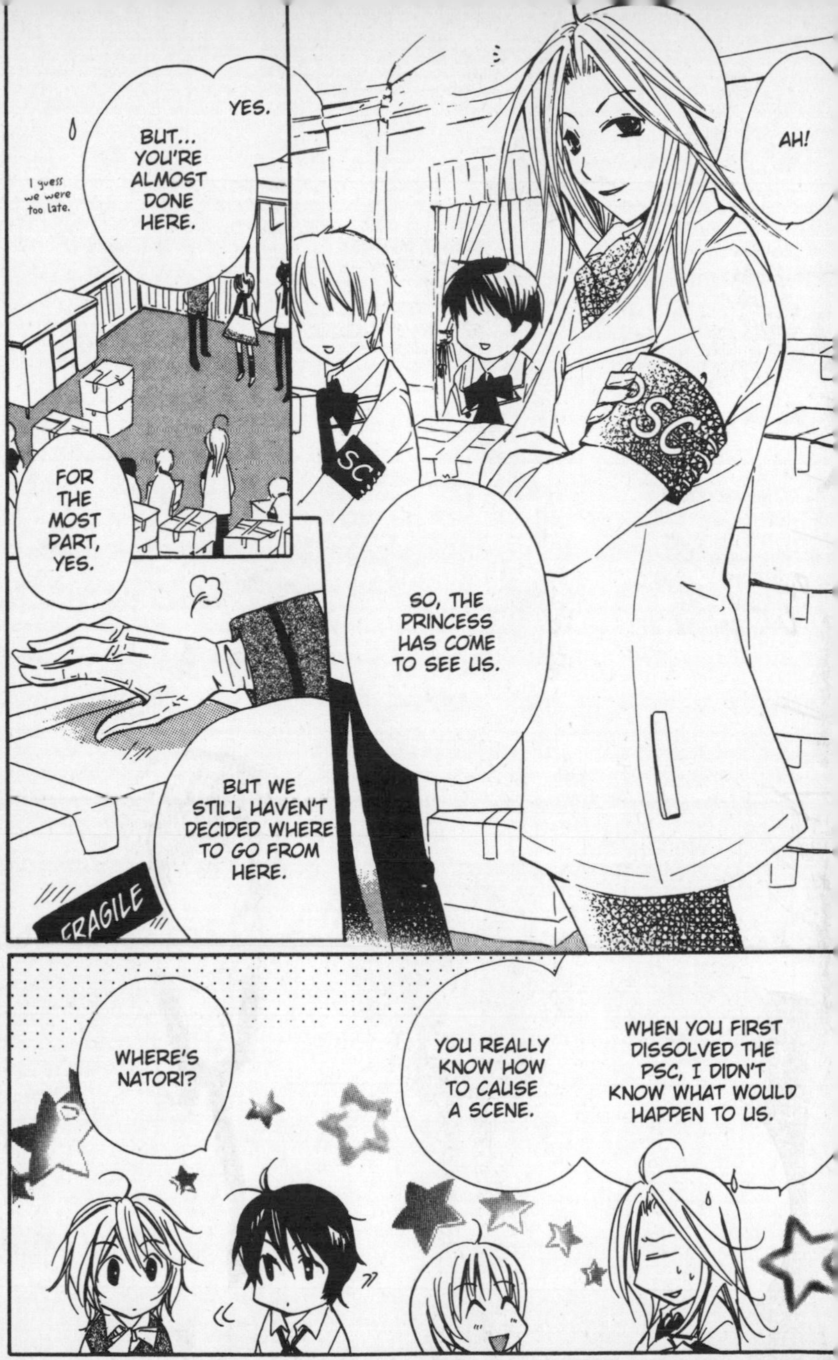
AH!
SO, THE PRINCESS HAS COME TO SEE US.
YES.
BUT... YOU'RE ALMOST DONE HERE.
I guess we were too late.
FOR THE MOST PART, YES.
BUT WE STILL HAVEN'T DECIDED WHERE TO GO FROM HERE.
FRAGILE
WHEN YOU FIRST DISSOLVED THE PSC, I DIDN'T KNOW WHAT WOULD HAPPEN TO US.
YOU REALLY KNOW HOW TO CAUSE A SCENE.
WHERE'S NATORI?

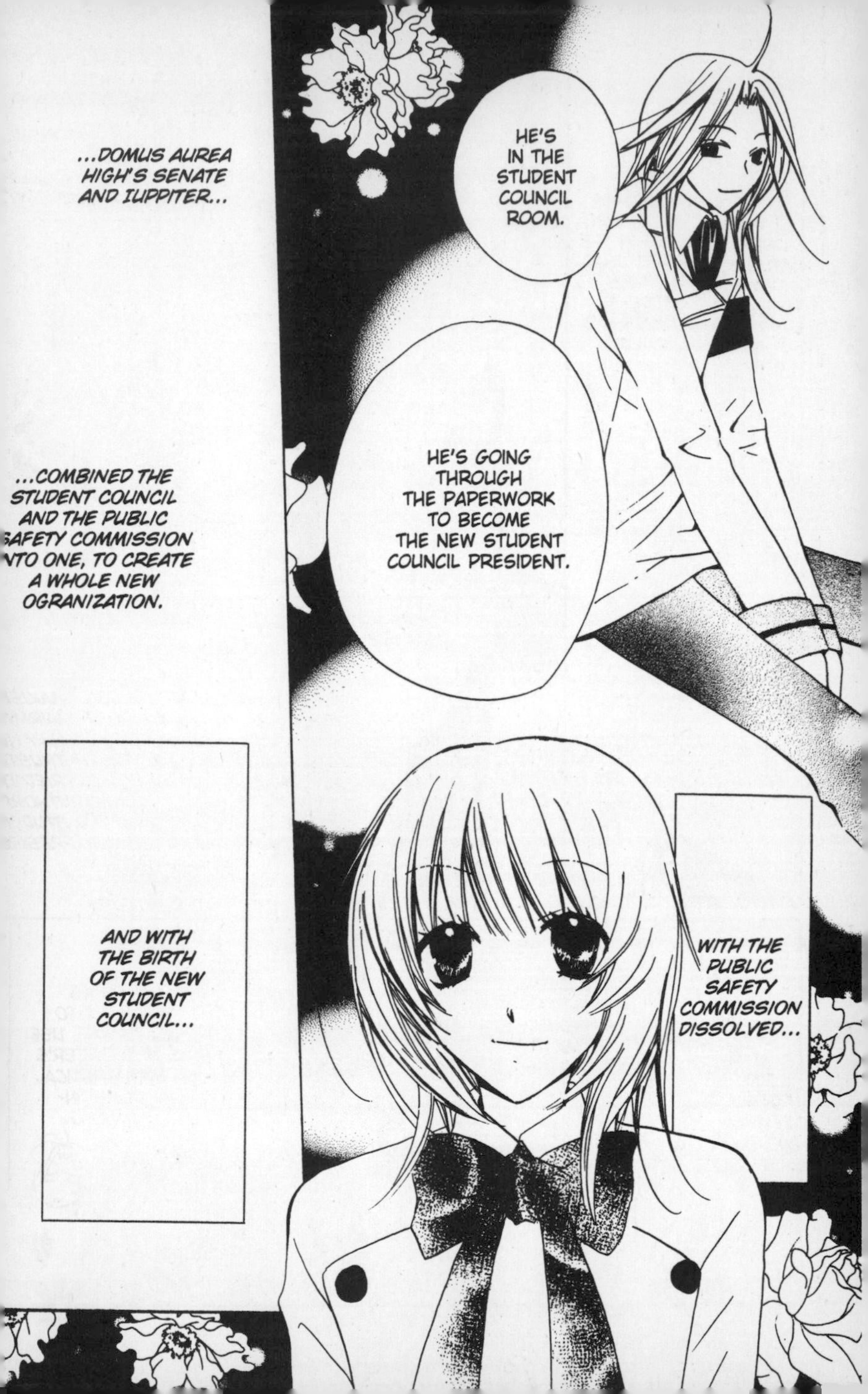
HE'S IN THE STUDENT COUNCIL ROOM.
HE'S GOING THROUGH THE PAPERWORK TO BECOME THE NEW STUDENT COUNCIL PRESIDENT.
WITH THE PUBLIC SAFETY COMMISSION DISSOLVED...
...DOMUS AUREA HIGH'S SENATE AND IUPPITER...
...COMBINED THE STUDENT COUNCIL AND THE PUBLIC SAFETY COMMISSION INTO ONE, TO CREATE A WHOLE NEW OGRANIZATION.
AND WITH THE BIRTH OF THE NEW STUDENT COUNCIL...

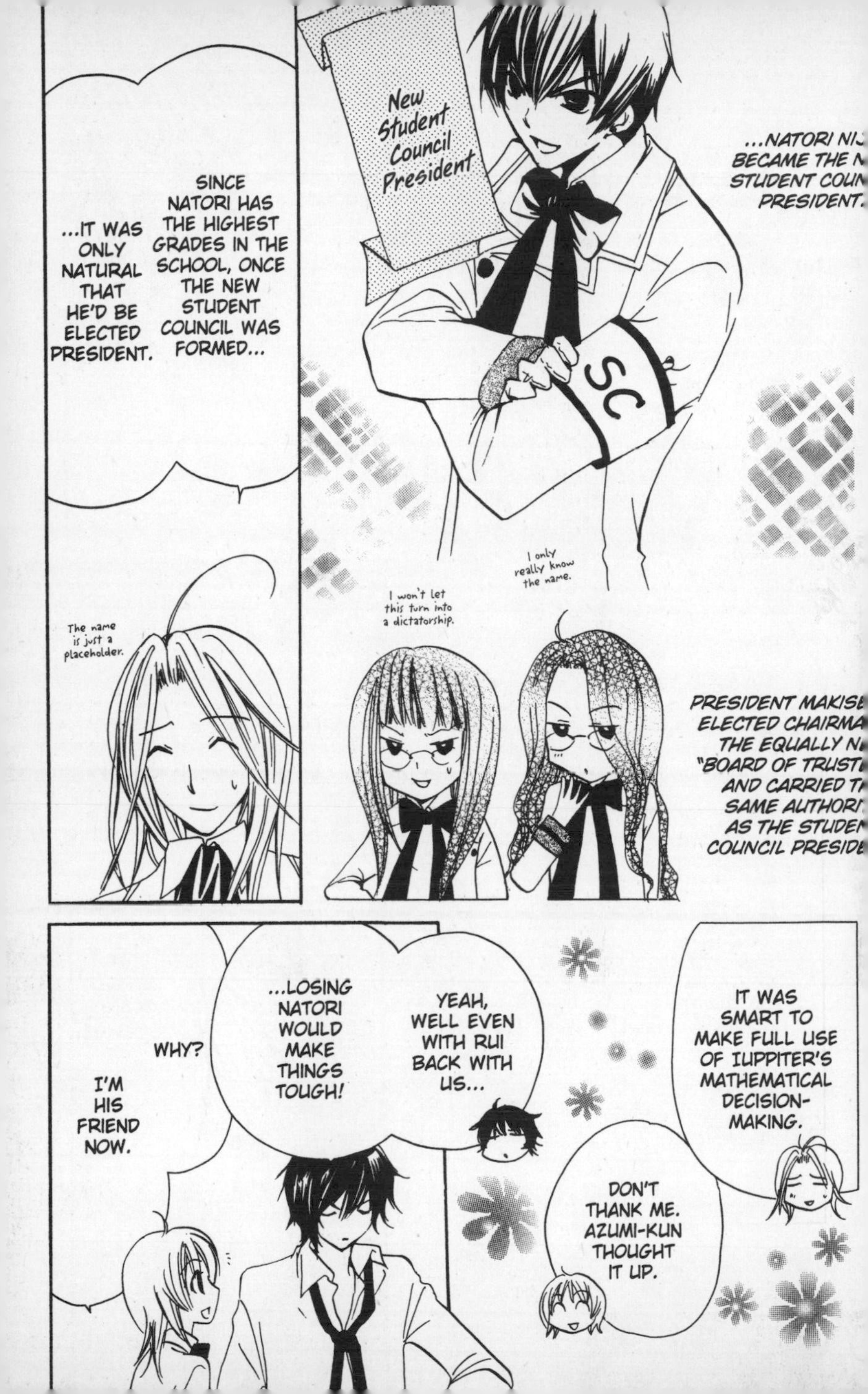

New Student Council President
SC
...NATORI NIJ BECAME THE N STUDENT COUN PRESIDENT.
I only really know the name.
I won't let this turn into a dictatorship.
PRESIDENT MAKISE ELECTED CHAIRMA THE EQUALLY N "BOARD OF TRUST AND CARRIED T SAME AUTHORI AS THE STUDEN COUNCIL PRESIDE
SINCE NATORI HAS THE HIGHEST GRADES IN THE SCHOOL, ONCE THE NEW STUDENT COUNCIL WAS FORMED...
...IT WAS ONLY NATURAL THAT HE'D BE ELECTED PRESIDENT.
The name is just a placeholder.
IT WAS SMART TO MAKE FULL USE OF IUPPITER'S MATHEMATICAL DECISION-MAKING.
DON'T THANK ME. AZUMI-KUN THOUGHT IT UP.
YEAH, WELL EVEN WITH RUI BACK WITH US...
...LOSING NATORI WOULD MAKE THINGS TOUGH!
WHY?
I'M HIS FRIEND NOW.

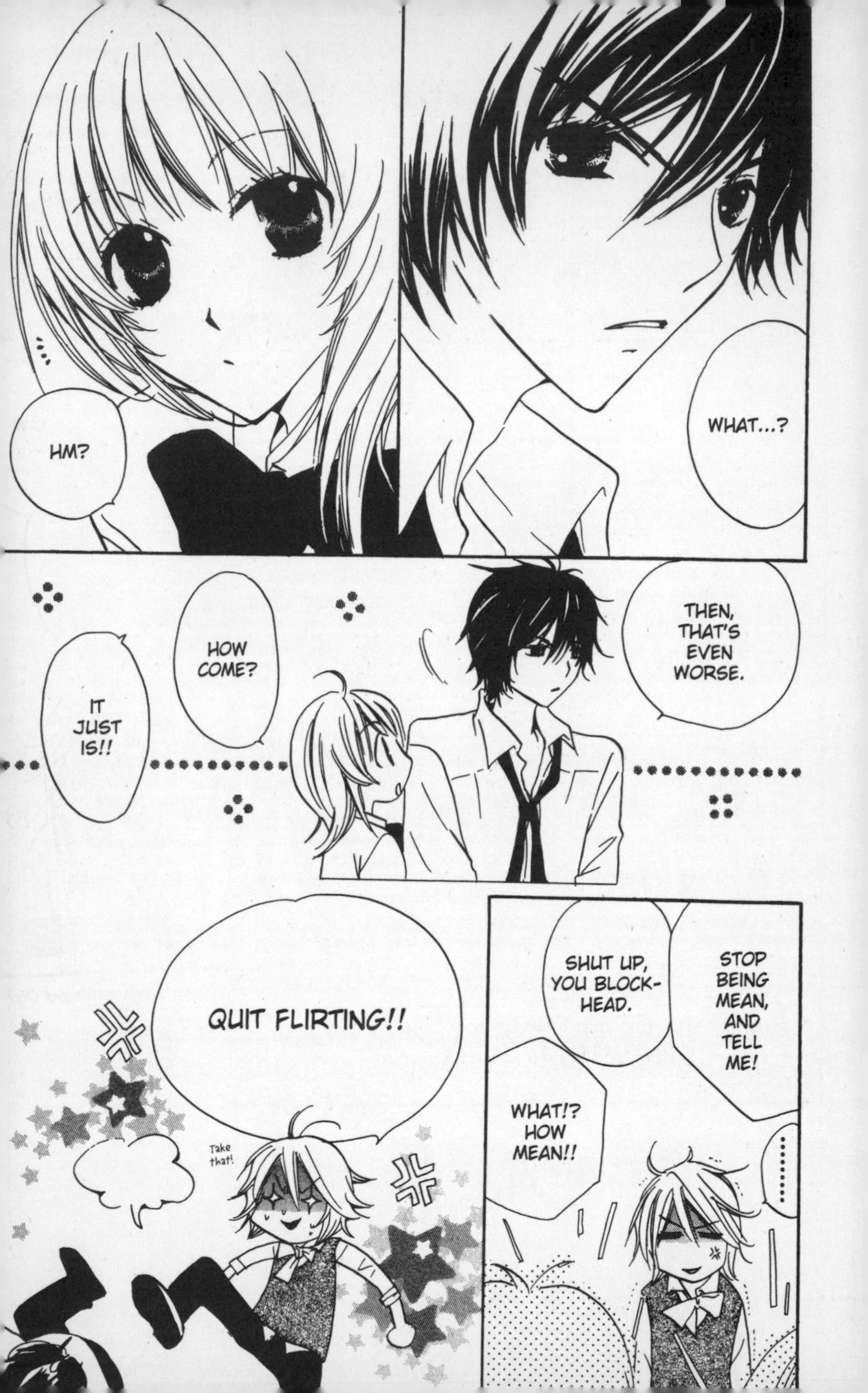
WHAT...?
HM?
THEN, THAT'S EVEN WORSE.
HOW COME?
IT JUST IS!!
STOP BEING MEAN, AND TELL ME!
SHUT UP, YOU BLOCK-HEAD.
WHAT!? HOW MEAN!!
QUIT FLIRTING!!
Take that!

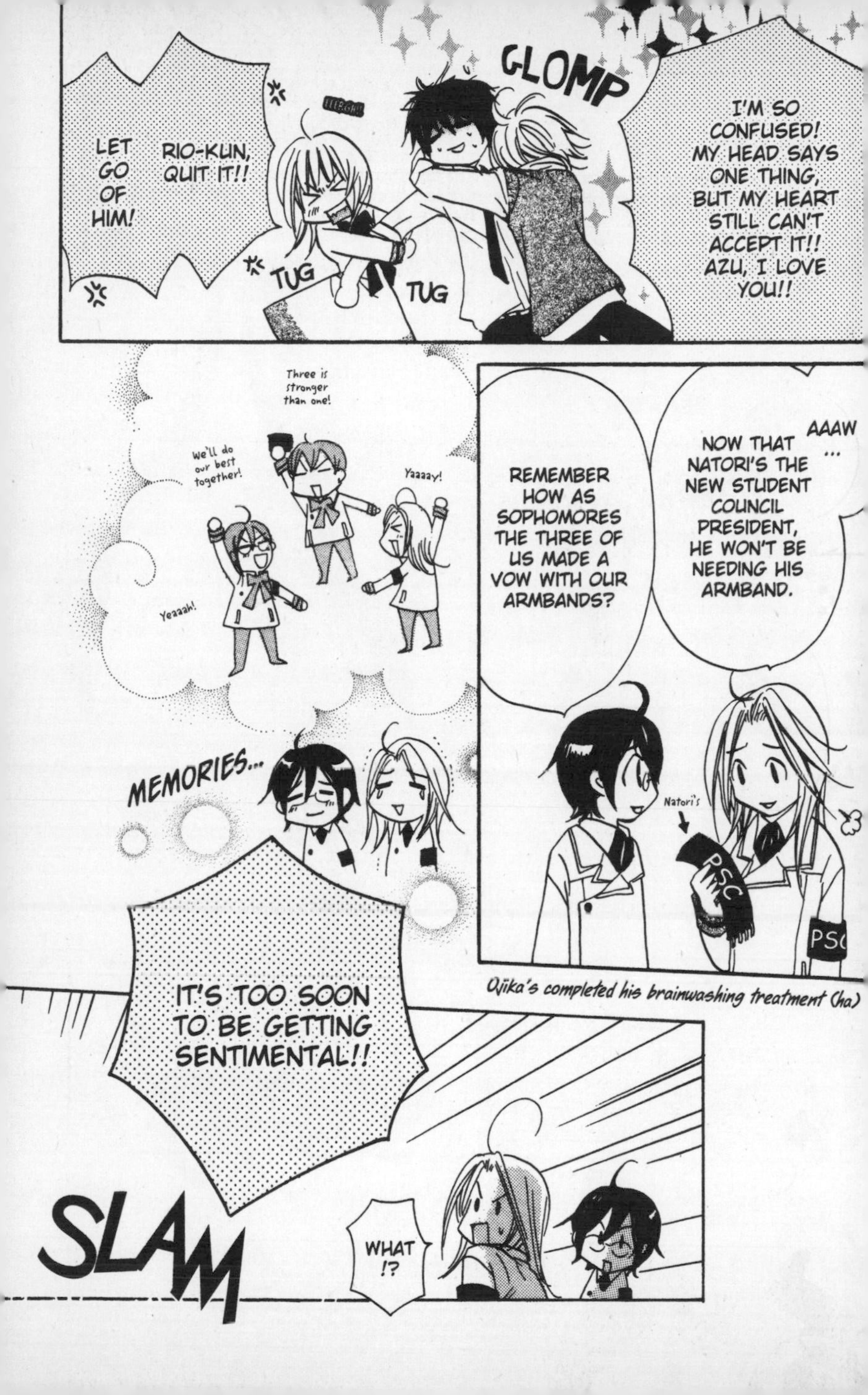
GLOMP
I'M SO CONFUSED! MY HEAD SAYS ONE THING, BUT MY HEART STILL CAN'T ACCEPT IT!! AZU, I LOVE YOU!!
RIO-KUN, QUIT IT!!
LET GO OF HIM!
TUG
TUG
AAAW ...
NOW THAT NATORI'S THE NEW STUDENT COUNCIL PRESIDENT, HE WON'T BE NEEDING HIS ARMBAND.
REMEMBER HOW AS SOPHOMORES THE THREE OF US MADE A VOW WITH OUR ARMBANDS?
Natori's
PSC
PSC
Ojika's completed his brainwashing treatment (ha)
Three is stronger than one!
We'll do our best together!
Yaaaay!
Yeaaah!
MEMORIES...
IT'S TOO SOON TO BE GETTING SENTIMENTAL!!
WHAT !?
SLAM

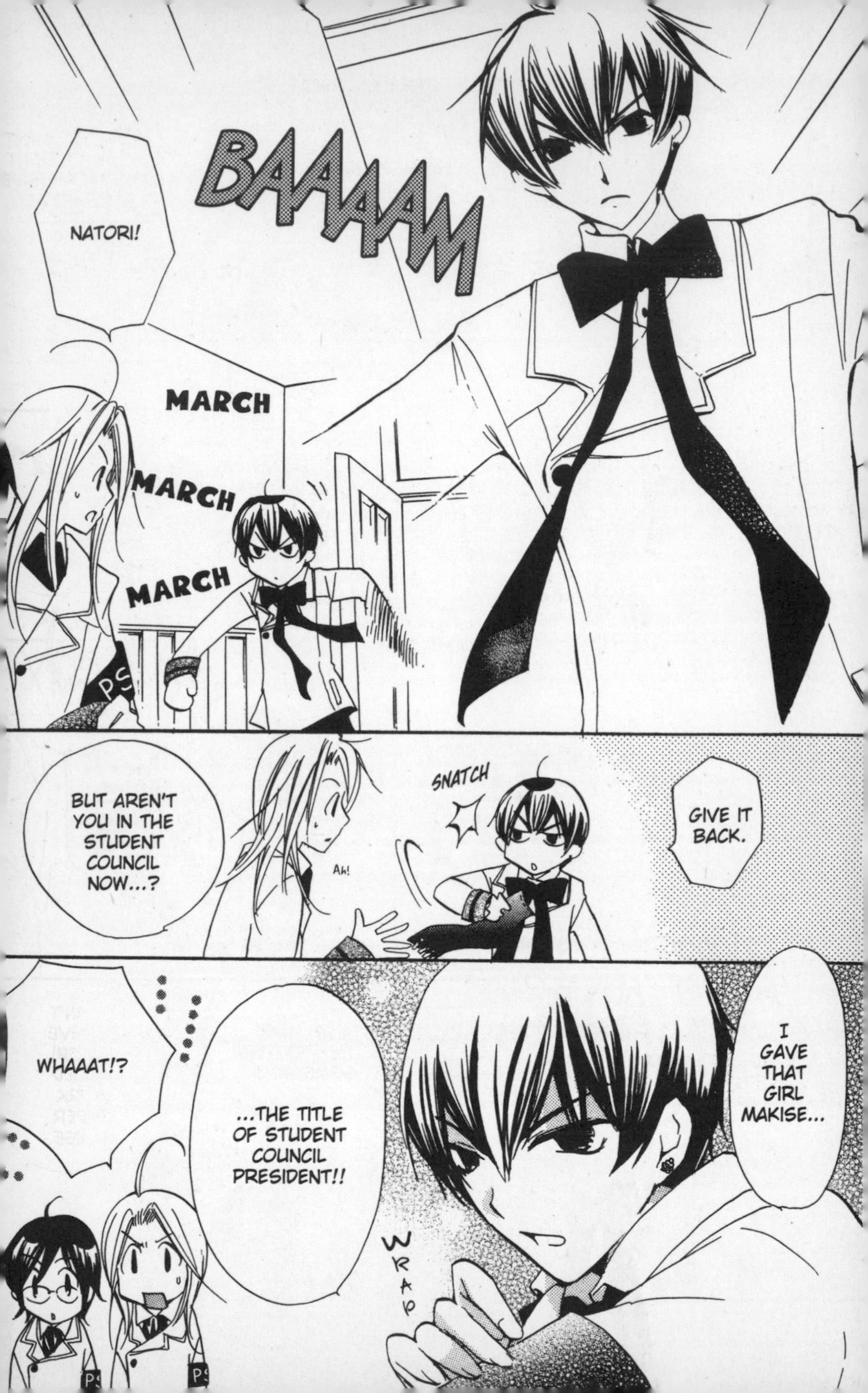
BAAAAAM
NATORI!
MARCH
MARCH
MARCH
GIVE IT BACK.
SNATCH
Ah!
BUT AREN'T YOU IN THE STUDENT COUNCIL NOW...?
I GAVE THAT GIRL MAKISE...
WRAP
...THE TITLE OF STUDENT COUNCIL PRESIDENT!!
WHAAAT!?

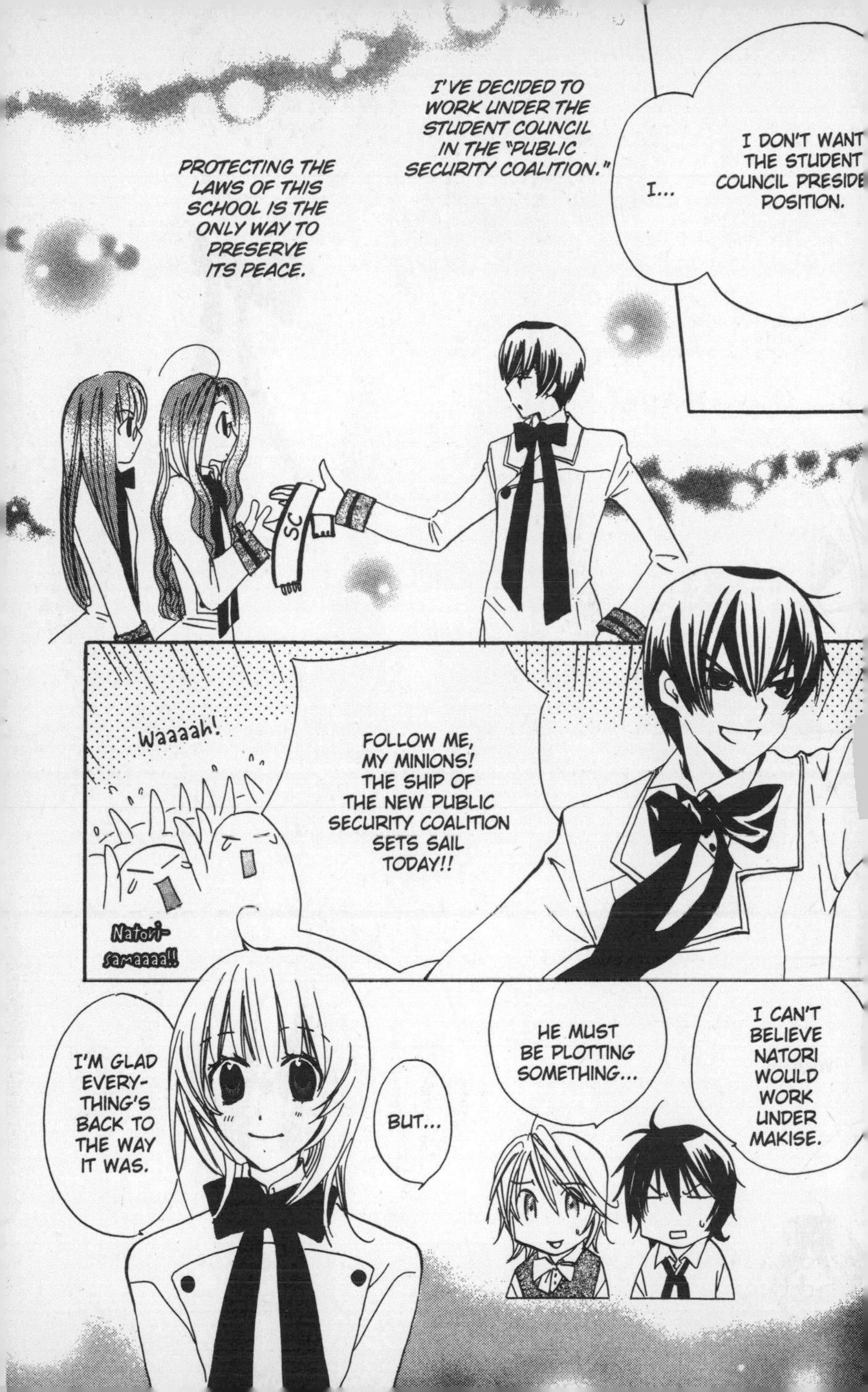
I...
I DON'T WANT THE STUDENT COUNCIL PRESIDE POSITION.
I'VE DECIDED TO WORK UNDER THE STUDENT COUNCIL IN THE "PUBLIC SECURITY COALITION."
PROTECTING THE LAWS OF THIS SCHOOL IS THE ONLY WAY TO PRESERVE ITS PEACE.
SC
FOLLOW ME, MY MINIONS! THE SHIP OF THE NEW PUBLIC SECURITY COALITION SETS SAIL TODAY!!
Waaaah!
Natori-samaaaa!!
I CAN'T BELIEVE NATORI WOULD WORK UNDER MAKISE.
HE MUST BE PLOTTING SOMETHING...
BUT...
I'M GLAD EVERY-THING'S BACK TO THE WAY IT WAS.

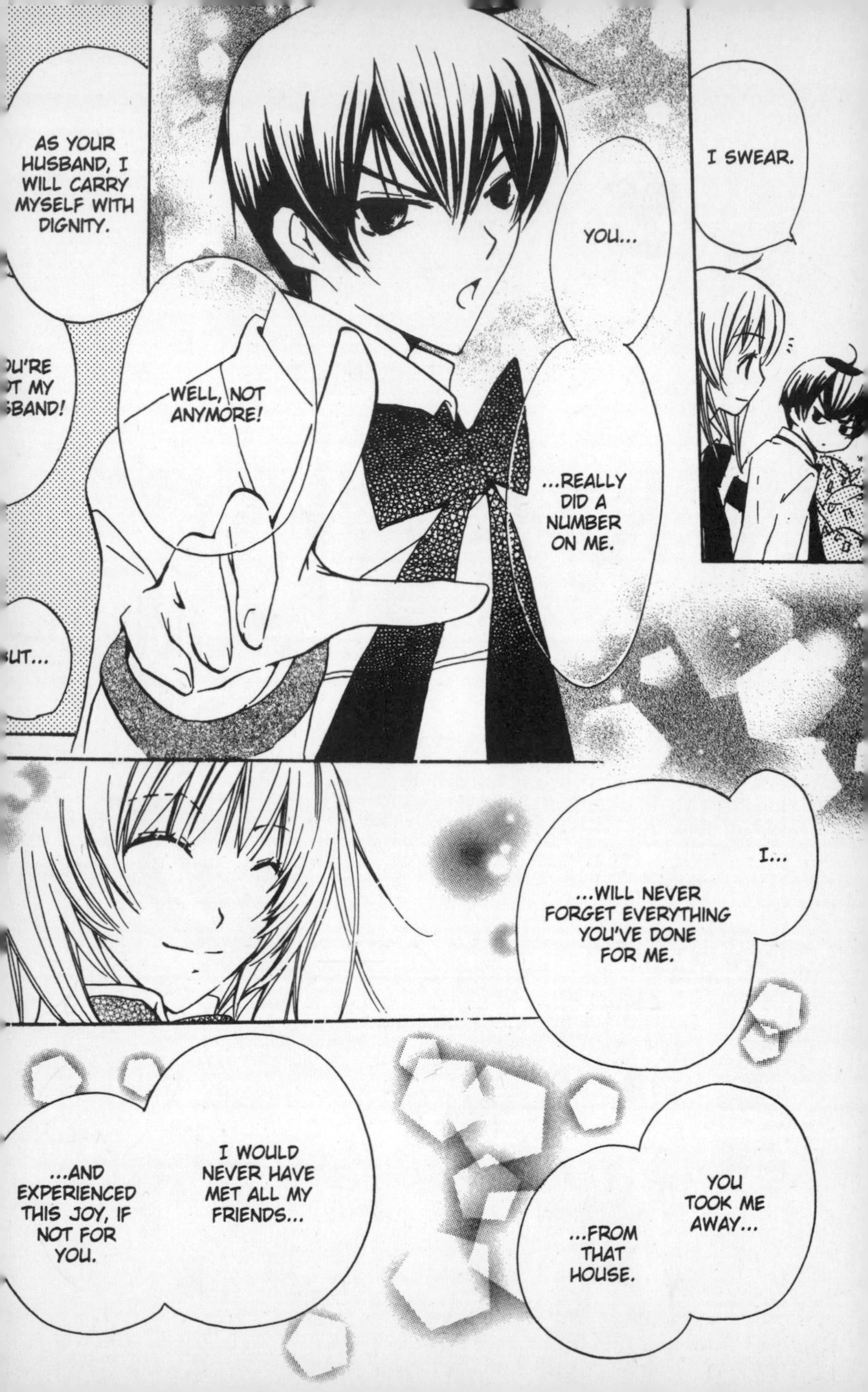
I SWEAR.
YOU...
...REALLY DID A NUMBER ON ME.
WELL, NOT ANYMORE!
AS YOUR HUSBAND, I WILL CARRY MYSELF WITH DIGNITY.
U'RE T MY SBAND!
UT...
I...
...WILL NEVER FORGET EVERYTHING YOU'VE DONE FOR ME.
YOU TOOK ME AWAY...
...FROM THAT HOUSE.
I WOULD NEVER HAVE MET ALL MY FRIENDS...
...AND EXPERIENCED THIS JOY, IF NOT FOR YOU.

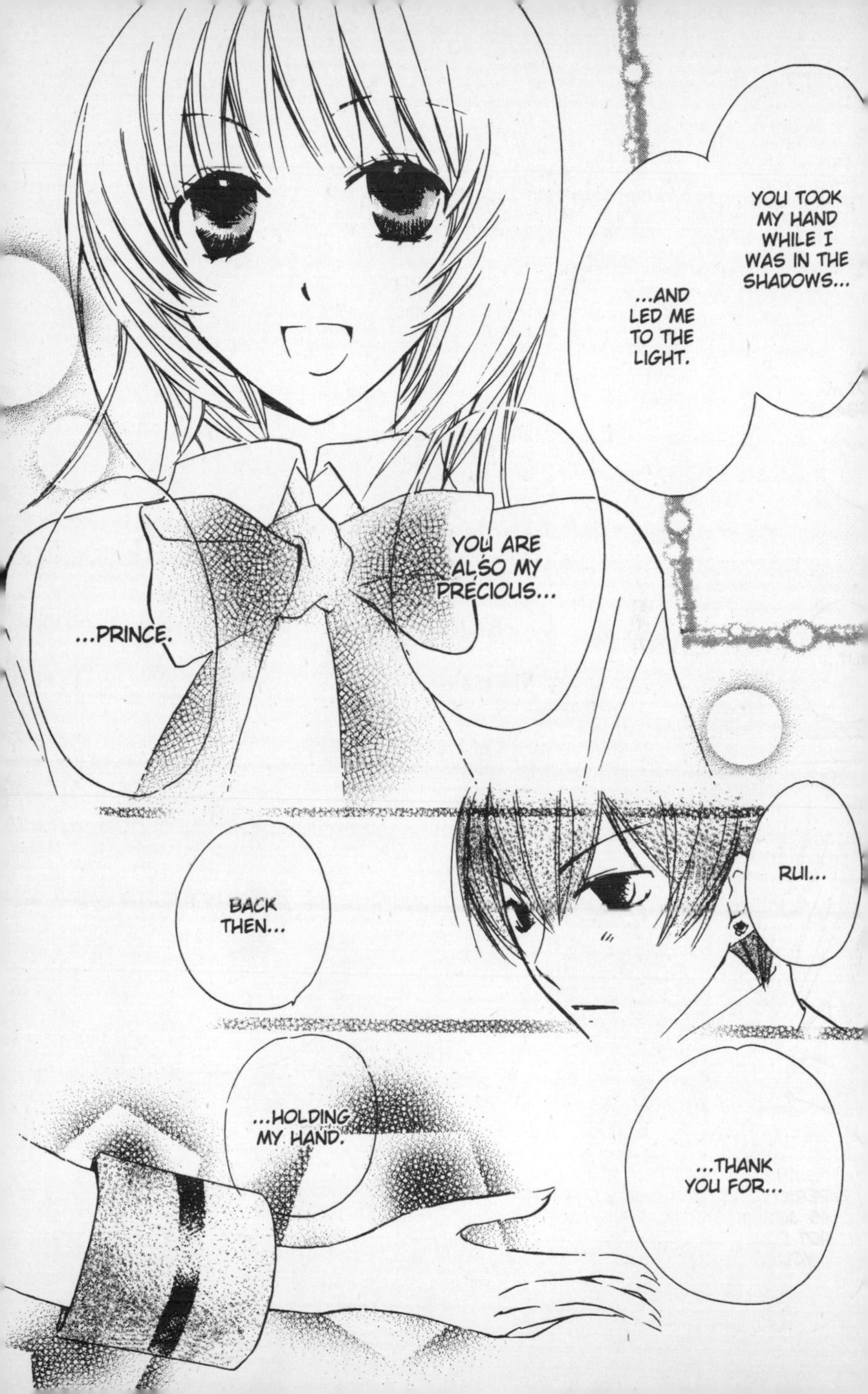
YOU TOOK MY HAND WHILE I WAS IN THE SHADOWS...
...AND LED ME TO THE LIGHT.
YOU ARE ALSO MY PRECIOUS...
...PRINCE.
RUI...
BACK THEN...
...THANK YOU FOR...
...HOLDING MY HAND.

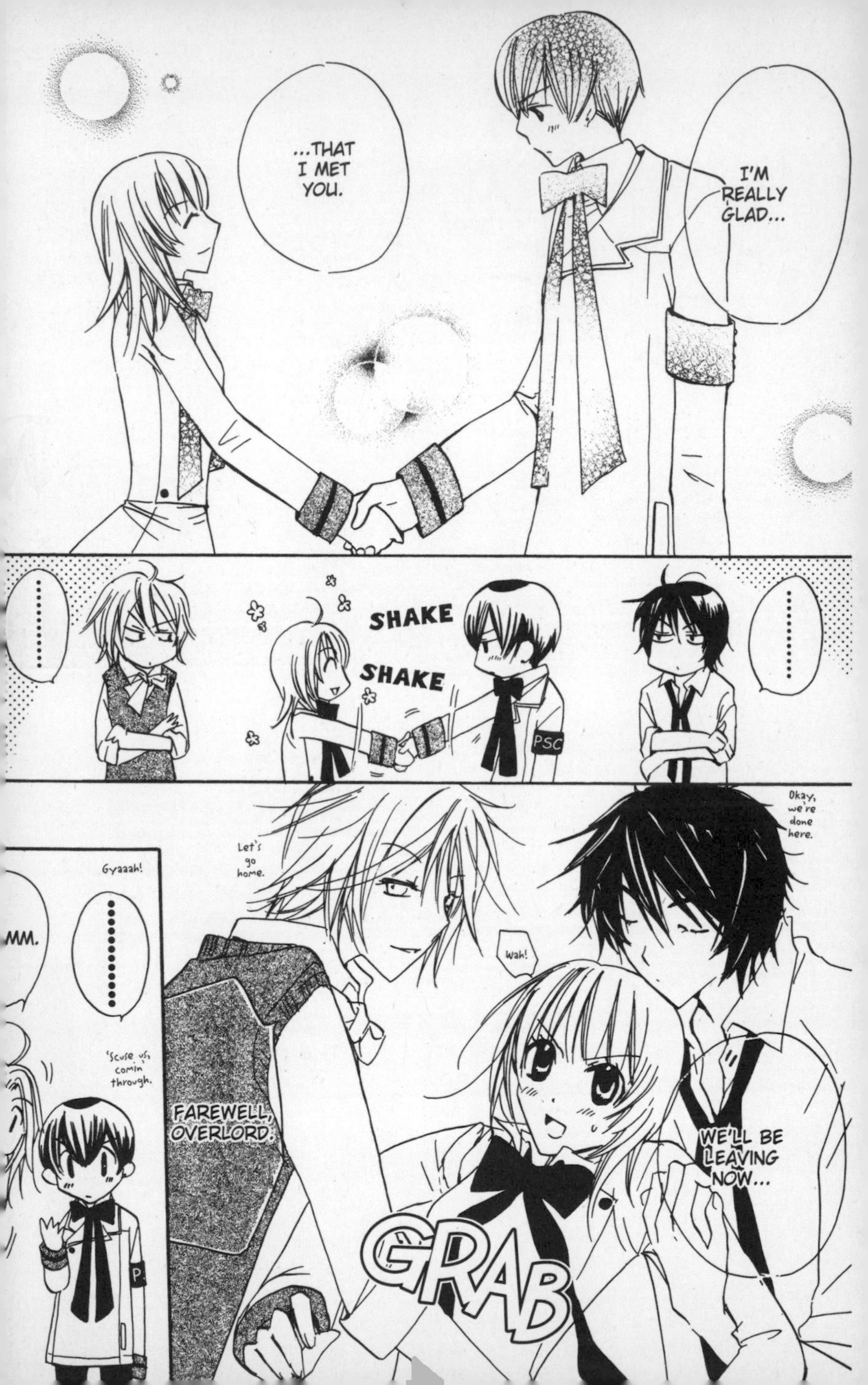
I'M REALLY GLAD...
...THAT I MET YOU.
......
SHAKE
SHAKE
......
Okay, we're done here.
WE'LL BE LEAVING NOW...
Wah!
Let's go home.
FAREWELL, OVERLORD.
GRAB
Gyaaah!
......
MM.
'Scuse us, comin' through.

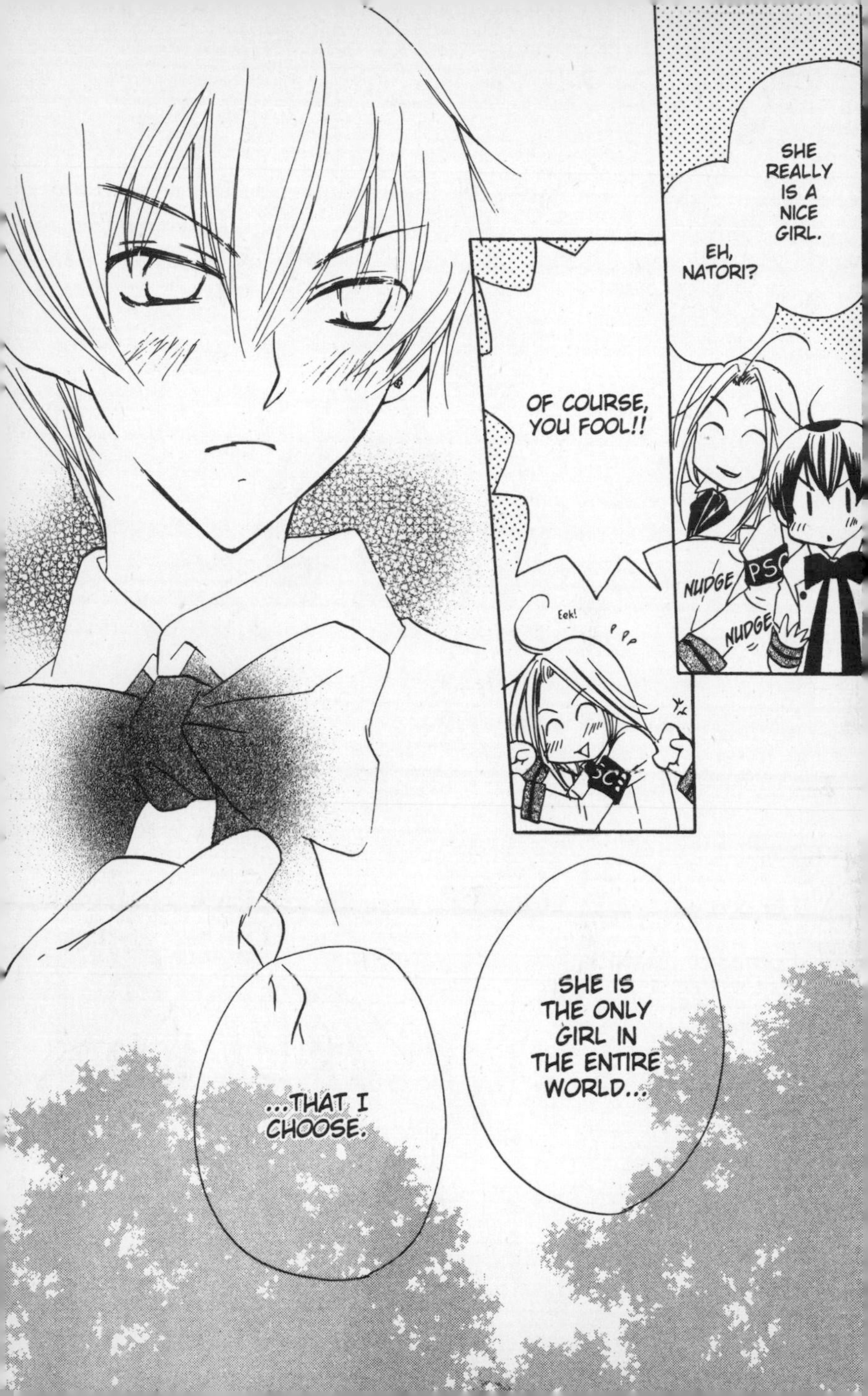
SHE REALLY IS A NICE GIRL.
EH, NATORI?
NUDGE
NUDGE
PSC
OF COURSE, YOU FOOL!!
Eek!
SC
SHE IS THE ONLY GIRL IN THE ENTIRE WORLD...
...THAT I CHOOSE.

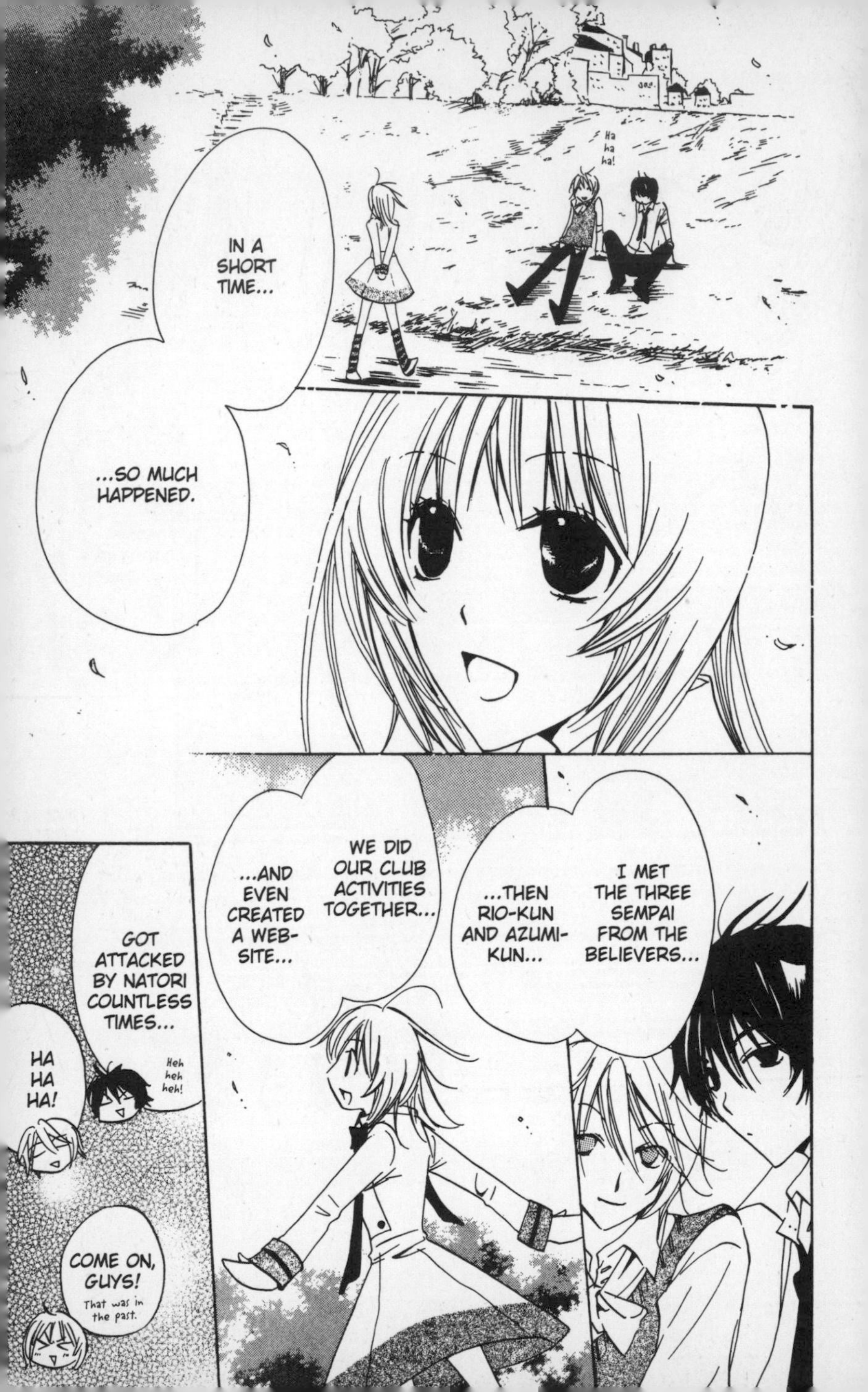
Ha ha ha!
IN A SHORT TIME...
...SO MUCH HAPPENED.
I MET THE THREE SEMPAI FROM THE BELIEVERS...
...THEN RIO-KUN AND AZUMI-KUN...
WE DID OUR CLUB ACTIVITIES TOGETHER...
...AND EVEN CREATED A WEB-SITE...
GOT ATTACKED BY NATORI COUNTLESS TIMES...
Heh heh heh!
HA HA HA!
COME ON, GUYS!
That was in the past.

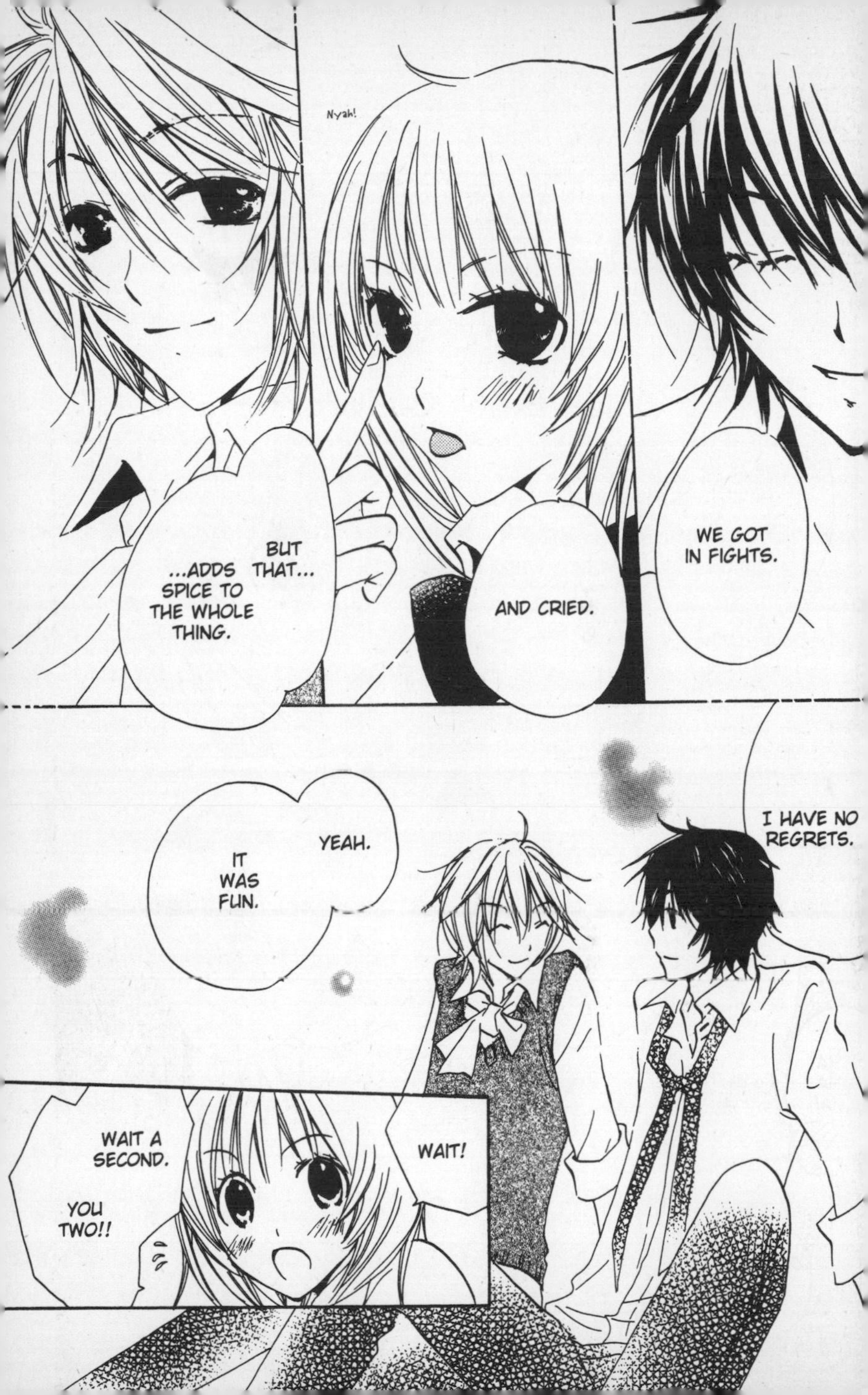
WE GOT IN FIGHTS.
Nyah!
AND CRIED.
BUT THAT...
...ADDS SPICE TO THE WHOLE THING.
I HAVE NO REGRETS.
YEAH.
IT WAS FUN.
WAIT!
WAIT A SECOND.
YOU TWO!!

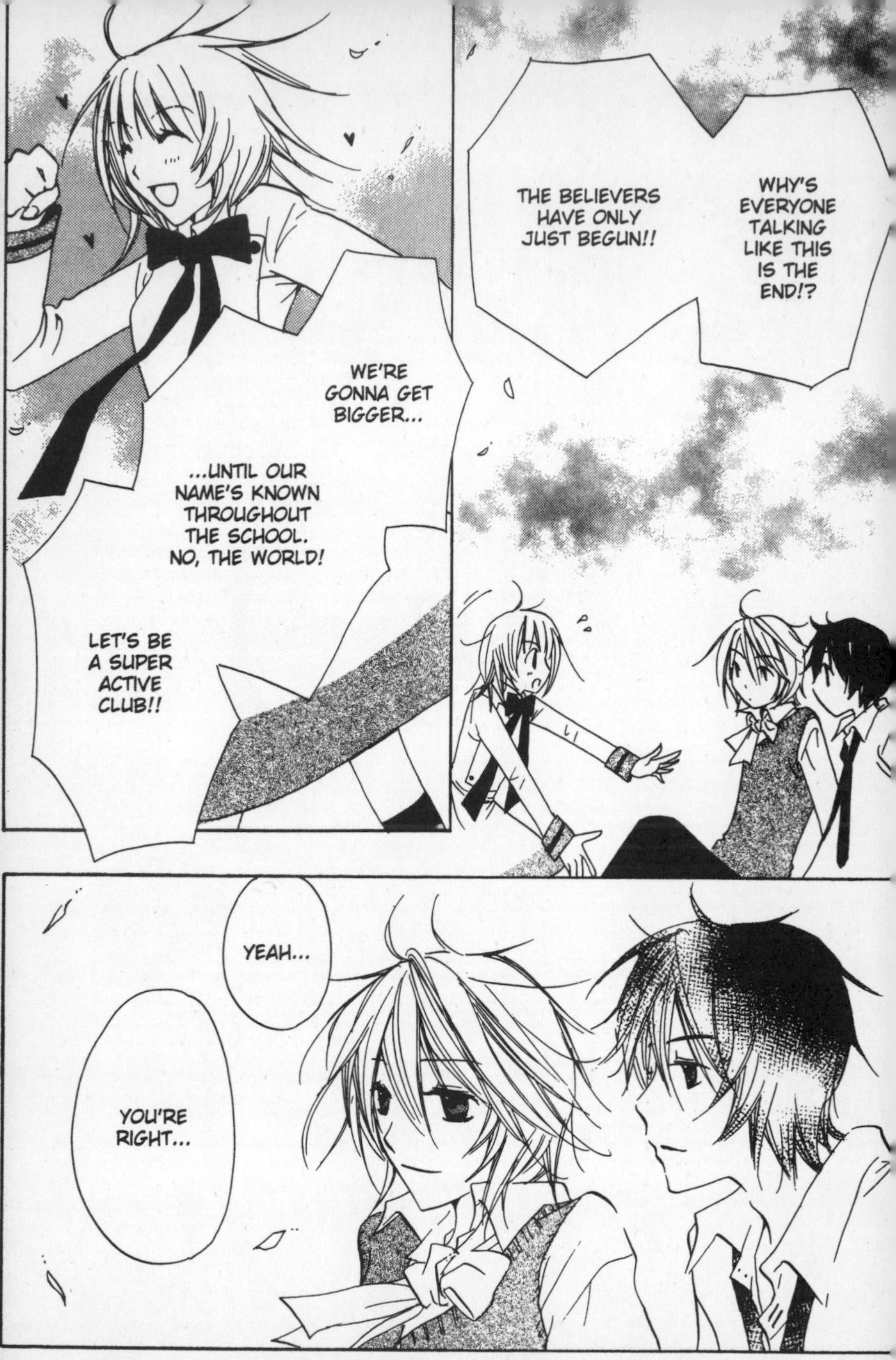
WHY'S EVERYONE TALKING LIKE THIS IS THE END!?
THE BELIEVERS HAVE ONLY JUST BEGUN!!
WE'RE GONNA GET BIGGER...
...UNTIL OUR NAME'S KNOWN THROUGHOUT THE SCHOOL. NO, THE WORLD!
LET'S BE A SUPER ACTIVE CLUB!!
YEAH...
YOU'RE RIGHT...

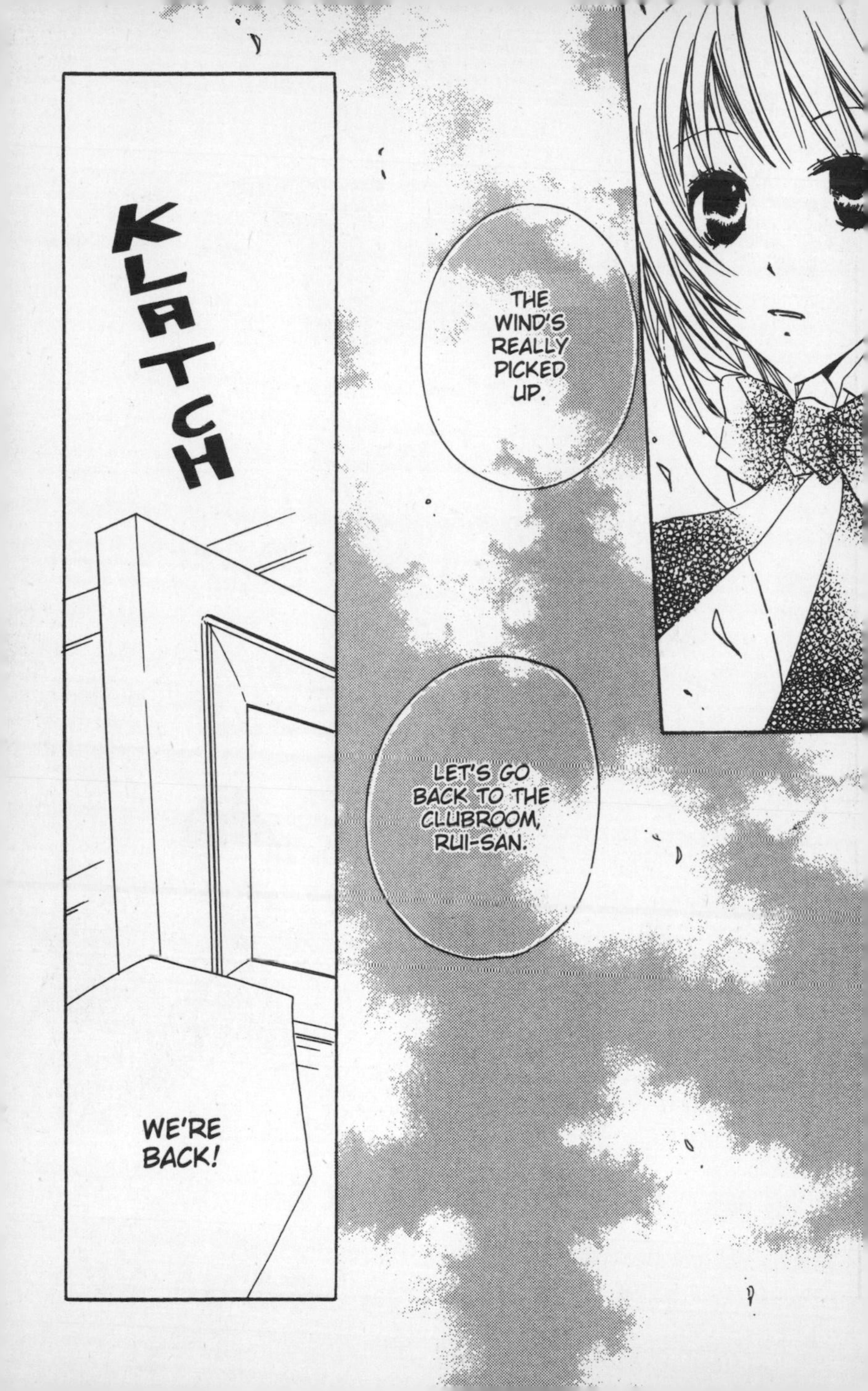
THE WIND'S REALLY PICKED UP.
LET'S GO BACK TO THE CLUBROOM, RUI-SAN.
KLATCH
WE'RE BACK!

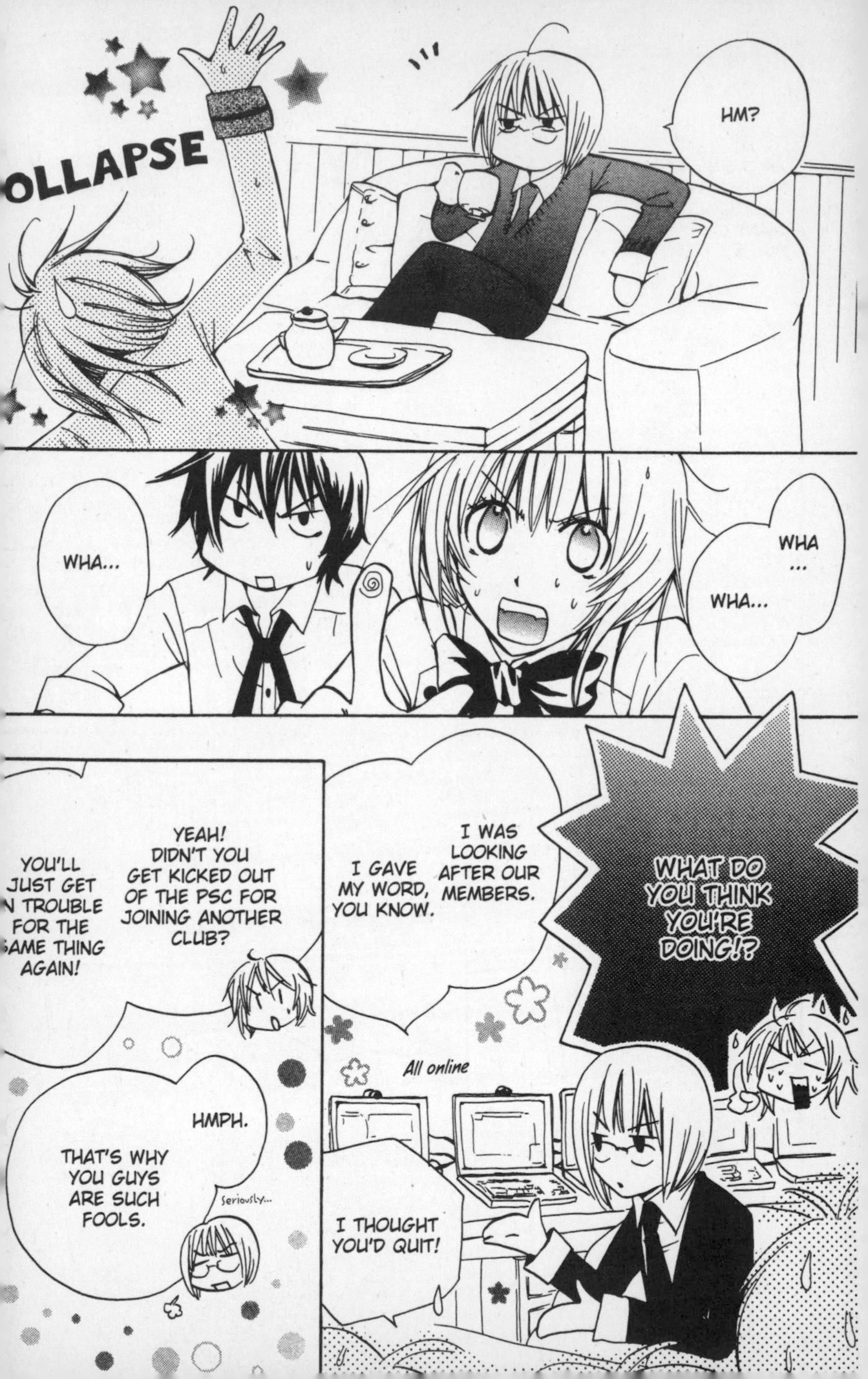
HM?
OLLAPSE
WHA... WHA...
WHA...
WHAT DO YOU THINK YOU'RE DOING!?
I THOUGHT YOU'D QUIT!
I WAS LOOKING AFTER OUR MEMBERS.
I GAVE MY WORD, YOU KNOW.
All online
YEAH! DIDN'T YOU GET KICKED OUT OF THE PSC FOR JOINING ANOTHER CLUB?
YOU'LL JUST GET N TROUBLE FOR THE AME THING AGAIN!
HMPH.
THAT'S WHY YOU GUYS ARE SUCH FOOLS.
Seriously...

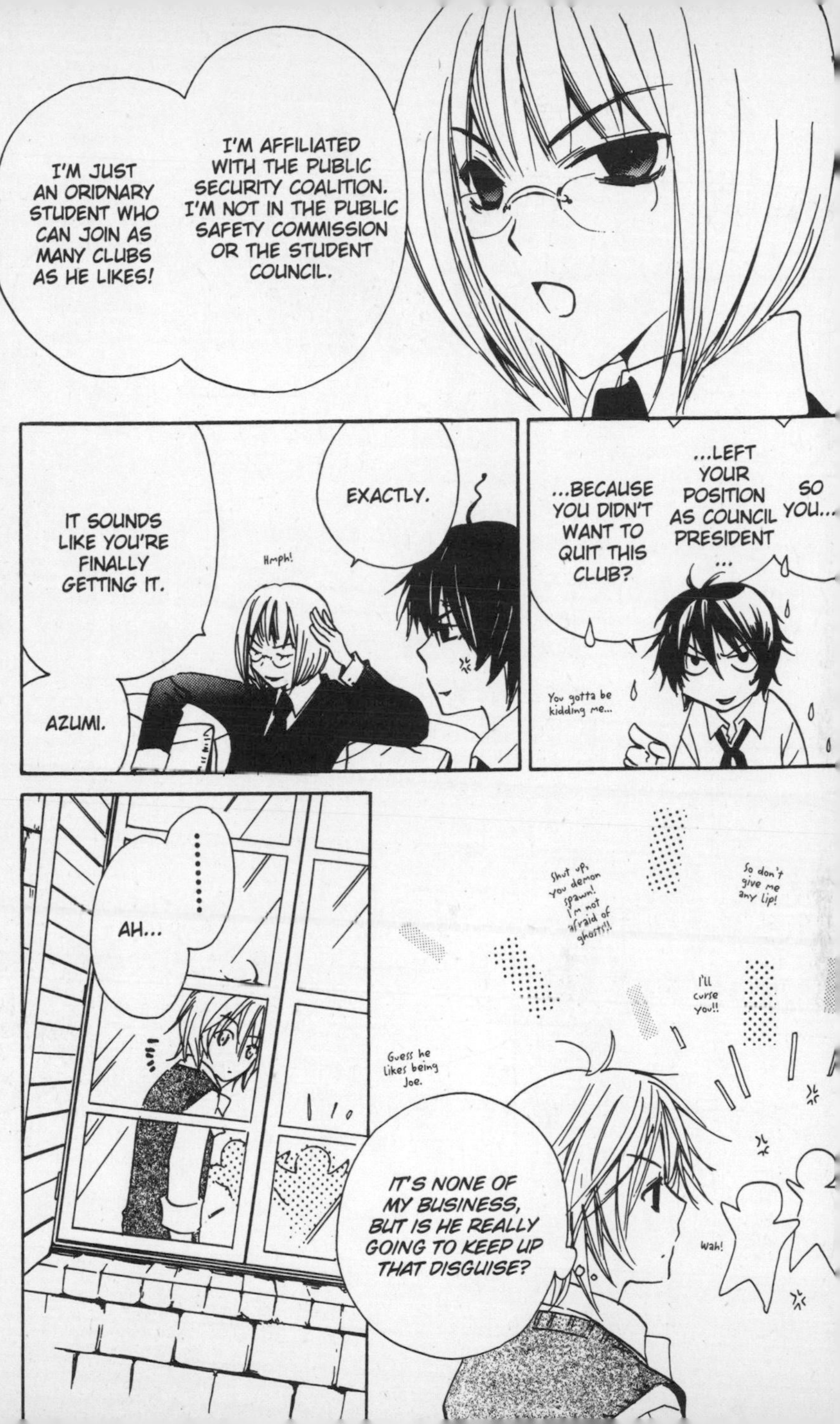
I'M AFFILIATED WITH THE PUBLIC SECURITY COALITION. I'M NOT IN THE PUBLIC SAFETY COMMISSION OR THE STUDENT COUNCIL.
I'M JUST AN ORIDNARY STUDENT WHO CAN JOIN AS MANY CLUBS AS HE LIKES!
SO YOU...
...LEFT YOUR POSITION AS COUNCIL PRESIDENT ...
...BECAUSE YOU DIDN'T WANT TO QUIT THIS CLUB?
You gotta be kidding me...
EXACTLY.
Hmph!
IT SOUNDS LIKE YOU'RE FINALLY GETTING IT.
AZUMI.
So don't give me any lip!
Shut up, you demon spawn! I'm not afraid of ghosts!!
I'll curse you!!
Guess he likes being Joe.
IT'S NONE OF MY BUSINESS, BUT IS HE REALLY GOING TO KEEP UP THAT DISGUISE?
Wah!
......
AH...

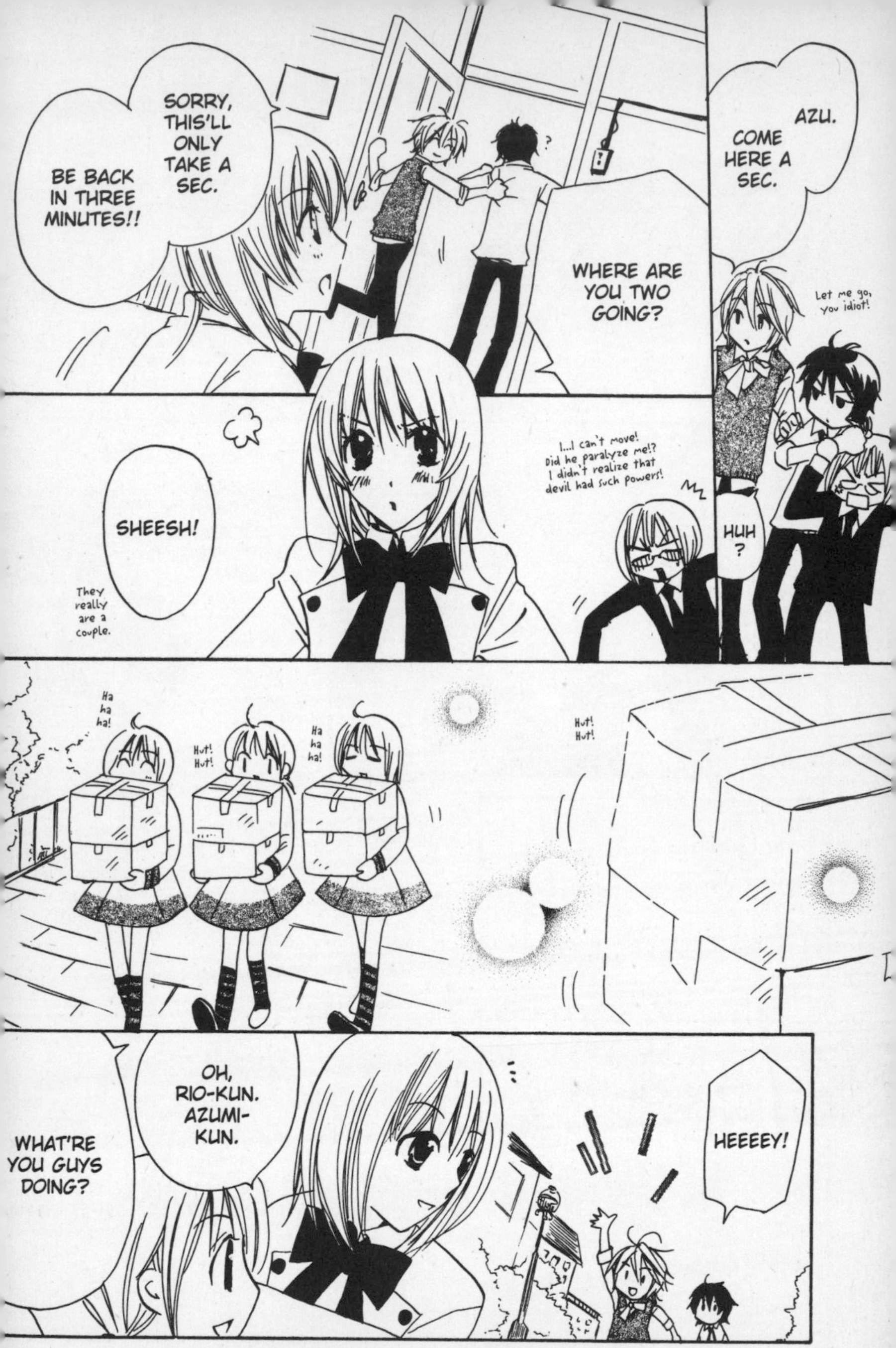
AZU.
COME HERE A SEC.
Let me go, you idiot!
WHERE ARE YOU TWO GOING?
SORRY, THIS'LL ONLY TAKE A SEC.
BE BACK IN THREE MINUTES!!
HUH?
I...I can't move! Did he paralyze me!? I didn't realize that devil had such powers!
SHEESH!
They really are a couple.
Hut! Hut!
Ha ha ha!
Hut! Hut!
Ha ha ha!
HEEEEY!
OH, RIO-KUN. AZUMI-KUN.
WHAT'RE YOU GUYS DOING?

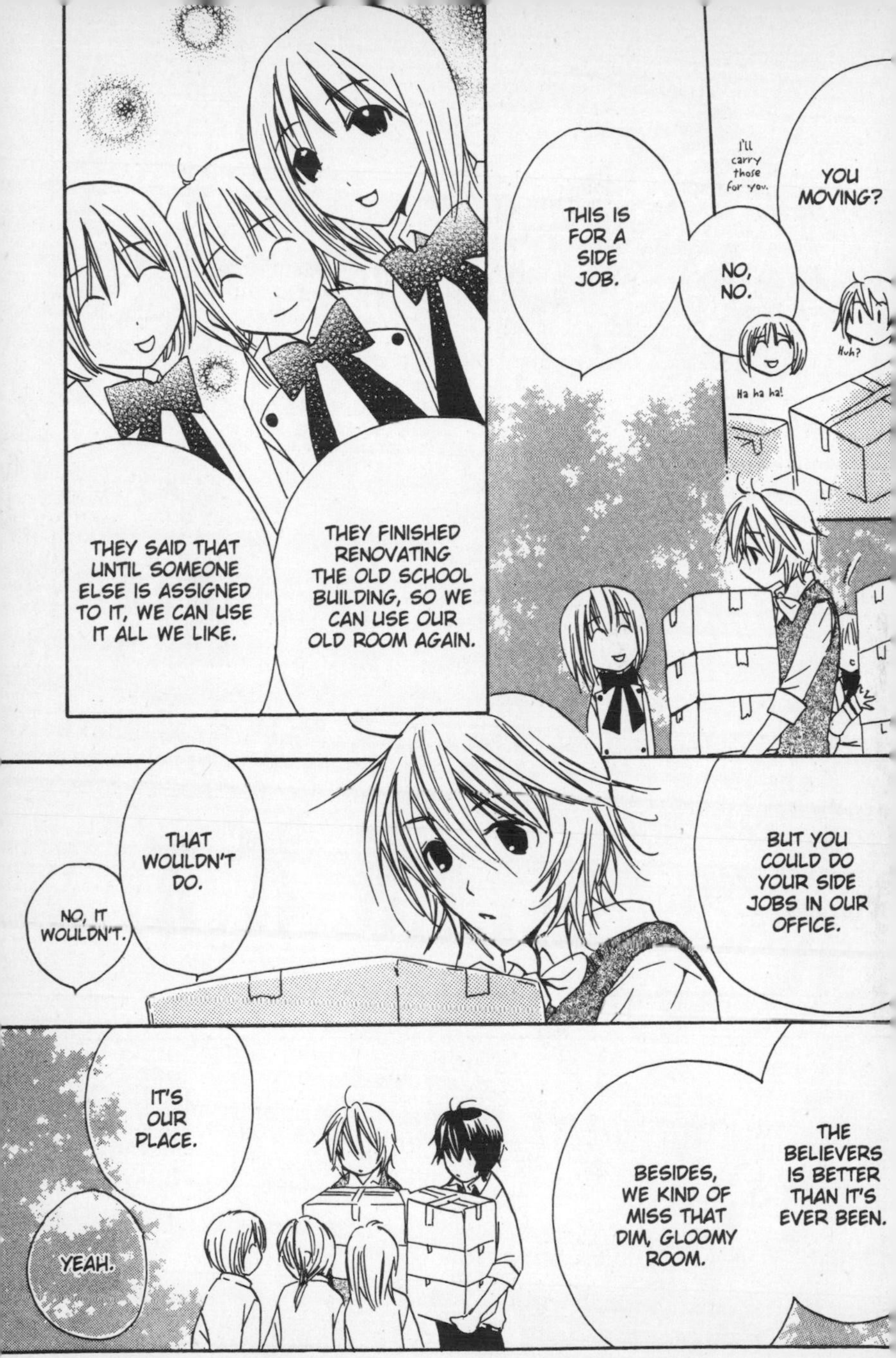
YOU MOVING?
I'll carry those for you.
NO, NO.
Huh?
THIS IS FOR A SIDE JOB.
Ha ha ha!
THEY FINISHED RENOVATING THE OLD SCHOOL BUILDING, SO WE CAN USE OUR OLD ROOM AGAIN.
THEY SAID THAT UNTIL SOMEONE ELSE IS ASSIGNED TO IT, WE CAN USE IT ALL WE LIKE.
BUT YOU COULD DO YOUR SIDE JOBS IN OUR OFFICE.
THAT WOULDN'T DO.
NO, IT WOULDN'T.
THE BELIEVERS IS BETTER THAN IT'S EVER BEEN.
BESIDES, WE KIND OF MISS THAT DIM, GLOOMY ROOM.
IT'S OUR PLACE.
YEAH.

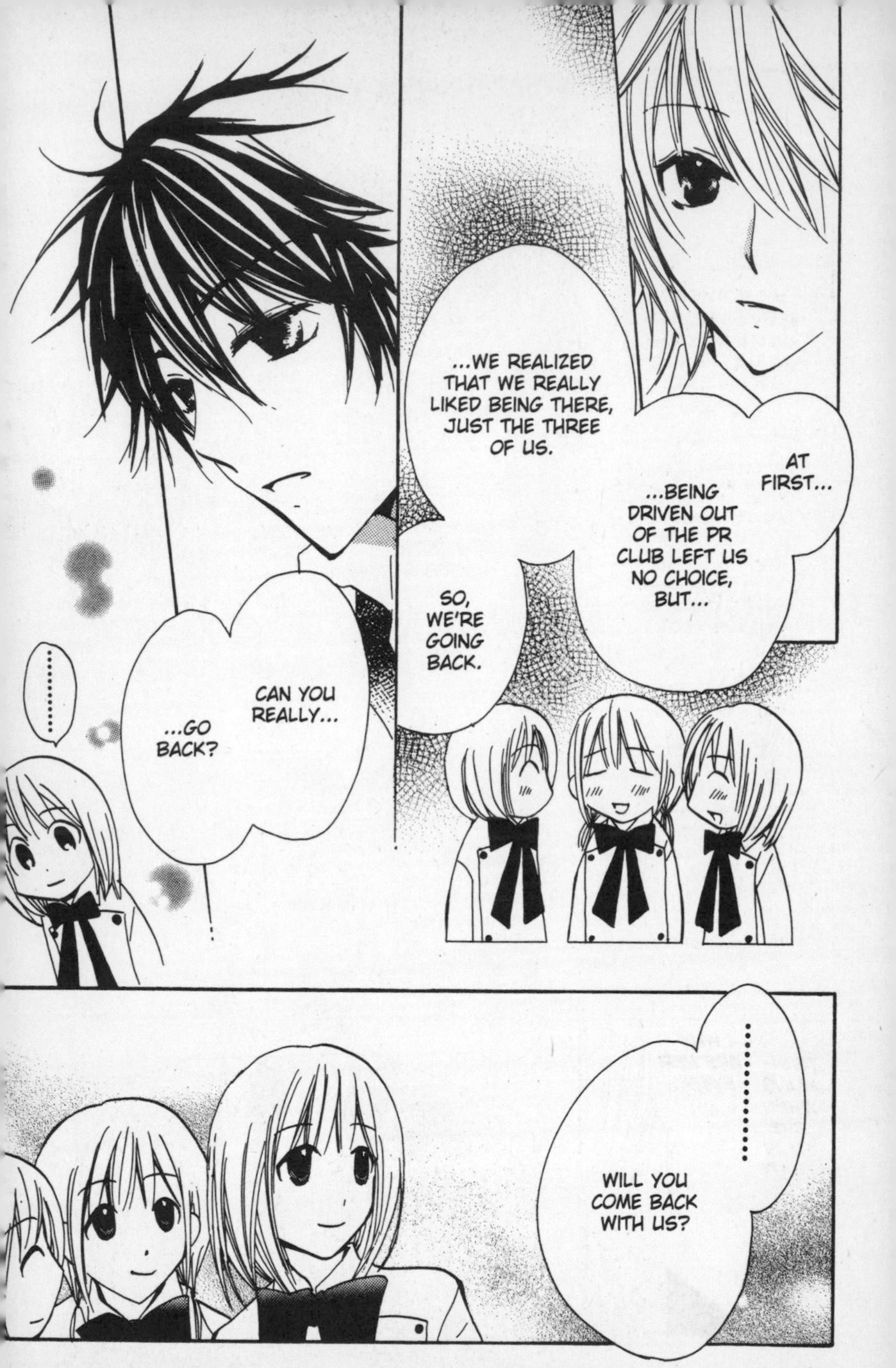
AT FIRST...
...BEING DRIVEN OUT OF THE PR CLUB LEFT US NO CHOICE, BUT...
...WE REALIZED THAT WE REALLY LIKED BEING THERE, JUST THE THREE OF US.
SO, WE'RE GOING BACK.
CAN YOU REALLY...
...GO BACK?
......
......
WILL YOU COME BACK WITH US?

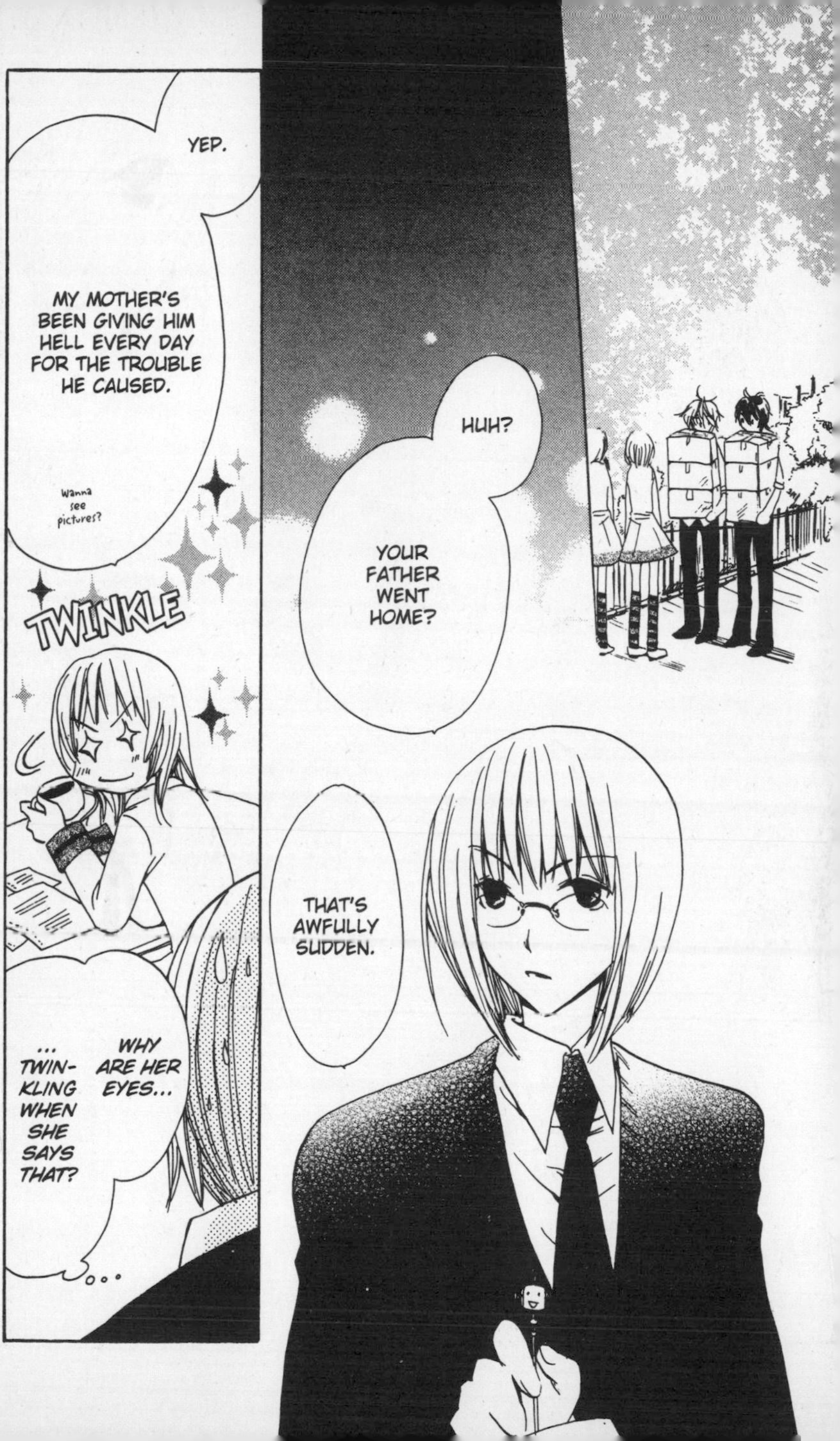
HUH?
YOUR FATHER WENT HOME?
THAT'S AWFULLY SUDDEN.
YEP.
MY MOTHER'S BEEN GIVING HIM HELL EVERY DAY FOR THE TROUBLE HE CAUSED.
Wanna see pictures?
TWINKLE
WHY ARE HER EYES... ...TWIN-KLING WHEN SHE SAYS THAT?

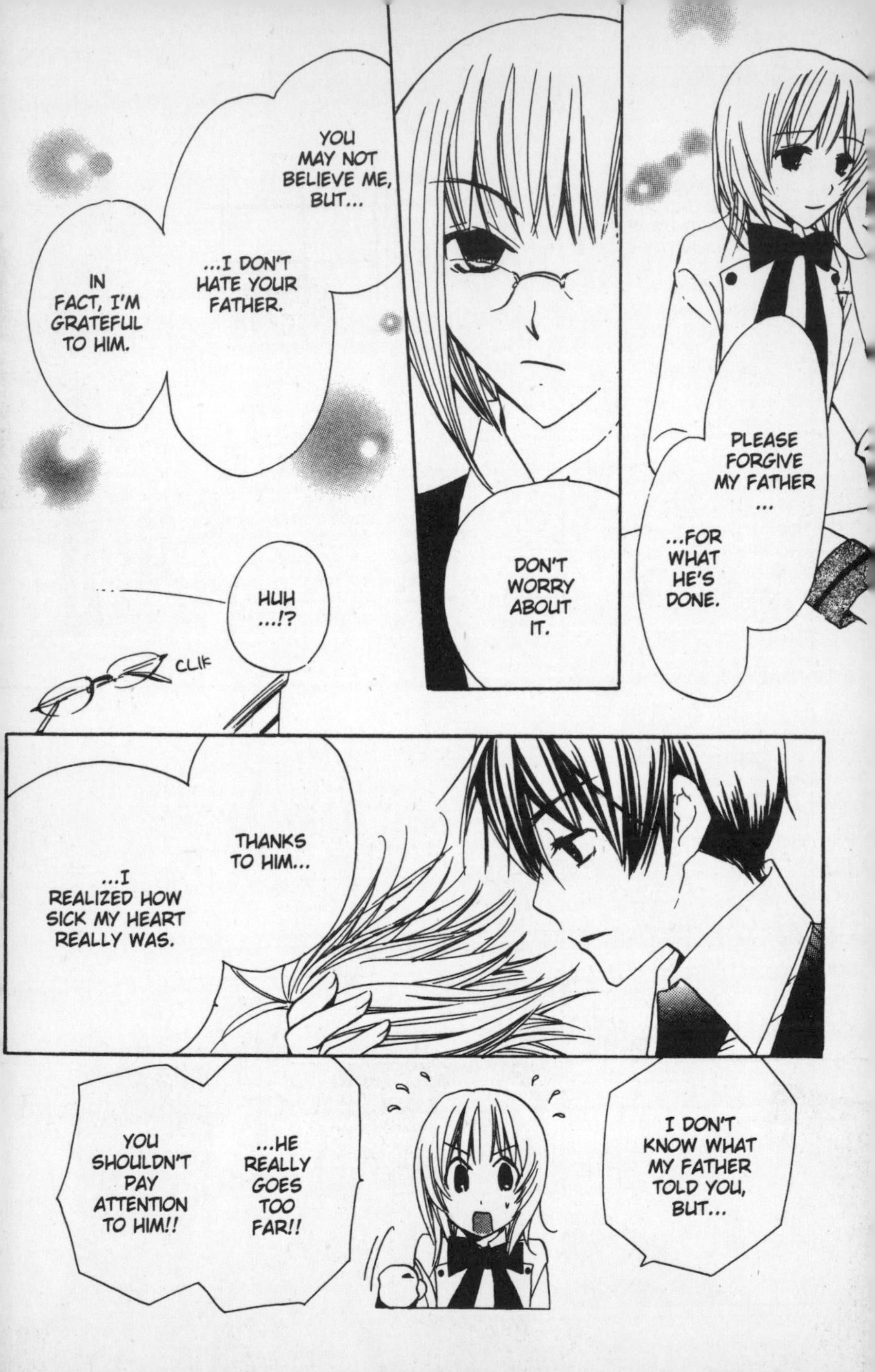
PLEASE FORGIVE MY FATHER ...
...FOR WHAT HE'S DONE.
DON'T WORRY ABOUT IT.
YOU MAY NOT BELIEVE ME, BUT...
...I DON'T HATE YOUR FATHER.
IN FACT, I'M GRATEFUL TO HIM.
HUH ...!?
CLIF
THANKS TO HIM...
...I REALIZED HOW SICK MY HEART REALLY WAS.
I DON'T KNOW WHAT MY FATHER TOLD YOU, BUT...
...HE REALLY GOES TOO FAR!!
YOU SHOULDN'T PAY ATTENTION TO HIM!!

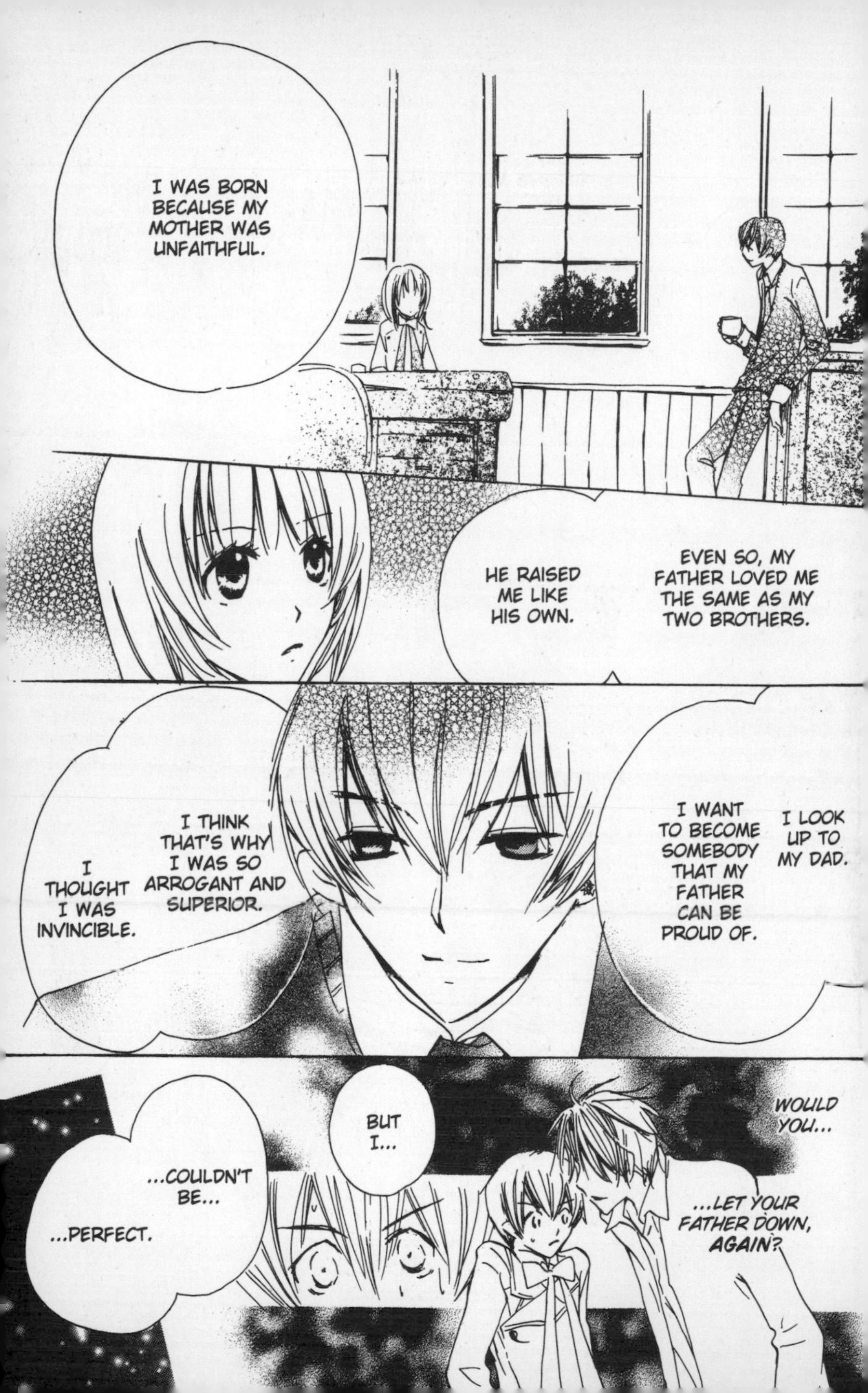
I WAS BORN BECAUSE MY MOTHER WAS UNFAITHFUL.
EVEN SO, MY FATHER LOVED ME THE SAME AS MY TWO BROTHERS.
HE RAISED ME LIKE HIS OWN.
I LOOK UP TO MY DAD.
I WANT TO BECOME SOMEBODY THAT MY FATHER CAN BE PROUD OF.
I THINK THAT'S WHY I WAS SO ARROGANT AND SUPERIOR.
I THOUGHT I WAS INVINCIBLE.
WOULD YOU...
...LET YOUR FATHER DOWN, AGAIN?
BUT I...
...COULDN'T BE...
...PERFECT.

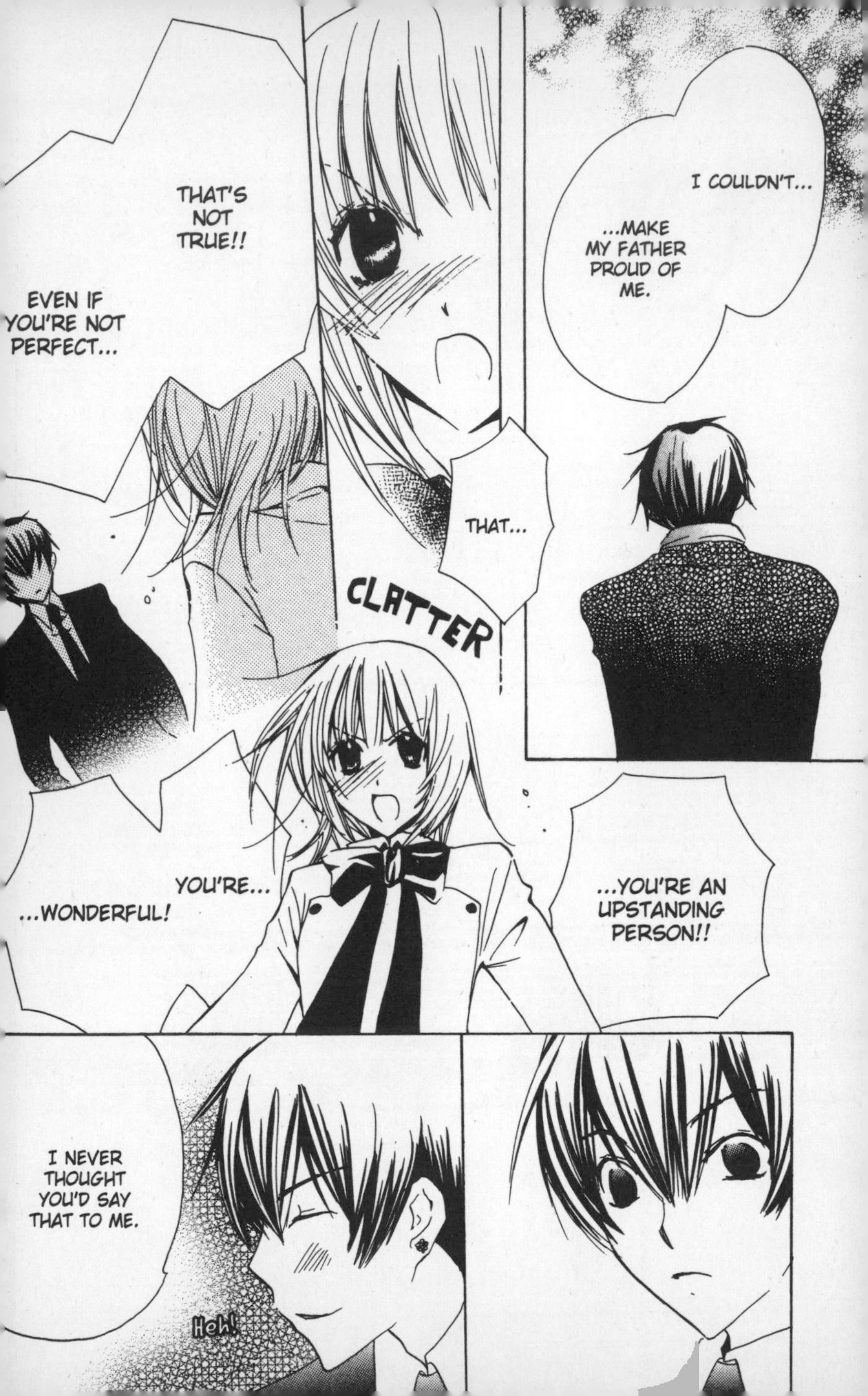
I COULDN'T...
...MAKE MY FATHER PROUD OF ME.
THAT...
THAT'S NOT TRUE!!
EVEN IF YOU'RE NOT PERFECT...
CLATTER
...YOU'RE AN UPSTANDING PERSON!!
YOU'RE...
...WONDERFUL!
I NEVER THOUGHT YOU'D SAY THAT TO ME.
Heh!

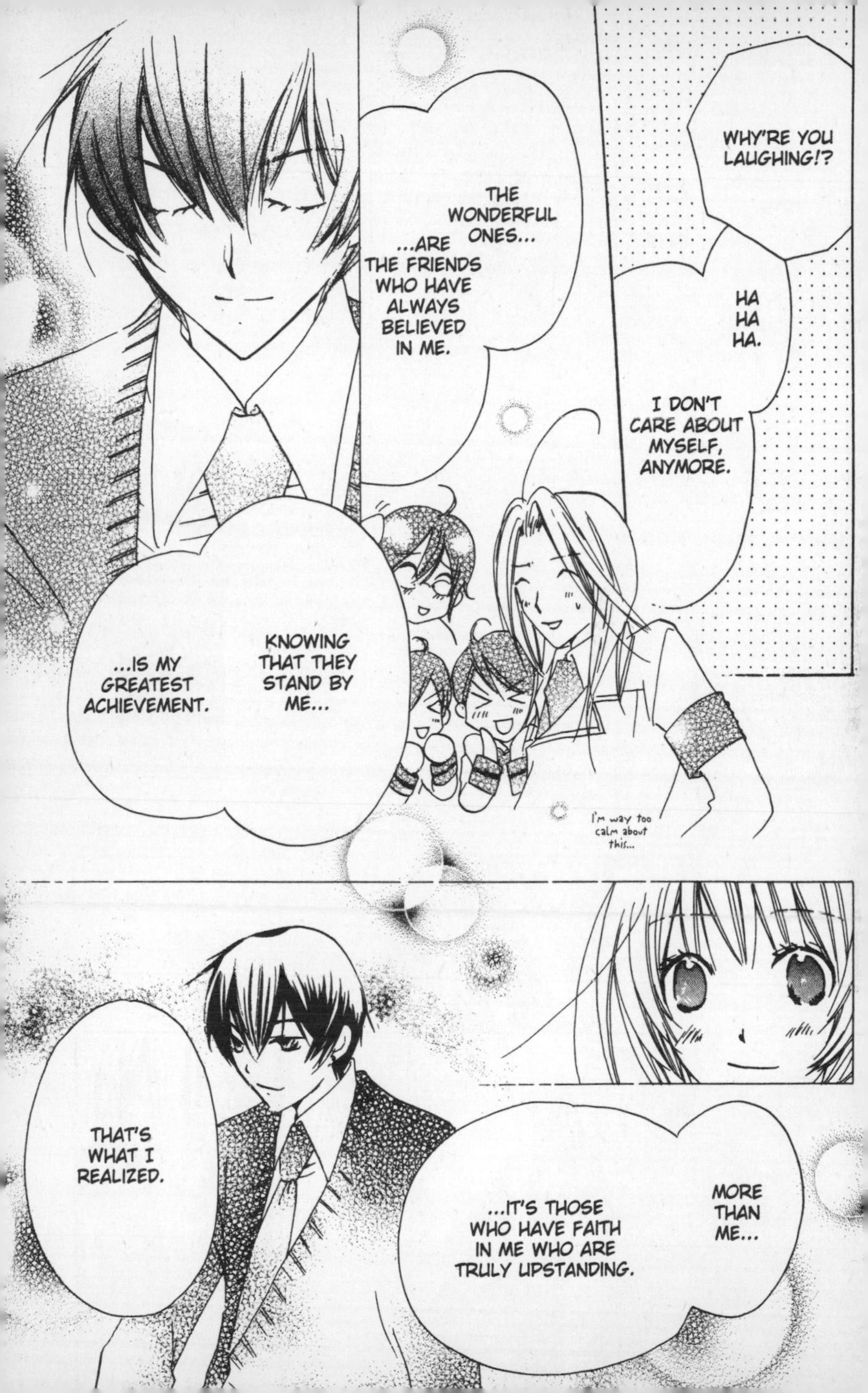
WHY'RE YOU LAUGHING!?
HA HA HA.
I DON'T CARE ABOUT MYSELF, ANYMORE.
THE WONDERFUL ONES...
...ARE THE FRIENDS WHO HAVE ALWAYS BELIEVED IN ME.
I'm way too calm about this...
KNOWING THAT THEY STAND BY ME...
...IS MY GREATEST ACHIEVEMENT.
MORE THAN ME...
...IT'S THOSE WHO HAVE FAITH IN ME WHO ARE TRULY UPSTANDING.
THAT'S WHAT I REALIZED.

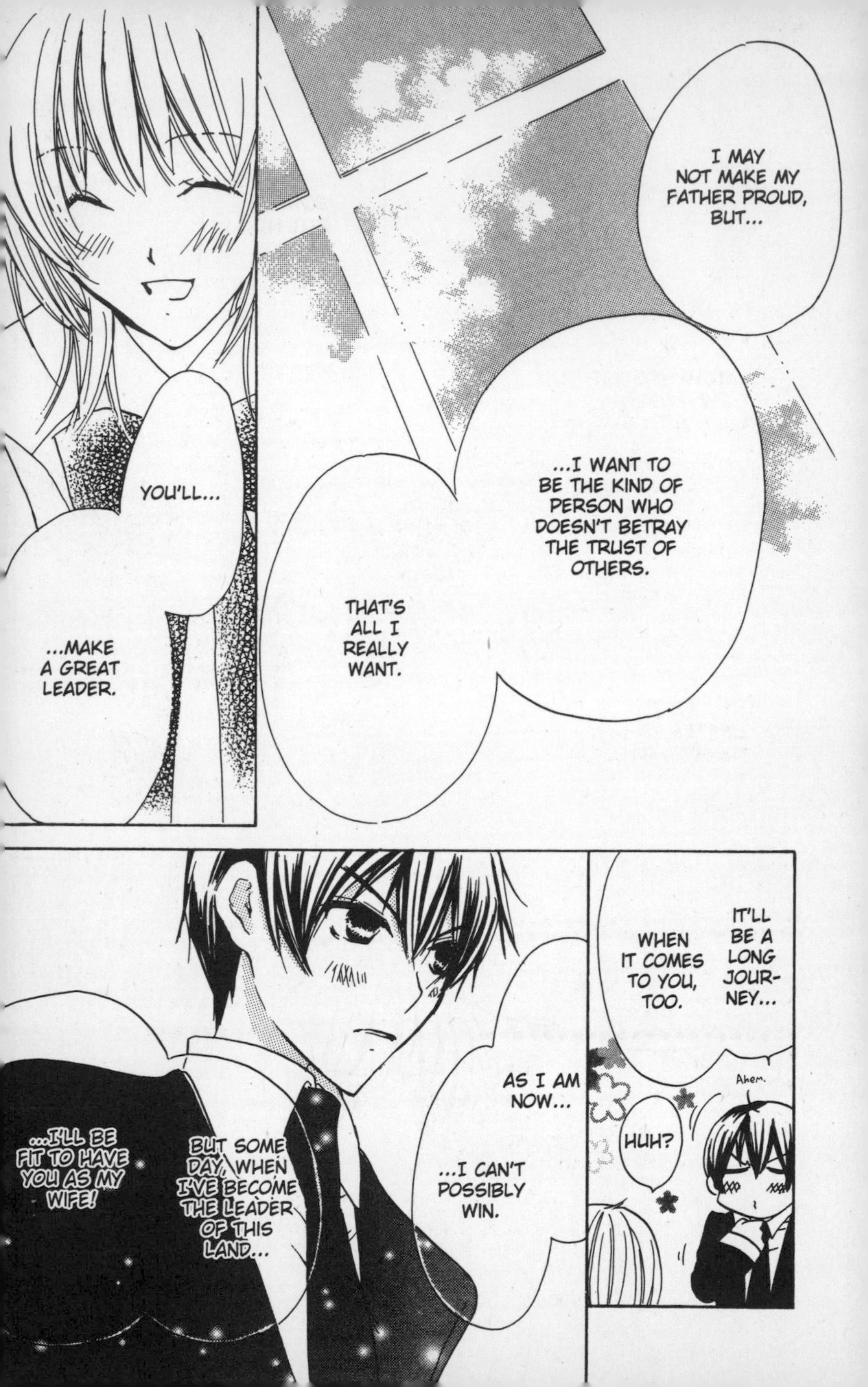
I MAY NOT MAKE MY FATHER PROUD, BUT...
...I WANT TO BE THE KIND OF PERSON WHO DOESN'T BETRAY THE TRUST OF OTHERS.
THAT'S ALL I REALLY WANT.
YOU'LL...
...MAKE A GREAT LEADER.
IT'LL BE A LONG JOURNEY...
WHEN IT COMES TO YOU, TOO.
Ahem.
HUH?
AS I AM NOW...
...I CAN'T POSSIBLY WIN.
BUT SOME DAY, WHEN I'VE BECOME THE LEADER OF THIS LAND...
...I'LL BE FIT TO HAVE YOU AS MY WIFE!

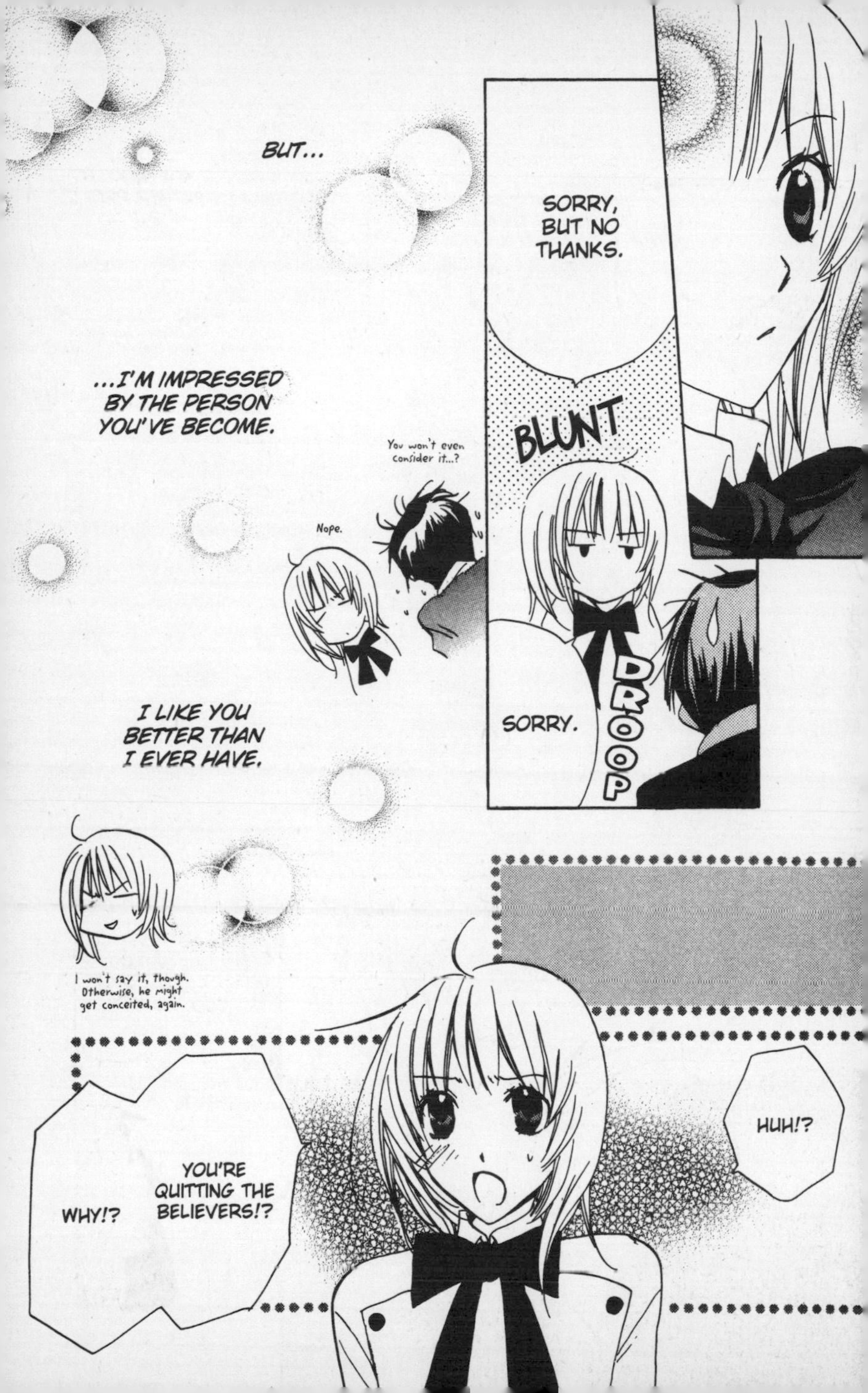
SORRY, BUT NO THANKS.
BLUNT
SORRY.
DROOP
BUT...
...I'M IMPRESSED BY THE PERSON YOU'VE BECOME.
You won't even consider it...?
Nope.
I LIKE YOU BETTER THAN I EVER HAVE.
I won't say it, though. Otherwise, he might get conceited, again.
HUH!?
YOU'RE QUITTING THE BELIEVERS!?
WHY!?

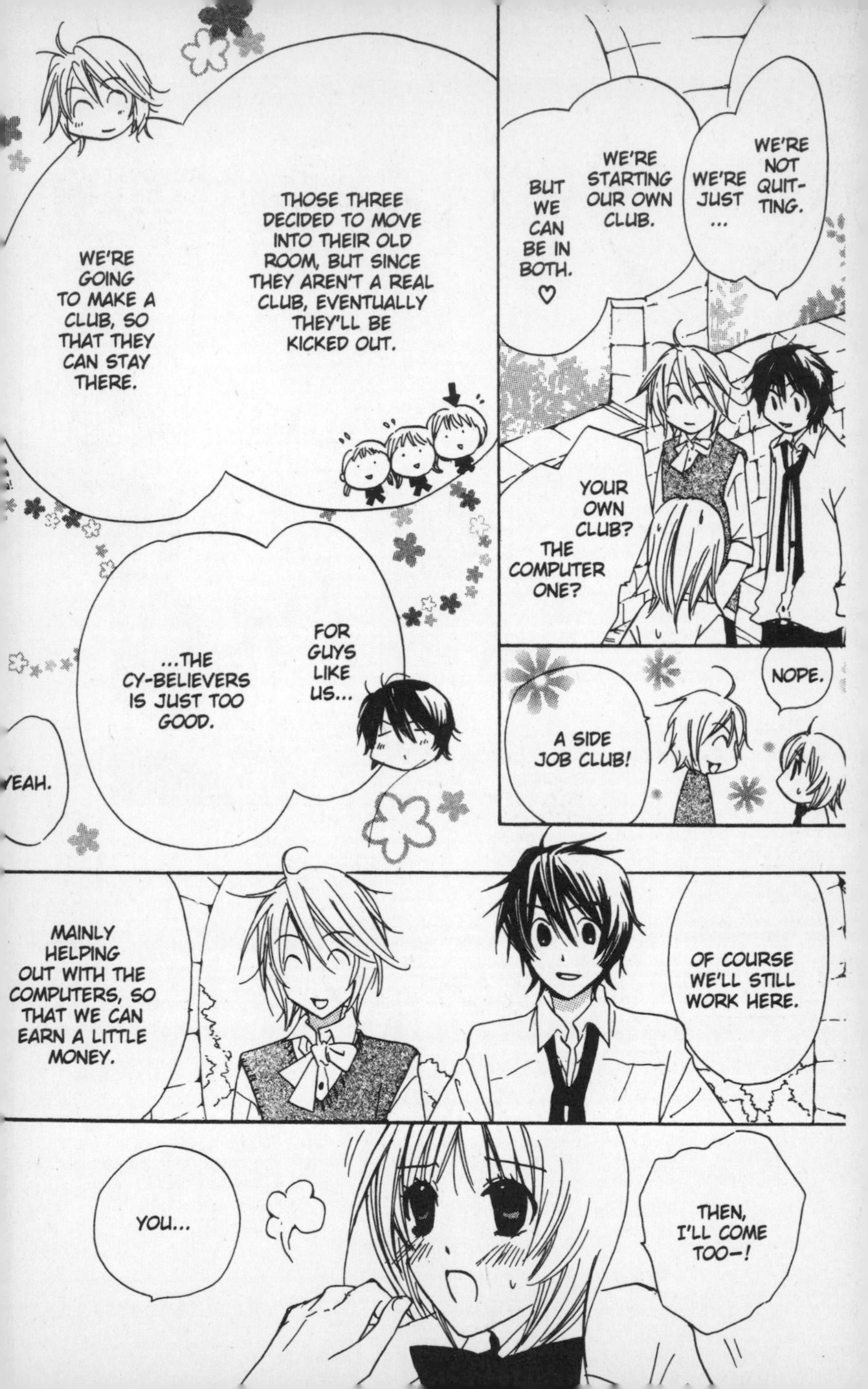

WE'RE NOT QUIT-TING.
WE'RE JUST ...
WE'RE STARTING OUR OWN CLUB.
BUT WE CAN BE IN BOTH. ♡
YOUR OWN CLUB? THE COMPUTER ONE?
NOPE.
A SIDE JOB CLUB!
THOSE THREE DECIDED TO MOVE INTO THEIR OLD ROOM, BUT SINCE THEY AREN'T A REAL CLUB, EVENTUALLY THEY'LL BE KICKED OUT.
WE'RE GOING TO MAKE A CLUB, SO THAT THEY CAN STAY THERE.
FOR GUYS LIKE US...
...THE CY-BELIEVERS IS JUST TOO GOOD.
YEAH.
OF COURSE WE'LL STILL WORK HERE.
MAINLY HELPING OUT WITH THE COMPUTERS, SO THAT WE CAN EARN A LITTLE MONEY.
THEN, I'LL COME TOO—!
YOU...

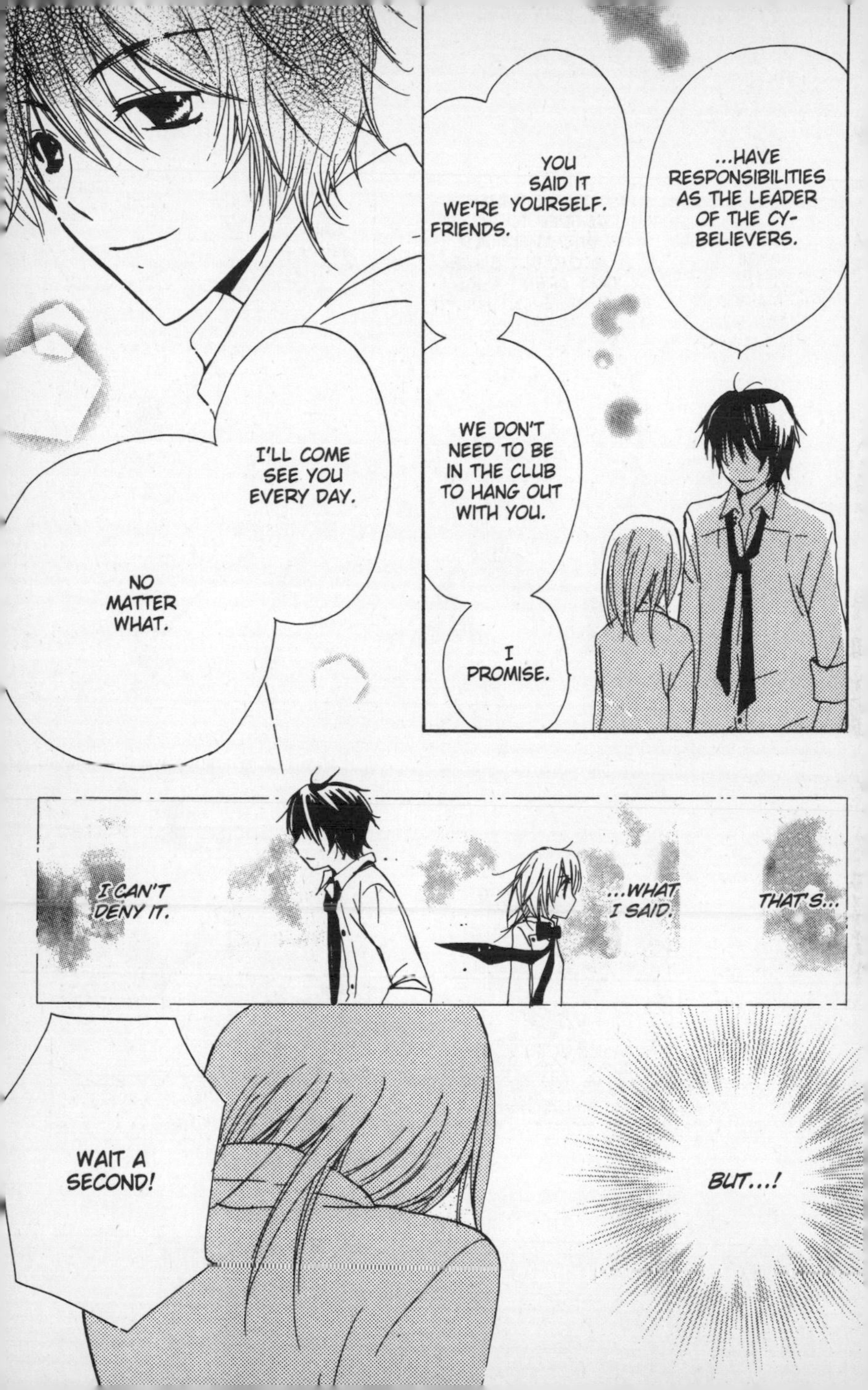
...HAVE RESPONSIBILITIES AS THE LEADER OF THE CY-BELIEVERS.
YOU SAID IT YOURSELF.
WE'RE FRIENDS.
WE DON'T NEED TO BE IN THE CLUB TO HANG OUT WITH YOU.
I PROMISE.
I'LL COME SEE YOU EVERY DAY.
NO MATTER WHAT.
THAT'S...
...WHAT I SAID.
I CAN'T DENY IT.
BUT...!
WAIT A SECOND!

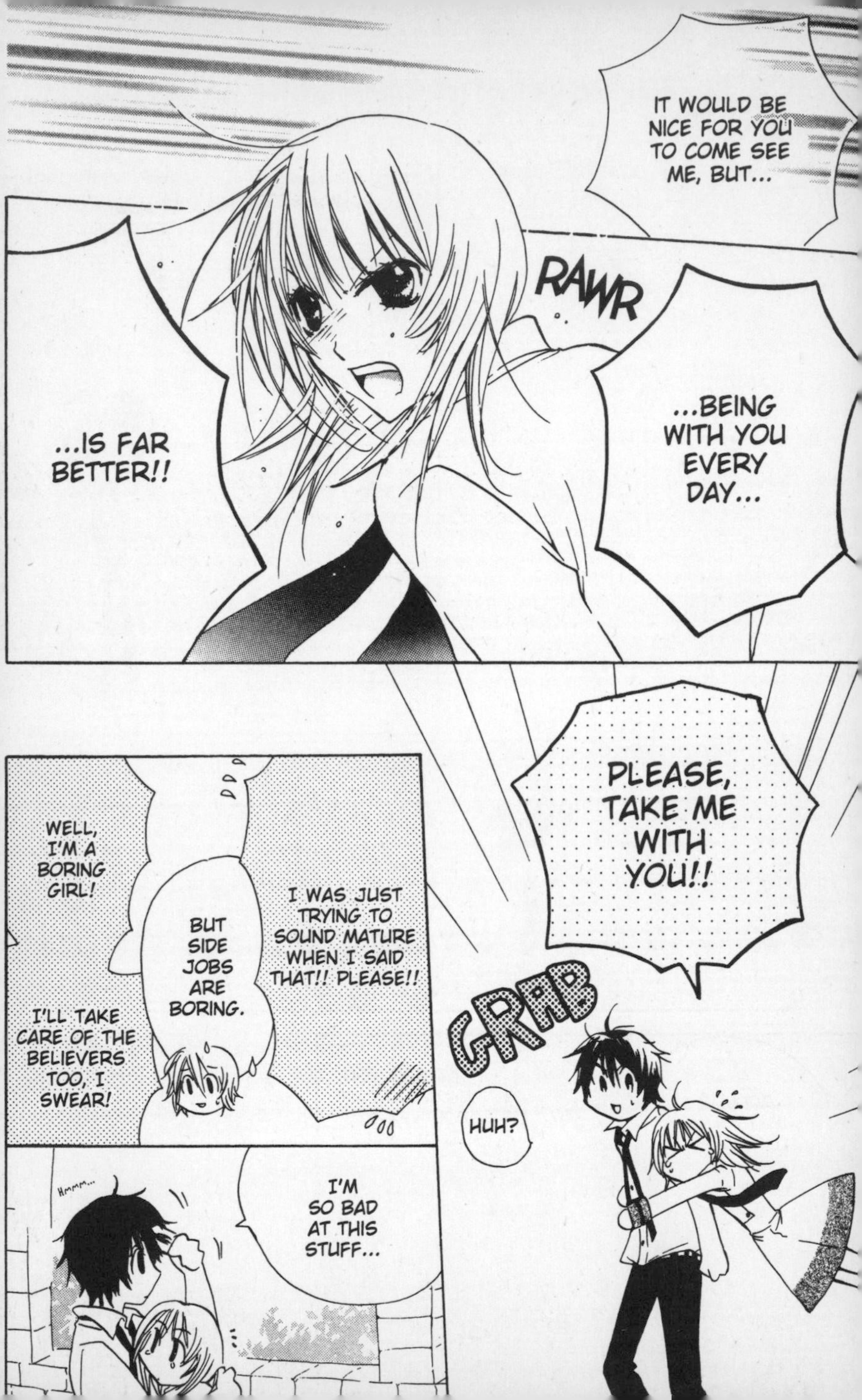
IT WOULD BE NICE FOR YOU TO COME SEE ME, BUT...
RAWR
...BEING WITH YOU EVERY DAY...
...IS FAR BETTER!!
PLEASE, TAKE ME WITH YOU!!
GRAB
HUH?
I WAS JUST TRYING TO SOUND MATURE WHEN I SAID THAT!! PLEASE!!
BUT SIDE JOBS ARE BORING.
WELL, I'M A BORING GIRL!
I'LL TAKE CARE OF THE BELIEVERS TOO, I SWEAR!
I'M SO BAD AT THIS STUFF...
HMMM...

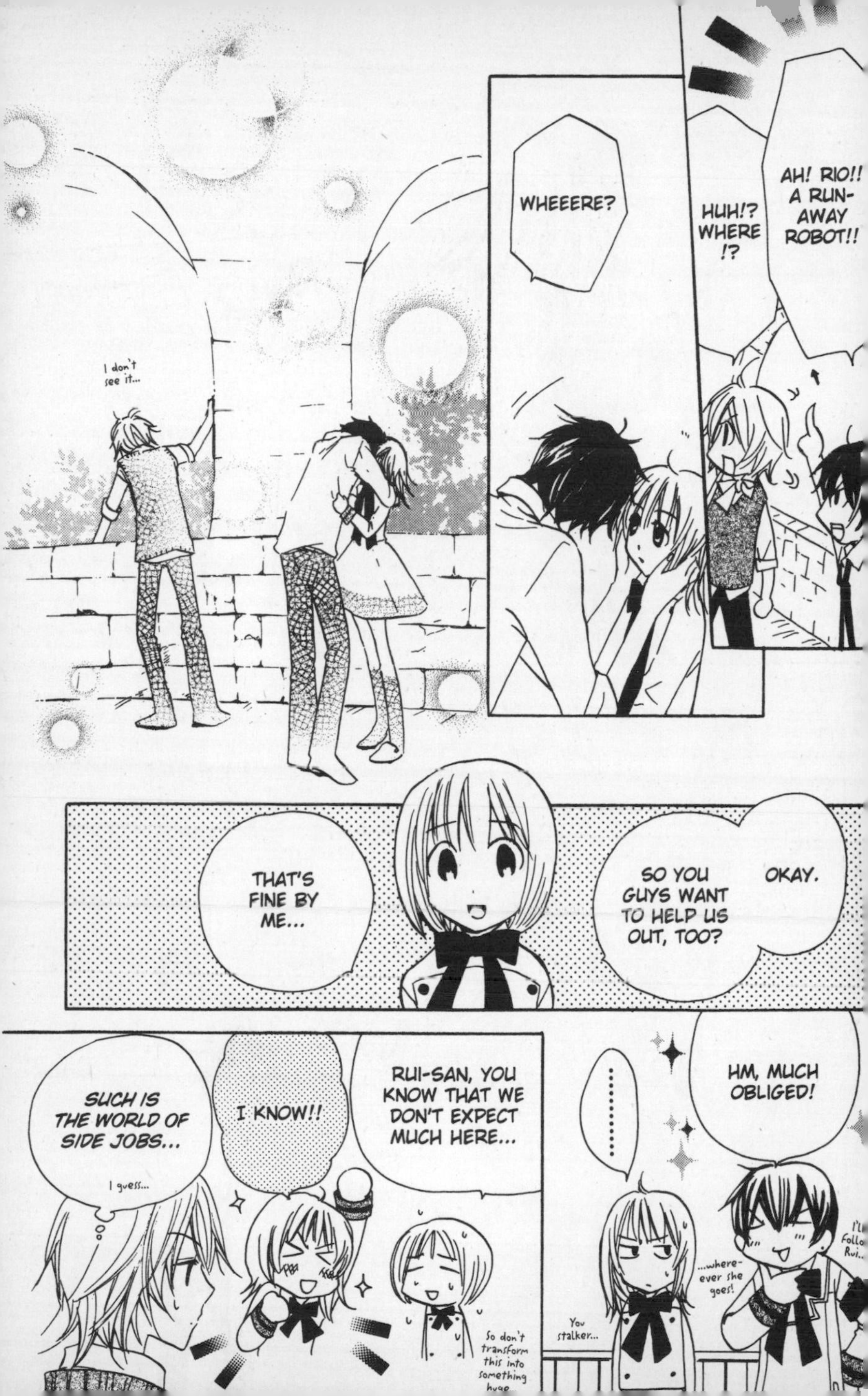
AH! RIO!! A RUN-AWAY ROBOT!!
HUH!? WHERE!?
WHEEERE?
I don't see it...
OKAY.
SO YOU GUYS WANT TO HELP US OUT, TOO?
THAT'S FINE BY ME...
HM, MUCH OBLIGED!
....
I'l Follo Rui...
...where-ever she goes!
You stalker...
RUI-SAN, YOU KNOW THAT WE DON'T EXPECT MUCH HERE...
I KNOW!!
SUCH IS THE WORLD OF SIDE JOBS...
I guess...
So don't transform this into something

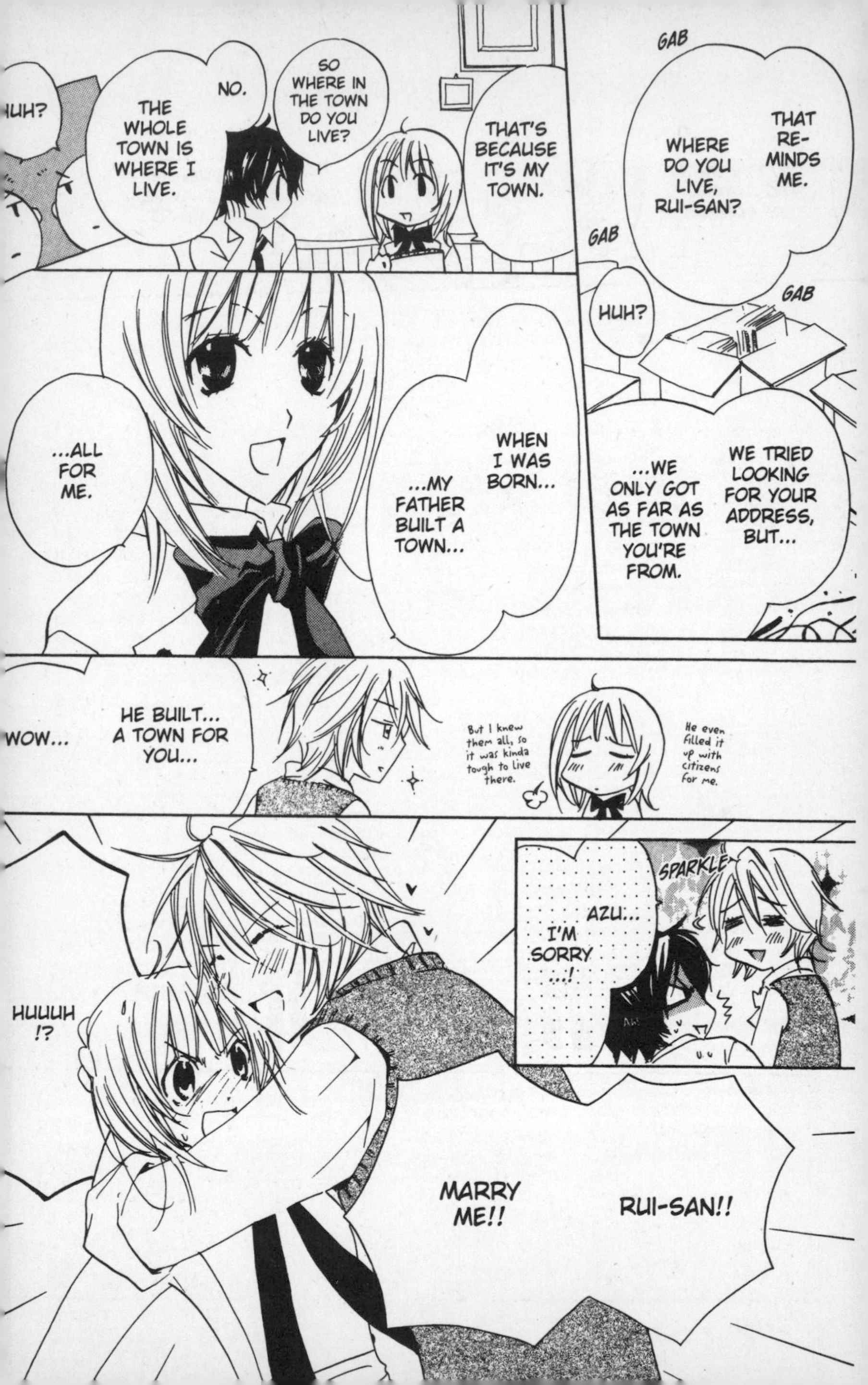
GAB
THAT RE-MINDS ME.
WHERE DO YOU LIVE, RUI-SAN?
GAB
HUH?
GAB
WE TRIED LOOKING FOR YOUR ADDRESS, BUT...
...WE ONLY GOT AS FAR AS THE TOWN YOU'RE FROM.
THAT'S BECAUSE IT'S MY TOWN.
SO WHERE IN THE TOWN DO YOU LIVE?
NO.
THE WHOLE TOWN IS WHERE I LIVE.
UH?
WHEN I WAS BORN...
...MY FATHER BUILT A TOWN...
...ALL FOR ME.
He even filled it up with citizens for me.
But I knew them all, so it was kinda tough to live there.
HE BUILT... A TOWN FOR YOU...
WOW...
SPARKLE
AZU...
I'M SORRY ...!
RUI-SAN!!
MARRY ME!!
HUUUH !?

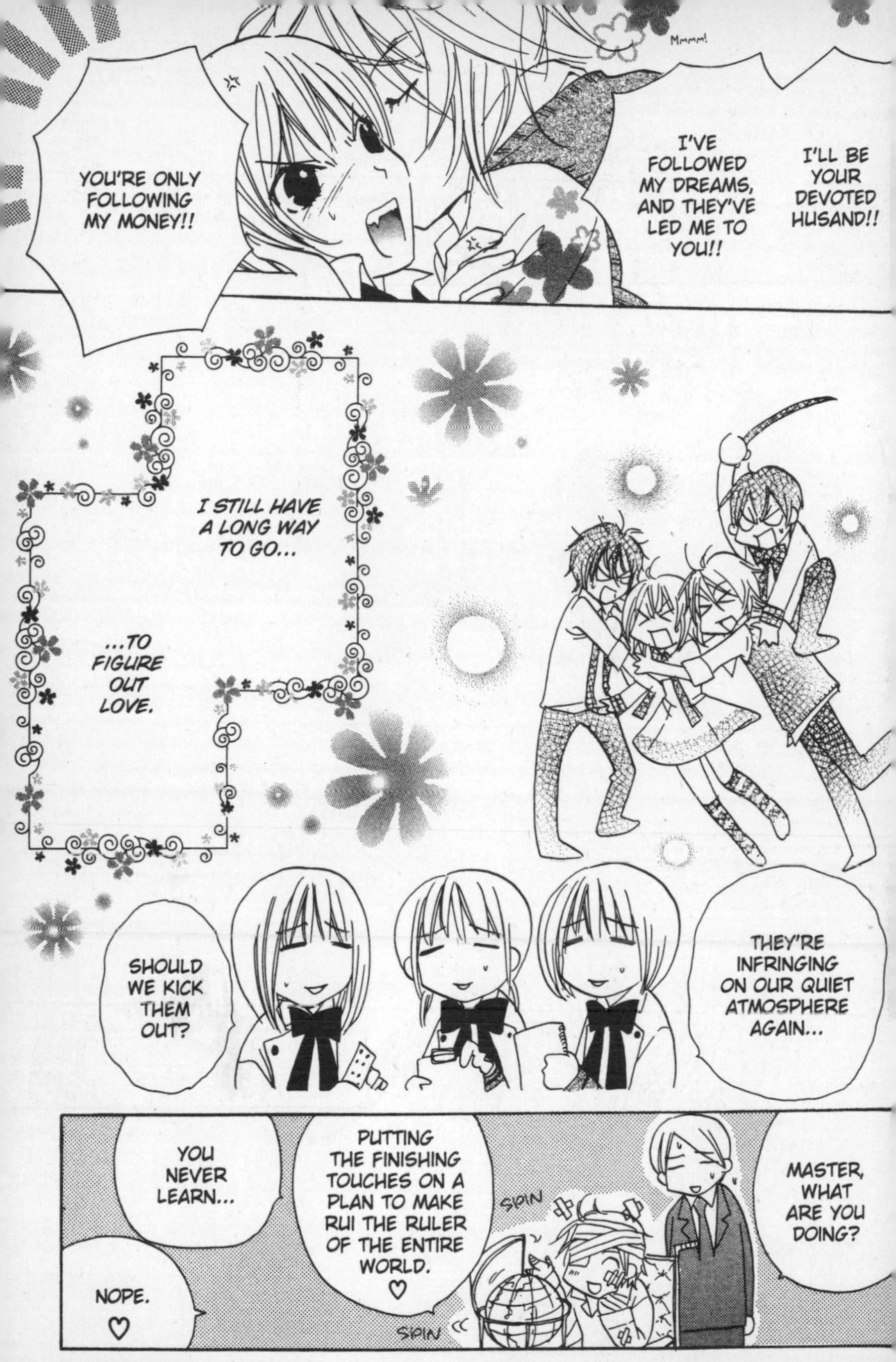
Mmmm!
I'LL BE YOUR DEVOTED HUSAND!!
I'VE FOLLOWED MY DREAMS, AND THEY'VE LED ME TO YOU!!
YOU'RE ONLY FOLLOWING MY MONEY!!
I STILL HAVE A LONG WAY TO GO...
...TO FIGURE OUT LOVE.
THEY'RE INFRINGING ON OUR QUIET ATMOSPHERE AGAIN...
SHOULD WE KICK THEM OUT?
MASTER, WHAT ARE YOU DOING?
SPIN
PUTTING THE FINISHING TOUCHES ON A PLAN TO MAKE RUI THE RULER OF THE ENTIRE WORLD. ♡
SPIN
YOU NEVER LEARN...
NOPE. ♡

#19 / END

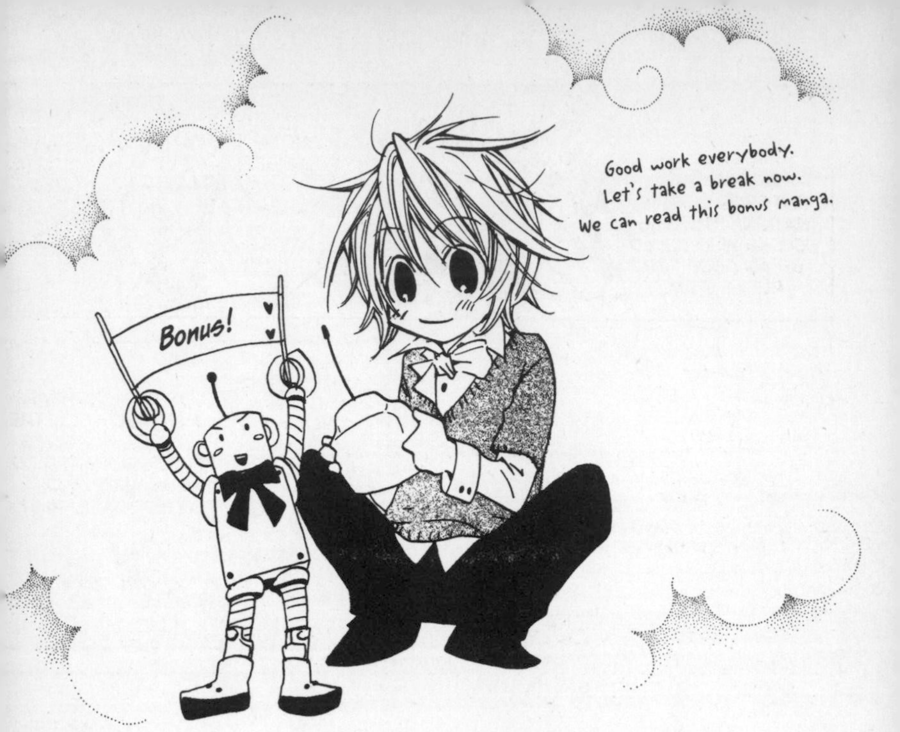
Good work everybody.
Let's take a break now.
We can read this bonus manga.
Bonus!

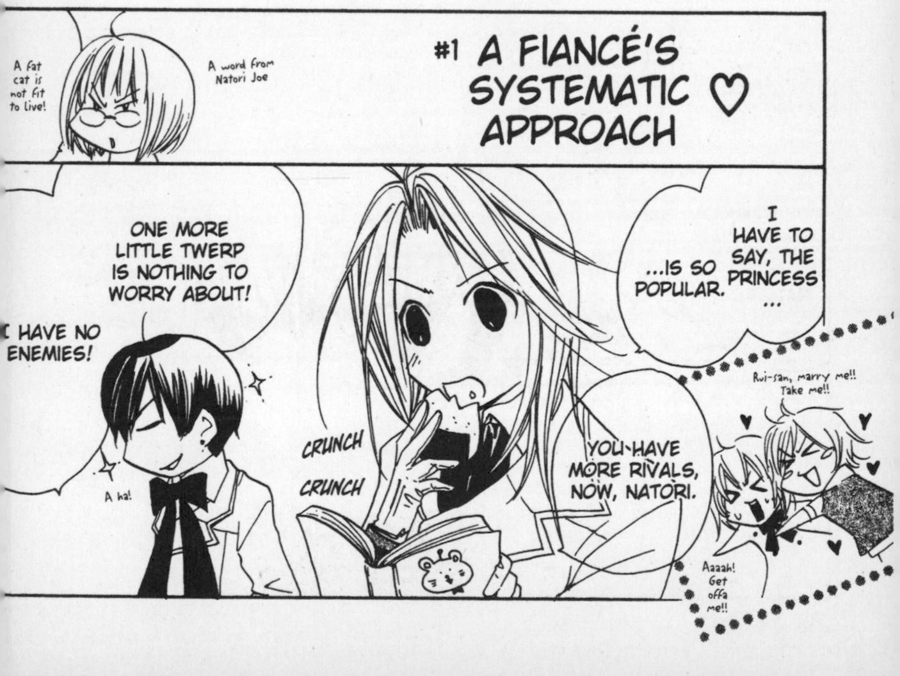
#1 A FIANCÉ'S SYSTEMATIC APPROACH ♡
A word from Natori Joe
A fat cat is not fit to live!
Rui-san, marry me!! Take me!!
Aaaah! Get offa me!!
I HAVE TO SAY, THE PRINCESS ...
...IS SO POPULAR.
YOU HAVE MORE RIVALS, NOW, NATORI.
CRUNCH
CRUNCH
ONE MORE LITTLE TWERP IS NOTHING TO WORRY ABOUT!
I HAVE NO ENEMIES!
A ha!

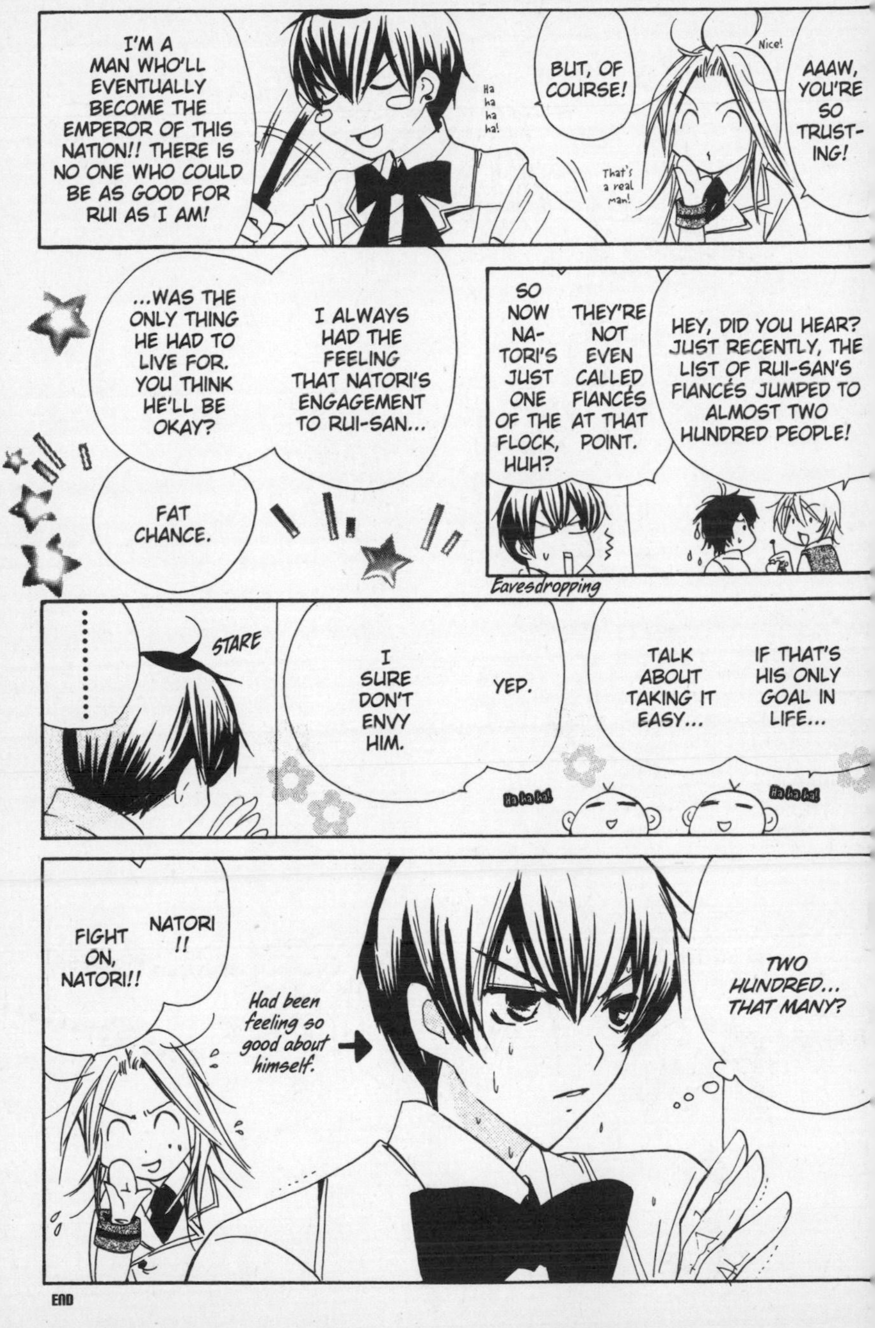
AAAW, YOU'RE SO TRUSTING!
Nice!
That's a real man!
BUT, OF COURSE!
Ha ha ha ha!
I'M A MAN WHO'LL EVENTUALLY BECOME THE EMPEROR OF THIS NATION!! THERE IS NO ONE WHO COULD BE AS GOOD FOR RUI AS I AM!
HEY, DID YOU HEAR? JUST RECENTLY, THE LIST OF RUI-SAN'S FIANCÉS JUMPED TO ALMOST TWO HUNDRED PEOPLE!
THEY'RE NOT EVEN CALLED FIANCÉS AT THAT POINT.
SO NOW NATORI'S JUST ONE OF THE FLOCK, HUH?
Eavesdropping
I ALWAYS HAD THE FEELING THAT NATORI'S ENGAGEMENT TO RUI-SAN...
...WAS THE ONLY THING HE HAD TO LIVE FOR. YOU THINK HE'LL BE OKAY?
FAT CHANCE.
IF THAT'S HIS ONLY GOAL IN LIFE...
TALK ABOUT TAKING IT EASY...
Ha ha ha!
YEP.
I SURE DON'T ENVY HIM.
Ha ha ha!
STARE
......
TWO HUNDRED... THAT MANY?
Had been feeling so good about himself.
NATORI!!
FIGHT ON, NATORI!!

END

#2 A CURSE'S SYSTEMATIC APPROACH ♡

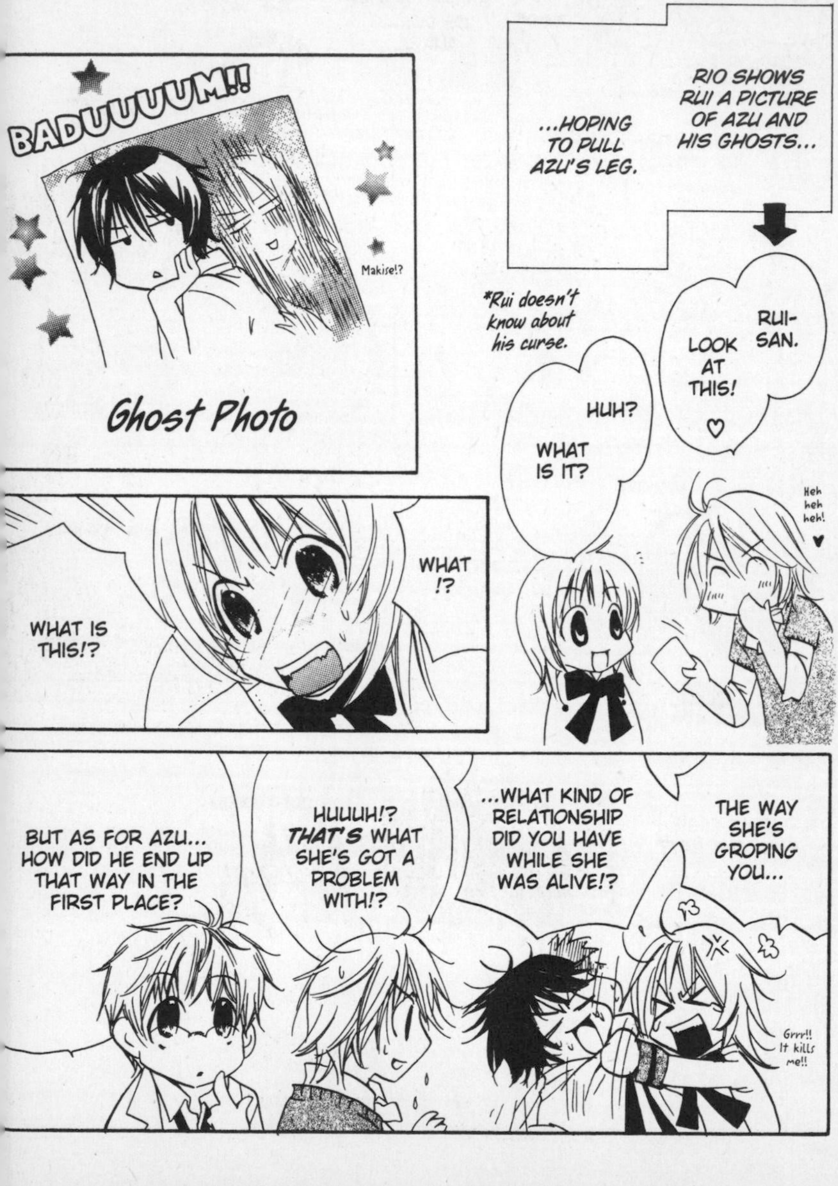

RIO SHOWS RUI A PICTURE OF AZU AND HIS GHOSTS...
...HOPING TO PULL AZU'S LEG.
RUI-SAN.
LOOK AT THIS! ♡
HUH?
WHAT IS IT?
*Rui doesn't know about his curse.
Heh heh heh! ♥
BADUUUUM!!
Makise!?
Ghost Photo
WHAT!?
WHAT IS THIS!?
THE WAY SHE'S GROPING YOU...
...WHAT KIND OF RELATIONSHIP DID YOU HAVE WHILE SHE WAS ALIVE!?
HUUUH!? THAT'S WHAT SHE'S GOT A PROBLEM WITH!?
BUT AS FOR AZU... HOW DID HE END UP THAT WAY IN THE FIRST PLACE?
Grrr!! It kills me!!

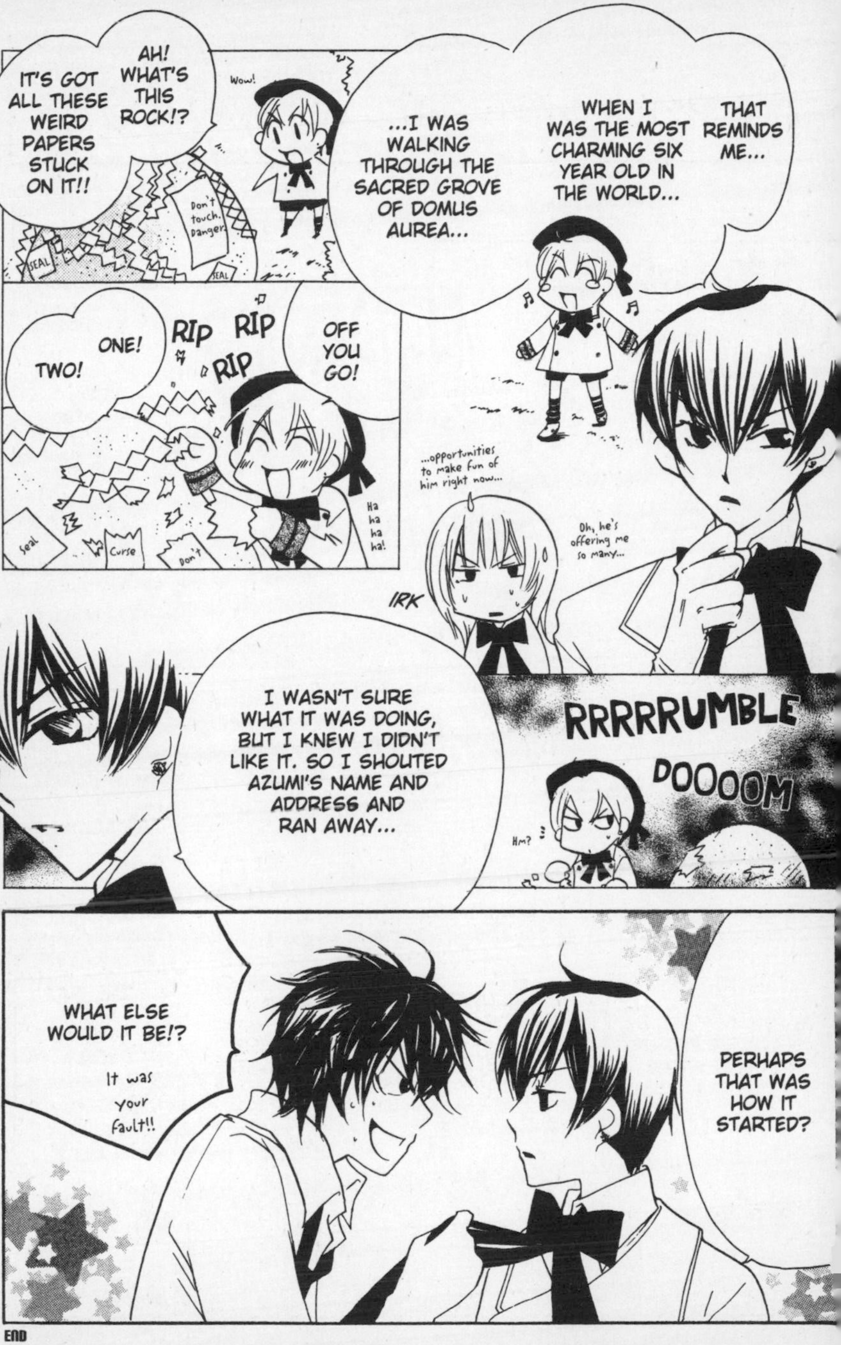
THAT REMINDS ME...
WHEN I WAS THE MOST CHARMING SIX YEAR OLD IN THE WORLD...
...I WAS WALKING THROUGH THE SACRED GROVE OF DOMUS AUREA...
Wow!
AH! WHAT'S THIS ROCK!?
IT'S GOT ALL THESE WEIRD PAPERS STUCK ON IT!!
Don't touch. Danger
SEAL
SEAL
OFF YOU GO!
RIP
RIP
RIP
ONE!
TWO!
Ha ha ha ha!
Seal
Curse
Don't
Oh, he's offering me so many...
...opportunities to make fun of him right now...
IRK
RRRRRUMBLE
DOOOOM
Hm?
I WASN'T SURE WHAT IT WAS DOING, BUT I KNEW I DIDN'T LIKE IT. SO I SHOUTED AZUMI'S NAME AND ADDRESS AND RAN AWAY...
PERHAPS THAT WAS HOW IT STARTED?
WHAT ELSE WOULD IT BE!?
It was your fault!!

END

Rui and Natori

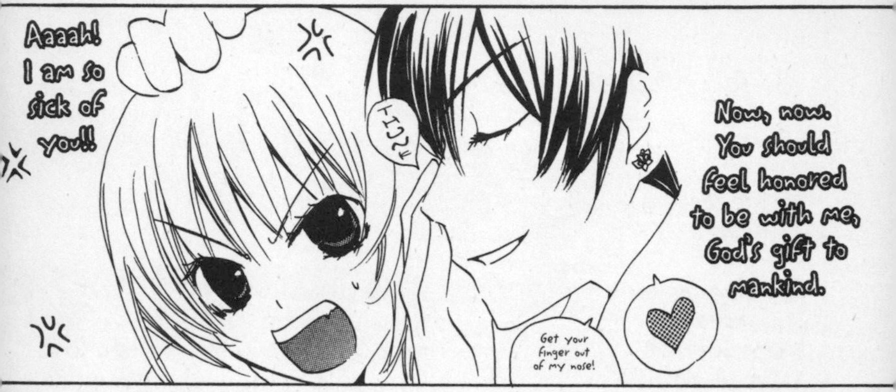
Now, now. You should feel honored to be with me, God's gift to mankind.
Aaaah! I am so sick of you!!
Get your finger out of my nose!

I just remembered that back in volume 1 I'd said I'd draw something about Rui and Natori, but only now at volume 4 finally do I write about them...

Rather than label Rui as a rich princess daughter, she's conceptualized as more of a strong girl who was raised in a strange environment, given strange studies, and uses strange words. But all in all, she's got a strong heart. Rui's positive attitude saved me countless times during the serialization of the story.

Natori is, well, what you saw. (ha) He's just that kind of guy. Yep. In letters, I've been asked if I am like Natori, but that's just ridiculous. (ha) Indeed, drawing sadistic characters is tons more fun than drawing masochistic ones. In a way, Natori is positive enough not to lose to Rui, too.

I think the two will get along just fine. Though I don't think they'd last long as lovers...

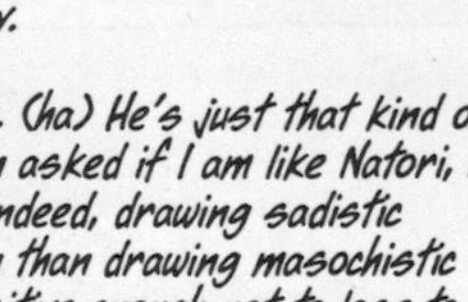
Poor thing...
What!?

Postscript

And so, Cy-Believers ends here.

Thank you so much for reading to the very end!

And to those who cheered me on during the serialization, my deepest gratitude.

Including the initial preparations, this work has been with me for about two years now. It really flew right by. And for me as the creator, since there was not one character that I had trouble drawing, it was a great story. It did all the work for me! Also, if any of you readers want to keep this story going even after it's over, it'd make me so happy.

Thanks a bunch!

With love,

Shioko Mizuki

Special Thanks:
To my brother, the professor, who taught me all about the Roman Empire, and to my mom who helped with the script: thank you. (I run a household industry...)

CY-BELIEVERS / END

Author's Note

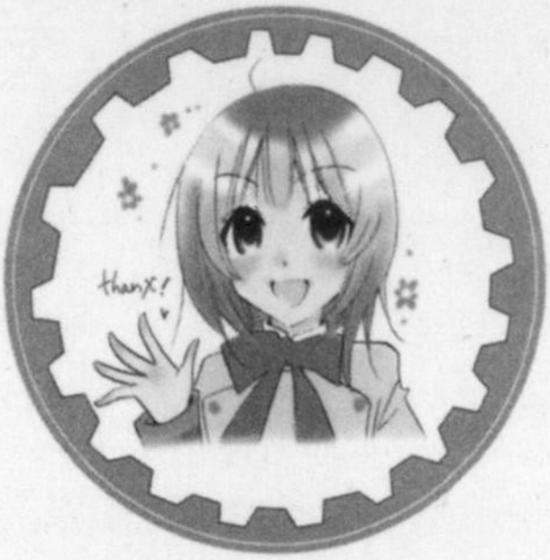
thanx!

Shioko Mizuki

While this story was running in the magazine, I had several other stories going on, too, so I'd draw it with the feeling that everyday was a desperate struggle. But looking back on it now, this story had the most lively characters of all the ones I've ever written, and I realized that they actually gave me energy in turn. It's my first work that really made me think about how drawing manga is a source of energy for me. From now on, I hope to write stories that will also give energy to those who read them. Thank you, everybody who cheered me on along the way.